CONTOURS *of*
CHRISTIAN
THEOLOGY

THE LAST
THINGS

T0324014

Titles in this series:

THE LAST THINGS

DAVID A. HÖHNE

CONTOURS *of* CHRISTIAN THEOLOGY

GERALD BRAY
Series Editor

INTER-VARSITY PRESS

INTER-VARSITY PRESS
36 Causton Street, London SW1P 4ST, England
Email: ivp@ivpbooks.com
Website: www.ivpbooks.com

First published 2019

British Library Cataloguing-in-Publication Data
A catalogue record for this book is available from the British Library.

ISBN: 978-1-78359-664-5
eBook ISBN: 978-1-78359-665-2

Set in Times New Roman
Typeset in Great Britain by CRB Associates, Potterhanworth, Lincolnshire

Inter-Varsity Press publishes Christian books that are true to the Bible and that communicate the gospel, develop discipleship and strengthen the church for its mission in the world.

Inter-Varsity Press originated within the Inter-Varsity Fellowship, now the Universities and Colleges Christian Fellowship, a student movement connecting Christian Unions in universities and colleges throughout Great Britain, and a member movement of the International Fellowship of Evangelical Students. Website: www.uccf.org.uk. That historic association is maintained, and all senior Inter-Varsity Press staff and committee members subscribe to the UCCF Basis of Faith.

For my beloved daughter and sons,
Anna, Joshua and Samuel:

'Whatever you do, in word or deed,
do everything in the name of the Lord Jesus,
giving thanks to the Father through him.'
Colossians 3:17

Contents

Series preface

Contours of Christian Theology covers the main themes of Christian doctrine. The series offers a systematic presentation of most of the major doctrines in a way which complements the traditional textbooks but does not copy them. Top priority has been given to contemporary issues, some of which may not be dealt with elsewhere from an evangelical point of view. The series aims, however, not merely to answer current objections to evangelical Christianity, but also to rework the orthodox evangelical position in a fresh and compelling way. The overall thrust is therefore positive and evangelistic in the best sense.

The series is intended to be of value to theological students at all levels, whether at a Bible college, a seminary or a secular university. It should also appeal to ministers and educated laypeople. As far as possible, efforts have been made to make technical vocabulary accessible to the non-specialist reader, and the presentation has avoided the extremes of academic style. Occasionally this has meant that particular issues have been presented without a thorough argument, taking into account different positions, but when this has happened, authors have been encouraged to refer the reader to other works which take the discussion further.

For this purpose adequate but not exhaustive notes have been produced.

The doctrines covered in the series are not exhaustive, but have been chosen in response to contemporary concerns. The title and presentation of each volume are at the discretion of the author, but the final editorial decisions have been taken by the Series Editor in consultation with Inter-Varsity Press.

In offering this series to the public, the authors and the publishers hope that it will meet the needs of theological students in this generation, and bring honour and glory to God the Father, and to his Son, Jesus Christ, in whose service the work has been undertaken from the beginning.

Gerald Bray
Series Editor

Preface

It is only fitting that this final volume in the series be entitled *The Last Things*. It is a rather cruel irony that the volume has taken so long to produce and that the editors have had to exercise such patience waiting for it. I am immensely grateful for the gracious forbearance shown to me by Philip Duce at Inter-Varsity Press and series editor Gerald Bray and for their steadfast commitment to our agreement to work together on this project. I am also very thankful for their expert advice that has made the manuscript far more readable than when it first left my computer. There are many others who ought to be acknowledged for their various contributions to this book.

Many students listened to the contents of these pages in class, both keenly and sceptically, and their questions have done much to sharpen my thoughts. I am particularly grateful for the encouragements of Revds Dan Anderson, Peter Baker, Dr Andrew Errington, Richard Glover, Matthew Moffit, Blake Hatton, Mat Aroney and Ms Laura Southam. Colleagues past and present at Moore College offered many timely words of encouragement to keep me going (or just keep running). I am especially thankful for Drs Robert Doyle, Michael Jensen, Bill Salier, Andrew Leslie,

Chase Kuhn and Bishop Greg Anderson. The Governing Board of Moore College has been both kind and generous with study leave.

I have never succeeded in any venture without the love and support of my wife Amelia and this book is no exception. Her 'work in faith, labour in love and steadfastness of hope in our Lord Jesus' have been a constant source of blessing for me, our family and all whom the Father brings into her path.

'The ends crown our works but Thou crown'st our ends' (John Donne).

David A. Höhne

Introduction

> When they came together they asked him, 'Will you be
> restoring the kingdom to Israel at this time?' But he said
> to them, 'It is not yours to know the times or seasons
> which the Father has appointed in his own authority.'
> (Acts 1:6–7)

In many ways and at various times since the resurrection of Jesus,
the church has agonized over the Father's plans to restore his
kingdom to the earth. If Jesus has ascended to the right hand
on high and the Holy Spirit has been poured out on all flesh,
then surely the *Last Things* have come to pass – or very nearly.
Of course, after nearly 2,000 years of anticipation Christians in
the West struggle to maintain a hope for the future exclusively
on the promises of the gospel and to resist the false optimism
of the Enlightenment. Ironically, even modernity's secular critics
have come to see that its determination to displace God as the
foundation of truth, meaning and purpose has failed miserably.
While promising 'a culture of unintimidated, curious, rational,
self-reliant individuals', it has instead delivered 'a herd society, a
race of anxious, timid, conformist "sheep," and a culture of utter

banality'.[1] In the twentieth century alone the paradoxes of our modern culture, especially the Romantic infatuation with change or revolution,[2] have given ample evidence of both our desire to preserve, at all costs, an individual's right to choose and, simultaneously, the potential to unleash technological forces capable of destroying human life entirely.

Throughout this modern period with its messianic aspirations and apocalyptic visions, Christian accounts of eschatology have expanded to include more than the traditional list or sequence of end-times events. During the twentieth century what has been called the 'now but not-yet' tension of the gospel message has become more prominent. Some movements in Christian theology have favoured the 'now' or realized elements of God's promises, while others have argued for emphasis on the 'not-yet' of God's rule over history. In this book I shall aim to keep these two poles in equilibrium by developing a biblically anticipatory and theologically experiential account of eschatology. That is, the Scriptures will determine what we can expect of God's will for creation in the future, and in the meantime our life will be guided and governed by reflecting on the promises that the God of the Bible makes to his people. As such, eschatology in what follows will mean 'the goal of history toward which the Bible moves' and 'the biblical factors and events bearing on that goal'.[3] One of the chief aims of this book is to construct an explicitly trinitarian description of eschatology that is at once systematic, generated from the theological interpretation of Scripture and yet sensitive to essential elements of Christian practice.

While there is no shortage of books on 'the end times', too few combine systematic theology with a theological interpretation of Scripture and Christian living. Regrettably, many books on the subject arise out of incoherent or superficial readings of the Bible that detract from, or even ignore, the 'once and for all' achievements of God through the death and resurrection of Jesus. The cost to the church is an eschatology that is insufficiently Christian despite its claim to be 'biblical'. Alternatively, many books on this subject fail to consider how God reveals himself through the Lord Jesus and by the power of his Spirit and are therefore not genuinely Christian, despite the claim to be 'theological'. Sadly, too many books on this subject fail to distinguish between the hope provided by the gospel and the superficial aspirations of a culture that is shaped by the tenets of free-market capitalism and Western political liberalism.

A biblical system of theology

Down through the ages Christian theologians have organized their accounts of eschatology according to a list of topics linked to the end of time. These events may include the kingdom of God, the return of Christ, the resurrection of the dead and the final judgment with its (usually) twofold outcomes of heaven and hell. In addition, some attention may be given to issues arising from millennialism and various other speculative questions like an intermediate state and/or purgatory. Their eschatology is systematic to the extent that the topics are expounded in the order with which one might die and come back to life again, depending on whether the Lord Jesus has returned or not. In contrast to this, I shall adopt a pre-existing system, or integrated collection of theological themes, that can be found within the Bible itself – the Lord's Prayer. Using the Lord's Prayer as a biblical system of theology, and of eschatology in particular, has a number of advantages. These will be discussed more fully in chapter 2, but by way of introduction I offer the following.

The first advantage of adopting the Prayer as the guiding system for expounding eschatology is simply that its eschato-logical tone is well recognized and, as a coherent collection of theological themes, it is not alien to the Scriptures themselves. Attempts at systematizing theology, even theology that is heavily dependent upon the exegesis of Scripture, invariably run up against the charge of forcing the Christian Bible to ignore contra-diction by ignoring parts of Scripture that do not fit neatly within an alien framework.

A second and immediately related advantage of expounding eschatology through the Prayer is that, as a biblical system, it is embedded within the apostolic reflection on the person and work of the Lord Jesus Christ. This means that we can expect the themes represented in the various petitions to align perfectly with the apostolic (dominical even) practice of rereading the Old Testament in the light of the person and work of Jesus Christ. When the Lord gathered his disciples after his resurrection he 'opened their minds to understand the Scriptures'. The immediate result was that they were able to perceive 'that everything written . . . in the Law of Moses, the Prophets, and the Psalms must be fulfilled' in the risen Jesus Christ (Luke 24:44–45). Each of the books in the New Testament is a theological interpretation of the Old Testament Scriptures and I shall attempt to follow that pattern as I expound the Prayer.

A third advantage of the Prayer for establishing a biblical system of theology is the fact that, taken together, the various requests outline the Lord's expectations for the fatherhood of God on the earth to correspond to what it is in heaven. From this perspective, the Prayer is intensely theological because each invocation gives us insight into the being and act of God in the economy of salvation. The Lord Jesus expects us to grow in our knowledge and love of God *as our Father* as a consequence of praying in this manner.

A final advantage, therefore, of shaping our theological description of eschatology via the Lord's Prayer is that it locates our theological reflection on the Scriptures in the context of discipleship at its most basic level – responding to God's word in prayer. Not only have Christians always looked to the Lord's Prayer to shape their theological enquiries; they have, at Christ Jesus' command, incorporated these requests into their basic piety both corporately and individually. For Christians, prayer is an eschatological experience to the extent that they pray on the basis of what they have/know *now* in anticipation of the Lord's answers that are *not-yet* a part of their lives with him. Therefore I shall proceed on the assumption that our theological description of eschatology will be experiential in accordance with the word of the Lord in holy Scripture.

A theological interpretation of Scripture

The practice of interpreting Scripture theologically has enjoyed a renaissance in recent years. I have already indicated something of what that will look like in the present work,[4] namely that I shall seek to read the whole Bible after the example of the apostles who wrote the New Testament. Specifically, I shall explore the canon of Scripture with Paul's stated rule of thumb that 'all God's promises have their "Yes" in Christ Jesus' (2 Cor. 1:20). The canon of Scripture is a narrative that is guided and governed by the gospel of the Lord Jesus Christ. I will take it that the gospel and the canon are constitutive of each other. The gospel determines the shape and scope of the canon, while the canon is the means through which I come to grasp the significance of the gospel.[5]

Putting this together with the biblical system outlined above will mean using each of the Prayer's petitions to clarify a specific divine promise to be explored throughout the canon of Scripture. Furthermore, since we are seeking to look over the shoulders of the apostles as we read the Bible, we shall first link the petition with a specific eschatologically orientated New Testament passage in order to establish a firm exegetical foundation for it. So, for example, in order to explore the hallowing of the Father's name on earth as it is in heaven, we shall begin with Paul's words to the Philippians in chapter 2, where he looks forward to every creature 'in heaven, on earth and under the earth' confessing that the name of the Lord has been given to Jesus the Christ (Phil. 2:10–11). We shall then look back into the Old Testament narrative through the lens of Philippians to grasp the eschatological significance of Christ Jesus' being worshipped with this name in terms of the fulfilment of God's promises concerning his name. The same pattern will be repeated in chapters 3–8 according to the ordering of the petitions in the Lord's Prayer with the purpose of understanding what we can hope for when the fatherhood of God on earth corresponds to what it is in heaven.

Reading the Scriptures for the sake of developing a theological description of something is a practice of the church past and present as much as, if not more than, developing the piety of an individual. Therefore as we reflect on the eschatological significance of each of the Prayer's requests we shall engage with a number of conversation partners. Since I intend this book to be a constructive contribution to modern eschatology studies, my main interlocutors will be Karl Barth and Jürgen Moltmann. These two writers, perhaps more than any others in the twentieth century,[6] have dominated discussions of Christian eschatology, for good and for ill, with their voluminous systematic contributions. Yet their theological input, especially in the case of Barth, is of value to the present project because of their habit in the first instance of reflecting on Scripture.[7] Both of them bring distinct perspectives on how the Bible should be read in the process of theological enquiry and therefore have distinctive emphases on the topic of eschatology. The point of engaging with them in dialogue is to 'let the word of Christ dwell among [us] richly in all spiritual wisdom, teaching and admonishing one another' (Col. 3:16). On the other hand, since understanding the Scriptures themselves is a key focus of what follows, we read them together, 'so that [we] may learn not to go beyond what is written' (1 Cor. 4:6). In that vein and because both Barth and Moltmann belong to the Reformed tradition broadly conceived, I shall also frequently consider what John Calvin wrote about various exegetical points. These eminent Bible readers have been included essentially to clarify the faith 'once and for all delivered to the saints' (Jude 3). Therefore our explorations of their eschatology are limited and students of Barth, Moltmann or Calvin may well find them inadequate. However, while I shall make every effort to outline their positions, it is not my primary intention to provide new insights into their work.

An experiential account of eschatology

To describe an account of eschatology as experiential, especially in our modern context, may seem precariously close to the Romanticism of Schleiermacher with his assertions that 'Religion's essence is neither thinking nor acting, but intuition and feeling'.[8] But, and as indicated above, the experience upon which this book will focus is the right response of any and every Christian to the promises of God, namely prayer. More than this, since Jesus exhorts us to call on '*our* Father in heaven', the prayerful response to God's promises or the experience of eschatology that will be a focus in what follows is that of gathering together as a church. It is among the family of God that we (most likely but not necessarily) hear the promises of the gospel and receive the gift of faith. It is as the body of Christ that we learn to live together in love and it is as the fellowship of the Holy Spirit that hope for the fatherhood of God is born. Throughout this book the experience of eschatology that characterizes the Christian life will be summed up in the phrase 'life in the Middle'. First, and most basically, it is the time between the ascension of the Lord Jesus as the Christ in the power of the Spirit and his return to perfect the Father's will for creation. Second, but no less importantly, life in the

Middle is the space marked out by the church as it is constituted by the Spirit as a testimony to the coming kingdom of the Lord Jesus. Most importantly, though, life in the Middle is characterized by joining with the Lord Jesus himself to call on God as our Father. The goal to which the Bible story moves is the glorious future of the royal and eternal Son of God in the power of God's Spirit. Therefore throughout this book our experience of eschatology will be revealed in what Jesus knew, what he did and for what he hoped.

So then, let us begin by describing eschatology as it is recorded in the Bible. We turn first to life in the Middle as hearing God's promises, responding in hope and embodying that hope in our prayers.

1

LIFE IN THE MIDDLE?

In response to the Brownshirts building the Third Reich on piles
of burning books outside his lecture hall, Dietrich Bonhoeffer
challenged the ability of any modern culture to understand
history:

> Humankind no longer lives in the beginning; instead
> it has lost the beginning. Now it finds itself in the
> middle, knowing neither the end nor the beginning, and
> yet knowing that it is in the middle. It knows therefore
> that it comes from the beginning and must move on
> toward the end. It sees its life as determined by these two
> factors, concerning which it knows only that it does not
> know them.[1]

According to Bonhoeffer, modern German culture was adrift in a
history that had lost its foundational markers. Modern science
had divorced European culture from its traditional Christian
beginning – the creation accounts of Genesis 1 and 2. Meanwhile
the growing shadow of National Socialism menaced the Weimar
Republic with a future described as a putative thousand-year

reign of the Third Reich. To Bonhoeffer, the beginning had been lost and the end was unthinkable. Hence the world was marooned in the middle of history. More than seven decades after the Second World War, after the Cold War, and even after the second millennium, is the world, or just the liberal Western part of it, still in the Middle? Surely the current global threats of terror and of ecological crisis mean that *The End* is nigh. Even if these *ends* do not prove to be *The End*, was it reasonable for Bonhoeffer to assert that the world knows nothing of its end?

Of course, according to our modern scientific culture the answer must surely be, no! Since 1850 exponents of thermodynamics have discussed the possibility of the universe succumbing to an eventual heat death. Based on the principle of 'closed systems degenerat[ing] from order to disorder' some scientists somewhat pessimistically predict the far-future dissolution of life as we currently experience it.[2] Naturally the timescale being referred to as *The End* here is too long to have any meaningful connection to the average individual's end after roughly three-score-and-ten years. Consequently, many in our Romantic Western culture are optimistic about what lies ahead and are happy to accept that the world is in the Middle of history or at least at a turning point prior to a brighter future. For example, Yuval Noah Harari opines that since 'the average human is far more likely to die from bingeing at McDonald's than from drought, Ebola or an al-Qaeda attack',[3] we should strive ahead with ever empowered imagination. Harari backs up these startling claims with an impressively broad sweep of human history as a series of famine, disease and warfare to show that in the early twenty-first century the average Western person (at least) could and should be more optimistic than is in fact the case. When these disasters occur, we need only marshal the considerable resources available to our globalized culture, address the problem and look to a better future that we shall make for ourselves.

In this modern context the Christian gospel comes to us as a promise from the past and for the future, a future with a very definite end – the return of Jesus the Christ to receive his inheritance from God the Father and the establishment of a new creation. From the perspective of the gospel the world is in the Middle between the resurrection of Jesus of Nazareth from the dead and his return that will mark *The End* of a dysfunctional creation ruined by sin, death and evil.

What is more, our place in the Middle of this gospel history also has a spatial aspect. Bonhoeffer described it well: the Lord Jesus meets us as the ultimate truth about the reality of God and the world,[4] and its future, amid the everyday activities of the community, the church.

> I hear another human truly proclaim to me the Gospel; he hands me the sacrament; you are forgiven; he and the community pray for me and I hear the Gospel, pray with and know myself in the Word, sacrament and prayer of the community of Christ, the new humanity, be they here now or elsewhere.[5]

In this book these everyday experiences of Christian living will serve as a starting point for developing a description of eschatology. My proposal is that life in the Middle consists of hearing God's promises and responding with a hope that is embodied in our prayers. Praying together in response to God's promises will serve as the most basic experience of life in the Middle. This is to ensure that, from the outset, the theological description of eschatology that emerges is not 'simply a plausible intellectual vision but more importantly, a compelling account of a way of life'.[6] Each of the three proposed elements of life in the Middle – hearing God's promises, responding in hope and embodying that hope in our prayers – needs clarification, but first we must define what is meant by the term 'eschatology' in Christian doctrine.

What is a Christian doctrine of eschatology?

For most of the last 2,000 years, when Christians spoke of eschatology they described the sequence of events surrounding the return, or second coming, of Christ to the earth. These events included (with some additions and variations) a general resurrection of the dead, a final judgment of the living and the newly resurrected, with the blessing of heaven for the elect and the curse of hell for the reprobate. However, the social and political turmoil of the twentieth century was matched by parallel theological upheaval in the way Christians understood eschatology.

3

Cardinal Ratzinger described it as the shift of eschatology from 'the quiet life as the final chapter of theology' to 'the very centre of the theological stage'.[7] This was the work of biblical scholars and systematic theologians alike. Their common theme was a call for Christians to expand their understanding of eschatology from the events of the end of time to the arrival of God's reign in the world, but how much of that do we have now and how much is still to come? At the risk of oversimplifying, the key theological question changed from 'What happens when the world ends and when will that be?' to 'What effect should the world's approaching end have on our everyday existence?' How should life in the Middle be affected by, from or for *The End*?

The twentieth-century revisionists of eschatology wanted a more *theologically* driven 'self-control'[8] in the manner with which Christians discussed history. Throughout the course of the eighteenth and nineteenth centuries, a combination of factors and ideas led liberal Protestant theologians to speak of history as the process of divine education through reason and for the sake of human freedom.[9] The concept of a cataclysmic end to history was abandoned. Instead, Christianity (read, the moral teachings of Jesus of Nazareth) was held to contribute to 'the moral and cultural progress of humanity'.[10] As Jesus himself taught, 'the kingdom of God is within you' or 'in the midst of you' (Luke 17:21).[11] Modernist ideas of progress via human achievement abounded, whether these were the increasingly ambitious claims for the supremacy of human reason in all human affairs or 'a belief in, if not the perfectibility, then at least the improvability of mankind'.[12] These ideas in turn rested on Hegel's philosophy of history, which saw 'the movement of Absolute Spirit through the various points of transition that are the existence of finite beings on the way to the Spirit's absolute fulfilment'.[13] The net effect was the transformation of Romantic Europe's under- standing of the kingdom of God with a liberal Protestantism filled with a cultural eschatology of heaven being realized on earth in the form of rational and free individuals establishing modern nation states.[14]

Against this popular tide, at the turn of the twentieth century, Johannes Weiss argued, 'actualisation of the Rule of God by human ethical activity is completely contrary to the transcenden- talism of Jesus' idea'.[15] Jesus' teaching about the kingdom of God

4

was thoroughly futurist and instituted exclusively by God. Jesus, according to Weiss, 'had hoped to see the establishment of the Kingdom' but realized that he must 'make his contribution to . . . the Kingdom in Israel by his death'.[16] Albert Schweitzer later added chidingly, 'Men feared that to admit claims of eschatology would abolish the significance of His [Jesus'] words for our time.'[17] Schweitzer applauded Weiss's work and added, 'With political expectations this Kingdom has nothing whatever to do.'[18] The tragic irony is, of course, that both of these scholars considered that the failure of God's kingdom to arrive on the earth, either in the life of Jesus himself or by the time the first generation of followers died out, meant that God had been defeated. Jesus of Nazareth too, it would seem, was lost in Bonhoeffer's 'Middle'.

The idea that Christian eschatology is primarily a *theological* question – what God does in and with history – returned to prominence via the early writings of Karl Barth. After the horrors of the First World War, the idea of God's judgment as a catastrophic end to the world, previously dismissed by liberal Protestants as archaic, returned as a transcendent reality that overshadowed the present. Christians began again to focus on the relationship between time and eternity, as the resurrection became 'the model for the confrontation of time through the eternal'.[19] Full of sensational and distinctly existential rhetoric, Barth's *The Epistle to the Romans* proclaimed of Romans 8:11:

> We cannot question Truth [the Spirit] as to why it is what it is; for it has already asked us why we are what we are; and in the question has provided also the rich answer of eternity: 'Thou,' it says, 'art man, man of this world; thou dost belong to God, Creator and Redeemer' . . . Because Truth is eternally pre-eminent over all that we have and are, it is our hope, our undying portion, and our indestructible relation with God.[20]

The Spirit's action of giving life to our mortal bodies is at once wholly future and yet secretly present. The confirmation of such a promise was not to be in the advances of Western culture – now lost in the quagmires of Europe's battlefields. Instead, the Middle is history bounded by God's transcendent and eternal apocalyptic incursion. In the gospel we hear, 'By hope we are saved – inasmuch as in Jesus Christ the wholly Other, unapproachable, unknown, eternal power and divinity (i.20) of God has entered into our world.'[21] Barth too advocated the thoroughly eschatological nature of the ministry of the Lord Jesus: 'If Christianity be not altogether thoroughgoing eschatology, there remains in it no relationship whatever with Christ.'[22] Yet, unlike Weiss and Schweitzer, Barth insisted that Jesus could not be left behind in history, because he is the Lord of history. A thoroughly eschatological Christianity must understand the Middle as the time between the resurrection of the Lord Jesus and the earthly consummation of his kingdom – his defining of our history.

Barth's revision of modern eschatology renewed the discipline of understanding the pre-eminence of God's freedom over creation and the gracious nature of his saving actions within it when discussing history. Consequently, there is a distinctly 'now' emphasis on God's kingdom – we understand eschatology based on what he has revealed of his actions already completed. The extent to which life in the Middle should be affected by, or even effected from, *The End* became an acute matter amid the social and political upheaval of the 1960s. The importance of the future hope in Christian theology was the subject of Jürgen Moltmann's *Theology of Hope*. Broadly influential on both sides of the Atlantic,[23] Moltmann's work argued for what he saw as a distinctively Christian theology shaped by the future:

> From first to last, and not merely in the epilogue, Christianity is eschatology, is hope, forward looking and forward moving, and therefore also revolutionising and transforming the present. Thus eschatology is not one element of Christianity, but it is the medium of Christian faith as such, the key in which everything in it is set, the glow that suffuses everything here in the dawn of an expected new day.[24]

Moltmann's dedication to the centrality of hope for eschatology was, in his mind, an attempt to return Christian theology to a biblical emphasis on the importance of promise and fulfilment – especially in the exodus and the prophetic writings of the Old Testament. In contrast to these, Moltmann claimed that Christian theology, especially in the West, had too readily adopted the

Hellenistic notion of the immanent presence of absolute being – 'the god of Parmenides' – that negates any meaningful sense of history. Moltmann understood himself to be taking the discussion beyond the emphases of the early Barth.[25] He complained that Barth's stress on the self-revelation of God meant an 'eternal presence of God in time', a 'present without any future'.[26] This, according to Moltmann, resulted in 'the future redemption [promised] in the revelation of Christ [becoming] only a supplement, only a noetic unveiling of the reconciliation effected in Christ'.[27] Barth's insistence on the transcendent intervention of God's eternal present undermined the reality of history and therefore diminished the sense in which the gospel of the risen Lord Jesus could be understood as a promise. In contrast, Moltmann's desire was for something more than another metaphysical description of the world. He argued that because it is rooted in the resurrection and cross of Christ, eschatology 'must formulate its statements of hope in contradiction to our present experience of suffering, evil and death'.[28] Thus hope for the future becomes the basis for mission in the present. This is not to return to the ethical reconstruction of a new Christian civilization but to the Spirit's work of constituting a church in the world, a church that proclaims Christ while waiting in hope for the coming of God. The theology of hope was not to be understood as a quietist vision of life in the Middle – Moltmann's theology was (and is) always revolutionary in its ethos. Not surprisingly, then, an eschatology that understood the coming of the rule of God as 'the coming of righteousness, peace, freedom and human dignity' found great support in environments that experienced the opposite – among liberation theologians of Latin America, for example.[29]

From these twentieth-century revisions in Christian eschatology a theological description of life in the Middle must include the expectation that the rule of God in the world will be a *divine achievement*, not the gradual outcome of human civilization. This divine achievement has already entered apocalyptically into world history with the resurrection of Messiah Jesus from the dead. But this divine intervention remains a promise for the future that is yet to be *perfected*. The promised future provides hope by contradicting our present experience in a world distorted by sin, death and evil. The hope that God will bring about such an end

7

shapes the gospel that is preached and upon which our prayers are based in the everyday experience of life in the Christian community. With these broad theological disciplines for our eschatology in place, we must now consider more carefully what the Bible says about God's making of promises, what is involved in our response of hope and what this hope must look like as we pray.

Promises, hope and prayers in the Bible

Before prayers can be offered, promises must be given and that action of God must be understood theologically. To make a connection between our prayers and the promises of God is hardly revolutionary. Calvin commented on praying in response to God's promises, 'among the duties of godliness, the Scriptures commend none more frequently'.[30] Still, in order to gain a stronger grasp on the everyday impact of the gospel's now–not-yet tension and to refine further the sense in which this must be understood as a theological issue, more needs to be said regarding the nature of God's promises and our prayers as the basic eschatological experience of them. Furthermore, the nature of Christian hope and significance of that hope for life in the Middle must also be taken into account.

God's promises for the Middle

When individuals are drawn into the community of Messiah Jesus by his Spirit they gain perspective on life in the Middle through promises like these:

> At the name of Jesus every knee in the heavens, on the earth and under the earth will be bent and every tongue will confess that Messiah Jesus is Lord to the glory of God the Father. (Phil. 2:10–11)

> When all things have been subjected to him, then the Son himself will be made subject to the one who subjected all things to him so that God will be all in all. (1 Cor. 15:28)

> God's plans for all things, in heaven and on the earth, have been (and will be) revealed to be summed up in the Messiah. (Eph. 1:10)

8

The specifics of these kinds of promises will be addressed in the chapters that follow but for now a theological definition of promise-making will depend on what we learn about God and how he relates to his human creatures as a consequence of making promises to them. How God makes promises and then fulfils them is the key to understanding eschatology in the context of life in the Middle. Barth suggested that we should consider two key biblical promises: God's promise to be present in creation and his covenantal promise to perfect a people for himself. We shall start with these two fundamental promises because an eschatology derived from the whole Bible will be more 'holistic' than just a list of things to expect at the return of Christ.[31] To be theological, our eschatology must be a product of weaving together the actions of the Father through the Son and in the Spirit from creation to new creation.

God gives himself to us through promises

In discussing 'The Work of God the Reconciler', Barth sought to encapsulate 'the whole complex of Christian understanding and doctrine' on the subject (reconciliation) in the phrase 'God with Us'.[32] According to him, this is a statement that Christians in their community make to one another and to any who as yet do not, but should, belong with them in the community of God's people – 'God is the One who is with them as God.'[33] The phrase belongs most importantly to Matthew's Gospel, where the evangelist recounts Joseph's dream in which he is told that Mary, though a virgin, will give birth to a son, giving him a name that means 'salvation' (Matt. 1:18–25). Matthew then interprets the birth of this child of promise as the fulfilment of the promise made by YHWH through the prophet Isaiah: 'The virgin will conceive, have a son, and name him Immanuel' (Isa. 7:14). This name, adds the evangelist, means 'God with us'. From the very beginning of the Gospel accounts Jesus is depicted as the one through whom God will bring salvation. The Isaianic promise is not just that in Jesus we are able to declare that 'God is on our side,' but that God will be personally present as our saviour in Jesus.[34] What is of significance for a discussion of God's promise-making is this central claim that when God makes a promise, he gives himself in it.[35] Barth wrote:

9

> What unites God and us men is that God does not will
> to be God without us, that He creates us rather to share
> with us and therefore with our being and life and act His
> own incomparable being and life and act.[36]

Putting these two ideas together, without compromising his
absolute otherness as the transcendent creator of all things, God's
desire is to share himself – his life as Father, Son and Holy Spirit –
and to be present with us as this God, and he achieves this in his
promises and their subsequent fulfilment for us and among us.[37]
This is what the prophet Isaiah foresaw, through God's word and
by his Spirit, and what was subsequently fulfilled, or perfected, in
Jesus; God not only promises to be present with his people but is
in fact present in the promise through his word and by his Spirit.
Whatever the contemporary significance of the prophecy was for
Israel, the concept of God's sharing himself with his people is
echoed in various places in the Old Testament where YHWH is
referred to as 'the portion' of various people. Hence Moses is told
that Aaron and the Levites will be given no part of the land
because YHWH himself will be their 'portion' (Num. 18:20).[38]
Likewise, the psalmist praises the promise-making God, 'You are
my portion, Lord . . . my portion in the land of the living,' and
the prophet Jeremiah referred to the Lord as 'the Portion of
Jacob'.[39] What has been experienced from the time of Pentecost
in terms of the Spirit of God among his people was foreseen by
Ezekiel, through whom the Lord promises, 'I will place My Spirit
within you' (see Ezek. 36:27; 37:14).[40] Life in the Middle must
therefore be understood in terms of God's sharing himself with
his people in his promises. God makes promises through his word
and by his Spirit. He fulfils these promises through his Son and in
his Spirit. This can be understood even more concretely when we
look to the covenant promise 'I will be your God and you will be
my people.'[41]

God makes promises and in them gives himself in order to
perfect the relationship between himself and his creatures. As
Barth wrote:

> When (in Jesus Christ) we look into the heart of God –
> for in Him He has revealed to us: 'I will be your God'
> – we are permitted, indeed we are constrained, to look

at ourselves, that what is proper to and is required of us is: 'Ye shall be my people.'[42]

The gospel of the Lord Messiah Jesus commands and enables us, in the power of the Spirit, to hear God's gracious promise to us in the Lord Jesus, that we are the body of the Messiah, the fellowship of the Spirit and the children of God (cf. 1 Cor. 12:27; 2 Cor. 13:14; John 1:12). The writer to the Hebrews confirms this observation with his interpretation of the promises made through the prophet Jeremiah. In the context of explaining the superiority of the covenant that God establishes through Jesus over and against the old Sinai covenant, he cites Jeremiah 31:31–34, especially 'This is the covenant I will establish with the house of Israel after those days, says the Lord . . . I will be their God and they will be my people' (Heb. 8:10).

The age-old formula of the promise finds its perfection through and in the person and work of the Lord Jesus.[43] In fact, John's Apocalypse appeals to this promise as a description of the experience in the new creation: 'God will dwell with them, they will be his people and God himself will be with them and will be their God' (Rev. 21:3). Consequently, as has been suggested, God not only gives himself to us in his promises, but gives these promises in order to renew and perfect a relationship with him. Sin, death and evil are constant barriers to the creator God's purpose to share his life with his creatures and the reason why the relationship requires renewal. However, in the Lord Jesus and by the power of the Holy Spirit God's determination to fulfil his promises is indomitable, even if their achievement is not immediately obvious. This is where the creaturely response of hope to God's promises becomes significant.

Hope as a passion for the possible

If understanding the nature of God's promise-making in the Bible is one key aspect for life in the Middle, theologically describing human experience of those promises as hope is another. Even if God gives himself in his promises and definitively in Jesus, Moltmann's observation still holds: 'fulfilment unexpectedly gives rise in turn to another promise of something greater still'.[44] There is always more to God's promises even when it seems they have been fulfilled. For example, when the disciples came to the empty

11

tomb the angels said, 'He is not here; he has risen' (Luke 24:6). Yet the resurrection of Jesus and even his subsequent exaltation 'to the right hand of God' introduced a further 'until' for Jesus himself as he awaits the time in which God 'make[s] [his] enemies a footstool for [his] feet' (Acts 2:33, 35; cf. Ps. 110). As with Jesus, then, so also with us, on the basis of the promise that 'God has made this Jesus whom you crucified, Lord and Messiah,' we await the day when 'in the name of Jesus, every knee will bow – on earth and in heaven – and every tongue will confess that Messiah Jesus is Lord' (Acts 2:36; Phil. 2:10–11). We have to wait for God's promises to be fulfilled because of what Moltmann referred to as 'the overspill' of promise: 'The overspill of promise means that they have always a provisional character . . . Hence the history that is thus experienced and transmitted forces every new present to analysis and to interpretation.'[45] We shall construct a theological definition of hope within the context of 'living in the overspill of God's promises'.

It is a basic axiom of Reformation theology that we are saved by grace and through faith, so to propose that we respond to God's promises in hope needs some explanation. In relation to the promises of God Moltmann also wrote, 'faith is the foundation upon which hope rests, hope nourishes and sustains faith'.[46] One must trust the promises of God before there is hope, yet trust and hope are equally proportional and mutually constitutive.[47] There must be knowledge of and hence trust in God's promises in the Lord Jesus to ensure that hope is not confused with utopia. Yet faith without hope soon falls to pieces in the experience of a world frustrated by sin. Hope 'sees in the resurrection of Christ not the eternity of heaven, but the future of the very earth on which his cross stands'.[48] Paul Ricoeur, in conversation with Moltmann's *Theology of Hope*, suggested that for hope to be meaningful it ought not merely to point 'to a specific object but to a structural change within . . . [our] discourse'.[49] His proposal was that the substance of hope ought to be understood in terms of a way of being in the world above and beyond acknowledging a particular historic event – like the resurrection. Ricoeur appreciated Moltmann's understanding of hope as 'nothing else than the expectation of those things which faith has believed to have been truly promised by God'.[50] That is, hope is a verb before (and more importantly than) it is a noun because it is our way of participating in the divine dynamic of promise and fulfilment – along with love, hope is a personal engagement in God's promises. Hence Ricoeur adopted the expression 'a passion for the possible' as a philosophical description of hope and our way of living in the Middle or in the context of the overspill of God's promises.[51] In developing Moltmann's concepts, Ricoeur also pointed to the significance of Paul's 'how much more' meditation on the triumph of God's grace in relation to sin (Rom. 5:12–20; see esp. Rom. 5:17). Here Paul juxtaposes the sin of Adam and its subsequent effects on humanity with the free gift of life in Christ Jesus and the vastly superior transformational power of God's grace in perfecting the intentions revealed in the gospel. This 'wisdom of the resurrection', according to Ricoeur, implies 'a logic of surplus and excess' in Christian hope: 'This wisdom is expressed in an economy of superabundance, which we must decipher in daily life, in work, and in leisure, in politics and in universal history.'[52]

So hope is living with a 'passion for the possible' in the 'overspill' of God's promises. It is certainly a rich description and a fairly optimistic view of hope in the Middle. However, this definition needs to be qualified in a number of areas if only to distinguish our intentionally theological description from the aspirations of modern Romantic culture. First, while there is a degree of alignment between Moltmann and Ricoeur, the latter was drawn more to the symbolism of the resurrection than to the future of Jesus that the resurrection reveals.[53] Hence when Moltmann discussed the effect of promise on revelation in relation to the Easter events, promise is not *merely* 'a word-event which brings truth and harmony between man and the reality that concerns him'.[54] The resurrection of Jesus does far more than give us a different way of establishing meaning and action in the world: with the objectivity of divine revelation, 'promise announces the coming of a not yet existing reality from the future of the truth'.[55] Hence *possibilities* that arise from promise '[go] beyond what is possible and impossible in the realistic sense'.[56] God the Father's intentions are revealed in the perfection of his promises and far surpass our imagination or intellectual intuition.

Second, and following immediately on from the above, using the perspective of the resurrection of the crucified Messiah, the

13

sense in which hope might be optimistic arises when 'the man of hope' endures suffering in a world contradicted by the promise of a new creation.[57] It is through suffering 'participation in the mission and the love of Jesus Christ' that individuals suffer 'the passion for what is possible, for what is coming and promised in the future of life, of freedom and of resurrection'.[58] Moltmann appealed to Paul's words to the Corinthian church, 'As he was crucified through weakness, yet liveth by the power of God, so we also are weak in him, but we shall live with him by the power of God' (2 Cor. 13:4).[59] *The passion of those who hope in the promises of God the Father is for vindication in the face of death through the power of resurrection.* Modern Romantic culture has, by way of contrast, elevated the power of human imagination or intellectual intuition to the point that art, in a wide range of technological forms, 'has the power to create an entire world through imagination'.[60] It has this power, apparently, due to the creative potential of 'intellectual intuition' to rationalize facts that are not otherwise given to the senses. It is a view of art based on the conviction that 'it [is] through the intellectual intuition of the infinite in the finite, the absolute in its appearance, or the macrocosm in the microcosm'.[61] As we shall come to see, modern culture invests the individual with a largely sentimental kind of passion for predominantly aesthetic possibilities.

The third qualification of the idea of hope as a passion for the possible was raised by Eberhard Jüngel, and it relates to the importance of understanding the possible as a free act of God as opposed to the human achievement just mentioned. In discussing history as eschatological, Moltmann drew attention to the way in which the event of the resurrection completely changes our view of what could or could not happen in history given the right circumstances: 'The resurrection of Christ does not mean a possibility within the world and its history, but a new possibility altogether for the world, for existence and for history.'[62] For Jüngel the resurrection of the Lord Jesus is an *ex nihilo* event in world history – like the creation of the world itself – that must completely undermine any progressivist view of history, no matter how rational it may appear. Jüngel takes this basic idea of the resurrection and applies it to individual human experience. His chief concern is to point out the difference that justification by faith makes to our understanding of what is possible in human existence. He argues that, thanks to Aristotle, the Western world view has always given priority to 'the actual' over 'the possible' when it comes to describing our existence.[63] At first glance this seems obvious: 'the actuality of this world arises from its possibility not as from nothingness but as from a "not yet" which as such participates in being [existence] even though it is not yet'.[64] Hence the Romantic aspiration to discern the infinite *in the finite* or intuit the *Big Picture* of history from a specific number of particular events. However, Jüngel argues, this Aristotelian way of thinking is not the same as the 'now–not-yet' tension of the gospel. The New Testament apocalyptic description of the actions of God in the world 'represent[s] a complete metamorphosis of both the apocalyptic material [of the Old Testament] and also the world view inaugurated by Aristotle'.[65] That is, the Gospel accounts of Christ Jesus' resurrection introduce a *type* of event for which there is no precedent in the biblical story. To grasp the significance of this, the Aristotelian mindset must be deconstructed at the most basic human level. That, according to Jüngel, is found when we revisit hope's complement that was mentioned above, the Reformation doctrine of justification by grace, through faith alone.

Using Luther's criticism of Aristotle's basic concept of the righteous person, Jüngel points to the prevalence in Western thinking of the idea 'We are what we make ourselves.'[66] What Luther showed, from the perspective of the gospel, was the complete opposite. That is, what we attempt to make of ourselves is 'the nothingness of sin' as opposed to the 'new creation' (from nothing in terms of our own efforts) we are through the gospel. Jüngel points to Paul's description of 'the justifying God . . . who gives life to the dead and calls into being the things that are not (Rom. 4:17)' as a warrant.[67] Hence the resurrection of Jesus completely changes the existence of the individual because 'Jesus' resurrection from the dead promises that we shall be made anew out of the nothingness of relationlessness [sin], remade *ex nihilo*.'[68] In relation to the idea of hope as a passion for the possible, Jüngel wanted to change radically the definition of the possible: '*Theology does this by establishing the distinction between the possible and the impossible as incomparably more fundamental than the distinction between the actual and the not-yet-actual.*'[69]

15

For hope to be a passion for the possible, it must be a passion for what God makes possible and declares to be impossible in the gospel of the Lord Messiah Jesus. It is in this fashion that 'the Word of God occurs as a word of promise and judgement'.[70] Hope that grows from the gospel, according to Jüngel, cannot look to the actual for signs of the possible nor consider the possible as somehow already existing in the actual. Instead, hope must look to what God has made possible in the resurrection of the Lord Jesus and what God has declared to be impossible – the world governed by sin: 'the justified person hopes for the world, not as hope for any particular future worldly actuality, but only as hope in God's creative Word'.[71]

To sum up, hope is a passion for the possibilities that are latent in God's promises. It is grounded on God's key achievements in the resurrection and anticipates the perfection of those achievements in the future. Given the overspill of God's promises, such a hope will recognize an appropriate degree of openness concerning the future: 'a hope which is seen is no hope at all' (Rom. 8:24). This is primarily because the resurrection, though foretold, was an event that defied intellectual intuition. Therefore hope in God's promised future powerfully contradicts an individual's or churches' present experiences of participating in the suffering love and mission of the Lord Jesus because 'if we are hoping in that which is not seen, through perseverance we wait eagerly' (Rom. 8:25). Nevertheless, neither suffering nor the lack of it will contribute to this future hope, as the life that springs from the promise of the gospel is always and in every way a gift of God's grace.

To ensure that this hope that we have defined is not simply a baptized version of intellectual intuitions, it must be embodied in our responses to God's grace, since 'faith without works is dead' (Jas 2:17). Hence we shall proceed to explore hope embodied in prayer as the quintessential eschatological response to God's promises. Before we do that, however, we need to reflect further upon two aspects of the overspill of God's promises. The first is our historical experience of the provisional nature of God's promises, an experience that fashions our hope and refines our faith. The second is the sovereign activity of God by the power of his Spirit that perfects our history in fulfilment of his promises.

The provisional nature of God's promises

I defined hope in the context of what Moltmann called the overspill of God's promises: 'The overspill of promise means that they have always a provisional character . . . Hence the history that is thus experienced and transmitted forces every new present to analysis and to interpretation.'[72] Our experience of history is directly related to the time that it takes for God's promises to be fulfilled. The provisional nature of God's promise-making establishes the broad contours and temporal direction of life in the Middle as part of the history created by God's promise to be present with his people. Hence, as human beings understand who they are and where they fit in history, they hope, as a consequence of remembrance and expectation, 'by the anamnesis [remembrance] by which he retains his past and the prognosis [anticipation] by which he lays hold of what is to come'.[73] The promises of the gospel come to us as both remembrance and expectation. We remember that Messiah Jesus was raised from the dead by the Spirit to sit at the right hand of God the Father. This fact has been an essential element of gospel preaching from Pentecost onward: 'God has raised this Jesus to life . . . [he has been] exalted to the right hand of God,' declared Peter (Acts 2:32–33). At the same time, and on this basis, we also anticipate the 'day when he [Jesus] comes to be glorified by his saints and to be admired by all those who have believed' (2 Thess. 1:10).

The 'known from the past' but 'looking to the future' experience of provisionality is the 'now–not-yet' tension of life in the Middle and it is also one of the key challenges to faith and hope: 'How long, O Lord?' is the oft-repeated call of the biblical writers, as in Psalm 13. It is a challenge in so far as it requires a careful understanding of what can be read in the Bible about God's making promises and fulfilling them; for example, the millennium in Revelation 20. The various genres of biblical literature reflect the provisionality of the promise given. Brueggemann from the exodus narrative identifies two distinct forms of the promise-making that emerged in the life of Israel. The first group consists of the prophetic and messianic promises.[74] The substance of these promises concerns 'the public, concrete prospect of peace, justice, security and abundance',[75] and points to YHWH's intention that public institutions will eventually conform to his

17

purposes. Hence the hope of Israel rests on whether YHWH is willing and able to establish these institutions. However, the promises are messianic in so far as they anticipate that God's future will be enacted via the medium of human agency. Now Israel must not only entrust herself to the word of YHWH but also the human agent commissioned by him. The second group of promises, far more on the periphery of the Old Testament, take on an apocalyptic form. These originate neither through public processes nor by human agency. Instead, 'by the sovereign incursion of Yahweh, whose newness is not extrapolated from the present, something utterly new will be given'.[76] These apocalyptic promises anticipate an unmediated action of YHWH on behalf of his people.

In terms of the first group of promises, certain of them are repeated throughout the Israelite drama and are often provisionally fulfilled, whether in possessing the Promised Land or kingship in Israel. Yet the promises are not subsequently eclipsed by these provisional fulfilments.[77] Provisionality means that biblical promises ought not to be understood as mere predictions that come to an end once the time and place has arrived: they invariably retain some future aspect, some overspill. König points to 'the day of the Lord' as a prime example.[78] Possibly quite old by the time it first appears in Amos' ministry (Amos 5:20),[79] the prophecy seems to have been fulfilled with the fall of Jerusalem in 586 BC, as interpreted by Ezekiel (13:5) and Jeremiah (Lam. 1:12; 2:1, 22; cf. Isa. 13:6–9). Yet Malachi, after the return from exile, invokes the phrase in reference to a return of Elijah (Mal. 4:5) at some future 'day of the Lord'. A further variation on the theme is found when Peter invokes Joel's use of the phrase to interpret the events of Pentecost. Joel (Joel 2:28ff.) looked forward to God's pouring out his Spirit on 'the day of the Lord'. Peter (Acts 2:17) interpreted the day of Pentecost as 'the great and glorious day' to which Joel was referring. Nevertheless, even here, at what is a climactic event of the pouring out of God's Spirit in fulfilment of the ancient prophecy, Peter's sermon depicts the outpouring as an ongoing event ('In these last days') – the day of the Lord is projected into the future.[80] The one thing these promised 'days of the Lord' have in common is that he will appear.[81]

In reference to what has been said concerning God's giving himself in the promises, the provisional nature of the promises through time and space *could* depend on the extent to which God gives himself in the promise. Barth offered something like this in his discussion of Old Testament promises: 'God is present to man as the coming God. Present and coming are both to be stressed.'[82] Of course, there is a creaturely aspect or contribution to the provisionality of God's promises. Calvin drew our attention to the transient nature of the promise receivers: 'We hold that carnal prosperity and happiness did not constitute the goal set before the Jews to which they were to aspire. Rather, they were adopted into the hope of immortality.'[83] The implication here seems to be that because the promises ('by oracles, by the law and by the prophets') were so readily compromised by the experience of death, the promises must therefore be provisional in nature. In fact, Calvin argued, the very nature of the gospel promises reveals that they offer something far more necessary than creaturely institutions.[84] Since surely 'the gospel does not confine men's hearts to delight in the present life, but lifts them to the hope of immortality',[85] the Old Testament promises must point to the future. As we shall see, the human condition does have some significance for the provisionality of God's promises: 'Between promise and fulfilment there is a whole variety of intermediate links and processes, such as exposition, development, validation, assertion, renewal etc.'[86] Such a process does not take away from the authenticity of any of God's promises however, because 'the guarantee of the promise's congruity with reality lies in the credibility and faithfulness of him who gives it'.[87] God's promises are not provisional because he is somehow unable to fulfil them or unreliable in making them. Instead, as we shall see, in spite of the human condition, God governs the course of human history by the power of his Spirit, who provides both the promises and the fulfilment.

The Spirit of hope and the promises of God

If our passion for the possibilities of God's promises for life in the Middle is a gracious gift, as described above, it is because the risen Lord Jesus 'has received from the Father the promised Holy Spirit and poured out what you now see and hear' (Acts 2:33). In this way God continues to give himself in his promises throughout life in the Middle. At Pentecost Peter proclaimed to the gathered crowd that the promise of God through the prophet Joel had been fulfilled – 'the last days' had begun as seen in the power of the Spirit (Acts 2:14, 16–17). The church is now constituted by the power of the Spirit and into the history created by God's promises. By the Spirit God acts to make himself present to his people – Jew and Gentile – through the Lord Messiah Jesus. Therefore a church is a new temple, the dwelling place of God (Eph. 2:21–22). A passion for what is possible during life in the Middle arises from God's gift of himself through Christ and in the Spirit; as Calvin put it, 'by [the secret energy of the Spirit] we come to enjoy Christ and all his benefits'.[88] It is by the power of God's Spirit, by whom Jesus was raised from the dead, that the Christians 'can obediently take upon themselves the sufferings of discipleship and in these very sufferings wait the future glory'.[89] The possibilities of these benefits for life in the Middle will be explored further as the last aspect of responding to God's promises – in prayer – is considered. In anticipation of that, we must add that the importance of the Spirit for life in the Middle is not confined to the church. All God's activity in creation from the beginning is in the power of his Holy Spirit (Gen. 1:2; cf. Ps. 33:6).

Calvin, rightly, acknowledged a distinction between the way God's Spirit particularizes the church and the way God works by 'His second hand'[90] for the rest of creation:

> Nor is there reason for anyone to ask, what have the impious, who are utterly estranged from God, to do with his Spirit? We ought to understand the statement that the Spirit of God dwells only in believers [Rom. 8:9] as referring to the Spirit of sanctification through whom we are consecrated as temples to God [1 Cor. 3:16]. Nonetheless he fills, moves, and quickens all things by the power of the same Spirit, and does so according to the character that he bestowed upon each kind by the law of creation.[91]

The Holy Spirit mediates God's power in and over creation, thus ensuring that creation is distinct from God himself. This is not separate from God's actions in creation through his Son but rather, as Basil of Caesarea suggested, we may understand the Holy Spirit as 'the perfecting cause of creation'.[92] The Spirit perfects, that is, gives ontological direction to everything in creation towards the Father, through the Son. This is not a static notion of perfection but rather a sense of having come through a state of fallenness by means of redemption in order to be what all are meant to be in ongoing relationship with the living Creator. Colin Gunton summarized it thus: 'As the "perfecting cause" the Holy Spirit, the Lord the Giver of Life, gives reality to the world by perfecting what the Father does through his Son: originating what is truly other.'[93] The perfecting activities of the Spirit are focused most clearly in creation on the person of Jesus the Christ, for in him we have a preview of what will be achieved in the new creation. Again, Gunton summarized, 'God the Father through his Spirit shapes this representative sample of the natural world [Jesus Christ] for the sake of the remainder of it.'[94] The full significance of these ideas will be explored in due course, but for now two things need explaining.

First, and as mentioned above, the Spirit incorporates a church into the *whole* history created by God's promises. This action creates the continuity between those who received God's promises through the Lord Messiah Jesus *and* those who were promised he would come. For, as Peter remarks, the prophets of the old covenant were serving the church when they foretold the things of Messiah Jesus that were subsequently preached by the apostles in the Spirit: 'for though human, they spoke from God as they were moved by the Holy Spirit' (1 Peter 1:11–12; 2 Peter 1:21). It is in the power of the one Spirit that all God's promises are made. Yet it is in the power of the same Spirit that God's promises are received and the passion for the possible – hope – is born. In terms of the experience of provisionality discussed in the previous section, which fashions hope and refines faith, all our experience of history is guided and governed by the perfecting Spirit towards God's ultimate achievements for and in Jesus the Christ. The grace of God is revealed in that not only does he direct the history of the world towards his intended goal of the universal lordship of Jesus the Christ over sin, death and evil, but he also empowers his people by the same Spirit to hope in his promises despite their circumstances.

The second matter of importance concerning the eschatological work of the Spirit relates to some of the remarks made by Jüngel. While it is essential to uphold that 'it is by grace [we] have been saved through faith – and this not from ourselves, [but as] a gift from God' (Eph. 2:8) there are theological difficulties inherent in adopting creation *ex nihilo* as a description of God's *saving* actions. The resurrected Lord Jesus, though transformed by the power of the Spirit, is still the crucified Messiah – hence the reference to the scars of his passion in both the resurrection appearances and his apocalyptic glorification (John 20:25–27; Rev. 5:6–12). This continuity in the person of Jesus himself is not only essential to the gospel; from this foundation it is also essential to ensuring that God's work in creation is not somehow isolated from his work in redemption. Any description of eschatology must ensure that the person and work of the Lord Messiah Jesus is not, somehow, God's 'plan B' for creation. Hence to appropriate a perfecting work of God in creation to his Spirit is to make eschatology the direction to which God moves creation for his ultimate purpose. In this way the future direction or forward-moving aspect of history that makes it possible to speak of the 'not-yet' is a theological description of history and the key to understanding the provisional nature of God's promises; especially when it is recalled that God's purpose is the summing up of all things in the Lord Jesus, for 'all things are for him'. Of course, it is a purpose that is at all times and in all places through him because 'all things are through him' and 'in him all things hold together' (Col. 1:16–17). The sum total of these ideas is that hope becomes a passion for the possibilities of the triune God's perfecting work.

We must finally consider the last of the proposed aspects of life in the Middle, the embodiment of hope in prayer. To ensure that our definition of prayer is truly theological we must contextualize this basically creaturely experience within the focal point of the triune God's perfecting work, the cross of Jesus of Nazareth.

Prayer and the promises of God

So far the present description of eschatology has developed as a theological account of life in the Middle. The argument has focused upon God's promise-making, how we interpret the Bible as the history of God's promise-making and how, by the power of God's Spirit, God's promises give birth to hope – a passion for the possibilities of God's perfecting work. If hope is the starting point of a theological description of human experience or a response to God's promises, hoping and trusting need to be embodied in some kind of creaturely activity, because hope and faith are two sides of the same coin. The chief creaturely response to the promises of God, and therefore the quintessential experience of life in the Middle, is prayer. As Calvin said:

> It is, therefore, by the benefit of prayer that we reach those riches, which are laid up for us with the Heavenly Father. For there is a communion of men with God by which . . . they appeal to him in person concerning his promises in order to experience . . . that what they believed was not vain, although he had promised it in word alone. Therefore we see that to us nothing is promised to be expected from the Lord, which we are not also bidden to ask of him in prayers. So true is it that we dig up by prayer the treasures that were pointed out by the Lord's gospel, and which our faith has gazed upon.[95]

The ordinary human response to God's promises is prayer. As we pray, we look to the future – it is inherent in the promise–response dynamics of personal interaction. At the same time, the very notion that we can call on God as Father, through Jesus and by his Spirit, is evidence that God's fatherhood is open to us already. Therefore, in this sense, *prayer embodies the now–not-yet tension of eschatology*. For just as no one hopes for what he has, neither does he ask for it. Yet we call on God as Father only because God's Messiah, the Lord Jesus, has poured out his Spirit 'by whom we cry, Abba, Father' (Rom. 8:15). In the very act of praying we reveal what we believe and understand about the nature of God's promise to perfect a relationship between himself and his human creatures.[96] So, out of God's fatherly kindness towards us, his Spirit prompts us to pray in response to the promises God makes to us through his Son.[97] In order to make concrete the relationship between prayer and hope as a passion for the possibilities of God's perfecting work, this chapter will draw to a close with a meditation on the prayer of the Messiah Jesus. It is by his Spirit of sonship that we call out to God in prayer, and it is in response to God's promises to and through him that we pray (cf. Rom. 8:14–17). To guide the meditation we return to Ricoeur's essay 'Freedom in the Light of Hope'. There,

23

and by way of philosophical reflection on the issues raised by Moltmann's *Theology of Hope*, Ricoeur seeks 'a philosophical approximation of freedom in the light of hope'.[98] Here he delivers three questions for us to take to the Gospel accounts of Jesus' prayer: 'What can he know? What must he do? For what must he hope?'[99]

The Spirit of hope, the prayers of the Son and the promise of the Father

At some point in the middle of the night before he died, between his Passover meal with the disciples and his arrest at the hands of the temple guards, Jesus took the twelve to the garden called Gethsemane to pray (Matt. 26:36–46; Mark 14:32–42; Luke 22:39–46). The scene is shrouded in a darkness deeper than any evening: Satan has led the traitor to gather a posse of faceless antagonists, while despite Peter's passionate declaration of loyalty Jesus has responded with a shocking prediction of further betrayal and seems himself to be on the verge of being over-whelmed with anguish.[100] Within this context the first question is, *what can Jesus know?*

Jesus went to the garden to pray, knowing that he was the Spirit-anointed and therefore 'beloved Son, with whom [God] is delighted'.[101] As he prayed, he had the words of God's promise on his lips: 'My Father, if it is possible, let this cup pass from me' (Matt. 26:39–42). The cup from which Jesus sought deliverance was a symbol of God's wrath or fury that God promised would be drunk both by sinful Israel and the pagan nations. So Isaiah said to Israel, 'you . . . have drunk the cup of His fury' (Isa. 51:17), and Jeremiah was commissioned to prophesy with, 'Take this cup of the wine of wrath from My hand and make all the nations I am sending you to, drink from it' (Jer. 25:15; cf. Jer. 25:28; 49:12; 51:7). The long-promised, and provisionally enacted, judgment of God was to be 'poured out' and Jesus believed that he was the one upon whom it had to fall. He believed this because he likewise knew that he was the promised Servant of the Lord who, empowered by God's Spirit, would announce the year of the Lord's favour (Luke 4:16–20; cf. Isa. 61:1–2) and suffer the punishment 'for the iniquity of us all' (Isa. 53:6). So, as much as Jesus seemed to recoil in the face of his death, as the royal and eternal Son he anticipated wrath where there had only ever been blessing and joy.[102] The consuming fire of God's holiness was about to break out against sin, death and evil and the royal and eternal Son was determined to stand in the way for the sake of sinners (John 12:27) – an experience so dreadful that it distorted the creation, turning the midday sky to blackness and making the earth heave and quake. Thus he offered 'prayers and petitions with loud cries and tears to the one who could save him from death' (Heb. 5:7).[103] Jesus knew that he was God's promised saviour and that God is faithful to his promises. Therefore *what must he do?*

Throughout his ministry Jesus lived with God's promises as 'the law of his being'.[104] That is, enabled by the Spirit, Jesus freely submitted to the 'authority of God's grace'[105] by consistently choosing to interpret his identity and mission through God's word. The wilderness temptation is a perfect case in point (Matt. 4:1–11; Luke 4:1–13). Led by the Spirit into the desert, in response to Satan's offer to determine the nature of his sonship (If you are the son . . .), Jesus chose the way of discipline (suffering), he chose the Father's promised inheritance and he chose not to pre-empt the Father's promise to save him from death – all was 'as it is written'.[106] The Spirit would make effective the Father's promise to his messianic servant and would empower Jesus to face death. Later, and again in the power of the Spirit, Jesus returned to Nazareth to announce, via Isaiah 61, that he was the Spirit-empowered Servant of YHWH who had come to announce and enact the long-promised salvation of God. God endorsed Jesus' actions, as the narrative sews together the history created by God's promise-making. When Jesus went to Gethsemane to pray the narrative shows the same pattern of action: Jesus would do what he had always done.

As mentioned, Jesus had the word of God – the promise of God's judgment – in mind, and by the power of the Spirit Jesus freely submitted to his heavenly Father: 'Not my will but yours be done.'[107] Though clearly distraught at the prospect, Jesus entrusted himself to his 'Abba' Father, and God said 'Yes' to this prayer even while he said 'No' to Jesus' request that the 'cup might pass'. The Spirit was not merely 'with Jesus', but also ministering to him through the promises of God. In his later work *The Spirit of Life* Moltmann continues to promote the importance of the Spirit's ministry to Messiah Jesus during Jesus' mission, especially during 'his experience of God's hiddenness', right through to the 'experience of God-forsakenness on the cross'.[108] Moltmann depicts the Spirit's enabling Jesus to submit to the will of the 'hidden, absent, even rejecting Father'.[109] Hence Jesus endures godforsakenness vicariously for a godforsaken world. Moltmann emphasizes this notion of godforsakenness in all his deliberations on the cross, beginning with *The Crucified God*.[110] 'God-forsakenness is the final experience of God endured by the crucified Jesus on Golgotha, because to the very end he knew he was God's Son.'[111] But rarely, if ever, does Moltmann attend to the importance of God's promises mediated to his Son by his Spirit. Instead, to develop a theology of God's suffering, he focuses entirely on the opening lines of Psalm 22 uttered by Jesus on the cross. So that for the Christian, the God who saves is the Father of Jesus the Christ, the Father who forsakes his Son for the godless and godforsaken. With Jesus' cry of dereliction ('My God, my God, why have you forsaken me?', Mark 15:34) 'all disaster, forsakenness by God, absolute death, the infinite curse of damnation and sinking into nothingness is in God himself'.[112]

In contrast to Moltmann, I propose that the prayers of Jesus should be understood as a Spirit-enabled trust in the promises of God. We may even go so far as to say that God did not desert his Son but enabled him by the Spirit to achieve the salvation that God willed – *this was Jesus' passion*. Even in the infamous depths of the Golgotha event, when Jesus utters the opening words of Psalm 22 (and Matthew's Gospel especially proceeds to load his account of the crucifixion with allusions to the poem), may we not also allow the Spirit to minister the promises of vindication to Jesus?

> For He has not despised or detested
> the torment of the afflicted.
> He did not hide His face from him
> but listened when he cried to Him for help.
>
> (Ps. 22:24)

At the very least, the Father has gifted his Son with a word of lament in order to face his trials. In Gethsemane Jesus responds, or is empowered by the Spirit to respond, to the promises of God in prayer and in this we gain insight into his passion for the possibilities for God's perfecting work. Therefore *for what does Jesus hope?*

As Jesus kneels to pray in this garden the gospel story is fast approaching its climax, for the forces of darkness conspire together against God's Messiah.[113] Jesus knows that he is that Messiah – the one to bring the salvation of God – and he also knows that this salvation can come only through his death. Three times in conversation with his disciples Jesus predicts this to be the case (e.g. Mark 8:31; 9:31; 10:33–34).[114] Now, empowered by God's Spirit, the Messiah entrusts himself to his heavenly Father. Yet this act of submission is not one of resignation. For Jesus commits himself to God's will out of a passion for the possibilities of God's perfecting work for him (Jesus). I have already drawn attention to the prophetic possibilities involved in Jesus' self-understanding – and the Father underlined these through apocalyptic communications. If, as has been suggested, Jesus understood himself to be the suffering Servant of Isaiah, then not only does the prophecy anticipate Jesus' suffering, but also his vindication: 'After he has suffered, he will see the light of life and be satisfied . . . I will give him a portion among the great' (Isa. 53:11–12 TNIV). Each of Jesus' predictions of his death contains a commensurate forecast of his resurrection; 'till we come to his resurrection, in which the power of the Spirit shines brightly . . . faith will find no encouragement or support'.[115] In addition, in his inspired analysis of Jesus' death and resurrection, Peter makes an explicit appeal to Psalm 16 as the means of interpreting the Messiah's death:

> For David said about him, 'I saw beforehand my Lord always before me: because he is at my right hand I will not be shaken . . . because you will not abandon my soul in Hades nor will you permit your holy one to see decay. (Acts 2:25–28)

Thus it seems fair to conclude that Messiah Jesus' passion for the possibilities of God's perfecting work was grounded on God's promise of resurrection for his faithful messianic Servant.

The possibilities of God's perfecting work are, of course, far broader than the resurrection of his Messiah. As 'the pioneer and perfecter' of our faith, Jesus' prayer in Gethsemane, especially his inspired trust in God's promises, previews the goal of the gospel even as his death and resurrection will achieve it. For in Jesus, as Matthew's genealogy indicates, the whole span of the biblical drama of God's promise-making will be drawn together – from Abraham to Jesus (Matt. 1:1–24). Luke's genealogy goes even further and connects Jesus to Adam (Luke 3:23–38). Ever since Adam and Eve were cast out of the Garden of Eden, God has faithfully been working through the history of the world – as shaped by his various promises – to arrive at Jesus in the Garden of Gethsemane. In spite of, and because of, the sin of Adam that affected the whole world, God was working out his intentions so that his eternal and royal Son, Jesus of Nazareth, would pray the prayer 'not my will but yours be done'. In this history Jesus' words are the opposite of those implied by Adam. When Adam ate the fruit from the tree in the Garden of Eden he effectively said to God, 'Not your will but mine be done.' Now, outside the city of God in another garden, the sin of the world is on the verge of being undone because Jesus prays, 'Not my will but yours be done.'

In the end it was only Jesus who prayed this prayer – evidenced so painfully in the failure of his sleeping disciples. Nonetheless, it was the Spirit-perfected Son who prayed alone, and not only for the sake of the past but also for the hope of the future; for if Jesus had not so prayed, no others would ever have been able to. Thus, for example, the writer to the Hebrews emphasizes the fact that the Lord Jesus, as our high priest, 'entered, once and for all, the Most Holy place having found an eternal redemption' (Heb. 9:11–12). The words that Messiah Jesus prayed in Gethsemane 'Not my will but yours be done' become for us a basic response to God's promises. Furthermore, God's promise for us in the Middle is that the Lord Messiah Jesus 'is able to save completely those coming to God through him because he lives always to intercede on their behalf' (Heb. 7:25). As we shall see, regrettably absent from Moltmann's futurist eschatology is the significance of Messiah Jesus' heavenly session as the living promise of God's love for his creation. However, as Calvin so consistently maintained, 'it belongs to a priest to intercede for the people, that they may obtain favour with God. This is what Christ is ever doing, for it was for this purpose that he rose again from the dead.'[116] Critical to *our* passion for the possibilities of God's perfecting work in the future is the promise of the Lord Jesus living for us now, in the Middle. There is much more to be said regarding the everlasting mediation of Messiah Jesus for us. For now, let me summarize the dynamics of life in the Middle.

In the power of God's Spirit we long for the possibilities of God's promise to perfect a relationship between him and us through the Lord Messiah Jesus at his return. We know that God has promised to give himself to us by the Spirit and through the Lord Jesus during this time. We express our hope in prayer as a Spirit-enabled response to what God has achieved for us in the death and resurrection of his royal and eternal Son. In praying, we participate in the passionate struggles of the Spirit-empowered Messiah against sin, death and evil, even as his resurrection in the power of the Spirit stands as God's achievement that contradicts our present plight and guarantees Christ Jesus' (and through him our) future. What remains now is to construct an eschatology grounded on God's promises as they are revealed in Scripture so that we may discern a theologically informed yet modest set of possibilities for our passion. Most importantly we need to be taught how to pray in response to the promises that God the Father makes through his Son and by his Spirit and it is to this task that we turn first.

2

PRAYING FOR THE
PERFECTION OF LIFE
IN THE MIDDLE

Now we must learn not only a more certain way of
praying but also the form itself: namely, that which the
Heavenly Father has taught us through his beloved Son,
in which we may acknowledge his boundless goodness
and clemency.[1]

From the example of Jesus himself we have seen that life in the
Middle is characterized by praying in response to God's promises.
In the power of God's perfecting Spirit, we pray passionately
for the possibilities of God's perfecting work. However, if this
essential practice is going to play a formative role during life in
the Middle, then we need more than 'not my will but yours be
done'. Since we are joining in with the prayers of our great high
priest and in the power of his Spirit, we must, as Calvin suggests,
'learn not only a more certain way of praying but also the form
itself'. The Scriptures are filled with many and various prayers
that ought to play a role in teaching us to pray. Nevertheless, the
Lord's Prayer from the Gospel accounts is 'a form for us in which
he [Jesus] set forth as in a table all that he allows us to seek of him,
all that is of benefit to us, all that we need ask'.[2] The pedagogic

31

value of the Lord's Prayer has long been part of its history in Christianity.[3] Yet it is the eschatological tenor[4] of the prayer and the opportunities that it presents to assist us in establishing a systematic eschatology that is of greatest value in the present study.

The Lord's Prayer for life in the Middle

Ever since the time of Augustine 'God and the soul have gone together,' so that 'the fate of the soul' has been put 'at the centre of the ultimate questions'.[5] But the propensity of Western civilization to confuse the Bible's teaching regarding the millennium with the rule of the church (or the state) on the earth has meant that alternative views of the economy of salvation were treated as heresy – a threat to the established power. Yet another and distinctly Romantic option has been the outwardly pious calls from the likes of Schleiermacher or Feuerbach for humans to accept the finitude of their existence in a contingent universe (even after resurrection!) and leave eternal life to God and his glory.[6] Moltmann similarly contends:

> We shall only be able to overcome the unfruitful and paralysing confrontation between the personal and the cosmic hope, individual and universal eschatology, if we neither pietistically put the soul at the centre, nor secularistically the world. The centre has to be God, God's kingdom and God's glory.[7]

Indeed, let us put God's kingdom and his glory first but only if it is God the Father's kingdom realized in his glorified Messiah and in the power of his Holy Spirit. As Calvin saw,[8] the first three invocations of the Lord's Prayer are evidence of the perspective believers ought to have, as they consider their own lives in relation to the possibilities for God's perfecting work, and this for two important reasons.

The Lord's Prayer and systematic theology

The first reason for choosing the Lord's Prayer to structure our eschatology is its historic role in systematizing the Christian faith in general. As early as Tertullian in the third century AD Christians have recognized the potential of the Prayer for organizing Christian doctrine.[9] This is not to detract from the Prayer's obvious contribution to 'the meaning of the ascent to God which is accomplished through a sublime way of life', as Gregory of Nyssa referred to it.[10] Rather, it is simply a matter of recognizing that the Prayer consists of an arrangement of scriptural themes that describe the relationship of God to his creation in the light of the gospel. Hence Calvin included it as part of the structure of the *Institutes* from the first edition.[11]

The Lord's Prayer clearly distinguishes, but also combines, the purposes of God with the spiritual experience of his children. Each of the first three invocations calls for the fatherhood of God to be manifested on earth as it is in heaven.[12] We shall take this as the overall shape not only of the Prayer, but also for our eschatological vision. In the Lord's Prayer Jesus the Christ, who leads us in prayer, outlines the sense in which God's fatherhood is perfected on earth as it is in heaven – the hallowing of his name, the coming of his kingdom and the perfection of his will. At one level all these things are to be anticipated in the future. Yet, as we shall see, all three have been achieved, and therefore previewed, by the Spirit through God's Messiah, Jesus the incarnate Son. That is, God has chosen Jesus to receive 'the name that is above all names', the Father has designated, by the Spirit, Jesus the son of David to be king over his kingdom and it is in the rule of Jesus that the will of God is perfected by his Spirit for all creation. The second three invocations extend this schema in so far as we call on our heavenly Father to preserve us with his everlasting presence, to forgive our rebellion in the face of his coming kingdom and to deliver us from sin, death and evil in accordance with his will to perfect all things for the Lord Jesus. It is in this context of praying for the fatherhood of God to be manifest on earth as it is in heaven that we shall seek to articulate an understanding of God's economy of salvation. At the same time, since I have defined life in the Middle as a corporate experience, we shall explore the perfection of God's heavenly fatherhood for personal eschatology.

Allowing the Lord's Prayer to shape our doctrine of eschatology enables us to engage in the canonical practice of 'learning the meaning and correct grammar of God'.[13] Reading the Bible theologically not only provides God's account of the economy of salvation but also sets the norms for how God enables humans to participate in it – including the principles for interpreting the Bible itself.[14] This is particularly important for judging the relationship between biblical and systematic theology on the subject of eschatology. The Bible ought not only to provide the content of systematic theology beyond a set number of purple passages (or self-interpreting verses) but also to govern the forms that such systems take and the topics included in them.[15] This is particularly important for the doctrine of eschatology, considering the extent to which history and mystery are either divorced from each other or are homogenized, with the latter being lost in the former.[16]

The Lord's Prayer and apocalyptic

A second reason for employing the Lord's Prayer as a biblical system of eschatology relates to the important issue of apocalypticism. Whenever history and mystery have been confused in establishing a Christian eschatology, the inappropriate interpretation of apocalyptic texts has been the chief culprit. 'Apocalypticism' is a description of the world view that centres on 'the expectation of God's imminent intervention into human history'.[17] This world view is generated from various Jewish texts, both within and outside the canon of Scripture, that are classified as apocalyptic. Revelation, or the Apocalypse of John, while a unique and distinctively Christian example of this genre, is nonetheless an example of apocalyptic literature. All the New Testament documents are theological; that is, to borrow an idea from Ricoeur, they are theological configurations of a theological prefiguration to develop a theological refiguration.[18] The apostles' teaching, to which the church dedicated itself (cf. Acts 2:42) is, actually and already, a theological interpretation (configuration) of God's actions in the world from creation to new creation. The apostles, by the power of the Spirit, read the Old Testament (theological prefiguration) in the light of the death and resurrection of God's Messiah in order 'to proclaim the whole will of God' (cf. Acts 20:27). The apostolic configuration – the books of the New Testament – enabled the churches, in the power of the Spirit, to refigure their lives together in response to the gospel of Jesus. The apocalyptic books (or passages) in the Bible need to be read as a particular example of this genre of theological texts.

The distinguishing feature of apocalyptic texts is the style of the author's configuration: seers with visions of end-time scenarios containing elaborately symbolic depictions of the relationship between God and creation.[19] In addition the author/seer is invariably pessimistic in his assessment of 'this present age', regarding it as an era characterized by the dominance of evil forces – both human and non-human – yet at the same time emphatic that God will triumphantly intervene, revealing the true nature of his sovereignty over all things.[20] Broadly speaking, and as far as these matters can be determined validly and reliably, biblical scholars point to a historical context for the literature that is marked by a time of crisis in which God's people are persecuted because they will not conform to the demands of worldly powers.[21]

When it comes to the task of theologically interpreting apocalyptic texts a number of hermeneutical disciplines need to be observed. In this book all of them will be guided and governed by the biblical system provided by the Lord's Prayer. The first discipline is to recognize that signs and symbols that appear in a biblical text are distinct features of that text intended to convey meaning. In general 'a sign is immediately exhausted in a one to one relationship with its meaning'.[22] However, when we recall the provisional nature of God's promise-making in the Scriptures, the identification of a sign with its meaning ought not to imply that such a one-to-one relationship will be immediately obvious. So, for example, when the prophet Isaiah announces God's judgment upon Israel with the sign of a pregnant virgin, it takes a gospel interpretation in order to understand that Isaiah was referring to the Lord Jesus (Matt. 1:23; cf. Isa. 7:14). When symbolism is employed in an apocalyptic text, elements of a particular historical experience – kingship/power – are transformed via a symbol from a 'today and everyday' meaning to an urgent 'once and for all' icon.[23] It may of course be possible to associate a peculiar symbol with a specific historical event but such associations ought not to bind the symbol to a singular historical occurrence. Hence the apocalyptic of Daniel may well refer either to Babylonian exile or to Antiochus Epiphanes IV; and the Revelation to John most likely referred to the first-century Roman Empire, but it ought not to be bound to these or to any other single point in history. That said, the would-be modern interpreter must respect the prefigurative tradition from which the biblical author has drawn the various signs or symbols to establish his theological configuration of divine revelation for the audience to which he writes. So, for example, in the case of John's Apocalypse Bauckham comments that the whole of the Old Testament 'forms a body of literature which John expects his readers to know and explicitly to recall in detail while reading his own work'.[24] Of course, subsequent readers attempting theological refigurations of apocalyptic symbolism, particularly of the new creation, must resist the temptation to employ a kind of historicist 'principle of analogy' in which they project a future 'on the basis of what is known to be actual, probable and possible in the experience of the present'.[25] In addition, too many interpreters have exploited the overlap between history and mystery that apocalyptic literature presents, in the name of historical objectivity, and have simply assigned their contemporary concerns to apocalyptic symbols.[26] As we shall see, eschatology designed to organize God's promises in relation to divine presence (God's name), divine rule (God's kingdom) and divine intention (God's will) provides the appropriate equilibrium of sign–symbol and history–mystery.

The second discipline of interpretation of apocalyptic literature flows directly from the above in so far as apocalyptic texts as a genre are a literary style that function metaphorically. A metaphor is a literary device that produces a new meaning by connecting two otherwise disparate phenomena.[27] Through the prolific use of symbols, the apocalyptic writer configures a new rationality for life 'under the sun' (see Ecclesiastes *passim*) by linking divine actions to creaturely phenomena. At a basic level God is wholly and completely transcendent in relation to his creation. God is Father, Son and Spirit – holy, righteous and loving. Creation, as absolutely dependent upon this God, is subject to frustration by sin, death and evil. The apocalypticist's theological configuration brings these two domains together for a time in history when it appears that they could not have been further apart. From a theological point of view, however, what guarantees the legitimacy of an apocalyptic writer's metaphorical work as a medium for divine revelation is not the degree to which it might somehow be mapped onto a particular period of history.

Rather, it is the fact that the ability of any human theological configuration rests on the life, death and resurrection of Jesus, the eternal Word of God who became flesh and made his dwelling among us. In the power of his Spirit God the Father has provided what Barth referred to as 'the analogy of faith' between us and him in the incarnate Son.[28] The resurrected Jesus is the metaphor par excellence since, 'no one has ever seen God: God the one and only Son, who lives in the Father's heart, has interpreted Him to us' (John 1:14–18). Consequently though, the mode by which the Father speaks his word to us in the power of the Spirit acts as a precedent for the way we communicate with one another. Metaphors in general, and Christian apocalyptic texts in particular, are able to act as media of communication based on this principle. This is not to say, however, that apocalyptic texts ought to be regarded as *merely* poetic: not 'factual or scientific in kind', and therefore not invested 'with any serious intent to describe or to communicate "information" about the future at all'.[29] Consequently, the triune exposition of the possibilities of God's perfecting work presented in this book will be intentionally modest in detail regarding aspects of the new creation. Nevertheless, I reject any Bultmann-like interpretation that treats 'language about the kingdom of God, the end of the world, the last judgement', and so on, as 'a mythological way of speaking not about the future at all, but about the present'.[30]

A third discipline for interpreting apocalyptic literature concerns the genre's relationship to prophecy or prophetic ministry that I have already broached.[31] Apocalyptic literature serves to underwrite God's basic promise 'I will be your God and you will be my people' in circumstances that might otherwise imply that the promise has gone beyond provisionality to mere utopianism. So, whether it be the crisis of the exile or an apparent delay in the return of the Lord Jesus in the face of state persecution, by the same Spirit as the prophets, the apocalyptic writers explain that 'the whole world is now involved in God's eschatological process of history, not only . . . men and nations'.[32] The universal scope of salvation anticipated by the prophets is deconstructed to provide eternal perspective on the history of creation under the sovereign rule of the Creator. The apocalyptic texts are generated in a form that flows out of the reason for writing them: 'Without apocalyptic a theological eschatology remains bogged down in the ethnic history of men or the existential history of the individual.'[33] However, as with prophecy, the legitimacy of what is promised rests on the person and work of Jesus. This is because the definitive *apokalypsis* comes when God intervenes in history in the resurrection of the eternal and royal Son. There is no greater crisis in the history created by God's promises than when 'men of Israel . . . killed [the Messiah] with the hands of lawless men having nailed [him] to a cross' (Acts 2:23). Nevertheless, when, in the power of the Spirit, Jesus became 'the resurrection' (see John 11:25), history was redeemed since 'all other history is illuminated, called into question and trans-formed',[34] because 'all things are for him . . . and in him all things hold together' (Col. 1:16–17).

These disciplines are not expected to iron out every exegetical difficulty in reading apocalyptic texts – nor should they. Never-theless, by incorporating them into the practice of interpreting Scripture theologically and guided by the Lord's Prayer, a more gospel-focused depiction of eschatology will emerge. A doctrine of eschatology, shaped by the Lord's Prayer, would therefore be a reconfiguration of the apostolic configuration of God's relation-ship with the world. It would be a system that 'takes shape in a world [engaging] with reality and the implications of the economy of divine action in creation, reconciliation and redemption as it is recorded in Scripture'.[35] Our passionate prayers for the possibil-ities of God's perfecting work will better reflect the glory that the Lord Messiah Jesus deserves when they are a response to this reading of God's promises.

Praying for the eschatological fatherhood of God

Up to this point we have been working to establish the hermen-eutics of eschatology for life in the Middle. We *know* that God has promised himself to us in the Lord Jesus and this by the power of his Spirit. This is the sense in which God gives himself in his promises for the purpose of perfecting his relationship with human creatures – so that he may be our God and we be his people. We also know what we must *do*: in the power of God's Spirit of sonship we must join in with the prayers of Messiah Jesus, our great high priest. Our hope rests upon the possibilities of God's perfecting work in the Spirit and through the crucified Lord Jesus, whom God raised to life at his right hand. Furthermore, and in obedience to the royal and eternal Son, we shall prescriptively embody our hope using the structure of dominical prayer. Thus, as have the saints throughout the ages, in the Middle between the resurrection and the return and in the midst of any church, in every place, we pray, 'Our Father in heaven'. Let us now consider what it might mean to hope for the fatherhood of God to be perfected on the earth as it is in heaven.

For Jesus to instruct his disciples to call God Father in their prayers was unusual in the first-century Jewish context. Augustine noted:

> A great deal has been said in praise of God in a variety of ways and in many places in Holy Scripture which anyone can reflect on when he reads them; but nowhere is found a command given the people of Israel to say Our Father, or to pray to God as a father; but it was as Master that they knew Him, they being slaves, that is still living according to the flesh.[36]

The Jews were very careful about how they spoke to God and were often outraged at the level of familiarity exhibited by Jesus in relation to God. Yet *familial*-arity with God, in the strictest sense, was central to the purposes of the incarnate Son's journey into the world that God had made through him: 'To whoever received him [Jesus], to those believing in his name, he gave authority to become *children of God*' (John 1:12). Indeed, the first words spoken by the risen Jesus confirm this intent: 'Go to my brothers and say to them, "I am ascending to my Father *and to your Father*; to my God and your God"' (John 20:17). Certainly, particular individuals enjoyed a greater level of intimacy with the Lord in the history of Israel, and the prophets often implied that Israel could or should enjoy such intimacy with God.[37] However, what Jesus' language implies is a perfected sense of relation to God for his people that went beyond, or was at least always beyond, the reach of Israel. For though God referred to Israel as his son in confrontation with Pharaoh and en route to the Promised Land (Exod. 4:22; cf. Deut. 8:5; Hos. 11:1), there is, as Augustine noted, little evidence that the Israelites enjoyed

39

such familiarity with YHWH. However, what Augustine did not mention, at least in his commentary on *the Sermon on the Mount*, is the fact that this privilege was reserved for the Messiah, of whom God said, 'You are my son; today I have become your Father' (cf. 2 Sam. 7:14, Ps. 89:26–27 and David's description of Solomon in Ps. 72:1). With the application of this and other passages to the identity of Jesus by the Gospel writers, the sonship of Jesus in which the disciples are to be included takes on a much broader temporal significance. For the work of the Messiah, in the Spirit, is to achieve the long-promised salvation of God. *Therefore God's promise to save can be equated with the experience of God's fatherhood through Jesus, who is both the son of David and the Son of God.* Here we discover the surprising impact of the gospel on our understanding of eschatology. For the outward significance of events – the realization of a geopolitical kingdom, the defeat of enemies or even the judicial/cultic significance of expiation of sin and the propitiation of wrath – are encapsulated within a larger goal in an apocalyptic fashion. What might otherwise have been more readily understood in terms of personal intimacy – calling God, 'Father' – is actually the external state into which human creatures are being brought by the Spirit and through the Son. As Barth observed, 'The answer which the New Testament gives us here is a very different one from that which a natural and edifying but utterly arbitrary exposition of the word "father" might yield.'[38]

We must use the language of *experiencing* God's fatherhood judiciously however for (at least) two reasons. First, as a distinct person in the immanent Trinity, God the Father is 'the Lord of our existence. He is this in the strict sense to the degree that He is the Lord over life and death of man'.[39] The Father is the Creator of heaven and earth, as Athanasius stated it:

> [Against polytheism] For we must not think there is more than one ruler and maker of Creation: but it belongs to correct and true religion to believe that its Artificer is one . . . Who then might this Maker be? . . . the God we worship and preach is the only true One, Who is Lord of Creation and Maker of all existence. Who then is this, save the Father of Christ, most holy above all created existence, Who, like an excellent

pilot, by His own Wisdom and His own Word, our Lord and Saviour Christ, steers and preserves and orders all things, and does as seems to Him best?[40]

God is the transcendent creator of all things and is so in the power of the Holy Spirit as the Father of Jesus the Christ. More than this, God is Father as the one from whom the eternal Son is generated in the eternal Spirit. As I expound the various petitions of the Lord's Prayer we shall come to appreciate that just as it is essential that the immanent Father be so through the Son and in the Spirit, so also it is essential that God's transcendent fatherhood be mediated to creatures through the Son and by the Spirit. We must maintain an appropriate equilibrium between transcendence and immanence (or the distinction between the immanent and economic Trinity) in our eschatology because of the very real pressure in Romantic thought to compromise God's absolute transcendence for the sake of sentimentalist notions of his imma- nence.[41] We can see traces of it in Moltmann's description of God's fatherhood:

> The Father loves the Son eternally, and the Son also eternally returns the Father's love. But this inner- trinitarian love is the love of like for like, not love of the other . . . it is not yet creative love, which communicates itself by over-coming its opposite . . . It is not yet the love that responds out of the being that is the other.[42]

The Romantic tendency seen in Moltmann's words is to picture God's love and therefore his fatherhood as incomplete without creation, since to be so it must 'overcome its opposite'. In order to remain faithful to biblical Christianity we must avoid this even as we articulate eschatology as the perfection of God's heavenly fatherhood on the earth. Since it is towards this goal that Jesus directs our hopes in prayer, we must, with the writer to the Hebrews, describe the destiny of the 'many sons and daughters' as being acknowledged as such by the royal and eternal Son before the throne of God: 'I [Jesus] will proclaim your name [Father] to my brothers [and sisters], in the midst of the assembly I will sing you a hymn . . . Here I am and the children God has given me' (Heb. 2:12–13). Nevertheless, we must do so without compromising the absolute distinction between, and freedom from, Creator and creation. Therefore, and especially in a book on eschatology, it is essential that we give some thought to the relationship between eternity and history.

The time of the Father and the history of the world

If the eternal God is present in creation, will this somehow negate the extent to which creation can experience the changes and contingencies that might otherwise explain time? Are these elements simply a product of the fallenness of creation? At the end of all things, does time or history simply give way to eternity as complete changeless timelessness? Alternatively, must we hold open the option of God himself having a future in order to give due weight to the future of creation? Is the history of the world a reflection (somehow) of God's own history? Moltmann's futurist account of these issues has already provided us with much food for thought. Here I shall offer a brief sketch of the way Barth handled these questions in his *Church Dogmatics* and the ensuing objections raised by Moltmann.

In an effort to get away from the confusion of eschatology with history so prevalent in nineteenth-century liberal Protestantism, Barth emphasized the confrontation between eternity and history in *The Epistle to the Romans*. He later realized that he 'had not sufficiently considered the pre-temporality of the Reformers or the supra-temporality of God which Neo-Protestants had put in such a distorted way at the centre'.[43] Specifically, his description of eternity had not given sufficient weight to the sense in which *God is before creaturely time as well as above or outside creaturely time*. The result, as Barth admitted, was missing the significance of passages like Romans 13:11ff., where Paul encourages his audience to consider their salvation as 'nearer than when we first believed'. The issue here is 'the teleology which it ascribes to time as it moves towards a real end'.[44] That is, the net effect of Barth's original confrontation between time and eternity meant that there was 'no concrete hope or movement [in history] to what is absolutely beyond time'.[45] As we saw in the previous chapter Moltmann refuted this approach, claiming it had more to do with Hellenistic philosophy than the description of the promise-making God given in the Old Testament. Later, in his *Church Dogmatics*, Barth opted for a threefold description of eternity in order to develop a fuller understanding of God's eternity in relation to time: 'Pre-temporality, supra-temporality and post-temporality are equally God's eternity and therefore the living God Himself.'[46] To speak about eternity is actually just to speak about God in himself. It is not some different time or place in which God dwells: it is God himself – he is *not just eternal but is eternity itself*. Hence creaturely history is shaped by interaction with eternity – with God.

Moltmann was dissatisfied with this threefold expansion of the concept of divine temporality. He argued that it did not solve the problem of God's eternity in relation to creaturely time. In his later work on eschatology, *The Coming of God*, he complained, 'Is it really progress if . . . eternity then surrounds time from all sides and is contemporaneous with all times, not just to the present?'[47] To Moltmann this was simply a more elaborate form of Platonism that negated the reality and significance of creaturely time, thinking that it was ultimately to be abandoned in relation to God. The complaint has some validity when we consider what Barth wrote of God's post-temporality:

> We move to Him as we come from Him and may accompany Him . . . He is when time will be no more. For then creation itself, as a reality distinct from God, will be no more in its present condition in everything which now constitutes its existence and being.[48]

Taken at face value, this quote does seem to imply that at the consummation of all things there will be no more time; or, worse, there may not be the same kind of distinction between God and creation. This notwithstanding, the quote must be mitigated by other elements of Barth's account which are essential to ensuring that an appropriate distinction is maintained between the manner in which time could be described as a characteristic of divine life on the one hand and creaturely life on the other. The way forward, according to Barth, is to be mindful of the triune nature of the Christian God. In the first instance it means acknowledging the difference between Plato's monad (or Aristotle's Unmoved Mover) and the triune God of the Christian gospel. For the God and Father of our Lord Jesus Christ there is something going on in eternity even if the dynamic nature of that happening is quite unlike the phenomena that creatures experience. After all, 'Knowledge of the creator and of creation is creaturely knowledge; in knowing the creator and his act, and ourselves as creatures, we do not transcend our creaturely condition, but repeat it.'[49] Therefore let us consider how the gospel of the Lord Jesus might affect our understanding of God's time in relation to our own.

Eternity as God's life

In §31.3 of *Church Dogmatics* II/1 Barth acknowledges, 'A correct understanding of the positive side of the concept of eternity, free from all false conclusions, is gained only when we are clear that we are speaking about the eternity of the triune God.'[50] When eternity is understood as the immanent divine life of God in himself – the perfect life of Father, Son and Holy Spirit – 'free from all fleetingness and separations of what we call time . . . which cannot come into being or pass away', this then is God's time, 'a juxtaposition which does not mean any exclusion, a movement which does not signify the passing away of anything, a succession which in itself is also beginning and end'.[51] So eternity understood as a characteristic of the Christian God is a triune dynamic of interpersonal interaction, unlike the Platonic static monad, but not so much that it includes loss, decay or the kinds of change that we would otherwise associate with life in a creation distorted by sin, death and evil. As we shall see, it is only these elements of fallenness in creation that the presence of divine life negates. Furthermore, through his actions in the gospel God's time is opened to engage creaturely time when the royal and eternal Son, the Word, becomes a creature in his own creation:

> In Jesus Christ it comes about that God takes time to Himself, that is He Himself, the eternal One, becomes temporal, that He is present for us in the form of our own existence and our own world, not simply embracing our time and ruling it, but submitting Himself to it, and permitting created time to become and be the form of His eternity.[52]

44

It is in the person of the royal and eternal Son of God, Messiah Jesus, that time can be a characteristic of both divine and creaturely life. In the Lord Jesus eternal divine life, and hence eternity, is mediated to creaturely history. As a result, in Jesus a possibility exists for describing the dynamic nature of creaturely existence that is distinct from the changes that might otherwise be considered the consequence of sin, death and evil.[53] In Jesus creaturely history is mediated to eternity and vice versa.

Divine and creaturely time came together, according to Barth, from the perspective of the Easter events – especially the forty days between the resurrection and the ascension. Jesus, unlike other humans, has 'fragments of a second history' by virtue of his resurrection from the dead: 'It is the Easter history, the history of the forty days between his resurrection and ascension.'[54] During this time the apostles and their communities came to understand who Jesus really was, 'as the One who "was and is, and is to come"'.[55] Jesus' followers realized that, though veiled at the time, his words and actions among them before Easter had also been those of the holy one of God as God. Consequently, through their New Testament accounts we gain insight into the coming together of divine and creaturely time: 'It is the time which is the time of all times because what God does in it [Jesus' time] is the goal of all creation and therefore of all created time.'[56] That is to say, with the resurrection of Messiah his ordinary 'before, during and after' life as the man Jesus of Nazareth – the time that all creatures have – was revealed to be perfect participation in divine eternal life, the ultimate act of God's giving himself in his promise 'I will be your God and you will be my people.'

History as the time of Jesus the Christ

When God gives himself to creation in the Lord Jesus, as revealed in the resurrection, it changes completely the way we understand time or history as before, during and after. Beginning with what I have called life in the Middle, creaturely history between the resurrection of Jesus and the perfection of creation, 'the fact that He lives at the right hand of God means that even now He is absolutely present temporally' to all creatures.[57] By the gift of his Spirit Christians and their churches live their particular time 'in Christ', rejoicing in and proclaiming God's salvific achievements for them, since his death to sin has become theirs as well, just as his resurrection has become their hope (cf. Rom. 6). Throughout this time the Lord Jesus is genuinely but transcendently present to them 'yesterday and today' in perfect continuity with the apostles and their communities.

In addition, creaturely history, even that which seems to precede 'the time of His way from Bethlehem to Calvary', *the history captured in the Old Testament, is revealed at Easter to be Jesus Christ's past*: 'The Lord Christ was for it the Messiah to whom the Old Testament had pointed forward, the Son of Man and Servant of God.'[58] When the eternal Son comes into the world as the son of David – the royal son – that history becomes the time of the Lord Jesus. So, for example, the various sons (and descendants) of David do not lose their place as receivers of God's promise to David but rather gain a richer identity as anticipations of Messiah Jesus (2 Sam. 7:12–14). The distinction between them and him rests on God's decision not to fulfil his promise to any other than Messiah Jesus. Hence the history shaped by the promises of God from Abraham onwards becomes the past of the Lord Jesus, the one to whom all these promises looked forward (Matt. 1:1–6). Yet even this is not enough, for Jesus is the son of Adam (Luke 3:23–38) and more:

> If in the Old Testament the covenant is always eschato-logical and prophetic in character, and is never actually realised; if finally . . . Jesus is the One who was to come as the fulfilled reality of the covenant is it speculation to say that even the time of creation was His time?[59]

As the one 'through whom all things were made and without him nothing was made that has been created' (John 1:1–3) the past of the Lord Jesus stretches right back beyond 'the beginning'. Barth's point is not merely that God's promises create a history that finds its denouement in the person and work of the Lord Jesus. Rather, as McCormack has noted, 'If God's eternal act of self-determination is a determination for existence as human being in time, then it is the eternal decision itself *which founds time*.'[60] Far from robbing us of a distinctive sense of creaturely history, the presence of the eternal triune God in his promises that are fulfilled in Jesus *creates temporality and subsequently history*.

Hence, and finally, 'this living Lord Jesus yesterday and today could not be believed and loved as such without being expected in hope as the One who is *eis tous aiōnas* (into eternity), as the One who comes'.[61] Barth's portrayal of the future time of the Lord Jesus, or the sense in which he is the one to come (see Rev. 1:4), is framed over and against nineteenth-century liberal Protestant notions of 'an amelioration of present conditions or an ideal state'.[62] The culture of modernity sees history as the gradual advancement of Western history towards human perfection through education and especially scientific rationality. Instead, in the Gospel portrait of the Lord Jesus Christ, we have the apostolic testimony to 'his future for us', which from our perspective is life in the Middle, the distance in time between the resurrection and the perfection of Jesus' lordship on earth as it is in heaven. Yet because the time of the Lord Jesus is the centre of creaturely history, from the perspective of the eternal God giving himself to us in Jesus, 'The resurrection is the anticipation of His *parousia* as His *parousia* is the completion and fulfilment of the resurrection.'[63] In this way the Christian hope for the perfection of creation is not a matter of anticipating abstract 'spiritual, moral or material blessings in a future Kingdom of God'. Rather all these things contribute to the possibilities for which the gospel encourages us to be passionate for 'His glory: initially revealed in His resurrection, and finally to be revealed in His return'.[64] The gospel of the Lord Jesus creates in us a great expectancy for the glorious scope of creaturely living promised in the resurrection of Messiah Jesus as the first fruits of the new creation. His presence above and beyond the current grim circumstances of sin, death and evil is what gives the church a longing, a hope, along with all creation, for his general revelation (cf. Rom. 8). In addition, it connects the church with the history of anticipation found in the prophetic ministry in Israel. As Barth points out, all the prophetic ministry in the Old Testament, including the apocalyptic kind, 'only becomes vital in Christianity'.[65] As the history of Jesus appropriates the history of Israel (becoming his past), the prophet's future and apostle's present are incorporated into the future perfection of the Lord Jesus in all creation. Ultimately, the future of Messiah Jesus is shaped by his parousia, which for Barth is a threefold coming of the victorious Lord. Expanding the relationship between Easter and the parousia, Barth writes,

'As we must plainly distinguish the resurrection, the outpouring of the Spirit and the final return of Jesus Christ, so we must understand and see them together as forms of one and the same event.'[66]

The main concern in this clarification is to ensure that the 'not-yet' of the perfection of salvation is correlated with the 'now' of the churches' experience and the 'past' of the Easter community's experiences with the resurrected Lord. The one Lord Jesus risen from the dead comes to the disciples at Easter, again in the Spirit at Pentecost and finally at the perfection of all things. The perfection of creaturely history will be its terminus with the purposes of God summed up in the glorification of the eternal and royal Son at his ultimate coming.

Even in this all-too-brief sketch of Barth's eschatology, what seems clear is that there is ample evidence that Barth's description of temporality was as sensitive to history portrayed in Scripture as anything that Moltmann offered in *Theology of Hope*. If God's promise-making creates a history that is 'forward looking and forward moving, and therefore also revolutionising and transforming the present',[67] then 'permitting created time to become and be the form of his eternity'[68] in the person and work of the Lord Jesus is the gospel way of allowing time to be a characteristic of both creaturely and divine life.[69] Far from being a more sophisticated form of Platonism, when eternity is understood as a description of the triune God's transcendent life and this life freely involves creation through the person and work of the Lord Jesus, *history is not threatened by eternity but is instead glorified by it.*

The time of Christ as an advent in history

This excursus on Barth's description of time and eternity has focused our attention on the presence of God in Christ Jesus. From the perspective of the gospel this is appropriate and our approach throughout will be sympathetic, but the brevity of the sketch has not given sufficient attention to the logic of Barth's conclusions and neither should we accept them uncritically. Among other things, we must test this proposition that the Old Testament is the past of the Messiah Jesus. We need to clarify the presence of the Spirit with Jesus, not just the presence of Jesus in the Spirit during life in the Middle, and we ought to scrutinize the nature of New Testament testimony to the future of Christ for us. Furthermore, Moltmann for his part remained sceptical to the point of dismissive towards the later developments in Barth's eschatology: 'There are not three *parousias*: in the flesh, in the Spirit, and in the glory, as later theological traditions said, in an attempt to put the advent hope on ice.'[70] Instead, Moltmann contends that the notion of God's coming to creation in Messiah Jesus (his parousia) is better described in terms of advent – the long-awaited arrival – rather than simply marking time until what will inevitably be. This means adjusting normal experience of time (past/present/future), but it is warranted because, according to Moltmann, that which is real emerges only from some kind of potentiality: 'reality emerges from potentiality, all past and present realities being realised potentialities; but reality never again turns into potentiality'.[71] The present can be only what it is, and the past can only be repeated. As I noted in discussing Jüngel as to the effect of the resurrection on our understanding of hope, Moltmann held, against Aristotle, that potentiality surpasses reality and therefore the future as the one true source of potentiality surpasses the present and the past. With the future as the source, time becomes a transcendental that protects temporality, unlike 'timeless-simultaneous eternity', without being lost 'in the maelstrom of general transience of all temporal being'.[72] The outcome is an expectation of something that is at once completely new and yet analogical with what came before; since, like the resurrection, 'The new thing is the surprising thing, the thing that could never have been expected,' and that which is new 'does not annihilate the old but gathers it up and creates it anew'.[73]

The nature of the 'new thing' in Moltmann's eschatology developed more as philosophy of history with theological implications than as a theological description of temporality per se.[74] After a lengthy and largely abstract consideration of time and history, still influenced by Ernst Bloch but long after *Theology of Hope*, Moltmann settles on an essentially spatial metaphor:

> Just as the primordial moment springs from God's creative resolve and from the divine self-restriction on which God determined in that resolve, so the eschatological moment will spring from the resolve to redeem and the 'derestriction' of God determined upon in that.

> God does not de-restrict himself in order to annihilate his creation, and to put himself in its place and its time; his purpose is to dwell in his creation, and in it to be 'all in all'.[75]

Creaturely time emerges from the divine act of creation when God makes a space within himself for creation to exist and this creaturely temporality is transformed into eternal time at the point when God comes into this space of creation to dwell with his creatures.[76] There are obvious questions to be asked of Moltmann's description, especially with regard to his view of *The End* and how creation will remain a distinct entity when God is 'all in all'.[77] Needless to say, the difficulties inherent in Moltmann's counterposition of *The End* arose from the underlying assumptions of God's relationship with creation:

> The Spirit . . . is God himself. If God commits himself to his limited creation, and if he himself dwells in it as 'the giver of life,' this presupposes a self-limitation, a self-humiliation and a self-surrender of the Spirit. The history of suffering creation, which is subject to transience, then brings with it a history of suffering by the Spirit who dwells in creation.[78]

If Barth's explanation of eternity and time was problematic for understanding history, then it would appear that Moltmann's depiction of *both* God *and* creation is more problematic. As has been pointed out by a number of interlocutors, it is difficult to understand how creaturely existence, let alone temporality, has a distinct future in Moltmann's account.[79] Furthermore, as the above quote indicates, the sense in which time could be a characteristic of both creaturely and divine life results in a portrait of a Spirit who, as much as his creation, requires redemption.

In fact, in Moltmann's theology it would appear that God needs a future in order to deal with the contradictions within divine life itself: 'To recognise God in the cross of Christ . . . means to recognise the cross, inextricable suffering, death and hopeless rejection in God.'[80] Moltmann expands this thought such that 'the Son's sacrifice of boundless love on Golgotha is from eternity already included in the exchange of the essential, the consubstantial love which constitutes the divine life of the Trinity',[81] so that 'the pain of the cross determines the inner life of the triune God from eternity to eternity'.[82] With remarks such as these it is unsurprising that Moltmann's view of history's goal involves the ultimate justification of God himself: 'Even the universal salvation of the new creation is not yet in itself the goal but serves *the justification of God.*'[83] To be fair, there is much more to Moltmann's eschatological vision, as we shall see. However, these later developments make clear that even if eschatology is 'the medium of Christian faith as such',[84] it must provide an appropriate harmony between the absolute Creator and the absolutely contingent creation. In fact, the theological import-ance of mediation will be crucial to establishing and maintaining such harmony. The great strength of Barth's eschatology was that the transcendent and eternal God's presence was perfectly *mediated* to creation in, through and with the Lord Jesus. The Gospel description of God present to his creation establishes the appropriate theological framework within which the relationship between time and eternity can be explored. Furthermore, the Gospel description of God present to his creation is a configur-ation based on the prefigurative categories provided by the greater story of YHWH's covenant relationship with Israel. It is only by assessing the larger story of God's acts to vindicate his promises to and presence with Israel that we shall establish appropriate language for our eschatological hope in the Lord Jesus.

History in the mediated acts of the triune God for salvation

A second reason we ought to be circumspect with the language of God's fatherhood is to ensure that we faithfully represent the mediatorial work of Jesus Christ by the power of the Holy Spirit in the love of God for *salvation.* Neither Barth nor Moltmann would contest this statement in principle, yet it is how such a statement is articulated that makes all the difference to both history and eschatology.

Against the modern liberal Protestant tradition, and in keeping with Athanasius, we speak of God the Father as Creator but not as a mere universal progenitor of 'infinite[ly] valuable human souls', such that 'the whole of Jesus' message may be reduced to . . . two heads – God as Father, and the human soul so ennobled that it can and does unite with him'.[85] As we shall see, in the economy of salvation God is Father exclusively through Jesus the holy one and in the power of the Holy Spirit. It is the gracious death of the Christ for the 'enemies of God' (Col. 1:21–22) that makes them valuable to *his* Father, not the infinite value of human creatures that prompted the exemplary death of Christ to 'remind them of what they know already'.[86] In fact, as Barth commented:

> What may be known as the manward will of the heavenly Father in what takes place through and to Jesus does not lie primarily in the direction of a genial affirmation, preservation and insurance of human existence but rather in that of a radical questioning and indeed abrogation of it.[87]

Therefore if eschatology is to be the economic perfection of God's heavenly fatherhood it must be through the lens provided by the gospel message found throughout the New Testament. So, as Paul promised the Philippians, the eschatological glory of God's fatherhood will be perfected on the earth by the Spirit, in and through the Lord Jesus. Hence 'At the name of Jesus every knee in the heavens, on the earth and under the earth will be bent and every tongue will confess that Messiah Jesus is Lord to the glory of God the Father' (Phil. 2:10–11).

Here we have the future event of God's universal glorification as Father within the context of the name of the Lord being hallowed on earth as it is in heaven – the name given to the risen Jesus the Christ. As the first theme of the coming of God's fatherhood, the biblical story of God's name will be surveyed as the perfection of his presence with his people in his creation. This will be the *what* of our eschatology. At the same time, it will provide the first element of a description of God's final judgment – the vindication of his Messiah.

Following the logic of the Prayer, the coming of God's heavenly kingdom to the earth will be investigated in terms of Paul's promise to the Corinthians:

> The end will come, when he hands over the kingdom to God the Father after he has destroyed all dominion, authority and power. For he must reign until he has put all his enemies under his feet. The last enemy to be

destroyed is death. For he 'has put everything under his feet'. Now when it says that 'everything' has been put under him, it is clear that this does not include God himself, who put everything under Christ. When he has done this, then the Son himself will be made subject to him who put everything under him, so that God may be all in all. (1 Cor. 15:24–28)

The perfection of creaturely history arrives when God's Messiah has destroyed all opposition to his reign and has subsequently handed over (or returns) this dominion to the Father. This will be the *how* of our eschatology. Yet this is also the point at which the presence of God in creation is perfected 'so that God may be all in all'. The resurrection of the dead and prosecution of God's curse upon the enemies of salvation will mark the apocalyptic arrival of God's indomitable sovereignty.

Furthermore, God's desire to glorify himself through his Son, a desire that is perfected by his Spirit in the coming of his kingdom, will be the fulfilment of God's will on earth as it is in heaven or as the Ephesians were promised:

The Father made known to us the mystery of his will, according to his good pleasure, intended in the Messiah for the management of the fullness of time, to sum up all things in the Messiah, things in the heavens and on the earth. (Eph. 1:9–10)

In the gospel we are given a genuine insight into the great mystery of the ages: that God's will for heaven and earth in the economy of salvation is summed up in the person of the exalted Messiah Jesus. Barth's comment is apt: 'the totality of earthly and heavenly things . . . are to be comprehended in Christ . . . nothing has come into being or exists in itself as such, but only in this way and for this purpose'.[88] This will be the *why* of our eschatology. God's delight is to have all his plans for and actions in creation find their ultimate fulfilment in the glorification of his Son in heaven and on the earth.

Starting with the three propositions provided by the Lord's Prayer, we can construct an eschatology of the heavenly father-hood of God being perfected on earth at the apocalypse of

53

the universal rule of Jesus the Christ, in the power of the Holy Spirit.

On earth as it is in heaven

To address our prayers through and with Jesus to our heavenly Father is, as has been argued, the goal of the gospel. It is this hope that contradicts any present Gethsemane-like experience of entrusting ourselves to God's will that we might undergo. It is entirely appropriate for us to wonder and rejoice at such a privilege: 'we have no right to call Him Father, to be His children, to address Him in this manner'.[89] Even so, what we learn from the Lord's Prayer is that we are praying for God's heavenly fatherhood to be manifest, realized or, better still, perfected on earth. Most, if not all, of the great expositions of the Prayer attach this aspect to the third invocation: 'Your will be done on earth as it is in heaven.' However, there is no linguistic necessity for reading the Prayer in this manner. In fact, as has been hinted, 'The first three petitions are really expressing only different aspects of the same thought.'[90] This was Brown's assessment of the syntax of the Prayer and he took the single thought to be the eschatological glory of God. The present study will contest such a reading of the Prayer not because it is incorrect, but because it is insufficiently informed by the gospel – it is not as disciplined by the triune relations of God in the economy of salvation as it could be. With and through the Lord Jesus we pray passionately for that which is true in eternity to be mediated by the Spirit to creation: the fatherhood of God. This is the eschatological glory towards which we strive; this is the future hope that contradicts our present experience of sin, death and evil.

To refigure our future hope in terms of the coming fatherhood of God will provide a more explicitly theological depiction of the new creation or heaven. This is where the structure of the Prayer can best serve us, for our hope is for heavenly fatherhood *on the earth*. Hence our eschatology will employ the word 'heaven' in terms of 'what is coming to pass, in the sense of taking place, as distinguished from what is passing away'.[91] It will be a historical and, in fact creaturely, view of heaven as distinct from an ethereal upperworldly view of life after death. In other words, and more importantly in relation to what I have already said about

54

Moltmann, I shall attempt a theological description of the new creation that leaves adequate conceptual space for everlasting creaturely existence as distinct from the divinization of time and space that occurs when God's eternity absorbs history.

As far as what heaven on earth might look like, the possibilities in the biblical drama revolve around images of the new creation; 'the in-breaking of God at the consummation of history, as it is portrayed in Revelation 21–22, is treated as a new creation'.[92] This is a complete recreation of all that ever was, 'not merely the alteration of the existing order'.[93] Yet the recreation is a perfection of the *kind* of creation that God originally made, and hence the anticipated end-time scenarios depict a *purification* of createdness:

> I saw a new heaven and a new earth, for the first heaven and the first earth passed away and the sea no longer existed . . . death will not be there nor mourning, nor crying or pain, for the former things have passed away. (Rev. 21:1–4)

This new creation, a new heaven and a new earth, will be rid of sin, death and evil in all their modes, but what else can or should be said about its form? Strange and wonderful to our ears and eyes are the descriptions of vast cities,[94] flowing waters,[95] gathered peoples and creatures;[96] not to mention predators and prey lying together.[97] As has already been mentioned, these apocalyptic images need to be invoked with circumspection for they are symbols of what goes beyond human experience. The portrait of *The End* in Scripture is 'thematic rather than fictive'.[98] Chief among our tasks then is the careful articulation of the nature of continuity between the old and the new, on the one hand, and, on the other, appropriately maintaining the distinction between Creator and creation. I shall address these issues progressively as we consider each petition in the Lord's Prayer 'on earth as it is in heaven'.

For now, we note that in general, the Jewish expectation was for an earthly reality, as opposed to an ethereal heavenly existence, for the new creation. First-century Judaism reflects an essentially concrete view of the consequences of resurrection, namely the expectation that those who are raised to life again will do so in genuine bodily form.[99] Yet more important than this is the role of apostolic testimony to a physical resurrection of the Lord Jesus. Though raised imperishable, as Paul describes it in 1 Corinthians 15:42, the Messiah was raised in the body, as the Gospel writers were keen to point out. On this point rests our hope for the new creation, for, in the words of Gregory of Nazianzus, 'that which He has not assumed He has not healed; but that which is united to His God-head is also saved'.[100] So since Jesus the Christ was raised to life in bodily form, we hold that his physicality, his material human nature, is preserved even in his ascension and despite the particular way that he was able to manifest himself to the disciples. Consequently, at the very least, we expect a material physical state in the new creation.

We must continually emphasize the material nature of the new creation, albeit transformed, for the tendency to undermine the perpetuity of physical existence has consistently dogged Christian theology in the history of the church. From very early times Christian faith was compromised by various forms of Gnosticism that considered material existence something to be escaped in favour of a rational and spiritual salvation that moves the faithful to a higher spiritual realm. Unfortunately, even a non-Gnostic theologian like Origen of Alexandria was able to describe creation as a training ground for disobedient spirits, and Platonic notions of spirit versus matter have lurked in the corners of Christian eschatology ever since.[101] In fact, the great father of Latin theology, Augustine of Hippo, had an unfortunate tendency to dispense with the ongoing significance of the 'relevance in heaven of the person and earthly work of Jesus Christ'.[102] These and other compromises have left doubt in the minds of Christians about a genuine, earthly, physical existence in the new creation and have consequently devalued the experience of life in the Middle.

I have now established the main elements of Christian eschatology that will be explored in this book: during life in the Middle our hope is for possibilities involved in the perfection of God's heavenly fatherhood on the earth. Our hope is grounded on the gospel promises made by God our Father through his royal and eternal Son and in the power of his Spirit. With the passion of the Christ, we embody our hope for God's fatherhood in prayer amid the reality of sin, death and evil awaiting the perfecting work of the Spirit. So let us now turn to explore the promise of God's presence with us through the vindication of Jesus Christ as Lord.

3

THE NAME ABOVE
ALL NAMES

In search of theological perspective

The gospel message promises the perfection of God's heavenly fatherhood on the earth. The basic response to these promises is a Christlike passion for the possibilities of God's work to share himself with us. God's royal and eternal Son has taught us a way of embodying our hope by calling on our Father to act. Now we must consider the various petitions that we are to put before our heavenly Father to understand life in the Middle as shaped by his promises.

Augustine anticipated God's answer to the first petition in explicitly missional terms: 'the Gospel by being made known among all the different nations even in our own times commends *the name of the one God* through the operation of His Son'.[1] The promises of God are to be shared so that his life is manifested to all his creatures. Such a reading of the Prayer laid emphasis on the human activity needed to fulfil this petition, the grace of God notwithstanding. This subjective interpretation fits well with what we have identified as key to life in the Middle since it 'implies that God's name is known to him who prays'[2] and reflects the proposal that prayer is an eschatological experience. That is, we call for God to hallow his name because he has enabled us to do so in the power of the Holy Spirit, and as we do so his name is hallowed still further. From the perspective of mission we are four times further away in time from Augustine than he was from the apostles, and the gospel message has now spread all over the globe. Hence we have proportionally greater reason to point to the preaching of the gospel as the hallowing of God's name on the earth.

However, Barth asks an obvious question of the efforts of either the individual or the church when it comes to glorifying God's name: 'Have the church and Christians really been concerned about God? Is it really He whom they have made known in the world?'[3] Regrettably, the answer must be, not always or not enough. Calvin, for his part, took a sterner reading of the request: 'Here we are bidden to request not only that God vindicate his sacred name of all contempt and dishonour but also that he subdue the whole race of mankind to reverence for it.'[4] Calvin's choice of divine vindication as the main issue concerning God's name is a good one because it directs our attention towards a divine perspective on life in the Middle. Calvin's insistence on expounding the first petition from God's perspective ensures a genuinely *theo*logical description of eschatology and highlights the force of God's promise '*I will be your* God and you will be *My* people.' Calvin was concerned that God himself would act for his name's sake because human efforts certainly have *not yet* brought the Father's heavenly glory to the earth.

God's desire to vindicate his name on earth involves more than the limitations of his people. Calvin's comment highlights the genuine antagonism in the world towards God's intention to perfect his relationship with his creatures. From the perspective of creation, 'The heavens declare the glory of God' (Ps. 19:1), and 'there is an evident intelligibility of God to those [who suppress the truth] for God has made it plain to them . . . from the creation of the world' (Rom. 1:19–20). Yet, as Barth pointed out again, 'the statement that God is known and even well known to the world is too strong' because 'the world is guilty [since] God is also unknown to it'.[5] We must not forget that life in the Middle is only a specific chapter in the history of creation – the big picture of God's perfecting work. But God's actions in the death and resurrection of Jesus are unequivocal: 'It is in this sense that we say, "God's name is already hallowed."'[6] What God has definitively achieved in the person and work of his Son has *already* hallowed his name. The tension of life in the Middle is that what God has achieved in Jesus Christ is yet to be perfected in all creation. A critical element of our passion for the possibilities of God's perfecting work – our hope – is that God will apocalyptically, universally and everlastingly vindicate the sanctity of his name on earth as it is in heaven through the Lord Jesus. This is the *what* of our eschatology – what God is going to do to perfect his heavenly fatherhood on the earth.

The gospel promise of vindication

The petitions of the Lord's Prayer form a structure that enables us to understand the Father's promise to perfect his relationship with creation. The goal is to construct an account of eschatology that is shaped by the way God reveals himself in holy Scripture. This means reading the whole Bible, as far as possible, in the light of the way the apostles understood the person and work of Jesus. Let us begin with the gospel promise to the Philippians through the apostle Paul:

> Therefore God has highly exalted the Messiah and graciously given to him the name that is above every name, so that in honour of the name of Jesus every knee shall bow – in heaven, on the earth and under the earth – and every tongue shall confess that Messiah Jesus is Lord, to the glory of God the Father. (Phil. 2:9–11)

In this passage Paul gives us particular insight as to how God has achieved and will perfect the hallowing of his name on earth; as Calvin commented, God has 'vindicated His sacred Name' through the exaltation of the crucified Messiah and will perfect that vindication when 'the whole race of mankind' will 'bow their knees and confess that Messiah Jesus is Lord'.[7] Let us examine this a little further.

At first glance the passage points to the vindication of the incarnate Son who, 'though he existed in the form of God', did not strive for equality with God, but instead submitted himself to

59

a slave's death on a cross (Phil. 2:6–8). In response God the Father raised the Messiah to his right hand and bestowed his own name, Lord, on the royal and eternal Son. In effect Paul's words act as an exposition of Peter's Pentecost proclamation 'that man Jesus whom you crucified, God has made Lord and Messiah' (Acts 2:36). In Philippians 2 Paul is associating the exaltation of the risen Jesus with Isaiah's promise that everyone will bow before YHWH the saviour (Isa. 45:23). The name YHWH is the personal name of the God of Israel, which was not pronounced and is usually translated as LORD.[8] Paul informs the Philippians that the name of the Lord is, and will at some future point be, vindicated on earth and hence be hallowed as it is in heaven, when it is recognized to belong to the risen Messiah Jesus. What these verses imply is that the Father's name is, and will be, hallowed on earth as it is in heaven when the risen and ascended Messiah is acclaimed and proclaimed on earth as he is in heaven to be YHWH, the God of Abraham, Isaac and Jacob. As Barth remarked on the Philippian passage, 'What is revealed is that in His [Jesus of Nazareth's] identity with the Son of God this man was the Lord.'[9] This, writes Paul, will be 'to the glory of God the Father', on earth as it is in heaven.

The promise of salvation vindicated

There is, however, a deeper significance to the promise that the Father will vindicate Jesus as Lord to the glory of that name, which is that God gives himself in his promises in order to perfect his relationship with his creatures. From Philippians 2 we can deduce that the universal *affirmation* of the lordship of Messiah Jesus will coincide with the universal *confirmation* that the meaning of God's lordship over all the earth has been perfected in the *career* of his chosen/anointed king, and especially on the cross (Phil. 2:6–8). Our hope is grounded on God's vindicating his promise to be *with us* in Jesus' self-sacrificial actions as the saviour of sinners.[10] That is, the Father will vindicate the obedience of Messiah Jesus as *God's own* loving action towards his creation. Barth's comments are again worth heeding: 'As the Son of God humbled Himself and became a man, this man became the doer of the eternal will of God. He became the one who accomplished this work.'[11] God will hallow his name on earth as it is hallowed in heaven when the Father reveals his presence in the royal and eternal Son and justifies him over and against the sinners who brought about Jesus' death.

In addition, we must be able to discern a relationship between this promise to vindicate his name and the covenantal promise to be the God of his people. We shall do this, first, by rereading the biblical narrative in order to understand what God's name means. Second, we shall gain deeper insight into the way that God's presence through his name fulfils his promise to be the God of his covenantal people. The promise to be present will continually be challenged by sin, death and evil. However, in the gospel we understand that God has achieved glory for his holy name by the power of his *Holy* Spirit and through Messiah Jesus, the *holy one* of God.

Understanding the name of the Lord

The name as promise

From the beginning of the Israelite story, to learn God's name is to receive a promise. In Exodus 3, when Moses turns aside from keeping his sheep in order to investigate a burning bush that does not seem to be consumed by the flames, the issue of a divine presence is secondary to the question of the identity of the one who reveals himself to Moses.[12] God speaks to Moses and identifies himself thus:

> God said to Moses, 'I WILL BE WHO I WILL BE. This is what you are to say to the Israelites: 'I WILL BE has sent me to you.' God also said to Moses, 'Say to the Israelites, 'YHWH, the God of your fathers – the God of Abraham, the God of Isaac and the God of Jacob – has sent me to you. This is my name forever, the name you shall call me from generation to generation.' (Exod. 3:14–15)[13]

'I WILL BE' has been adopted as the translation of the underlying Hebrew verb *hyh* because it more readily allows *the narrative* to expand the meaning of God's name.[14] Admittedly, Christians down through the centuries have favoured the present tense of the verb, which in the Greek (Septuagint) is rendered 'I AM.' This has led many theologians to discourse at length on God's being the ultimate ground of all being, the one eternal God who upholds all things. Such claims are by no means unwarranted, but as abstract discussions of existence ought to take second place to considerations of what God has to say about himself in the biblical drama.[15] Explorations of the meaning of God's name that immediately move to questions of Being too readily lose the eschatological tension that is inherent in the narrative.[16] The Masoretic Text offers only *'ehyeh*, which even Calvin admits is in the future tense, but he was unable to avoid being drawn into discussion of the difference between YHWH and *to ōn* in terms of what it means for God to be eternal and the ground of all being.[17]

The speaker identifies himself as the 'God of your fathers, the God of Abraham, the God of Isaac and the God of Jacob'. Immediately something of the meaning of God's name is revealed. The one who speaks to Moses is the one who made promises in the past and hence 'one of the key characteristics of the one to whom the name YHWH belongs' that will distinguish this deity from others is 'the habit of declaring the intention to do something and then doing it'.[18] More significantly, to know God's name is to experience one who is 'known from the past' but who is also 'offering more in the future'. If we may rephrase Rahner's words, human beings understand the Christian God – who he is and how he shapes history – as a consequence of anamnesis and prognosis: 'by the anamnesis by which He has acted in the past and the prognosis by which He will act in what is to come'.[19] Life in relationship with the God of the Bible is a dynamic of then and not-yet. Contra Moltmann, while the promise may point away from the appearance in which it is uttered, this reference to the patriarchs means that it is the past reaching through the present towards the future. The future may be unrealized, but the past gives us hope for its shape.[20]

YHWH's characteristic of making promises is what necessitates this special presenting act to Moses and is the issue that highlights the importance of vindication. From the perspective of the narrative the descendants of Abraham, Isaac and Jacob desperately need God to act upon his promises. They may be great in number, but have no great name and no land, while those who curse them are prospering (Exod. 1:7ff.; cf. Gen. 12:1–3).[21] Therefore God must vindicate his name as the God of the patriarchs, the God of promise. What we find in the narrative is that he who was seemingly absent (from heaven?) has determined, in response to the cries of his people, 'to come down to deliver/rescue' his people from Egypt, and to take them to the land of their fathers.[22] Hence, in the face of Moses' qualms, which seem to foreshadow Israel's reluctance towards or even ignorance of God, God names himself as the 'One who will be.' God's name is not a limit that protects his inner self or forestalls Moses' questions.[23] Instead, the interchange with Moses reveals that God's name is a promise in keeping with his identification as the God who made promises to the fathers of the Hebrews.

In addition, to say that God will vindicate his name is to say that he will be present, in accordance with his promises, as saviour. The name YHWH or Lord is a new development in the narrative identity of God, as we are subsequently informed: 'Then God spoke to Moses, telling him, "I am Yahweh. I appeared to Abraham, Isaac, and Jacob as God Almighty, but I did not reveal My name Yahweh to them"' (Exod. 6:2–3). So God's name reflects the provisional nature of the promises he makes. Nevertheless, when commissioning Moses YHWH refers to himself as the God of the patriarchs, as he promises to reveal himself as saviour in sign and deed. The name YHWH means that God's identity is not merely future-oriented, as Moltmann advocated, but contains an element of promise as well.

For Moses and Israel, YHWH vindicates his name as the promise-fulfiller in his dealings with Pharaoh and Egypt. Moses and the Israelites in Exodus 15 then celebrate YHWH's reliability after the Red Sea crossing.[24] The exodus event is the hallowing of God's name on earth in the exercising of his sovereignty as Creator, the vindication of his claim to be the God of the promise made to Abraham, Isaac and Jacob and the fulfilment of his promise to rescue Israel as his people, his son. The promissory nature of the name YHWH has been vindicated spectacularly, for the Lord is a mighty saviour.[25] The God of their fathers will be Israel's great warrior and shepherd, and this forms an essential element of the meaning of the name of the Lord for the rest of the Old Testament story.[26] Therefore we must affirm that the almighty lordship of God is fundamental to who he is as the promise-fulfiller; he is his name:

> He is in himself the Lord, the Lord who makes himself known and acts this way. And he is the Lord not only in time but from eternity to eternity: not only in a particular provisional and transient economy, but as the One he was and is and will be; not only for us, but for us as and because He is in inward truth this One and not another – and for us in such a way that he does not have another being in which he can always be for us something different from his proclamation and action.[27]

With YHWH fidelity to his promise is the constant that provides stability for the name even while circumstances may change, and his promises have a contingent aspect to them. However, power and might to fulfil promises are not all there is to the fundamental nature of God in relation to creation. In another great episode in the naming of the God of Israel, which also involves Moses, YHWH adds more of his character to a description of the name of the Lord. This addition is particularly significant because of the counter-intuitive manner in which God will use his power and might in order to vindicate his name.

The name as a provisional promise

The promissory nature of YHWH's narrative identity means that there is always a sense in which the perfection of his promises is provisional. From the perspective of the exodus account his creatures, especially Israel, have to *wait and see* the perfected extent of who he will be in relationship with them. Yet there is more to the provisionality of God's promises than simply the passing of time. The shocking aspect of the narrative is that the chief recipients of the promises are also their principal opponents. God acts to share himself with his people, but they resist him or receive him in a manner that threatens the sanctity of his holy name and hence calls his presence among them into question. What we shall discover from this is the central place of forgiveness in the promises of God.

In Exodus 34 Moses is again in conversation with YHWH, this time upon Sinai. The narrative has just passed an extraordinary crisis in which Israel has fallen into idolatry with the golden calf and YHWH has had to vindicate his name *against his own people*.[28] Calvin grasps the significance of the extraordinary interchange between YHWH and Moses in chapter 33: 'It is plain, that when God bids Moses depart with the people, He utterly renounces the charge which He Himself had hitherto sustained.'[29] Yet Moses courageously and successfully advocates for the people, and the presence of YHWH will remain with them on their journey to the Promised Land.[30] Again Calvin's insights are perceptive: 'As the ground of his confidence in asking, he [Moses] adduces nothing but the promises of God . . . [Moses] contents himself with this brief statement, cause the event to correspond with Thy words.'[31] YHWH has adopted the people of Israel as his own, promising to be their God and that they will be distinguished among all the other nations as his (cf. Exod. 19:5–6). It is only 'just' therefore, says Calvin, that YHWH should vindicate himself before the people and hold to his covenantal promise.[32]

In chapter 34 the interchange between Moses and YHWH is full of allusions to presence in the form of facial propinquity.[33] The significance of this phenomenon is the way it emphasizes YHWH's active presence in the life of Israel. God freely gives himself to his people in order to fulfil his covenantal promise, but at the same time the sin of Israel creates a tension in the narrative and introduces a further provisional aspect to the covenantal promise. In this context Moses seeks a blessing from God in the form of seeing his glory, and YHWH's response is to proclaim his name in Moses' presence:

> Then the LORD came down in the cloud and stood there with him and proclaimed his name, the LORD. And he passed in front of Moses, proclaiming, 'The LORD, the LORD, the compassionate and gracious God, slow to anger, abounding in love and faithfulness, maintaining love to thousands, and forgiving wickedness, rebellion and sin. Yet he does not leave the guilty unpunished; he punishes the children and their children for the sin of the parents to the third and fourth generation.' (Exod. 34:5–7 TNIV)

Once again YHWH gives himself in his promissory name, which is 'his person, being and potency, his whole historical reality in its nature and essence'.[34] In giving his name, 'he opens himself up to dealings with others, he is engaged in such dealings, he goes among people and is with them'. Furthermore,

> he becomes and is a person who can be addressed, but who can also be claimed. In his name he can and will be burdened by them. In his name he turns to them and thus comes into their clutches.[35]

The one who promised to reveal himself in his actions, and consequently both destroyed the opposition of Pharaoh and redeemed his people, now stands on the earth interpreting his name to his servant Moses.

Since their first meeting and introduction it is clear that YHWH will be glorified on the earth by his grace and compassion. In keeping with the promise he made to their fathers, God will be generous towards his people.[36] The height of his power will be his 'goodness and gratuitous beneficence', as Calvin calls it.[37] *For God uses his might to be patient with a sinful people, in fact with a sinful world.* His almighty strength will be seen in his tenacious adherence to the promise he has made despite the failings of Israel. YHWH *will be* their God and hence 'He patiently waits for those who have sinned, and invites them to repentance by His long-suffering.'[38] Nonetheless, though he will be forgiving he will not be unjust, and so his power will be reflected by punishing sin 'to the third and fourth generation'. For Brueggemann this points to a tension within YHWH's covenantal promise and hence his name: 'the very God who is in inordinate solidarity with Israel and who is prepared to stay with Israel in every circumstance, is the God who will act abrasively to maintain sovereignty against any who challenge or disregard that sovereignty'.[39] While Brueggemann is correct in identifying an outward discrepancy in the description of YHWH's actions, to charge God with abrasive behaviour obscures the relational dynamics between YHWH and Israel that underlie their covenant relationship. YHWH has already vindicated himself as the promise-maker who gives himself to his people. He has already vindicated his promise to be the one who will deliver Israel from slavery and that as the

God of the promise to the fathers of Israel. Yet at no point has YHWH promised simply to overlook Israel's ever-present recalcitrance towards being the people of the promise. Hence YHWH has promised that he will sanctify his name on the earth against his people if need be. As Calvin paraphrases, 'Although God is pitiful and even ready to pardon, yet He does not therefore spare the despisers, but is a severe avenger of their impiety.'[40] The 'overspill' of YHWH's promises, so important to Moltmann,[41] will be realized in terms of God's patience and generosity towards his people as he vindicates his name upon the earth.

The question arises, however, as to the precise identity of *the people* who will be the beneficiaries of the promise. In giving his name to the people,

> his name . . . becomes a decisive factor for them too, for their person, being and potency, for their historical reality . . . He burdens them with what he is and does for them in his dealings with them . . . The name is always both the humiliation and exaltation, both the condemnation and glory.[42]

An element of ambiguity covers the identity of YHWH's covenantal partners. To coin Moltmann's phrase, the promise does point away from the event of revelation to 'the as yet unrealised future' *people*.[43] Nevertheless, YHWH is determined to be the God of the promises he makes and so our attention turns to the manner in which he will be present with his people *in the present*. The exodus event reveals God's name as Lord of the past and the not-yet, but what of the now?

The present name

The *now* experience of God's name for Israel incorporates the important concept of the *place* for God's name in the community (or the community constituted by the presence of the name), as the presence of the name brings a provisional fulfilment of the covenant promise. God's divinity is *mediated* to his people as his name dwells among his people. In the previous chapter we reviewed Moltmann's assertions that the future or the *not-yet* of God's promises takes priority over the *now* with its static

67

revelations of the eternal God. According to Moltmann, this explains the provisional nature of God's promises:

> The reason for the overplus of promise and for the fact that it constantly overspills history lies in the inexhaustibility of the God of promise, who never exhausts himself in any historic reality but comes 'to rest' only in a reality that wholly corresponds to him.[44]

In contrast to this we shall see in this section that God comes 'to rest' among his people in relation to the way they respond to his name present with them.

Thus far in the exodus story the name of the Lord is intimately bound to his saving actions, which are pre-eminent in the narrative as the means by which he is hallowed on earth as he is in heaven (Exod. 9:16). His actions vindicate his promises and intensify the meaning of his name. In addition, the exodus story also introduces the theme of YHWH's sharing of himself with his people. God is not merely *actively* present with his people but *personally proximate* in his actions. In both the episodes thus far considered YHWH is present with Moses – first in the burning bush and then on Sinai – as his name is revealed. This association between the place of and for YHWH's name throughout the rest of the Israelite drama will be integral for developing a description of the hallowing of God's name on the earth and will lead ultimately to a consideration of the pre-eminent presence of God in Jesus. At the same time, we shall gain insight into the way the Israelite drama develops the concept of mediation which is so important for understanding the relationship between the absolutely different life of God the Creator and the contingent life of the creation.

The name, the tabernacle and the temple

In the first meetings between Israel and YHWH at Sinai God speaks to Moses of places where he will cause his name to be remembered (Exod. 20:24). These places of remembrance are non-specific but do involve the offering of sacrifices upon a precise type of altar. Therefore, though not explicitly stated in the rest of the wilderness narrative, it seems reasonable to assume that once God comes down from the mountain to dwell among his people in the highly regulated sacrificial environment of the tabernacle, this is the place where God's name is hallowed on the earth as it is in heaven or the means by which his promise to be their God is vindicated.[45] It is reasonable to argue that the association of the glory/cloud of YHWH's presence with the tabernacle is far more prominent than the name in the exodus narrative.[46] However, considering the significance of YHWH's meetings with Moses in which his name is announced and expounded in his glorious presence, it does no violence to the existing narrative to allow the tabernacle to assume the role of the central place in which YHWH's name is and will be present on earth.[47] Hence, as Moses preaches the sermons of Deuteronomy to the people on the plains of Moab, we take it that '*the* place' where he chooses 'to have His name dwell' (Deut. 12:5, 11, 21; 14:23–24; 16:2, 6, 11; 26:2) is the tabernacle in the first instance. It is not until David raises the idea of a 'house' for YHWH that an explicit connection is made between the name of the Lord and the temple, which is subsequently built by Solomon: 'I have built the temple for the name of Yahweh, the God of Israel.' This is to be the place where the Lord chooses for his name to dwell (1 Kgs 8:20, 29, 43). Solomon's prayer at the temple dedication introduces a number of important distinctions in so far as God's actual dwelling is transcendent in heaven, and hence his immanent presence requires some form of creaturely mediation – the temple. Thus the manner with which YHWH responds to the prayers of the foreigner directed towards the place on earth where his name dwells has a significant result:

> Then all the people on earth will know Your name,
> to fear You as Your people Israel do.
>
> (1 Kgs 8:43)

YHWH's name will be hallowed on earth as in heaven as the temple and the surrounding cult mediates his presence in creation, and therefore we can see, even at this stage, a connection between divine and creaturely life.

Discussions among Old Testament scholars concerning God's immanent presence in the Israelite cult range widely depending on what position is taken concerning possible sources for the canonical texts. This has led many scholars to consider that

69

the Old Testament depictions of tabernacle and temple are at odds.[48] Such contentions notwithstanding, what is evident is that in ancient Jewish cosmology the heavens and the earth were bound together in relation to God their creator by an image based upon the tabernacle/temple.[49] The forecourt of the structure was the representation of the world with the holy place as the experience of the heavens. God's transcendent presence is hidden behind the clouds in the holy of holies – invisible heaven.[50] This cosmic temple is not so much a Ptolemaic schematization as an ontological characterization.[51] Neither should we confuse it with Platonic notions of the ideal form since, as Beale shows, the concept of the temple being both the model of the heavens and the connection between earth and heaven is a well-documented ancient Near Eastern idea.[52] As the meeting place between heaven and earth, what went on in the earthly tabernacle/temple was the symbolic manifestation of what God was doing in the universe.[53] Hence when God's name is glorified in the earthly temple/tabernacle it is because it is already glorious in heaven. The numinous interventions of God's presence in the history created by his promises do not compromise the progress of creaturely time. Instead, they catalogue God's perfecting work of establishing the conditions in which he shares himself with his people. He is their God and they are his people in an increasingly deeper way.

The name and presence in crisis

When Solomon ascends the throne of David in 1 Kings it seems that the promise to Abraham will at last be fulfilled and YHWH will be vindicated completely as the promise-making God. Israel are at their peak politically, and have become a great nation of many people drawing admiration from the surrounding nations. The rest that has come upon the land and the descent of the Sinai cloud over the temple mark the formal end to the exodus (1 Kgs 4:21; 5:4–5; 8:10–11).[54] Jerusalem has become a world centre since YHWH has 'chosen Jerusalem so that My name will be there' (2 Chr. 6:6). Thus the name of the Lord is hallowed on earth as it is in heaven.[55] Furthermore, YHWH's name as promise appears to be vindicated once and for all as his desire to give himself to his people to be their God is achieved in the permanent medium of his house as opposed to the obviously transitory tent.

However, from this high point the story of Israel's life with YHWH progresses along a tragically downward spiral of syncretism and idolatry. The warnings of Leviticus go unheeded as one king after another profanes the name of the Lord, even in the place where YHWH caused it to dwell; for example:

> Manasseh set up the carved image of Asherah, which he made, in the temple that the LORD had spoken about to David and his son Solomon, 'I will establish My name forever in this temple and in Jerusalem, which I have chosen out of all the tribes of Israel.' (2 Kgs 21:7)

Consequently, prophets like Jeremiah inform the people that they have taken God's promises for granted, viewing 'the temple as a guarantee of divine presence and as a talisman warding off destruction',[56] despite their syncretism (Jer. 7:10). The provisional aspects of YHWH's name reach a crisis point, as God must act to vindicate his name against the sinfulness of his people on the one hand and yet, on the other, fulfil his promise to be their gracious and tenaciously faithful saviour.[57]

In the first instance the crisis deepens in the form of God's ominous faithfulness to his promises to *punish* sin: 'For I am already bringing disaster on the city that bears My name . . . You will not go unpunished' (Jer. 25:29). As he promised Moses, YHWH does indeed 'not leave the guilty unpunished' (cf. Exod. 34:7). However, the punishment that God has in mind threatens to repeal the history of the covenant relationship between YHWH and Israel, because the Lord threatens to abandon this people who bear his name. In the language of the later prophets Israel's importance to God is strikingly relativized as seers like Amos chastise the people for their unfaithfulness (Amos 9:7). As we noted in relation to Exodus 34, 'being part of Israel offers no unconditional guarantees to people'.[58] Worse still is the prospect through Hosea (later depicted in Ezekiel's vision) of YHWH's glorious presence departing from the temple and Jerusalem (Ezek. 11:23; cf. Hos. 5:15). If God gives himself to his people in his promises, then the severity of his wrath is that he takes himself back from them even as he removes them from the Promised Land and sends them into exile.

71

At times the power of YHWH to vindicate his own name comes in the form of Israel's punishment, but as he revealed at Sinai, the Lord's first inclination is to forgive his people and to wield his power to save them, even if only to vindicate his name because the people bear his name. God's actions for his name are always towards the earth – to establish a place for his name on the earth and, consequently, for his name to be treated as holy on the earth. The tensions for God's promises – evidenced in his words concerning himself – are resolved in his actions and even in the responses of his people.[59] The lasting tension, if that is what it could be called, is the exact identity of the covenantal people. On the one hand, the story of Israel shows that the direct recipients are the principal antagonists of the covenant. On the other hand, the later prophetic tradition intimates strongly that the covenantal promise can and will go on, despite Israel. The exile experience shows that YHWH has no intention of confining his promises to Israel. The hallowing of his name will be before the whole earth, before all nations. In fact, Isaiah and Jeremiah (at least) indicate that the question is not so much whether all nations will have a share in the promise but whether Israel will evade exclusion (Isa. 18:7; Jer. 3:17)

In the name of the Father

In the first chapter we determined to read the Bible with the gospel-focused assumption that all the promises made by God are fulfilled in Jesus the Christ. Thus far in this chapter we have explored the canonical narrative to consider how the story of God's name could shape our understanding of Jesus' commendation as Lord. This is one aspect of the history that we expect to become 'the past' of the risen Jesus.[60] Our hope for life in the Middle is founded on the possibilities for the Father's perfecting work and that work begins by hallowing his name on earth as it is in heaven. As we have seen, this work depends on the readiness of the God known as YHWH to vindicate his name as the promise-maker. In addition, a significant aspect of any act of vindication is bound up with the conditions for the possibility of God's presence among his covenantal people, since he does literally give himself in his promises.

It is clear from the exodus account that YHWH will defend his name via spectacular intervention on the earth to the point of disturbing the coherence of creation if necessary. Yet the focus of YHWH's powerful self-vindicating actions is to ensure that he is known in all the earth as saviour. Hence YHWH's great power to hallow his name on the earth is revealed in grace and compassion towards sinners. The name of the Lord reveals resolute and tenacious faithfulness, generosity and kindness, and God's most glorious actions upon the earth are seen in his readiness to defer the vindication of his name when present to his people even to the point of forgiving their sin. When God does preserve his holiness against the sin of his people he does so in a manner that protects the integrity of his name among the nations as saviour.

The promise of a new saving presence

After the exile the Old Testament story finishes with great antici- pation for the future when God's name will be hallowed on earth as it is in heaven:

> 'For My name will be great among the nations, from the rising of the sun to its setting. Incense and pure offerings will be presented in My name in every place because My name will be great among the nations,' says Yahweh of Hosts. (Mal. 1:11)

Yet this promise is succeeded by 400 years of silence on the part of YHWH. Sometimes 'YHWH's withdrawal is a withdrawal into silence.'[61] In this silence a degree of ambiguity once more settles on the covenantal promise despite the return of the exiles. A new temple has been built and even expanded, but a question hangs over the presence of the name in this place.[62] Without the ark the holy of holies is empty and therefore the name is absent (cf. 2 Sam. 6:2). Though the Jews had returned from Babylon, spiritually, they appeared to remain in exile.[63] It is in this context that the Gospel writers announce that God has made himself present mysteriously in fulfilment of Isaiah's distant promise regarding the virgin's son 'she will call him Immanuel; which means God with us' (Matt. 1:23; cf. Isa. 7:14). This presence is for the purpose of salvation, and hence the child's name is given to Joseph as Jesus, 'because he will save his people from their sins' (Matt. 1:21). Yet, as Calvin points out, it is a mistake to conflate the name YHWH with the name of Jesus at this early stage in the Gospel narrative.[64] We must instead look to the hints in the various configurations that allow for the possibility that God's name is once again present among his people and that he will act to vindicate his name on the earth once and for all.

To attempt to solve this mystery via engagement with the Gospel narratives means that our eschatological journey through the Bible will interact with Christology or what we might confess concerning the person and work of Jesus. In general and following Colin Gunton, we shall hold to three maxims for the incarnation: (1) that the reason for the incarnation is grounded on the eternal will of God, not contingent upon the fall of humanity; (2) that the Son submits to the will of the Father in order to be made flesh and that the Spirit prepares the humanity of Jesus for him; (3) the incarnation is a kenosis 'but one understood as the expression of the inner dynamic of the Trinity, not as the sloughing off of certain attributes'.[65] Historically, at least in the Western tradition, the mystery of God incarnate has been approached in one of two ways depending on whether or not one chooses a Christology from above or below; that is, whether one starts with the divine nature of the eternal Son or Logos to develop the identity of Christ Jesus or, alternatively, with the historical man seeking to look through, somehow, to the divine Jesus Christ. A third possibility is to read all the Gospel portraits in concert in order to discern 'through the gift of the Spirit, the human Jesus as *also* the divine Christ'.[66]

Within the context of the story of God's name, a further question in addition to the long-running issue of when and how God will fulfil his promises emerges in the Gospel narratives. That is, is this *man*, Jesus of Nazareth, the one in whom God's promises will be fulfilled, the God of Abraham, Isaac and Jacob present here and now? The answer to this question will, of course, be *yes*. What is of interest to us here is the way in which the New Testament writers, using the metaphors of divine presence that were so important to the story of God's promissory name, depict Jesus as the mediator between divine and creaturely life. With this in mind we turn to the beginning of the Gospel accounts.

A mysterious place for the name

From the opening verse of John's Gospel the reader is introduced to the Logos or Word who was with God and who was God. This Word of God existed with God before creation and participates fully in the divine – their interrelation is one of shared being.[67] Yet the wonder of the Christian story is that the one 'through whom everything was made' becomes a creature in his own creation – 'the Word became flesh' (John 1:3–14).[68] John here is more concerned with 'the significance of the incarnation, not the fact'.[69]

The evangelist describes the enfleshed Logos dwelling (*eskēnōsen*) or tenting among us,[70] which is evocative of the Old Testament's description of God's dwelling among his people Israel. In Exodus 25:8 the Lord tells Moses to build YHWH a sanctuary so that he may dwell among his people. While *skēnoō* itself occurs only in John 1:14, the tabernacle appears in Exodus.[71] As we have already observed, the tabernacle was a central motif of presence for much of Israel's history. It was the palace and sanctuary of YHWH among his people, the place where his glory rested and therefore the home of his name with Israel.[72]

John's prologue presents us with the implication that by the Spirit YHWH is present in the virgin's son, Immanuel, as he was in the tent in the camp of Israel. The Logos took up residence in the flesh of the man Jesus of Nazareth. In the same way that the tabernacle did not cease, with YHWH's residence, to be a real tent, neither did Jesus cease to be truly human. Of course, the *sarx* of Jesus is distinct from the *sarx* of every other human and this can be articulated by the same image. The tabernacle was consecrated exclusively for the dwelling of God and in fact at the point at which the glory descended upon the tabernacle nothing sinful could be in it (cf. Exod. 40, esp. vv. 34–35). Similarly, the man Jesus so contains the Logos that he was like us 'in every way yet without sin' (Heb. 4:15). The chief difference, obviously, is the mysterious hiddenness of God in this second instance of dwelling among the people. The mystery deepens from John's perspective because although the Word comes into his own world in the prologue, he is hidden throughout the rest of John's narrative.[73] To strengthen the connection between the divine presence and the person of Jesus we must turn to Luke's account of the virgin birth that delves into the mystery left by John's silence.

In the interaction between the angel and Mary, Gabriel addresses the virgin's perplexity at the prospect of childbirth with the words 'The Holy Spirit will come upon you and power from the Most High will overshadow you' (Luke 1:35). The significance of the angel's words in Luke 1:35 is much discussed by commentators, especially in terms of the presence of God. Again, is it possible to view Mary's experience in comparison with the dramatic way in which the glory of YHWH in the cloud marked his coming down upon the completed tabernacle? Nolland opines that *episkiasei*, "will overshadow," like *epeleusetai*, "will come upon," has probably been influenced by the LXX text of Ex. 40:35'.[74] In contrast Brown argues:

> It is speculation to suggest from the verb *episkiazein* that Luke thinks of Mary as the Tabernacle or the Ark of the Covenant overshadowed by or containing the divine presence. To be precise, in the OT it is the cherubim rather than God that are said to overshadow the Ark (Ex. 25:20; I Chr. 28:18); moreover, the Ark and the Tabernacle are not the only places overshadowed by the divine presence (Deut. 33:12; Ps. 91:4).[75]

Brown's alternative to the tabernacle symbolism is to delve even further back in the prefigurative tradition drawing allusions to 'the Spirit hovering over the face of the waters' in Genesis 1:2. In this way Mary's child is a new creation *ex nihilo*.[76] Certainly Luke's configuration is attempting to deal with a phenomenon that is outside everyday experience, and from that point of view Brown's reference to the creation story, though no less speculative, is apt. In fairness to Nolland, however, the fact that the divine presence can overshadow more than one thing strengthens the possibility of inference. The extent to which we can be certain about influences is limited, but Nolland makes a useful remark when he writes that 'there is not the slightest evidence that either of the verbs involved have ever been used in relation to sexual activity or even more broadly in connection with the conception of a child'.[77] The focus in the Lukan narrative is God's work in the Spirit that produces the child's conception within the body of the mother. As Calvin commented, 'Mary brought forth not an ethereal body or phantom, but the fruit which she had previously conceived in her womb.'[78] This was the work of God's Holy Spirit so that the child in the virgin's womb might be born holy. What makes Nolland's suggestion attractive is its connection to the ongoing relationship between eternity and time. If we accept that there are allusions to the tabernacle story in the Gospel accounts then the prefigurative tradition, on which the Gospel authors drew, contains conceptual resources that assist our understanding of the being of God (eternity) embracing the being of creation (temporality) in the incarnation while maintaining an appropriate distinction between the two.

If we reconsider the account of God's initial presence among encamped Israel in the Septuagint (hereafter LXX) text of Exodus 40:35, we read, 'Moses was unable to enter the tent of meeting because the cloud rested on [*episkiazein*] it, and the glory of the LORD had filled the tabernacle.' The completion of the tabernacle and the entrance of YHWH therein mark a climax to the exodus account. The epiphanic presence of God at Sinai comes among the people in a more permanent way.[79] The living arrangements of YHWH incorporated in the Gospel narratives form a significant correspondence with the miraculously conceived child. With the approach of the cloud nothing sinful is able to be in the tent. The divine presence has especially sanctified the tent as a uniquely holy space. Yet the tent is made of the same materials as every other tent in the camp and remains a tent. The child born of the flesh of the woman is referred to as *to gennōmenon hagion* (the one begotten holy) through the Spirit, since God is peculiarly present as a human being. Though this is an extraordinary instance of it, the same YHWH has established the conditions for the possibility of his presence among the people in order to fulfil his promise to save. Through the work of the Holy Spirit the holy one born of Mary is to be the agent who will make the name of the Lord great among the nations.

The possibilities of incorporating tabernacle symbolism in the developing narrative identity of Messiah Jesus may be more allusive than substantial. However, returning to John's account we observe that, the details of the virgin birth notwithstanding, John does confirm the means by which the Word takes residence in the person of Messiah Jesus. The narrative has barely progressed beyond introductions before Jesus comes into conflict with 'his own' in the temple forecourts (John 2:13–22). Having entered the temple precincts at the time of the Passover, Jesus proceeds to drive out the merchants because they have turned his 'Father's house into a marketplace'. The scene is, of course, portrayed after the fact. However, the evangelist is careful to ensure that any subsequent insight into the event is included in the report.[80] The disciples recall that Jesus acted out of 'zeal for the Lord's house' as per Psalm 69:9.[81] But, more importantly, in the interchange between Jesus and the Jews regarding the destruction of the temple and its subsequent re-establishment, the disciples recall that Jesus considered the new temple to be his resurrected body:

> 'Destroy this temple and in three days I will raise it.' The Jews replied, 'It took forty-six years to build this temple and you will raise it up in three days?' But he was referring to the temple of his body. (John 2:19–21; cf. Matt. 12:6)[82]

The effect here is that the presence of God in the man Jesus has eclipsed the divine presence previously instituted in the temple: 'For we know that the Son of God clothed himself with our nature in such a manner that the eternal majesty of God dwelt in the flesh which he assumed, as in his sanctuary.'[83] Furthermore, all the theological and cosmological significance that might otherwise have been associated with the presence of God on earth is now transferred to the incarnation of the Word. That is, if the temple is the place on earth in which the Lord puts his name, then the person of Jesus is now the place in which the name of the Lord will be hallowed on earth as it is in heaven.[84] There is a new mediation, a new giving of God in and for his promises to save.

A further instance of this kind of association between the person of Jesus and the place for God's name occurs in the transfiguration accounts (Matt. 17:1–7; Mark 9:2–10; Luke 9:28–37). Jesus and the three ascend a mountain to pray and God addresses the transformed Jesus as his chosen Son. Through an apocalyptic intervention Jesus appears in the presence of two of Israel's *great and good*. Both Moses and Elijah experienced the presence of YHWH on a mountain (Sinai, Exod. 24:15–16; Horeb, 1 Kgs 19:8–9). Now by the Spirit the Father publicly addresses the Son as the perfect mediator between heaven and earth, with the glory vindicating the perfected status of this mediation.[85] Even as he once spoke to Moses and Elijah in the clouds upon a mountain, God now speaks directly to the disciples, endorsing Jesus as the Messiah. In the presence of two of Israel's great mediators, the Father endorses Jesus of Nazareth as the one through whom he will address Israel – 'listen to him' (Luke 9:35). In terms of Luke's configuration, God vindicates the Messiah as one who enjoys immanent divine presence in an unprecedented manner. Nolland notes that the verb 'to flash or shine like lightning' (*exastrapton*) appears in the LXX of Ezekiel 1:4, 7 in connection with the outskirts of God's glory as Ezekiel sees *God* upon his throne. Similar is the effect upon Moses of speaking with God upon Mount Sinai (Exod. 34:29, 30, 35).[86] In both of these episodes the issue of God's presence is paramount.

Throughout the Israelite drama the tabernacle and the temple acted as divinely appointed media for God's desire to give himself to his people in his promises. As we have seen, the Gospel writers make important allusions to these symbolic types in expanding the Isaianic promise that God will dwell in the virgin's son. Suggestion of this fundamental Israelite symbol is even richer in the transfiguration episode. The reference to the cloud over-shadowing (*episkiazein*) those gathered with Jesus is strongly allusive to the birth announcement, and it is not difficult to envisage the glory of Jesus' face being the shekinah glory that settled upon the tabernacle (Exod. 40:35) as YHWH descended from the mountain to dwell among his people. Nolland opines:

> The cloud is the sign of God's (hidden) presence (Ps. 18:11; Ex. 19:16 etc.) and the mode of his transportation (Is. 19:1; Pss. 18:10; 104:3). Here the correlation of the 'cloud' and 'voice' points uniquely to God's speaking from Mt. Sinai (Ex. 19:16; Deut. 5:22).[87]

By the power of his Spirit, the name of the Lord is present in the man Jesus of Nazareth, who has eclipsed both the temple and the tabernacle as the locus of mediation par excellence between divine eternal life and creaturely temporal life. He is the place of the name. As such, he will also be not only the point from which God's name is hallowed among the nations. He will also be the one whom God promised as saviour and through whom YHWH will be the promise-making God.

'I will be' Messiah Jesus

The mysterious presence of the name of the Lord in the person of Jesus of Nazareth gives us the opportunity to consider how the work of Messiah Jesus will lead to the fulfilment of YHWH's promise to be the God who saves. If, during the exodus narrative, God's actions vindicated his personal proximity with Israel, then in the gospel story the personal proximity of the Lord will need to be vindicated by the extent to which the Messiah's actions are YHWH's.

The prophet Ezekiel anticipates God's glorifying his name among the nations when he saves Israel from exile: 'This is what the Lord GOD says: It is not for your sake that I will act, house of Israel, *but for My holy name*, which you profaned among the nations where you went' (Ezek. 36:22; emphasis added). What the Gospel writers, and John in particular, reveal is that the God of Abraham, Isaac and Jacob, who gave his promissory name to Moses, fulfils his promise *to be* in the actions of Jesus who will save his people from their sins. I draw particular attention to John's configuration because in this biography we find the consistent association of the name of the Lord with the identity of Jesus. *Egō eimi* as the Greek version of the name given to Moses in Exodus 3:6 has long been interpreted as a highly compressed formula with great theological significance. What we shall see in even a brief examination of John's use of the construction is that Messiah Jesus is the one whom God promised Israel he would be.

Throughout John's configuration the most frequent use of the formula is in conjunction with metaphors.[88] Schnackenburg has observed that 'all the symbols are connected with the *zōē* which Jesus is and gives to believers'.[89] That is, all the images are interpreted as referring to the significance of Jesus Christ for believers in terms of the promise of John 3:16, 'Whoever believes in him has eternal life.'[90] The significance of Jesus for the characters in the narrative (and to a large extent the reader[91]) varies depending upon the metaphor in question. It has been suggested that a primary function of the *egō eimi* in John is to take an Old Testament image and apply it to the person of Jesus.[92] Thus in a number of cases the formula and metaphors convey information about Jesus in relation to Israel (the light of the world, 8:12; 9:5; and Isa. 42:6; 49:6; 51:4), while in others Jesus speaks of his role in the work of God for the salvation of his people (e.g. the good shepherd of John 10).[93] The result is to show the continuity between YHWH's actions for Israel in the past and his actions in the person of Jesus in the present. The last example, from John 10, is most pertinent to the issue of presence and actions and so we shall consider it in more depth.

In John 10 Jesus adopts the phrase *egō eimi* without a specific Old Testament quotation, as in John 6, or a particular Old Testament phrase, as in John 8. Nevertheless, 'the passage is full of Old Testament allusions, which demonstrate John's complex but subtle use of the Old Testament'.[94] Significantly, as Calvin points out, the confrontation in this passage occurs in the temple during the Feast of Dedication – the annual festival marking the renovation of the temple after the persecutions of Antiochus.[95] As we have seen, John's narrative builds an expectation that Jesus' person will eclipse the role of the temple as God's presence on earth. Now, when the Jews celebrate the renovation of the temple, Jesus uses this significant season to contextualize his relation to God by identifying his actions with those of his Father. The main allusion in John 10 is to the prophecy in Ezekiel 34.[96] There the prophet is told to prophesy against the 'shepherds of Israel' who are the leaders of God's chosen people. In the Ezekiel passage God states that he will be the good shepherd (34:15) of his sheep. At the same time, he will set up his servant David (v. 23) as shepherd. By the words *egō eimi* in John 10 Jesus identifies himself with the role that God would accomplish as the promised good shepherd. At the same time Jesus fulfils the role of God's servant, David. Jesus' close relationship with the Father (John 10:14–15) is thus paralleled in Ezekiel by the thought that both God (vv. 11–16) and his servant David (vv. 23–24) are to be the shepherd of the flock. In Ezekiel the relationship between God and his servant is so close that God speaks of there being one shepherd (Ezek. 34:23; cf. 37:24), a fact also emphasized in John (10:16; cf. 10:30). Thus the evangelist's use of the *egō eimi* formula makes Jesus both the God who shepherds Israel and the human agent through whom God acts. It is no surprise that Jesus goes on to say in 10:30, 'I and the Father are one.' In Barth's words:

> The Father who is one with the man Jesus His Son . . . is the God who years before was not too good, and did not count it too small a thing, to bind and engage Himself to Abraham and his seed, and to be the God of this particularity and limitation – 'I will be your God.'[97]

81

Thus in certain instances the *egō eimi* formula is a device whereby John expands and enlarges the notion of the presence of the name in Messiah Jesus.[98] Jesus is far more than a 'sent ambassador' or representative who carries out the work of God. Rather, the name of the Lord, YHWH, is present in him as the eternal and royal Son, such that fulfilment of God's promise to save will be enacted in the ministry of the Messiah. The actions of Jesus will be the actions of YHWH to sanctify his name among the nations on earth as it is in heaven.

Vindicating the name in Jesus

While the Gospel narratives build a strong expectation that YHWH's saving actions for the sake of his promises will come to fruition through his presence in the person and work of Messiah Jesus, nothing tests this possibility like the climax of the story itself – the cross. I have gone some way in aligning the Old Testament tabernacle/temple motif with the story of Messiah Jesus. In this context, this is the Old Testament acting as the past of the Lord Jesus. I have alluded to the presence of the Spirit with Jesus in my discussion of the presence of the name in him. Now we need to consider the relationship between Jesus and the Spirit and the Spirit's preparation of him to be present with his people after his resurrection. It remains important to consider the role of the temple at this crucial part of the narrative.

For Moltmann one of the essential aspects of Christian confession is that God was *absent* from the cross. As mentioned in the previous chapter, the leitmotif of Moltmann's theology is the cry of dereliction from Psalm 22:1, which acted as the foundation of his landmark contribution in *The Crucified God*:

> In the total, inextricable abandonment of Jesus by his God and Father, Paul sees the delivering up of the Son by the Father for godless and godforsaken man . . . It may therefore be said that the Father delivers up his Son on the cross in order to be the Father of those who are delivered up . . . if Paul speaks emphatically of God's 'own Son,' the not-sparing and abandoning also involves the Father himself. In the forsakenness of the Son the Father also forsakes himself. In the surrender of the Son the Father also surrenders himself.[99]

Even much later, in *The Way of Jesus Christ*, though Moltmann enriched his exposition of the Christ's death from a number of angles, all of them found a nexus in messianic rejection. Hence he sums up the passion of Jesus as the child of God dying in abandonment.[100] To be fair, throughout Jesus' ministry, Moltmann sees the Spirit's empowering him and accompanying him along his cruciform path. Thus '[the Spirit] is drawn into his sufferings and becomes his *companion* in suffering'.[101] This, according to Moltmann, means the Spirit becomes 'the transcendent side of Jesus' immanent way of suffering'.[102] Nevertheless, as mentioned previously, Moltmann's Spirit-Christology sees the Spirit accompanying Jesus in the 'experience of God's hiddenness' right through to 'experience of God-forsakenness on the cross'.[103]

While Moltmann rightly acknowledges the importance of Jesus' claiming the Isaiah 61 promise (Luke 4:16ff.) as a foundation for messianic ministry,[104] he otherwise seems indifferent to the way the Spirit empowers Jesus with the *Scriptures*. Jesus' appearance in Nazareth in the Spirit's power follows directly from his triumph in the wilderness over Satan, a triumph enabled by the Spirit through the Scriptures. In response to Satan's offer to determine the nature of his sonship ('If you are the Son'), in the Spirit, Jesus chooses the way of discipline (suffering?), he chooses the Father's promised inheritance and he chooses not to pre-empt the Father's promise to save him from death, all 'as it is written'.[105] In this reading the Spirit makes effective the Father's presence via his word of promise to his messianic Servant to empower Jesus to face death.

When it comes to the Gethsemane agony, as we observed in chapter 1, we find Jesus again enabled by the Spirit to submit to God's word in the face of death, here described as 'drinking the cup'.[106] Since we understand 'the cup' in terms of God's wrath against unfaithful Israel (Isa. 51) and the nations (Jer. 25), the Gethsemane crisis for Jesus is less a matter of inexplicably facing God's silence than of submitting to God's spoken word, to the reality that 'this [cup] cannot pass unless [Jesus] drink[s] it' (Matt. 26:42) so that the Father's will might be done. As obviously terrible as the experience is, the Spirit mediates to Jesus the presence of God through his promise. As I have previously argued, this dynamic is nowhere more important than when the Messiah is inspired to exegete the Golgotha events through

Psalm 22. Matthew's account is pregnant with allusions to this lament such that the poet's answer to Jesus' cry 'My God, my God, why have you forsaken me?' is

> For He has not despised or detested
> the torment of the afflicted.
> He did not hide His face from him
> but listened when he cried to Him for help.
> (Ps. 22:24)

Even so, the distortion of the world order that marks the death of this man Jesus of Nazareth (darkness and earthquakes) might well have been understood as a sign that God had departed from *that* place and hence the faith of Messiah Jesus required vindication. After all, the narrative conflict over God's dwelling place in Israel re-emerges at the foot of the cross: 'You who are going to destroy the temple and build it in three days, save yourself! Come down . . . if you are the Son of God!' (Matt. 27:40). The taunt reflects the mischievous charges brought against Jesus at his trial, 'We heard him say, "I will destroy this temple made with human hands and in three days will build another, not made with hands"' (Mark 14:58). Together these two references bring to a head one of the essential conflicts between Jesus and the authorities throughout the Gospel narratives.[107]

Particularly in the synoptic tradition, the temple cleansing separates Jesus' triumphal entry into Jerusalem as Zechariah's Messiah of peace (Mark 11:9–10; cf. Zech. 9:9) from Jesus' explosive denunciation of the Jewish leaders through the parable of the wicked tenants (Mark 12:1–12). The net effect is that on coming to Jerusalem in quasi-royal fashion, Jesus not only announces his status as Messiah but also enacts the role of the agent of God's judgment towards those who have long been the principal antagonists to the promises of YHWH.[108] His actions amount to a prophetic announcement that YHWH has rejected Israel's idolatrous approach to the temple (cf. Jer. 7:9–11): 'there is no reason to doubt that he declared himself to be both King and High Priest, who presided over the temple and the worship of God'.[109] With this conflict as a major contributor to the act of crucifixion, it is all the more significant that the Gospel writers make mention of a crisis in the temple at the point in the narrative that otherwise appears to be a crisis of presence for the Messiah.

In the Synoptic Gospels, at the exact moment of Jesus' death, 'the veil of the temple was torn in two from top to bottom' (Matt. 27:51; Mark 15:38; Luke 23:45). The traditional Reformation understanding of this event, among other apocalyptic signs, is that

> the rending of the veil was not only an abrogation of the ceremonies which existed under the law, but was, in some respects, an opening of heaven, that God may now invite the members of his Son to approach him with familiarity.[110]

Later commentators have gone further, adding that due to the cosmic symbolism inherent in the veil, the event marks 'access for all believers to God's holy presence in a way that was not available in the old creation'.[111] Either way, in terms of God's presence – the hallowing of his name on the earth takes place in the death of the Messiah on the cross *as opposed* to the temple. The event anticipates the fact that 'God was in Christ, reconciling the world to Himself' (2 Cor. 5:19). His name was present at Golgotha, not Zion. This connection is again perhaps more allusive than substantial, and so we must look further to the Spirit-driven testimony of the apostles for confirmation.

It takes the perfecting work of the Spirit at Pentecost to reveal the active unity of God, the Father, and his royal Son in the work of salvation. In Paul's words, the resurrection by the Spirit reveals Messiah Jesus to be both son of David and Son of God (cf. Rom. 1:3–4). Peter explains through Psalm 16 that God has vindicated the faith of Jesus the Nazarene by his resurrection (Acts 2:24ff.). This act of God's Spirit is the culmination of many instances when Jesus is designated as God's holy one (Acts 2:22). The perfection of all these is the outpouring of the Spirit, which according to Peter is proof that Messiah Jesus is the one of whom Psalm 110 spoke:

> Therefore, since He has been exalted to the right hand of God and has received from the Father the promised Holy Spirit, He has poured out what you both see

and hear. For it was not David who ascended into the heavens, but he himself says: The Lord said to my Lord, 'Sit at My right hand until I make Your enemies Your footstool.' Therefore let all the house of Israel know with certainty that God has made this Jesus, whom you crucified, both Lord and Messiah! (Acts 2:33–36)

Having submitted to suffering, the exalted Messiah receives his inheritance at the right hand of God on high. Messiah Jesus is the son of David par excellence who is granted not an earthly throne but to sit at the right hand of God as his Son.[112] The coming of the Spirit is a *coronation gift* of God the Father to his Son that vindicates his sonship by making what was otherwise implicit, hidden in the narrative, explicit in the experience of his followers. Jesus is perfected as Messiah by the Spirit, as Immanuel and therefore Son of God, a fact that is now to be testified publicly. Yet there is more to the apostolic testimony, for not only was God present in the person of Jesus of Nazareth; God was in Christ Jesus for salvation. The crowds are 'cut to the heart' on hearing the proclamation of the lordship of Jesus and are told repeatedly throughout the rest of the Acts account that they must call on this name in order to be saved:

Let it be known to all of you and to all the people of Israel, that by the name of Jesus Christ the Nazarene . . . by Him this man is standing here before you healthy . . . There is salvation in no one else, for there is no other name under heaven given to people, and we must be saved by it. (Acts 4:10–12)

Salvation for all is now found in the name of Messiah Jesus, who is the Lord, the God of Abraham, Isaac and Jacob. The promissory name of YHWH the saviour is revealed by the Spirit to be Messiah Jesus, Immanuel. Calvin remarks, 'God hath made him Lord and Christ; that is, you must look for none other than him whom God hath made and given.'[113] Thus the name of the Lord is hallowed as Jesus among the nations gathered at Pentecost in Jerusalem (cf. Acts 2:5), as it will be throughout all the cosmos when the last days have been completed – a scene that Paul previews in the Philippian hymn.

86

Our Father, hallowed be your name

On earth

The Pentecost proclamation of Jesus as Lord brings us back to the front door of life in the Middle. In chapter 1 we nominated the resurrection of the Lord Jesus as the beginning point of history for the Christian life based on the promises of the gospel to which we respond in prayer. I began this chapter by asking how it might be that the name YHWH could be vindicated when revealed to belong to Messiah Jesus as Paul anticipates. From its introduction at the exodus event, the name YHWH has been the promissory act of God to the people of promise. It is a name with a long past of fidelity to promises (to Abraham, Isaac and Jacob) and an open future provisioned by God's constant desire to be gracious and compassionate. On the other hand, his reliability includes a refusal to act arbitrarily or unjustly towards his creatures, especially towards the recipients of his promises. Hence in the face of their continuous antagonism and in line with his deliberate, symbolic acts in making himself present with his covenantal people, YHWH will vindicate his name *against the recipients* of the promises by acting as their saviour, so that his name might be hallowed on earth. All this is achieved when the eternal Son *tabernacles* among us as Immanuel, the virgin's child. Furthermore, as God's actions during the exodus vindicated his personal proximity to Israel, so also in the gospel story the personal proximity of the Lord was vindicated by the fact that the self-sacrifice of the royal Son served and achieved God's long-promised salvation for the sinners at whose hands he died, *seemingly* abandoned by God. Hence the risen Messiah Jesus is the one whom YHWH promised Moses he would be. We have reread the canonical story through the lens of Philippians 2 in order to test the proposition that the universal *affirmation* of the lordship of Messiah Jesus will coincide with the universal *confirmation* that the meaning of God's lordship over all the earth has been perfected in his saving acts in the *career* of Immanuel – especially on the cross. Now we turn our attention to the possibilities involved in God's vindicating his name in Jesus, the holy one, the saviour of sinners.[114] How will this anticipated future shape our passions during life in the Middle?

87

In terms of the *now* for life in the Middle, our hope is shaped by the promise that to call on the name of the Lord Jesus is to receive forgiveness for opposing God's promises and the Holy Spirit, in order that God's name might be hallowed within us (Acts 2:38). In fact, the Christian practice of baptism, inaugurated at Pentecost, finds its eschatological significance in the public adoption of the name of Jesus as both the sign of salvation and incorporation into a new community of promise. As mentioned previously, life in the Middle has a spatial component, and in continuity with the word of the Lord to Israel, those baptized in the name of Jesus receive the Spirit and become the heirs of Abraham (Gal. 3:14). In this way, as the holiness codes provided the opportunity for Israel as a nation to bear the name, the gift of the Holy Spirit of Christ (Rom. 8:9; 1 Peter 1:11) signifies that Christians have a claim upon YHWH as their God – they know themselves to be blessed as YHWH's people in the name of Jesus. In the gift of his Spirit among the people, YHWH's heavenly glory is mediated to the earth through Messiah Jesus when 'all the peoples of the earth will see that you are called by the Name', the name of Jesus (cf. Num. 6:27; Deut. 28:10). In fact, those bearing the name of the Lord Jesus are, on the earth, a new temple in the Spirit (Eph. 2:22).

As we have seen, the *now* experience of God's presence for the people of promise was dominated by the tabernacle/temple – the place of the name. The coming of Immanuel has eclipsed this structure as God's act of giving himself to his people in his promises. Yet with the resurrection and ascension of the Lord Jesus the question of God's presence among the *new* people of promise has not been an easy issue. From the Pentecost story we have gleaned the Spirit is the agent by whom the name of the Lord Jesus is present with his people.

Colin Gunton pointed to two specific problems in Western Christianity's traditional ecclesiology. The first results from a Christology that focuses too closely on the divine nature of Christ at the expense of his human nature. According to Gunton it reveals itself either in a view that all humanity is ultimately the church of Christ or that the church eclipses Jesus of Nazareth as the one through whom God effects salvation.[115] The consequence is a view of the church in Western ecclesiology that gives it greater omniscience and/or infallibility than might be claimed for Jesus himself.[116]

This leads to a second problem for a Christological determination of ecclesiology – authority. Gunton asserts, 'It is only through the Spirit that the human actions of Jesus become ever and again the acts of God.'[117] In contrast, the church sometimes appears to claim a logical link between Spirit and institution with the result of undue confidence in claims to possess divine authority on the church's part. The chief difficulty in both these situations, for our argument's sake, is that it distorts the sense in which we might appropriately speak of those bearing the name of the Lord as having 'God with them'.

From our brief examination of the Pentecost story, the ascended Christ is present in the church via the Spirit. The Spirit enables the church to anticipate genuinely, but not continuously, life in the coming kingdom of God. This life is first revealed in the incarnate Son, and is occasionally experienced as a foretaste of his perfected state as his Spirit constitutes churches in various places and at different times. These churches, together and distinctly, live *leaning forward* towards the revelation of the Lord Jesus Christ, as 'aliens and strangers' (1 Peter 1:1). This statelessness 'lies not so much in the story of Abraham and Sarah and the story of Israel as it does in the destiny of Jesus Christ, his mission and his rejection which ultimately brought him to the cross'.[118] Once more, our passion is that of the Christ, awaiting his vindication, and therefore 'we do not colonise – recreate the old country – nor do we segregate a space within the new reminiscent of the old, nor do we simply accommodate to the new'.[119] I shall clarify these statements in subsequent chapters as we consider the kingdom of God being perfected on earth, and this as the fulfilment of our heavenly Father's will. For now I shall draw this chapter to a close with some consideration of the *not-yet* hope of the earthly hallowing of God's name as it is in heaven.

As it is in heaven

The apocalyptic images of a new creation that come to us through the Revelation, dominated by the throne of the Ancient of Days, focus on the slain Lamb in the centre of all proceedings. Through this image-rich medium, John portrays what Peter announced at Pentecost and Paul anticipated for the Philippians. That is, every creature variously symbolized is gathered before Jesus in order to worship him as the Lord (Rev. 5). As we consider our hope for the future perfection of God's promise to vindicate his presence in the Messiah, two images in John's visions demand our attention.

The first image is developed in chapters 4 and 5 and concerns the vindication before the Ancient of Days of the Lamb who was slain. The scene represents the one God in heaven presiding over a perfectly ordered creation.[120] Here we see 'the punitive and redemptive purpose for the world', achieved in the death and resurrection of Messiah Jesus, 'through whose reign God's purposes for creation will be consummately executed and divine glory accomplished'.[121] John employs echoes of Isaiah's temple vision (Isa. 6:2–3) and Daniel's vision of the Son of Man coming before the throne of heaven (Dan. 7:12–14) to represent via metaphor the enthronement of Jesus, the risen Christ, at the centre of divine will.[122] That is, there are not two enthronements – one of God the Father and another of the Lord Jesus, or one of the risen Jesus and a future repetition – but one mimetic depiction of God's sovereign reign as Creator and Saviour.[123] Of particular interest for us when considering the perfection of God's presence to his people is the prospect of God the Father mediating his presence to creation everlastingly through the Lord Jesus. Alternatively, we might ask, will God the Father cease to mediate his presence to us through the Lord Jesus once the Spirit perfects all things in creation – as one might interpret from reading Revelation 4 and 5?

Christians throughout the centuries have struggled with this idea of everlasting mediation of the Father to creation through Christ Jesus. For example, we can see the difficulties in Augustine's 'Letter 92' (AD 408).[124] Written to a certain Lady Italica concerning the death of her husband, the discussion soon moves towards the idea of seeing God in the new creation. The dilemma that Augustine addresses concerns what we ought to make of the words of John and Paul when put together to form an eschatological description. John writes, 'Dear friends, now we are children of God, and what we shall be has not yet been made known. But we know that when he appears, we shall be like him, for we shall see him as he is' (1 John 3:2). While Paul writes, 'For now, we see obscurely in a mirror; then we shall see face to face. Now I know in part; then I shall know fully, even as I am fully known' (1 Cor. 13:12).

Augustine comments that 'the likeness spoken of [by John] is therefore in the inner man', and hence we 'shall become the more like unto Him, the more we advance in knowledge of Him and in love'. This likeness, however, cannot be so perfected that we might see God 'face to face' as Paul indicates. Augustine then writes:

> If by these words we were to understand the bodily face, it would follow that God has a face such as ours, and that between our face and His there must be a space intervening when we shall see Him face to face. And if a space intervene, this presupposes a limitation and a definite conformation of members and other things, absurd to utter, and impious even to think of, by which most empty delusions the natural man, which 'receiveth not the things of the Spirit of God,' is deceived.[125]

Two things stand out in this quote. First, Augustine rightly upholds the wholly other, transcendent divine nature and will not allow that to be compromised in the new creation. But secondly, the bishop fails to mention that in his Son, the Christ, God does have a face, of which Paul also writes: 'God, who said, "let light shine out of darkness," has shone in our hearts the light of the knowledge of the glory of God which is *in the face of Messiah Jesus*' (2 Cor. 4:6). Bauckham and Hart suggest, with Augustine, that our heavenly vision of God will be a matter of 'creatures in their redeemed perfection [reflecting] God precisely in being their own true reality', since the heavens declare the glory of God and human life reflects the grace of God (cf. Pss 8; 19). Hence the unmediated vision of God need not obscure our experience of the new creation.[126] All the same, it seems tragic to think that the glorified Lord Jesus might be eclipsed in such a scenario. Therefore when Paul refers to our seeing God face to face in the new creation, we understand him to mean that it is in and through his Son that God will be known – as he always was. Ultimately, we need hope for nothing more than what the Lord described to Philip:

> Philip said to him, 'Lord, show us the Father and that will be enough for us.' Jesus said to him, 'So much time I am with you and you still do not know me, Philip? The

one who has seen me has seen the Father. How can you
say, show us the Father?' (John 14:8–9)

In Revelation 5 there is a distinction between God and the Lamb,
with both being depicted in heavenly glory. As I have mentioned,
the scene is parallel with that portrayed in Revelation 4, bringing
a number of Old Testament theophany images to bear.[127] The
development of the imagery in Revelation 5 is for the sake of
depicting in terms reminiscent of Daniel 7 that Jesus the Christ is
not visible to the churches because he has fulfilled God's saving
purposes and is now in and with God *in heaven*. John's audience
do not need to be reminded that God is in heaven. However, since
it is the role of apocalyptic literature to underwrite God's promises
when the historical circumstances would argue otherwise, John
depicts the risen Jesus as with God in glory. Hence all the mimetic
importance of Old Testament theophany is associated with
Messiah Jesus, who has been, since Pentecost, proclaimed and
acclaimed as Lord.

This leads directly to the second image of importance for our
current exploration. Near the close of Revelation, in chapter 21,
we read, 'I did not see a sanctuary in it, because the Lord God the
Almighty and the Lamb are its sanctuary' (Rev. 21:22).

The new creation or New Jerusalem is without a temple for
exactly the reasons we might expect given the flow of argument in
this chapter. God's name is present in the person and work of the
risen Lord Jesus, who has eclipsed the tabernacle and temple as
the dwelling place of God on the earth. Though many Old Testament prophets looked forward to a replacement for Solomon's
temple (Ezek. 40 – 43; Hag. 2:9; Isa. 65:17), the Gospel accounts
lead us to expect that Jesus the Messiah is above and beyond any
structure 'made with hands'.[128]

All this points to a critical aspect of our understanding of the
new creation and the ultimate experience of God's heavenly
fatherhood on earth, not to mention the future of Jesus Christ.
As we let the gospel shape our passion for the possibilities of
God's perfecting work, our hope, we ought not to expect unmediated access to our eternal God and Father in the new
creation. The return of the Lord Jesus to the earth will mark the
perfection of God's promise to give himself to his people. His
presence among them, however, will be through his holy one and

by the power of his Holy Spirit, so that his name will be hallowed on earth as it is in heaven. In the next chapter we shall meditate on the coming of God's kingdom, and key to this will be Paul's words in 1 Corinthians 15 that envisage the Messiah's laying his victory at the foot of the Father's throne. This notwithstanding, as we consider this we must, concurrently, uphold the strength of the Father's promise to the Son that his messianic reign will be for ever. Indeed, it is the Father's good pleasure to exercise his universal dominion through his Son everlastingly (cf. 2 Sam. 7:16). In addition, and in conjunction with this, the role of mediator to which the Son has been appointed is one without end because he is the royal *and* eternal Son. The ultimate significance of the appellation Messiah/Christ lies in the Father's eternal choice to relate exclusively to the creation by his Spirit through his Son, 'through whom and for whom all things have been created and in whom all things hold together' (Col. 1:16–17). I shall take up this issue in chapter 5 when we consider the perfection of the Father's will on earth as it is in heaven.

4

GOD'S KINGDOM
ALL IN ALL

To argue that God's name will be universally and everlastingly hallowed on earth as it is in heaven says both a great deal and very little about the possible outcomes of God's perfecting work. To argue that this is the fulfilment of God's covenantal promise to be present among his covenantal people might give our life in the Middle a sense of direction, but it does not offer much in terms of our expectations for the new creation or explain how we might move towards it. On the one hand, as Karl Rahner commented, we have professed 'the most improbable truth, namely, that God in God's very self with infinite reality and glory, with holiness, freedom and love, can really and without any holding back enter the creatureliness of our existence'.[1] On the other hand, my statement and description of Christian eschatology has said little of 'the experience one has . . . of this reality, however *subjective* this may seem'.[2] Nevertheless, the presence of God through Jesus and in the Spirit is the *what* of eschatology, the kernel of our hope: the perfection of God's promises to 'be with us' and 'to be our God'. To give more substance to our hope we need to turn our attention to *how* God perfects his promises to us.

The previous chapter has prepared the way forward via the relationship between the lordship of Jesus and the kingdom of God. There we equated the lordship of Jesus with God's act to vindicate his promise to be present as the redeemer of his people. We looked to Peter's Pentecost testimony as the primary announcement of Jesus' vindication and were given the link between lordship and kingdom: 'God made . . . Jesus . . . both Lord *and* Messiah' (Acts 2:36). Consequently, we ought to anticipate the coming of God's kingdom in parallel with his presence or lordship.

Discerning the kingdom

In the framework of the Lord's Prayer, Jesus exhorts his disciples to call on their heavenly Father to establish his kingdom on earth as it is in heaven. Yet, as Gregory of Nyssa asked, 'Could this really mean that He who is King of the universe should become King? . . . What, then, might this petition mean that asks for the Kingdom of God?'[3] Gregory's answer was to long for God's kingdom to come to *him*, 'so that the passions which still rule me so mercilessly may depart from me, or rather may be altogether annihilated'.[4] Gregory's thoughts reflect our common desire for a change in the manner, perhaps, with which God rules creation so that what is eternally true in heaven can be everlastingly true for the earth – particularly at a personal level. The focus of the kingdom here is the Father's act of reigning or intervening as much as the location in which such actions take place. Gregory took it as given that the locus of God's rule is the creation in general and the *soul* of the individual in particular. The eschatological tension is the extent to which, or the manner in which, God's rule over his creation reflects his life in eternity and how this is manifested in individual experience.[5]

In the modern era the question of how God's kingdom might be manifested in individual experience has been answered in terms of human (esp. cultural) activity – the ennobled human soul united itself with the eternal.[6] In contrast to this, I have maintained that *God gives himself* in his promises and therefore the promise of the coming kingdom means, 'God's kingdom is God Himself . . . it is God Himself as He not merely *is* somewhere and somehow . . . but as He *comes*.'[7] The attractive aspect of

Barth's emphasis on revelation is the object freedom of God in coming to that which is his own: 'He creates the righteousness which is the right order of the world that belongs to him.'[8] God does not reveal himself for the sake of any religion, morality or with any purpose whose execution relies in any way on the co-operation of the world or the church. Consequently, the coming kingdom is an entirely divine achievement: 'The second petition . . . looks to an unequivocal act of the grace of God, to the mystery of the kingdom of God which encounters all that history and limits it in its totality and its hope.'[9] In keeping with the last chapter we shall look to the broad sweep of the biblical narrative in order to understand how God does his work through his Son and in his Spirit. In addition, we shall look to one of the New Testament configurations of the perfection of the kingdom promise in order to draw the kingdom thread from the larger canonical tapestry.

The gospel promise for the kingdom

The ultimate goal of the kingdom of God is proclaimed to us in Paul's first letter to the church in Corinth:

> The end will come, when the *Messiah* hands over the kingdom to God the Father after he has destroyed all dominion, authority and power. For Christ Jesus must reign until *God* has put all *Christ's* enemies under his feet. The last enemy to be destroyed is death. For he 'has put everything under his feet.' Now when it says that 'everything' has been put under him, it is clear that this does not include God himself, who put everything under Christ. When he has done this, then the Son himself will be made subject to him who put everything under *Christ*, so that God may be all in all. (1 Cor. 15:24–28)

According to Paul, the economy of salvation, including the reign of Jesus, is perfected when the Messiah hands over his rule to the Father and all opposition to the reign of God is destroyed.[10] At that point all powers in the creation will give way to God's kingdom, which will be 'all in all'. This passage suggests at least two characteristics of the coming heavenly kingdom of God: the kingdom as the relationship between the reign of God and the reign of the Messiah, and the perfection of that reign in the context of the defeat of the Messiah's enemies. These characteristics allow us to ask two important questions, the answers to which will shape the broad structure of this chapter.

First, this passage suggests that the kingdom of God is a function of a particular relationship established between the Father and his incarnate Son, the Messiah, in the economy of salvation. What does it tell us about God's kingdom and its coming? Second, 1 Corinthians 15 locates the promise of God's ultimate victory over the enemies of the Messiah in relation to the resurrection from the dead. Consequently, we ask, what significance should we attach to the designation of death as 'the final enemy' of the kingdom of God?

The kingdom of the Father and the Son in the Spirit

As I begin my exposition of the kingdom as a particular expression of the relationship between the Father and the Son in time and space, I shall explore Paul's description of the defeat of the Messiah's enemies alongside the institution of God's kingdom for two reasons. First, because as Brown indicates, the phrase *kingdom of God* does not appear in the Old Testament as such. Rather than speak of 'the coming of God's kingdom', the Old Testament writers 'promise a universal kingship of God (Jer. 10:7, 10; Mal. 1:14)'.[11] Brown also observes, 'Is. 24:23 connects the signs of the last times . . . with the reign of the Lord of Hosts . . . and the manifestation of his glory.'[12] In addition, he notes, 'Dan. 7:18 has the saints of the Most High receiving the kingdom after all the earthly kingdoms have passed away.'[13] This, according to Brown, is evidence that the story of Israel is full of eschatological kingship language. The second reason for pursuing the Old Testament background of Jesus' kingship is related to the contribution of eschatology to the doctrine of God. In the previous chapter I adopted three maxims offered by Colin Gunton: (1) the reason for the incarnation is grounded on the eternal will of God, not contingent upon the fall of humanity; (2) the Son submits to the will of the Father in order to be made flesh, and the Spirit prepares the humanity of Jesus for him;

(3) the incarnation is a kenosis, 'but one understood as the expression of the inner dynamic of the Trinity, not as the sloughing off of certain attributes'.[14] We have already established the importance of narrative elements for our doctrine of God. Hence we looked to the importance of the tabernacle/temple motif for understanding how the canon provides a way of understanding God's presence in creation – especially in relation to Jesus Christ. Since we proposed that the kingdom of God is a particular temporal expression of the relationship between the Father and the Son in the Spirit, the Old Testament background will provide the broadest context in which to 'draw on the human career of Christ to characterize who he is as divine'.[15] This is not to assume that God's triunity is bound by time and space but to ensure that our perceptions of God's inner life are governed by divine revelation as presented in the whole Bible.

YHWH and his spiritually empowered agent

We have established that the hallowing of God's name occurs in the vindication of his presence in the person and actions of Jesus as Messiah. The Old Testament provides us with a steadily developing portrait of two distinct narrative identities – YHWH and his Messiah – that come together as the achievement of God's heavenly kingdom on earth.

From the exodus onward the Lord, YHWH, is portrayed as Israel's king.[16] YHWH alone defeats and conquers the Egyptians and reveals himself as the one who 'will reign forever and ever' (Exod. 15:18). In Exodus 25 – 40 the tabernacle is set out like a palace, the ark like a throne and YHWH is the 'Suzerain' ruler who makes the covenant with Israel his vassal.[17] The journey towards the Promised Land is that of Israel's warrior king, who goes before them in order to give them a place where they will dwell in the presence of their creator, redeemer and ruler. Described in Eden-like terms, the land of promise is the place from which the rule of YHWH will spread to the ends of the earth.[18]

Once Israel have entered and become settled in the land, God periodically raises up leaders in order to continue his work of saving his people from their enemies – principally the Philistines.[19] From a narrative point of view these leaders (or judges) are not extraordinary. They follow in the footsteps of both Moses and

Joshua in so far as they are endowed with God's Spirit for leadership in the community (Num. 11:25; Deut. 34:9). In contrast to Moses and Joshua, however, the judges have ambiguous personal qualities and/or are of questionable character, with the result that they serve mainly as narrative foils for YHWH's continued rule over a disparate and anarchic Israel.[20] The chief sign of this anarchic streak in the nation is that Israel seek to establish their own monarch. The people try to make Gideon ruler (Judg. 8), and Abimelech, Gideon's son, makes an abortive attempt to establish himself as a king (Judg. 9). Yet Gideon, his father, reminds the people, 'The LORD will rule over you' (Judg. 8:23), and YHWH does, in fact, rule over the people despite the virtual lawlessness that Israel continually edges towards. The ambiguity surrounding YHWH's rule is summed up by the author of Judges: 'In those days there was no king in Israel; everyone did whatever he wanted' (21:25).[21] Throughout the Judges period the covenant people failed to vindicate the holiness of God's name before the nations, which in turn obscured the reign of YHWH in the land or the world.

The theological significance of this divinely appointed and endowed leadership throughout the Judges cycle can be heightened if the Ruth narrative is allowed to make a contribution.[22] Set during 'the time of the judges' (Ruth 1:1), this story revolves around the idea of God's providing a 'kinsman redeemer' figure to save the poor in a time of distress. Of course, the male lead, Boaz, can be considered a hero figure only in the broadest sense compared to the designated judges in the cycle. However, Boaz is the godly kinsman redeemer who is to Naomi and Ruth what YHWH is to the embattled and embittered Israel during the Judges era.[23] Furthermore, through Boaz a path is laid for the emergence of Israel's greatest king, Boaz's great-grandson, David.[24] The eventual covenant made between David and the elders of Israel confirms the former's kinsman-redeemer status as the elders declare, 'Here we are, your own flesh and blood . . . The LORD also said to you, "You will shepherd My people Israel and be ruler over Israel"' (2 Sam. 5:1–2). The canonical role for Ruth as an apology for the house of David is widely recognized in critical studies of the book.[25] For our purposes we need only note that as the Israelite drama progresses from conquest to monarchy, kingdom in Israel contains within it the concept of God's selecting and spiritually enabling a saviour for his people from their midst. God's kingdom will be mediated to the earth for the people through a specifically chosen and spiritually empowered individual – a kinsman redeemer.

YHWH and his spiritually empowered Son

As the canonical drama proceeds, the pattern of this spiritually empowered leader makes an important transition as judgeship gives way to monarchy. Yet the development is more complex than Boaz's genealogy makes it appear. We have become familiar with the concept of YHWH's giving himself to his people in his promises. In the monarchy YHWH *takes* something, or, more importantly, *someone*, for himself *from* Israel. As Brueggemann has observed, the status of the human king in the story of Israel is ambiguous to say the least: 'kingship . . . was wrought out of felt practical necessity and settled upon through acute interpretive dispute'.[26] Be that as it may, at YHWH's instruction the prophet Samuel certainly realizes God's choice of monarch for Israel through a secret anointing of David. From here there is a basic pattern for recognizing God's Messiah in the narrative. Saul and David were both subjects of deliberate divine choice (1 Sam. 9:16; 16:1). Both men were anointed by Samuel, an event that brings them into special relationship with YHWH as Messiah (1 Sam. 10:1; 16:13). Both were empowered for office with the Spirit (including for prophecy), and finally, both were publicly attested through mighty acts (1 Sam. 11; 17).[27] In this way the monarch can be seen as an expansion and extension of the judge character from the conquest period. The Messiah is a charismatic individual, chosen out of Israel and empowered to save *the whole nation* from its enemies. In fact, Psalm 72:14 refers to the king as the kinsman redeemer (*gō'ēl*) and we read in 2 Samuel 7:1, 'When the king had settled into his palace and the LORD had given him rest on every side from all his enemies ' (cf. 2 Sam. 7:9–11). The Messiah becomes the instrument through whom YHWH establishes *his reign on the earth* for the people.

In 2 Samuel 7, however, something extraordinary happens for Israel as the relationship between God and the Israelite king is enshrined in God's promise that David's son will sit on his throne for ever. As Brueggemann has noted:

> In one sweeping assurance, the conditional 'if' of the
> Mosaic Torah (Ex. 19:5–6) is overridden, and David is
> made a vehicle and carrier of Yahweh's unqualified grace
> in Israel . . . this particular human agent (and his family)
> is made constitutive for Yahweh's way with Israel.[28]

The promises made to David and for his son seem to eclipse the
Sinai promises or at least to transcend them, and yet as Barth
indicated they are in keeping with the basic covenantal promise 'I
will be your God and you will be my people.'[29] But Barth seemed
not to notice the manner in which the Davidic promise anticipates
the means by which the covenant promise and the *Immanuel
promise* (Isa. 7:14) could ultimately be united.

In the last chapter I drew attention to the growing portrait of
YHWH's giving himself to his people in his promises symbolized
by the tabernacle/temple. In this chapter I have added the theme
of YHWH's reign for the people of promise mediated through
the spiritually designated leader. With the Davidic promise, the
fact of YHWH's presence and the *act* of YHWH as ruler come
together through the new relationship promised between YHWH
and the son of his spiritually empowered son Solomon. At this
point in the narrative much of what was promised to Abraham
appears to have been fulfilled. All that remains is provision for a
permanent dwelling place for YHWH's name among the people.
That task was to fall to David's son, but it does so with the promise
that the house of David will be intimately linked with the presence
of YHWH for ever. The depths of this bond between YHWH
and the Davidic line are celebrated in Psalm 89:28–29:

> I will always preserve My faithful love for him,
> and My covenant with him will endure.
> I will establish his line forever,
> his throne as long as heaven lasts.

Hence the king of Israel will not only be David's son, according
to Psalm 2:7 (cf. 2 Sam. 7:12–14); he will also be considered by
God to be God's *own* son.

Brueggemann argues that while this is an 'exalted political title',
we ought not to infer that it has any ontological or metaphysical
significance.[30] According to Goldingay, such language of divine

patronage is common among Middle Eastern peoples and is designed to give a theological mandate to the king's reign.[31] No doubt this is an accurate reading in the historical context. However, we should note that Psalm 110 (quoted by Paul in 1 Cor. 15) introduces a number of other elements into the portrait of the spiritually empowered son of God. That various forms of ancient Near Eastern language have been incorporated into the identity of the Israelite Messiah is less important than how they have been used and what they anticipate for the definitive relationship between Father and Son. YHWH's Messiah enjoys absolute sovereignty over the world, 'at the right hand of YHWH'. He also performs this task as a sacred mediator – the Messiah is to be both king and priest; that is, he mediates both YHWH's divine rule to the earth and the worship of the people to God: 'Forever, You are a priest like Melchizedek' (110:4). Whether this psalm refers specifically to David or is anticipated for his sons, the role of Israel's king will be intimately connected with the cult, and the narrative plays this out.[32] The book of 1 Samuel begins with pagan idolatry next to the ark at Shiloh, and 2 Samuel concludes with David's purchasing land for the site of the temple. In between the narrative describes a great many reforms to the Israelite cult – elimination of abuses, the purification of worship, the provision of a centralized shrine.[33] Most importantly, David leads the worship as the ark is brought into the city of Zion (2 Sam. 6), and his son Solomon leads Israel in the commissioning of the temple (1 Kgs 8). The Messiah is the chief custodian of the name's place on the earth even as he is the one through whom the kingdom of YHWH will be mediated everlastingly. *The kingdom of YHWH through the Messiah is the principal means by which the name is hallowed on the earth as it is in heaven.*

As the kinsman redeemer of Israel YHWH's messianic son is promised the complete subjugation of his enemies –YHWH will place the Messiah's enemies under his feet. YHWH's rule spreads over the earth in proportion to the rule of the Messiah (cf. Ps. 2). Throughout the Psalms this image of divine victory delivered to the Messiah is repeated frequently. For example, Psalm 18 begins with the words

For the lead player, for the Lord's servant, for David, who spoke to the Lord these words of this song on the day the Lord saved him from the grasp of all his enemies and from the hand of Saul.[34]

This is complemented in the narrative with the accounts of David's military victories over his enemies; the battle is David's but the victory is YHWH's. David himself declares this at his typological battle with Goliath: 'All this assembly shall know that not by sword and by spear does the Lord deliver, for the Lord's is the battle and he shall give you into our hand!' (1 Sam. 17:47).[35] Through the narrative, and supplemented by the psalms, the Messiah is presented as the *now* of God's kingdom on the earth.

As a Father disciplines his son

As we noted when exploring the presence of the name with the people, Solomon's ascension to the throne of David in 1 Kings makes it seem that the promise to Abraham will at last be fulfilled and that YHWH will be vindicated completely as the promise-making God. Nevertheless, though it lasts for the better part of a century, the Davidic kingdom of God on earth, or at least the mediation of YHWH's heavenly rule to the earth, inevitably declines. The warnings of Leviticus go unheeded, as one king after another profanes the name of the Lord, even in the place where he caused it to dwell. Despite the unconditional nature of YHWH's promise to David regarding his son, the Lord does insist that he will have to endure discipline for waywardness: 'I will be a father to him, and he will be a son to me, so should he do wrong, I will chastise him with the rod men use and with the afflictions of humankind.'[36] Thus the fortunes of the sons of David, and later the two kingdoms, wax and wane.

The decline of Israel in terms of failing to honour the name of YHWH was, in no small way, led by the king (2 Kgs 21:7) – especially the northern one. Throughout Kings and Chronicles the lives and times of these ignominious rulers are summed up in the grim refrain 'he did evil in the eyes of the LORD' (TNIV). The various kings are often successful leaders who build cities, empires and win wars, but they lead the people away from the central tenets of Israelite faith.[37] In keeping with this assessment, the prophets Jeremiah and Ezekiel are scathing as they condemn 'the shepherds who destroy and scatter the sheep' – that is, lead the people into exile (see esp. Jer. 23:1–2; Ezek. 34:3–6).[38] As with the covenantal promise, so with the monarchical oath: the human partner plays a principal role in antagonizing God in his desire to perfect a relationship with his creatures. Nevertheless, and again as with YHWH's desire to give himself to his people, the Lord's promise concerning his chosen one is indomitable. At times there is considerable uncertainty over the status of monarchy in Israel – especially when competing voices are given different and distant sources in the editorial history of the Old Testament.[39] But just as YHWH is reluctant to vindicate himself against his people once he has given them his promises, he is patient with the Judean kings 'for the sake of My servant David' (2 Kgs 19:34; 20:6). Furthermore, while there is obvious difficulty for the northern kings who have broken away from Jerusalem, the temple and all other aspects of the presence of the name of the Lord, for Judah also the identity of the recipients of the promises inherent in receiving the name is provisional, and so also is the identity of the son of YHWH. YHWH remains the heavenly king but the son of YHWH retreats into the shadows. The people's *experience* of God's rule becomes provisional – the *not-yet* element of the kingdom of God on the earth once again becomes a growing issue for the promises of God. This time the tension is heightened for the people of promise as to whether they will return to the time of David or should look instead for something else.

The Spirit and the monarchical promise

That the identity of the son of YHWH should be provisional has led commentators like Brueggemann to lament, 'Interpreters are at a loss to know why this [Davidic] promise, now removed from political reality and carried only in Israel's liturgical, visionary, ideological hopes, continued to have shaping power for the life and imagination of Israel.'[40]

Perhaps an explanation can be found in the narrative context enhancing the events surrounding David's selection. God's choice of Saul and David is continuous in nature with the judges that preceded them – God raises up a saviour for his people from their midst. This is the 'known from the past' ingredient for the identity of the son of YHWH. While on the surface the covenant with David naturally leads to the designation of the Judean king as the son of David, the true significance of David as king is found in

105

the fact that he is YHWH's choice. As Goldingay has observed, 'David is a king, "according to Yhwh's heart" (eg. 1 Sam. 13:14). Other occurrences of such phrases demonstrate that this need not suggest that he is a king who shares YHWH's priorities or way of thinking.'[41] This phrase simply identifies David as the one to whom YHWH makes a personal commitment. What is of greater significance, in keeping with the nature of God's promises to his people, is that this choice connects David to the history of God's mediated leadership of Israel and forms the vital foundation for anticipating the return of such a king in post-exilic Israel: *YHWH gives himself, or of himself, to his chosen one.* That is, the chrism of oil that designated both Saul and David as God's choice was symbolic of the greater chrism – God's Spirit. It is the expectation that the son of YHWH will be anointed with the Spirit of YHWH that both relativized the claim of every son of David who sat on the throne in Jerusalem without it, and maintained the hope of Israel that was in reality bereft of any king. The kingdom of God would come to the earth when the Spirit empowered God's specially chosen king to reign.

As the line of David in Judah gives every indication of failing before the might of Assyria, the prophet foresees a virgin birth and an especially selected son for the line of David who will signify YHWH's presence with the surviving remnant[42] (Isa. 7:13–14). The nature of this divine presence takes on a startling character when the prophet announces that the son of David will be called

> Wonderful Counselor, Mighty God,
> Eternal Father, Prince of Peace.
>
> (Isa. 9:6)

While the first and last titles are readily associated with human governance, the middle two introduce a divine aspect, or, better, realign the rule of David's son as the rule of YHWH 'from this time on and for ever' (Isa. 59:21 TNIV). The divine nature of Davidic rule is ensured when we read that God will give himself to the Messiah in the form of spiritual presence:

> The Spirit of the LORD will rest on Him –
> a Spirit of wisdom and understanding,

a Spirit of counsel and strength,
a Spirit of knowledge and of the fear of the LORD.

(Isa. 11:2)

The Messiah will once again be distinguished as the one through whom and for whom YHWH rules, ushering in a new hope of peace for God's people and for the whole world (Isa. 11:10–11). There will be a relationship between God and his son, but the kingdom of God is *still coming* to the earth, yet in a long-remembered and long-promised form.

Messiah Jesus: son of David and Saviour

If the presence of YHWH with the returned exiles was ambiguous, despite a rebuilt temple and city, the long-promised reign of an heir of David seems to have disappeared into the silence that characterizes the intertestamental period.[43] The royal covenant between the Father and his son appears to have lapsed and thus YHWH must vindicate himself as the promise-making God. However, just as in the previous chapter we explored the way Gospel writers used linguistic and narrative connections between Jesus and the temple in order to announce the promised presence of YHWH with his people to save them from sin, in what follows we shall focus on significant events in the Gospel narratives that establish a portrait of Jesus of Nazareth as the promised Messiah, the son of David. What the greater story has provided for us is an expectation that the king of Israel will be the spiritually empowered son of God and kinsman redeemer who defeats the enemies of God's people. What we shall also discover is the manner in which Jesus as Messiah re-establishes the conditions for the possibility of right worship and so becomes the one to whom Paul alludes in 1 Corinthians 15: the priestly king of Psalm 110.

Jesus of Nazareth: the kinsman redeemer

The Gospel writers outline the portrait of Jesus as a *kinsman* redeemer by using genealogies. Matthew's account opens with a simple statement that immediately links Jesus 'born of Mary' to both David and Abraham: 'a book of lineage *for* Jesus son of David, son of Abraham' (Matt. 1:1). Luke does a similar thing, although he takes the line back to Adam in an ascending rather

107

than a descending order (Luke 3:23–38). What concerns us here is that from the very beginning Jesus of Nazareth is explicitly linked to the history of God's promises to his people in general and to the Messiah in particular. The Gospel writers *themselves* make the Old Testament the past of the Lord Jesus.[44]

As we reviewed the monarchy narratives above we noted that the Messiah was a deliberate divine choice. That this is true of Jesus of Nazareth becomes explicit through the various annunciation scenes. For example, in Luke's account the angel informs Mary that she will bear a son whom 'the Lord God will give . . . the throne of his father David' (1:32). Furthermore, Jesus will not be just another man in the line of David – the angel brings word that as *the* son of David the full extent of God's promise will be fulfilled: 'He will . . . be called the Son of the Most High . . . and he will reign over the house of Jacob forever, and of his kingdom there will be no end' (1:32–33; cf. 2 Sam. 7:13–16). The exalted and everlasting nature of Jesus' kingship will mark the perfection of God's promises to David since Jesus will be the son whom God will call his own and there will be none to succeed him. At the risk of contradicting Calvin,[45] the *future* aspect of the language used by the evangelist ought not to be glossed over by too quickly interpreting the phrase 'Son of the Most High' as a reference to Jesus' divine nature. The words spoken to the virgin are a promise and the details of their perfection are yet to be seen – not simply because they are words spoken of one who is yet to be born. The angel's explanation for this miraculous birth rests on the perfecting work of the Holy Spirit. As such the child bears that deliberate messianic mark that links him to the words of Isaiah (11:2ff.) but, more importantly, to David himself as the spiritually empowered chosen one of God. Jesus of Nazareth is God's Messiah because God chose him to be. Moreover, not only will Messiah Jesus' reign be extraordinary because he will save his people instead of the Gentiles 'from their sins', his reign (unlike any other) will not be compromised by death. Even as Immanuel, it is by no means clear that the everlasting nature of Messiah Jesus' rule will be due to the essential presence of eternal Son in and with the child. Rather, Mary and the readers will have to look forward to the way in which God's ancient promises will be perfected and the extent to which the nature of this reign will be related to the primary task of the spiritually empowered Messiah – the defeat of Israel's enemies and the establishment of God's kingdom over all the earth.

Jesus of Nazareth: the perfect king for the ultimate enemy

The deliberate divine choice that led to the kingship of both Saul and David was embodied in the anointing act of Samuel but also in a concurrent anointing with the Holy Spirit (1 Sam. 10:1; 16:13; 1 Sam. 11; 17). In addition, once they had been so designated both Saul and David were publicly attested through mighty acts whereby they mediated YHWH's rule to save his people from their enemies. The manner in which Jesus of Nazareth follows his forebears throughout the Gospel narratives is more profound yet more mysterious. As we have already established, the promises of God establish the history of the whole world over which God's kingdom will come. We know that YHWH intends that his name be hallowed universally on the earth through the saviour, the Lord Jesus, and in the power of the Spirit. Throughout our survey a consistent feature of YHWH's rule has been against the external threat to his people. From a historical point of view this was certainly the expectation of Jews in Jesus' time.[46] In the Gospel narratives, however, Messiah Jesus will face an external and *universal* antagonist, but it is one both more ancient and more insidious than any Gentile overlord.[47]

The first (explicit) encounter with this antagonist comes just after Jesus' baptism at the Jordan – his anointing with the Spirit. Among the crowd of devotees Jesus is identified as YHWH's choice – Messiah – by the presence of the Spirit.[48] The scene blends a collection of anticipations concerning the son of David and the Servant of YHWH as God speaks the words 'You are my son, the beloved. In you I am delighted' (Luke 3:22). In this short utterance we have an allusion to the Davidic covenant (2 Sam. 7:12–14) that was celebrated in the life of Israel (Ps. 2:7; cf. Ps. 144) and associated with Isaiah's Servant of YHWH (Isa. 42:1). The presence of the Spirit is strongly allusive of David's anointing in 1 Samuel 16:13, when David is distinguished as God's choice of king.[49] Furthermore, the scene is a fitting enactment of Isaiah's anticipation for the child of the virgin: 'The Spirit of God will rest upon him, the Spirit of wisdom and understanding, the Spirit of counsel and strength, the Spirit of knowledge and godliness' (Isa. 11:2 LXX).[50]

Following his baptism in the Jordan the Spirit-empowered son of David embarks upon a journey into the wilderness to face the one enemy that has assaulted the promises of God since the garden. Luke's account highlights this by his placement of a genealogy that links Jesus not just to David and Abraham but to the very beginning of the human story: Jesus is the son of Adam. Hence the extent to which Jesus is to be a *kinsman* redeemer has the potential to far exceed the nation of Israel. Barth seems sympathetic to this reading in so far as he also focuses on Jesus as 'the Son of God . . . who has come to us and become one of us'.[51] Yet he chooses to interpret the whole encounter (especially the forty-day fast) in reference to 'penitence of Jesus and His fulfilling of all righteousness in the baptism of John'.[52] As we shall see, the significance of this pericope lies in the insight we are given into the manner in which Jesus as *Son of God* will follow and yet surpass his great ancestor David.

We have already established that throughout his ministry Jesus lived with God's promises as 'the law of his being'.[53] The confrontation with *The Enemy* clarifies what that means for Jesus' office as king since it revolves around the meaning of God's declaration at his baptism 'You are my Son' (Matt. 3:17 ['This is']; Mark 1:11; Luke 3:22). Satan does not, for example, challenge Jesus with 'Did God really say that you are His Son?' after the fashion of the question posed to Eve in the garden (cf. Gen. 3:1). Contra Moltmann, in the previous chapter, we noted that the chief ministry of the Spirit to Messiah Jesus was to make the Father present by his word – the promises of Scripture. Consequently, throughout this trial we see Jesus appeal consistently to the history of God's promises to his people in order to explain what kind of Son he will be. In reference to going hungry Jesus appeals to Deuteronomy 8:2–5, where Moses exhorts Israel to consider the purpose of their time in the wilderness. The people were led there as a test of their faithfulness – they were 'disciplined as sons' (Deut. 8:5) to teach them to rely on God and what it meant to receive his promises.[54] Hence for Jesus, as with his kin before him, the *fact* of his suffering is the *sign* of his sonship.[55] We might say that, according to Scripture, it is his hunger/suffering that designates him as the Son of God more than his ability to exercise power for himself. Barth is again sympathetic to the place we have given God's word for Jesus in the encounter (though with no reference to the Spirit). Nevertheless, Barth's focus is on Jesus of Nazareth as 'the one great sinner who allows that God is in the right'.[56] This is too little: the repeated challenge regards the nature of *sonship* – if Messiah Jesus is 'the Son', what kind of son of God will he be? This title is integral to the royal covenant and therefore the first characteristic of messianic victory is introduced – the Spirit has empowered the Messiah to triumph while suffering in submission.

In the second challenge (in the Lukan account) Satan seeks to supplant the Father as the Messiah's patron: 'I will give you all this authority [the kingdoms of the world] . . . if you bow down before me . . . it will be yours' (Luke 4:5–8; Matt. 4:8–10). Since the Father's words at Jesus' baptism echo Psalm 2:7 we might have expected Jesus to respond with a reference to Psalm 2:8: 'Ask me and I will give you the nations as your inheritance and the ends of the earth as your possession' (LXX). To be addressed as son by YHWH is to be offered global rule as an inheritance (Pss 2; 110). However, in the Spirit, Jesus appeals to the leitmotif of his people's faith, the Shema. In Deuteronomy 6:10–14 Israel are exhorted not to forget YHWH when they enter into their inheritance – YHWH alone, not other gods, is their benefactor.[57] Barth is close to this reading but again interprets Jesus' actions not as messianic but rather as penitent: 'As the one great sinner in the name and place of all other sinners . . . he willed to continue worshipping and serving God alone.'[58] Certainly, entrusting oneself to the faithfulness of God is essential, as Deuteronomy makes plain. The dramatic situation of Moses' admonition is for Israel to remember God as the source of their blessing *before* they come into their inheritance so that they will serve him faithfully when they do. As we saw in the previous chapter, the Father promises to vindicate the faithfulness of his chosen one. Just as importantly for Jesus of Nazareth, the Messiah should anticipate kneeling before no one but rather 'sit[ing] at [the Father's] right hand' (Ps. 110:1). Messiah Jesus will be *that* kind of Son – one for whom an inheritance is the promise of vindication by his Father. Hence the kingdom will be a function of the dynamics between a heavenly Father and his messianic Son and victory will come to the submissive Son from the Father in the power of the Spirit.

In the third scene Satan focuses his attention on the source of God's presence with the Messiah – his written promise. Yet he

111

does so in a context of great significance for the Messiah, on the temple where YHWH has promised that his name will dwell. The Messiah is challenged 'to commit an act of supreme, unconditional, blind, absolute, total confidence in God':[59] 'throw yourself down from here [the highest point of the temple]' (Luke 4:9; Matt. 4:6). After all, Satan reminds Jesus, YHWH has promised that his angels will 'keep you and take you in their hands' (Ps. 90:11 LXX). The opening verses of Psalm 90 LXX are, in part, a commentary on the whole encounter thus far. Jesus has made God's word his refuge and the extent to which Jesus has shown deference to scriptural propositions could well be seen as hoping in God (cf. Ps. 90:2 LXX). Now the promissory sense of God's word is introduced where, before, Jesus has invoked commands. The devil gives the Messiah an opportunity to fulfil the promise in the most spectacular way. On the highest point of his Father's house (cf. Luke 2:49) Jesus is challenged to show that he is the Son of God by casting himself upon God's promise to save him from certain death.

Nevertheless, Jesus' reply follows his previous pattern of appealing to God's command. He refuses the opportunity to prove that the promise is sound by declaring that to do so would be to tempt God, which is sinful. He repeats words from the Shema of Deuteronomy 6. His quote follows on almost immediately from the one in the inheritance temptation. Yet the rationale for this appeal is not clear. Israel is exhorted to 'be careful not to forget the LORD' (Deut. 6:12) and not go after the gods of the Canaanites. To do so would be to 'test the LORD your God' (Deut. 6:16). Barth continues to interpret the incident through the lens of Jesus as the penitent, claiming that had Jesus jumped 'He would have tried triumphantly to maintain His rightness with God instead of persisting in penitence, instead of allowing God to be in the right against Him.'[60] Yet the challenge from Satan is, again, in reference to *sonship*. Should the son confess that he is unworthy of YHWH's promise? What we observed from the monarchy narratives is that YHWH's Messiah (his son) leads the people in establishing the possibility of the conditions for right worship of God through the temple and then leads the people in that worship. If Jesus of Nazareth is to be *that* kind of son, *that kind of king* and particularly if he is to be the king who suffers while waiting on the vindication of God as he has already shown Satan, he must not presume upon the gracious promises of God as so many of his forebears have done. In addition, it may be that Jesus, as the Christ, already understands that it is death *in all its fullness* from which he needs salvation, not merely the event of dying. So, in this context, the Messiah suffers, trusting that 'You will not forsake my life to Sheol, You won't let Your faithful one see the Pit' (Ps. 16:10).[61] The issue is ultimately resolved in Gethsemane, as we have observed. For now, we need only acknowledge that these trials or encounters provide a model of how the Spirit-empowered Messiah will triumph over the enemy. In the power of the Spirit the Messiah will submit himself freely to the promises of God and be the Son who suffers, so that the Father may overcome the ultimate source of opposition to his reign.

Messiah Jesus: mighty over sin, death and evil

If Jesus of Nazareth is truly to be the spiritually designated kinsman redeemer, then he must be publicly attested with mighty acts. From our reading of 1 Corinthians 15 we are naturally expecting the ultimate messianic victory to be over death. Furthermore, all of this must fulfil God's promise to save his people from their sins even as YHWH fulfils his promise to the son of David that he will be the everlasting mediator of a divine kingdom. Therefore we shall refigure the Gospel narrative in terms of the suffering Messiah's combat against sin, death and evil.

In keeping with the prophetic ministry of Saul and David,[62] Jesus begins the public aspect of his campaign with the Spirit's empowering him to announce just that. He invokes Isaiah 61 as his mission statement: 'the Spirit of the Lord is upon me because he has anointed me to proclaim good news to the poor. He has sent me to preach release to the captives and recovery of sight for the blind, to send in freedom the ones who were oppressed' (Luke 4:18). The programme seems fitting for a military leader of the likes of Saul or David, but Jesus of Nazareth as Messiah will achieve these mighty works through obedient suffering and, adding to the dramatic tension of the narrative, will reveal the true nature of the captivity: blindness and oppression.

The Messiah's mighty acts of liberation, in and through the Spirit, are evidenced in the various miracles Jesus performs, particularly the exorcisms. The contest with Satan that began in the wilderness forms the backdrop of this messianic liberation movement, as Jesus himself explained in the strong-man parable.[63]

113

On the occasion of a particular exorcism (Matt.12:29; Mark 3:27; or Luke 11:21) Jesus is accused by the scribes of being empowered or possessed by Beelzebul – the prince of demons. Jesus refutes the claim with the simple logic that 'if Satan stands against himself then he is divided, he cannot stand and is coming to an end' (Mark 3:26). More importantly Jesus goes on to explain to the crowd that the strong man's time is, in fact, coming to an end. As Calvin remarks:

> Every benefit which the bodies of men received from Christ was intended to have a reference to their souls. Thus, in rescuing the bodily senses of men from the tyranny of the devil, he proclaimed that the Father had sent him as a Deliverer, to destroy his spiritual tyranny over their souls.[64]

From the monarchy narratives we are expecting the Messiah to defeat the enemies of God's people, and the first step is for them to understand who their real enemy is. The strong man, leader in the creaturely revolt against the promises of God, is 'the one to be feared' (Luke 12:4–7; Matt. 10:28–31).[65] This is the enemy against whom the spiritually empowered Messiah fights (and ultimately triumphs).

Of course, the spiritual conflict between the Messiah and the strong man will be carried out in the mundane aspects of social and cultural life – not just in spectacular battles. Hence Moltmann interprets the Isaiah 61 prophecy as such:

> The justice of God is presented as the right to have pity on the most pitiable; on the other hand the future of the kingdom of God begins among the people who suffer most from the acts of violence and injustice – and that is the poor.[66]

Moltmann claims that Jesus' gospel message is 'realistic, not idealistic', and hence his mission is to bring freedom in the form of dignity for the poor and release from the social/political structures that oppress them.[67] The category 'poor' is broad to say the least, covering as it does anyone who is 'subjected, oppressed and humiliated [for whatever reason]'.[68] Moltmann claims precedent for this by privileging the testimony of eighth-century prophets, and Isaiah in particular.[69] Accordingly, the opponent of the poor in the Gospel narrative (especially Luke's Gospel) is 'the man of violence, "who makes someone else poor and enriches himself at the other's expense"'.[70] Jesus begins and pursues his mission to and among the poor because they are 'blessed' and 'theirs is the kingdom of heaven' (Matt. 5:3). Naturally the gospel preached by the messianic prophet does not offer the poor 'health, wealth and comfort'; Moltmann recognizes that much. Instead, they are comforted with the message of the Messiah's solidarity with them: '*God* is on their side and *God's future* belongs to them.'[71] The rich or the 'oppressors' receive a call to conversion from 'violence to justice, from isolation to community, from death to life'.[72] Together, though, these two groups (poor and rich) represent all the godforsaken and the godless of the world.

As the kinsman redeemer, Jesus has come 'to bring down the mighty from their thrones and exalt the humble in estate' (Luke 1:52). However, while Moltmann's sociopolitical reading of Messiah Jesus' ministry has some presence in the Gospel narratives (especially Luke's Gospel), it fails to attend to the massive devolution that has taken place in human sin that we have already identified as opposition towards God's promises. Perhaps the most shocking aspect of the strong-man parable is the way that it foreshadows the nature of the conflict that will steadily grow between Jesus and the Jewish leaders throughout the entire gospel story. Hinted at by Simeon (Luke 2:34), the strong-man story characterizes opposition to Jesus at a human level and this as 'blasphemy against the Holy Spirit' (Matt. 12:32; Mark 3:29; Luke 12:10), an unforgivable sin. In so far as sin can be described as antagonism towards the promises of God in general, antagonism towards the Son will become the most fundamental definition of sin. Hence John the Baptizer proclaims, 'The one who is disobedient to the Son will not see life. On the contrary, God's wrath will remain on him' (John 3:36). Worse, though, if that were possible, those who oppose the mission of Jesus as God's Messiah are themselves agents of this strong man and co-conspirators in the evil that leads to death.

This association is made explicit only in the Fourth Gospel and it is only in John's biography[73] that the evil one retains a distinct identity as the plot progresses.[74] Of particular interest for us is the interaction between Jesus and the Jews in John 8. It is here that Jesus denounces the Jews as the sons of Satan, but more importantly provides a key description of their father:

> You are of your father the devil, and you want to do your father's will. He was a murderer from the beginning and has not stood in the truth, because there is no truth in him. Whenever he tells a lie, he speaks from his own nature, because he is a liar and the father of liars. (John 8:44)

The Jews are intent on killing Jesus, who comes from God (v. 40), and this, as Jesus points out, is because they follow 'the will of [their] father'. As Calvin put it, 'He calls them children of the devil, not only because they imitate him, but because they are led by his instigation to fight against Christ.'[75] They are, as Paul describes them, unbelievers blinded by 'the god of this world' (2 Cor. 4:4), who walk 'according to the ways of this world, according to the ruler who exercises authority over the lower heavens, the spirit now working in the disobedient' (Eph. 2:2). The Messiah denounces their father as 'a murderer from the beginning'. Many exegetes see this as a reference to the Eden confrontation, where the lies of the serpent result in the death of the man and the woman (Gen. 3:4–5, 10).[76] Calvin adds, 'for as soon as man was created, Satan, impelled by a wicked desire of doing injury, bent his strength to destroy him'.[77] For our purposes the significance is a direct link between the death of Messiah Jesus at the hands of the Jews and the schemes of the evil one whose instruments they become. The enemy will seek to thwart the sonship of the Messiah and his mission to bring about the salvation of God by championing the evil desires of those who oppose the Messiah to that end.

Modern theologians like Moltmann are evasive about 'forces conceived of in personal terms, which are destructive of life and annihilate being itself'.[78] For him the devil belongs with these 'earlier personal imaginings' like all 'fallen angels' and is metaphorical of the forces of evil in creation that 'rouse the death-wish in human beings'.[79] Hence his preference for a messianic mission against social structures that are either godless or godforsaken.

116

While we must maintain a distinction between the evil that humans do and that which is done through them, or even the extent to which evil gains a structural effect in human culture, there is little exegetical reason to consider the evil one as merely metaphorical – the Lord himself did not.

Far beyond simply resisting the promises of God, Jesus identifies his opponents, even the dissatisfied disciple Judas, as the instruments of the ancient enemy of humanity. Beyond all Gentile empires and opponents, those who claim the promises handed down from Abraham have now become the principal (human) opponents of the kingdom of God on the earth. One aspect of the ambiguity about the recipients of God's promise has been clarified in a horrifying manner: Israel will be excluded from the promises of God in so far as they fail to recognize Messiah Jesus as their kinsman redeemer. The tragic irony is that the one group against whom the Messiah will be most vindicated consists of those who would claim the kingdom of God for themselves without God's king.

Messiah Jesus: leading the people in worship

For Jesus to be the Messiah, the son of David, he must establish the conditions for the right worship of YHWH, as his ancestor did, and lead the people in that worship. In fact, Hezekiah in 2 Chronicles 29 – 30, Josiah in 2 Kings 22 and Ezekiel in chapters 40 – 48 are all instances when particularly royal action in the temple was associated with restoring the kingdom and preparing the temple for the new era.[80] So in his own way Jesus heads to the city of David in the week before Passover, as the Messiah who 'did not come to be served but to serve and give his life as a ransom for many' (Mark 10:45; Matt. 20:28; cf. Luke 22:27; John 13:12–15). As Jesus rides across the Kidron Valley from the Mount of Olives up to the Temple Mount, his actions announce the coming of Israel's Messiah, but it is done through the lens of Zechariah's promises:

> Look [Zion/Jerusalem], your King is coming to you;
> He is righteous and victorious,
> humble and riding on a donkey,
> on a colt, the foal of a donkey.
>
> (Zech. 9:9)

117

God's Messiah has come to bring peace to Israel and to the nations. The gathering throng responds almost liturgically with words from Psalm 118:26: 'He who comes in the name of the Lord is the blessed one.' The crowds recognize and welcome the coming of YHWH's Messiah to inaugurate the kingdom of God on the earth. While the conditions of this 'triumphal entry' seem perfect, Jesus' own interpretation of the situation offers a dramatic counterbalance to the celebratory mood:

> If you knew this day . . . the things that make for peace –
> but no, they have been hidden from your eyes. The days
> will come when your enemies will set up barricades
> against you . . . because you did not know the time of
> your visitation. (Luke 19:42–44)

Despite the people's enthusiasm Jesus continues to distance himself from their expectations. They have not understood him and therefore have misunderstood the kingdom of God. In fact, from prior events in the narrative we are made aware that Jesus' enemies have decided once and for all that he must be destroyed: 'From that day on they [the chief priests and the Pharisees] moved a resolution that they should kill Him' (John 11:53). In the context of Jesus' arrival in Jerusalem the conspiracy council means, 'The leaders of Jerusalem have decided to do away with Jesus to save the city from the peril of the Romans, yet in Jesus' eyes they are signing the nation's death warrant.'[81]

In keeping with his royal entrance, Jesus proceeds to the temple in order to take charge there too. Since he bears the name of the one who will cleanse and re-establish the temple after the exile (Zech. 3:7), Jesus' entry into and actions in the temple ought to be viewed in this light.[82] Jesus takes up this historic task as an opportunity to pronounce the judgment of God against the Jewish establishment that he has previously denounced as an agent of the evil one. Accordingly, and in the words of Isaiah and Jeremiah, the Messiah accuses the recipients of God's promises of having turned 'a house of prayer for all nations' into 'a den of robbers' (Isa. 56:7; Jer. 7:11; cf. Matt. 21:13; Mark 11:17; Luke 19:46). The issue is less one of the business being carried out in the temple courts than of the fact that Israel has come to treat the 'house, which is called by My name' as an idol that will save them from their antagonism towards Jesus the Messiah.[83] Hence the spiritually empowered son of David takes custody of 'the temple made with hands' in anticipation of purifying the worship of Israel once again.

Having completely disrupted the sacrificial system, Jesus proceeds to make the temple his seat of prophetic interpretation and for the next week clashes with the Jewish leaders multiply. The constant focus of debate is over the authority of Jesus, with the Messiah continually gaining the upper hand and leaving the chief priests admitting their impotence (cf. Matt. 21:46; Mark 12:12; Luke 20:19). Of particular note for this chapter is the interaction between Jesus and the Pharisees over the interpretation of Psalm 110:1:

> This is the declaration of the Lord
> to my Lord:
> 'Sit at My right hand
> until I make Your enemies Your footstool.'

The psalm from which Jesus quotes refers to the enthronement of the Messiah, to his victory over the kings of the earth and to his appointment as 'a priest in the order of Melchizedek'. The implication is that the Messiah is staking a claim not just for governance of the temple but over the very business of the cult that is processed there.[84] Considering that we expect Messiah Jesus to eclipse the temple as the place of God on the earth, the prospect of Messiah Jesus' likewise eclipsing the sacrificial system through an everlasting priestly service follows on naturally (note Ps. 110:4; cf. Heb. 5:7–10).

Finally, Jesus, via Isaiah 5, denounces his opponents in the parable of the wicked tenants, in which he depicts God as the patient landlord overlooking the history of Israel's recalcitrance towards his promises, up to the point where he sends his son. The tenants (as disobedient Israel) conspire together to murder the Son (Messiah Jesus), and what was agreed in secret is revealed to all 'who have ears to hear'.[85] The story ends full of foreboding; though without mystery, because the meaning of the story is obvious to all. Hence the possibility of Israel's exclusion from the promises of God, which we have previously entertained, will become a certainty. The reign of YHWH will come to the earth because 'He will come and destroy the farmers and give the vineyard to others.' God's promised kingdom will go out into all the earth but not through Israel as it currently exists, and the Son's death at the hands of Satan's sons will be an integral part of this change.[86]

The penultimate acts of worship performed by Jesus the Christ are private but in them we are shown how God's promised salvation from sin is inextricably bound up with the mission of the suffering Messiah. On the night before his death Jesus celebrates the Passover with his disciples, the archetypal practice for the people to participate in YHWH's victory over their enemies.[87] The central focus of the original rite was the slaughtering of a lamb and the spreading of blood over the doorways of each household (Exod. 12 *passim*). The blood of the firstborn lamb served as a substitute for the firstborn son(s) of the people and was a sign to YHWH that the household had come under the protection of his promise (Exod. 12:7, 12–13). At the same time, 'this moment is the one when YHWH is declaring ownership of Israel as firstborn (Exod. 4:22–23) but the king of Egypt is disputing YHWH's claim'.[88] Because of the shed blood the angel of YHWH passed over the people of promise and they were saved from YHWH's wrath against Egypt. Hence the Passover meal is a memorial of God's mercy towards his people in the face of wrath against Pharaoh and an annual reminder that salvation comes through judgment. Furthermore, to the first-century Jew, the meal 'pointed to the return from exile, the new exodus, the great covenantal renewal spoken by the prophets – the forgiveness of sins'.[89]

There is, however, a significant variation in the proceedings of this last Passover meal that Jesus shares with his disciples and we notice it in the words that Jesus says to them as they eat the bread and drink from the cup:

> While they were eating, Jesus took bread, gave thanks and broke it, and gave it to his disciples, saying, 'Take and eat; this is my body.' Then he took the cup, gave thanks and offered it to them, saying, 'Drink from it, all of you. This is my blood of the covenant, which is poured out for many for the forgiveness of sins.' (Matt. 26:26–28; Mark 14:22–24; Luke 22:19–20)

Jesus naturally assumes the role of the household head; but instead of rehearsing the events of the exodus and their traditional theological significance, Jesus explains to his disciples that the imminent shedding of *his* blood ought to be understood as the perfect paschal sacrifice 'for the forgiveness of sins'.[90] That is, Messiah Jesus adds an explicitly penal or expiatory meaning to what was otherwise a feast of propitiation. The Passover sacrifice averted wrath but there was no explicit Israelite sin to atone for in Egypt – at least not as was subsequently codified in the Torah of Israel. Now, however, through the shedding of the Messiah's blood, YHWH's actions to vindicate his name even against his own people will be achieved in the most remarkable fashion. By incorporating the Passover symbolism, Jesus teaches that the heavenly kingdom of God will come to the earth as the Messiah perfects the conditions of worship. Jesus, our Passover, provides himself as the sacrifice that will enable God to forgive the intractable recalcitrance of his people. Nevertheless, 'Although God is pitiful and even ready to pardon, yet He does not therefore spare the despisers, but is a severe avenger of their impiety.'[91] The difference is that the name of the Lord will for ever be avenged (and hence hallowed) through the self-sacrifice of the Messiah and hence the temple as the traditional location for the name is decommissioned in apocalyptic fashion when Jesus dies on the cross (Matt. 27:51; Mark 15:38; Luke 23:45).

Vindicating the Messiah as triumphant

It takes the perfecting work of the Spirit to reveal the unity between the heavenly rule of YHWH and the messianic victory of Jesus that Paul described in 1 Corinthians 15. Thus we find ourselves returning to the narrative at Pentecost. Jesus went to Golgotha crowned with thorns while 'the peoples plot in vain . . . the rulers conspire together against the LORD and His Anointed One' (Ps. 2:1–2; cf. Acts 2:23). Defied and defiled the 'King of the Jews' is executed as an insurrectionist and in the company of the same.[92] From Matthew's perspective the scene is an enactment of Psalm 22 and the taunts of Satan are now heard in the mouths of his sons, 'If you are the son of God' (Matt. 27:40). As the wrath of God settles over the scene, darkness shrouds everything and the Messiah breathes his last.[93] The Messiah's mightiest act, leading the people in worship, was in 'offering himself by the eternal Spirit to purify' the people (Heb. 9:14). Yet this is not the end.

By the power of the Spirit Jesus is raised to life (cf. Rom. 1:3–4), and as the Spirit is poured out at Pentecost Peter proclaims that this resurrection has vindicated the faith of Jesus (Acts 2:24ff.; cf. Ps. 16). Jesus' thrice-uttered prophecy made en route to Jerusalem 'He will be raised/raised up or resurrected on the third day' has been fulfilled (Matt. 16:21; 17:23; 20:19). At Pentecost Psalm 110 is cited again and this time expounded by Peter to show that 'it was not David who ascended into the heavens' but rather 'God has made this Jesus, whom you crucified, both Lord and *Messiah*!' (Acts 2:36). The long-anticipated outpouring of the Spirit is a sign that the Messiah has taken up his office of universal ruler. The heavenly reign of God is now the right of Messiah Jesus twice vindicated: 'After making purification for sins, he sat down at the right hand of the Majesty on high' (Heb. 1:3). Christ Jesus' 'worship of God alone' as his patron has been vindicated – there is no kneeling for this king (cf. Luke 4:8). The narrative tension between the promises of God and the faith of the Messiah has been resolved and the royal covenant has been fulfilled. The most high God rules through his exalted royal Son and in the power of his Holy Spirit.

Finally, the conditions for right worship have been established. As we noted in the previous chapter, the crowds are exhorted to be baptized in the name of Jesus 'for the forgiveness of your sins, [so that] you will receive the gift of the Holy Spirit' (Acts 2:38). With the benefit of hindsight we might say that looking for salvation by casting himself off the temple was the wrong *kind* of death for the son of David. Messiah Jesus *replaced* the temple in the hope that the Father would save him from the consequences of this death and deliver him into his rightful inheritance. It was not from dying that he required salvation but from death, and from the evil one who wielded its power (cf. Heb. 5:7). Still, that the son of David would triumph through suffering was the great mystery of the Gospel narratives, especially since his suffering was not sympathetically substitutionary, as Moltmann claims, but penal.

Moltmann concedes that these ideas about atonement and reconciliation 'go back to the Jewish-Christian community', where Jesus' death is interpreted as expiation and the preaching of the cross contains 'echoes of Leviticus 16 and Isaiah 53 (cf. 1 Cor. 15:3)'.[94] However, he claims that this is not compatible with the resurrection. Moltmann admits the possibility of Christ's death portrayed as an 'expiatory sacrifice [that] takes our sins and God's judgement . . . and saves us from them and their consequences'.[95] Yet on the basis of the resurrection he claims that such notions are 'bound to disappear once the sin disappears'.[96] He asserts that neither the scapegoat nor the 'Suffering Servant' could return by way of resurrection, and this despite the poet's mention that

> He [the Servant] will see His seed, He will prolong
>   his days . . .
> Therefore I will give Him the many as a portion,
> and He will receive the mighty as spoil.
>
> (Isa. 53:10, 12)

Moltmann complains that notions of an expiatory death by Christ for sin separate his death from his resurrection.[97]

We have already entered into some of the details surrounding God's vindication of himself as the promise-giver through the vindication of Messiah Jesus as Lord. Surely the most significant aspect of this vindication is that *the one so ignominiously executed as a seemingly unsuccessful insurrectionist was divinely confirmed to be none other than the Messiah of God*, the genuine king of Israel and especially as the Suffering Servant of YHWH (cf. Phil. 2:5–11)? As we have noted, the Pentecost testimony via Psalm 16 is that the Father honours the trust of the Messiah by rescuing him from death: 'you will not abandon me in Hades, nor allow your holy one to see decay' (Acts 2:27). The Father's Spirit specifically intervenes in the ordinary processes of death in order to preserve his royal son. Even so, it is not without continuity with the cause of his dying. Both Luke and John draw attention to the fact that Jesus bore the scars of his death when he appeared to the disciples (Luke 24:39; John 20:20). The implication is that the *risen* Lord is none other than the *crucified* Messiah. More than this, it seems fair to contend, against Moltmann, that in this way Messiah Jesus' victory over sin *as well as death* is preserved as part of his victorious kingship. That his sacrifice should act as an everlasting offering is integral to the testimony of Hebrews:

> For the Messiah did not enter a sanctuary made with
> hands . . . but into heaven itself, so that He might now
> appear in the presence of God for us. He did not do this
> to offer Himself many times, as the high priest enters the
> sanctuary yearly with the blood of another . . . But now
> he has appeared one time, at the end of the ages, for the
> removal of sin by the sacrifice of himself. (9:24–26)

It is critical to our passion for the possibilities of God's perfecting
work in the future that the ascended and *crucified* Messiah present
the fruits of his paschal sacrifice, his death scars, to the Father
now. Traditionally the phenomenon has been associated with
testimony to the bodily nature of his resurrection – that he was
not a ghost. For example, Calvin comments, 'He calls upon their
bodily senses as witnesses, that they may not suppose that a
shadow is exhibited to them instead of a body.'[98] Calvin considers the phenomenon an 'extraordinary act of condescension
towards the disciples' to choose support for their faith over a
physical perfection suitable to his glory. For, 'it was a foolish and
an old wife's dream, to imagine that he will still *continue to bear
the marks of the wounds*, when he shall come to judge the world'.[99]
Two things could, and possibly should, be raised against the
tradition at this point. First, as is generally recognized among
biblical scholars, including Calvin himself, John portrays Jesus
praying that the cross will be his glorification: 'Now, Father,
glorify me in your presence with that glory I had with you before
the world existed' (John 17:5). The battered and bloodied form
of the Messiah *is* his glorious state (cf. 1 Cor. 1:24–25). There is
no *scriptural* reason why his ascension à la Psalm 110 should
be considered his glorification without this. Furthermore, John's
Apocalypse similarly contains a vision of the glorified Messiah as
'one like a slaughtered lamb standing between the throne and the
four living creatures and among the elders' (Rev. 5:6). This is one
of the few apocalyptic metaphors that are readily connectable
with the concrete events of history; namely, the risen Jesus
remains the crucified Messiah and is glorified universally as
such: 'You are worthy to take the scroll and to open its seals,
because you were slaughtered, and you redeemed people for
God by your blood from every tribe and language and people
and nation' (Rev. 5:9).

124

If the reference in the apocalypse was the only indication that the Messiah would be for ever identified by his death, then it would be appropriate to treat his death on a par with other metaphorical representations – the same Lamb mentioned in Revelation 5 has seven horns. However, considering the amount of attention given to the genuine bodily nature of Jesus' resurrection in Luke and John, and that his death scars are included in this portrait, it seems perfectly reasonable to consider their preservation in his otherwise transformed and transcendent state. There is much more to say on this matter and we shall revisit its significance as in chapter 7 we call on the Father to 'forgive us our sins'. For now, though, we have established, contra Moltmann, that the resurrected Jesus is the vindicated Suffering Servant of YHWH and is vindicated as such for the promised forgiveness of sins to be the *now* of God's kingdom on the earth.

Our Father, your kingdom come

On earth

The kingdom comes when our heavenly Father establishes the reign of Messiah Jesus as the spiritually empowered kinsman redeemer of Israel and the Suffering Servant whose substitutionary death creates the conditions necessary for God's wrath to pass over the history of human recalcitrance to his promises. The Messiah's ascent to the Father's right hand spells defeat for all the enemies of God's reign in all the creation: 'He disarmed the rulers and authorities and disgraced them publicly; he triumphed over them by him' (Col. 2:15). This is the *means* through which YHWH's promissory name is vindicated, since he is both tenaciously gracious and compassionate and the faithful and just creator of the universe (cf. Rom. 3:26). YHWH (The Lord) has vindicated his name against the intractable recipients of his promises, and against all humankind. Yet, spectacularly and extraordinarily, he has done this in and through the self-sacrifice of his spiritually empowered Servant for forgiveness of the children of Adam. This is what we know from the past as we anticipate the future when 'God will be all in all,' which must at least coincide with the covenantal promise culminating with the Immanuel promise via the royal promise. Our hope lies in the

125

possibilities inherent in this perfecting work of our heavenly Father. We must now consider how the coming kingdom of God affects or shapes life in the Middle. We began this chapter considering that we ought to anticipate the coming of God's kingdom in parallel with anticipating his presence or lordship. We shall tease out these possibilities on the way to understanding what it means for God to be all in all by examining Moltmann's position on the relationship between the kingdom of God and his lordship.

As I have already discussed, Moltmann's insistence upon a realistic description of history (as opposed to Barth's alleged indifference) favours the future in reference to the kingdom. He writes, 'If according to Jesus' gospel the kingdom of God is "close," then it is already present, but *present* only as the *coming* kingdom.'[100] There is a distinction to be made (according to Moltmann) between the lordship of God and the kingdom of God:

> What can actually be experienced is the immediate lordship of God in the liberation of those who have been bound, and the healing of the sick, in the expulsion of devils and the raising up of the humiliated. But the conquest of death's power, and the experience of eternal life, are undoubtedly future.[101]

So, in terms of the fulfilment of Isaiah 61 (as acknowledged in Luke 4 for example), the Spirit-empowered mighty acts of Jesus (healing and deliverance) represent the lordship of God, who rules in history through Spirit and word.[102] However, this rule is constantly opposed (as we have seen from the time of the exodus not just in the life of Jesus) as it moves the world towards the perfection of God's promises. Hence 'It [the kingdom] is therefore aligned towards a point beyond itself,'[103] when God's lordship will be uncontested. This future state is, for Moltmann, most appropriately expressed as a 'kingdom'.[104] The divine interventions of God (lordship) represent a preview of the kingdom that is launched against the forces that have opposed it throughout history: 'God's *lordship* is the *presence* of his kingdom and God's *kingdom* is the future of his *lordship*.'[105] God's lordship is what the Father does through his Son and by his Spirit, to make

126

creation conform to his promises, in accordance with 'his good pleasure' (Eph. 1:9). God's kingdom is how creation will exist through his Son and by his Spirit when this series of actions has reached its goal: 'The kingdom of the Father consists of the creation of a world open to the future and the preservation both of existence itself and its openness for the future of the kingdom of glory.'[106]

Moltmann's distinction between lordship and kingdom is useful in so far as it will enable us to align the conclusion of this chapter with the theme of the previous one. In the previous chapter the mysterious presence of the name of the Lord in the person of Jesus of Nazareth gave us the opportunity to consider how the work of Messiah Jesus led to the fulfilment of YHWH's promise to be the God who saves. Thus far in this chapter we have read the story of the covenant people as God's saving actions that vindicate his kingship over Israel (cf. Ezek. 36). In the gospel story the kingdom of God has been a function of the extent to which the Messiah's saving actions are YHWH's. Hence in this chapter we have focused on the manner in which the kingdom of YHWH is revealed to be the salvation of his Messiah. Ladd again summarizes well: 'before the eschatological [end of the world] appearing of God's kingdom at the end of the age, God's Kingdom has become dynamically active among men in Jesus' person and mission'.[107]

The lordship of the Messiah in the Spirit

The Pentecost proclamation of the Lord Jesus as Messiah heralds the dawn of a new era in the history shaped by God's promises. Now is the time of the lordship of the Messiah in the Spirit as the Father's rule is mediated to the earth from his right hand in heaven. The kingdom of God on earth can be understood as his reign because YHWH has fulfilled his vow and installed his monarch to rule. Life in the Middle is the creaturely time of the 'until' of Psalm 110:3 when in the Spirit the historical intervention of YHWH is the reign of his Messiah, Jesus, who moves creation towards the eradication of enmity towards the Father in creation – the defeat of the *final* enemy (1 Cor. 15:26). The economic resolution of the relationship between Father and Son means that where YHWH worked for his royal son in the Spirit to mediate his rule to the earth as we saw in the history of Israel, now the

Father reveals his working through his eternal Son in the Spirit to mediate his rule to all the earth.

The Acts narrative portrays this era beginning with the agency of the Spirit in the fulfilment of Joel's prophecy:

> In the last days, says God, I will pour forth from my Spirit on all flesh. Your sons and daughters will prophesy. Your young men will see visions and your elders will dream dreams. And even upon my servants in those last days I will pour forth from my Spirit and they will prophesy. (Acts 2:17–18)

A primary aspect of the Messiah's lordship is the time when his Spirit will speak generally through members of the community and at the same time distinguish a new community of promise.[108] Considering the greater narrative as we have, it ought to be no surprise that God's actions by his Spirit are explicit in their anticipation of the kingdom. At the same time that he looked forward to the return of the Spirit-empowered son of David in the kingdom of God, Isaiah also saw a somewhat different activity of the Spirit among the people of the promise. While the main emphasis of Isaiah's visions is the ministry of the Spirit to and for the virgin's son and/or the Servant of YHWH, there are also signs that when the kingdom comes it will involve the work of the Spirit for the people of the promise. So Isaiah writes:

> I will pour water on the thirsty land
> and streams on the dry ground;
> I will pour out My Spirit on your descendants
> and My blessing on your offspring.
>
> (Isa. 44:3)

Similarly, Ezekiel looks forward to a democratization of Spirit endowment for all the people: 'I will place my Spirit within you and cause you to follow my statutes and carefully observe my ordinances' (Ezek. 36:27). As we have seen repeatedly, YHWH gives himself in his promises, and the resurrection and ascension of the victorious Messiah marks a further opportunity for YHWH to act in this way. The consequences of these visions are commensurate with what Jeremiah (Jer. 31:31–34) and Isaiah

(Isa. 54) anticipate for Israel under the new covenant to be established between YHWH and his new people.[109] For us this dawning of a new era is the advent of life in the Middle, but *does the constitution of the church equal the arrival of the kingdom of God on the earth?* After all, Joel's prophecy anticipates a universal agency of revelation for the Spirit on 'all flesh'. If ignorance or even recalcitrance is all that impedes God's kingdom on the earth, then it seems reasonable to assume that as the church spreads geographically, as sinners believe the Pentecost testimony, then that which is true in heaven will be true on earth – God reigns.

The agency of the Spirit and the presence of the kingdom

There are two things, however, to consider in understanding what it means for God to be *in* creation. In the first instance, to say that God is *in* creation is to say that he is *active*: he is doing something with our space and time. The Pentecost event with all its spectacular phenomena is a case where we see explicit divine intervention and therefore presence. There are echoes of Sinai, 'where God appeared in the midst of loud "voices and torches and a thick cloud" and "fire"' (Exod. 19:16–20; 20:18).[110] In addition, the phrase 'tongues of fire' appears in Isaiah 30:27–30, where YHWH descends upon his holy mountain and is cloaked in 'dense smoke . . . his tongues like consuming fire'.[111] Furthermore, within this scene of divine immanence the disciples are described as '*filled* with the Holy Spirit'. Here the disciples are individually touched by and baptized with the Spirit as both John the Baptizer and Jesus had promised. In fact, the Spirit rests upon them as he did with Jesus (cf. Luke 3:20–22). This is not to say that the flame is the Spirit any more than the dove was for Jesus at the Jordan. Nevertheless, the language in these verses equates easily with immanent intervention or action by the Spirit upon an individual. The story certainly mentions that the disciples were 'enabled by the Spirit', to speak in other tongues. The Spirit's active presence among a new people of promise has the potential to be at least a temporal aspect of the coming kingdom, but what of the actual spatial nature of the kingdom? Can the agency of the Spirit among this newly designated community (and therefore the presence of Messiah Jesus) be equated with a realm of activity, a new kingdom on earth as distinct from the state of Israel, where God reigns?

A number of commentators point to the event of Pentecost as the reversal of the curse of Babel: 'Jews from many nations, hearing the wonders of God in their own tongue.'[112] Whereas at Babel God confused the language of the nations and they were scattered over the earth, here at Pentecost the nations are gathered together again in order for God to address them. However, those gathered hear of the wonders of God 'in their *own* native language' (2:8). It is the plurality of address that is the most prominent feature considering that the universal language of the crowd is *koinē* Greek. The Spirit's actions do not diminish the natural ethnic particularities of this new community – they remain Jews 'from every nation under heaven' (2:5). At the same time a group is being *particularized* through this address. It is from a larger, predominantly Jewish, group that *converts* will be taken in the first instance (cf. Acts 2:47), which will later cut across another important distinction within the drama of Scripture, namely that between Jews and Gentiles: 'The ones from the circumcision group who had come with Peter were amazed, because the gift of the Holy Spirit had also been poured out upon the Gentiles' (Acts 10:45).

Throughout the Acts narrative both Jews and Gentiles who receive the gift of the Spirit are implicitly distinguished from 'the sons of Israel' (cf. Gal. 3:14) such that, as Paul writes in Ephesians 2:14–16, 'He might create in himself one new man from the two.'[113] Thus the lordship of the Messiah in the Spirit will constitute a community within those who might otherwise be considered the people of God, but the space or realm of God's messianic reign is determined by the location or propinquity of the people gathered in the Spirit as much as, if not more than, by the geographic location. Nevertheless, this Spirit-empowered community is commissioned by the Messiah to testify to his lordship 'in Jerusalem, Judea and Samaria and to the ends of the earth' (Acts 1:8; cf. Matt. 28:18–20). The Acts story has this testimony radiating out from Jerusalem as, in the Spirit, the lordship of Messiah Jesus commissions Philip, then Peter and then Paul to proclaim the coming kingdom, while geography and ethnicity proportionally diminish as key indicators of the people of promise. In the light of this primarily divine activity we might rightly consider our question above to be answered: *the spread of the church throughout the earth reveals the present reality of God's kingdom*. However, as we discovered in the previous chapter, while the lordship of the Messiah is present and active among the church and in the Spirit, we must maintain an all-important distinction between the transcendent Messiah and the Spirit-constituted church. Alternatively, to say that Jesus and through him the Father is present in the church is not the same as saying that the Father is present in Jesus as the Son, despite the fact that *both presences involve the agency of the Spirit.*

Therefore we must consider whether the weight of our emphasis should shift towards viewing even the spread of the church (which includes the presence of the name) as a lordly activity of the Father in creation that anticipates something else – the bodily presence of the one who bears the name, Messiah Jesus. As Moltmann suggested, 'The Kingdom of God is present as promise and hope for the future horizon of all things, which are then seen in their historic character because they do not yet contain their truth in themselves.'[114] For, while the daily activities of a church during life in the Middle might be the fruit of divine achievement or the lordship of the Messiah in the Spirit, *they are only creaturely activities in the name of the king, not as the king.* There is a second and most important way that we speak of God's being in the world, in the material person of the Lord Jesus.

Church and kingdom

From the previous chapter we identified two important challenges for Christians when it comes to understanding (eschatologically) the presence of God in their midst as the church – the extent to which church or churches could be thought of as *Christ towards the world* and, therefore, the extent to which the church exercises any kind of *authority in the world.* If we look again closely at the events of Pentecost, we shall see how the narrative depicts the relationship between Christ and the church in terms of the activity of the king as Lord.

When Peter addresses the crowd, the Spirit enables him to interpret for those gathered the true mechanism of authority in God's kingdom. The hearers are drawn into the story of Jesus, who was previously attested to them as one through whom God did 'miracles, wonders and signs' (Acts 2:22). Yet it is neither his deeds nor his death that is the ground for Jesus' sovereignty. It is the fact that God has vindicated him as Messiah by the lordly act

131

of raising him from the dead and subsequently that the Messiah (now revealed as Lord) has poured out God's Spirit. In what follows, Peter invokes Psalm 16 to explain the relationship between God and Jesus so that the crowd might realize the new status of God's kingdom among them:

> For David said about him, 'I saw beforehand my Lord always before me: because he is at my right hand I will not be shaken. Because of this my heart is gladdened and my tongue rejoices; because you will not abandon my soul in Hades nor will you permit your holy one to see decay. You have made known to me the way of life. You will fill me with the joy of your face.' (Acts 2:25–28)

In the original psalm (LXX 15) David calls on God for protection, confident that he will be preserved (that the Lord will intervene), *not necessarily from death* but rather decay in the place of the dead. In the Spirit Peter reads this as David's inspired foresight into the experience of God's holy one. The implication for Peter's hearers is that the experience of the 'I' in Psalm 16 is the experience of *Jesus* in the face of death – he did not falter but instead entrusted himself to the Father's refusal to allow him to remain dead. In the resurrection of Jesus of Nazareth the Spirit *preserves* the royal sonship of the Messiah by resurrecting him as the holy one of God. More to the point, the first activity of the Spirit among the church is vindication of the reign of the Messiah *in* the church *and* the distinction of the king *over* the church.[115]

The promised Spirit has enabled the followers of the risen Jesus to recognize him as the perfect Son of David (and therefore Son of God) (cf. Luke 24:45–47). Having submitted to suffering, the exalted Messiah receives his inheritance at the right hand of God on high. Messiah Jesus is the son of David par excellence, who is granted a throne, not on earth but at the right hand of God his Father.[116] That the Messiah is the one who pours out the Spirit of God gives us insight into the inauguration of his kingdom over the earth. The coming of the Spirit is a *coronation gift* of God the Father to his Son that vindicates his sonship by making what was implicit in the narrative explicit in the experience of his followers. Jesus has been perfected as Messiah by the

Spirit as son of David and therefore as Son of God, a fact that is now to be proclaimed publicly. The key thing to note here is that God is *in* the lordly and immanent activity of the Spirit through the transcendent activity of his Son, the Lord and king. The activity of the kingdom or rule of the king is among the church in the Spirit, while the king himself, who is the Lord, is transcendent with the Father.

There is a final aspect to the lordly work of the transcendent king in the Spirit-constituted church – the forgiveness of sins. We have established that to call on the name of the Lord Jesus is to receive forgiveness for antagonizing God the Father, with regard to his promises, and the Holy Spirit in order that God's name might be hallowed among us (Acts 2:38). Through the Messiah and by his Spirit the church is constituted for the Father as an outpouring of his reign; they are 'set apart by the Spirit for obedience and for sprinkling with the blood of Jesus Christ' (1 Peter 1:2). Thus the Spirit applies the benefits of the messianic sacrifice to the church so that they may bear Jesus' name.[117] The Spirit 'comes from the Father and calls us into the body, of which the Son is the head . . . the presence of Christ is not as but *through* the Spirit, who is the mediator of both Christ's presence and his (eschatological) otherness'.[118] Thus in his oneness with the church the Messiah remains the transcendent Lord. The church in turn comes to the Father in the Spirit and through the crucified Son – their great high priest: 'The intercession of Christ is a continual application of his death for our salvation. That God then does not impute to us our sins, this comes to us, because he has regard to Christ as intercessor.'[119]

As the Spirit gathers a church by mediating the promises of God's word of forgiveness through the Messiah's sacrifice we discover the importance of the church's other sacrament, the Lord's Supper. In this practice, instituted by the Messiah at his last Passover, he is celebrated both for his saving sacrifice in the Spirit (cf. Heb. 9:14) and his heavenly reign during life in the Middle: 'until He comes' (1 Cor. 11:26). The church is the place where the kingdom of God is echoed in the world at different times and in various places as the Spirit 'seals' the church as '*the down payment* of their inheritance, for the redemption of the possession, to the praise of His glory' (Eph. 1:14). The church, then, as an anticipation of the kingdom is the spatial Middle (in fractal form[120]), where the gospel of Jesus' lordship in the forgiveness of sins is proclaimed, as such:

> The space of the church is not there in order to fight with the world for a piece of its territory, but precisely to testify to the world that it is still the world, namely, the world that is loved and reconciled by God.[121]

Barth reminded us of the historical failures of Christians and the church to honour their king and hence echo the heavenly reign.[122] Nevertheless, the victory remains Messiah Jesus' for the church. This is the *now* of the kingdom that solidifies our hope for a future when the reign of God will be present on earth in all its fullness.

Our Father, your kingdom come

As it is in heaven

When we return to Paul's picture of *The End* in 1 Corinthians 15, which refers to the Messiah's reign culminating when 'he has put all his enemies under his feet', we need not fear a contradiction. In the light of what we have already seen, the Messiah acts to defeat the enemies of his kinsmen. As Paul explains to the church in Ephesus, 'God's multifaceted wisdom *is* now made known through the church to the rulers and authorities in the heavens' (Eph. 3:10). This human activity of the church must be understood as a divine regal achievement. A tension remains because, as Tom Wright has observed, Psalm 110 has the same phrase as Psalm 8 for universal dominion, which is a meditation on the Genesis mandate given to Adam.[123] Therefore we would expect the Messiah to reign openly over all the earth. However, as the writer to the Hebrews acknowledges, 'He subjected all things under his feet. For in subjecting everything to him, he left nothing not subject to him. As it is, *we do not yet see everything subjected to him*' (Heb. 2:8). So Paul writes of 'death as a final enemy' that prevents God's kingdom being 'all in all' (1 Cor. 15:26).

In 1 Corinthians 15 Paul refers to the risen Messiah Jesus as 'the first fruits' of the resurrection and this gives substance to the

possibilities of a general resurrection of all the dead as integral to
the kingdom of God. Calvin described it thus:

> For as in the first-fruits the produce of the entire year
> was consecrated, so the power of Christ's resurrection is
> extended to all of us – unless you prefer to take it in a
> more simple [*sic*] way – that in him the first fruit of the
> resurrection was gathered. I rather prefer, however, to
> understand the statement in this sense – that the rest of
> the dead will follow him, as the entire harvest does the
> first-fruits.[124]

The resurrection of the Messiah from the dead marks the advent
of the new creation in which death will no longer overshadow
the lives of human beings. The risen Messiah, having defeated the
devil, 'free[s] those who were held in slavery all their lives by
the fear of death' (Heb. 2:15).

The resurrection of the dead is the penultimate moment in
history shaped by God's promises marking the end of all opposition to the reign of God in the world: 'the last enemy is defeated'.
Now all those who have lived, all creation, are ready to be brought
before the enthroned Messiah to confess, 'Messiah Jesus is Lord,
to the glory of God the Father' (Phil. 2:11). The crucified Son and
Servant is vindicated everlastingly against his enemies and before
his church. This is *The End* that the gospel promises (1 Cor. 15:24)
and hence the point at which, through the Messiah and in the
Spirit, the fatherhood of God is perfectly all in all. There is still
more to discover concerning this vindication and in chapter 6 we
shall explore the possibilities as we consider God the Father's
gracious act of preserving a people for himself. In the meantime
we need only note that the perfection of the kingdom of God
on the earth is entirely dependent upon two things: *the bodily
presence of the king and the cessation of death.* Until the king
returns and human beings no longer die and, more specifically, all
those who have died are raised to life again, the experience of the
kingdom of God on earth will not be what it is in heaven. No
human activity has ever, or will ever, gain sufficient dominion
over creation to effect such an event and therefore there can be no
realization of the kingdom until God the Father acts through his
Messiah and by his Spirit. Only in this divine intervention will

history reach its perfection and also its glorification – with the return of the king, when the dead are raised before the throne of the one through whom the fatherhood of God will be everlastingly mediated in the Spirit.

5

THE FATHER'S WILL
FOR ONE AND ALL

Of men and angels

The fatherhood of God will be all in all when the Messiah, Jesus, is proclaimed Lord of heaven and earth by all God's creatures. When Christ the king returns to the earth and the dead are raised, then the last obstacle to the kingdom's arrival will have been defeated. When the paschal Servant is vindicated before all creation, then the presence of God will be with his people and they will celebrate his reign for ever. The possibilities contained in these promises are the source of our passion for the new creation – our hope. For when these things are mediated to earth from heaven the Father's covenantal and royal promises will be perfected. In the light of this, life in the Middle will consist of the Holy Spirit's constituting churches in the name of Jesus, and these churches will celebrate the victory of God's royal and eternal Son. As they do, there will be a genuine anticipation of right order for a world that belongs to the Father – the coming kingdom of Messiah Jesus will be previewed on the earth.

These conclusions, gleaned from the first two petitions of the Lord's Prayer, represent a broad-strokes picture of both the *what* and the *how* of eschatology. They are the substance of our hope and of our prayers for life in the Middle. The third petition in the Lord's Prayer leads us to reflect on the *why* of eschatology. In this chapter we shall consider the will of the Father for the earth that lies behind God's promises to be present with us as his people.

To presume to understand God's will and to make prescriptive statements about how this will governs the history of God's promises is no small thing. Here we do well to heed Calvin's warning:

> Seeing therefore we have so sufficient testimonies, shall we demand that Angels come down from Heaven, and that God will yet open unto us that [which] is hidden from us? But let us . . . content ourselves with the Holy Scripture. . . For . . . the Gospel containeth all perfection of doctrine: and also behold the only mean, whereby we may be thoroughly satisfied, and have our minds settled and stayed.[1]

In order to discern the will of God for his creation we must look to the Scriptures. In the Christian tradition, to call on the Father for his will to be done on earth is, as Augustine puts it, simply to 'let obedience be given to Thy precepts . . . by men as it is by angels'.[2] It is when humans do God's will that it is accomplished, 'not because they make God will but because they do as he wills, that is, they act according to his will'.[3] This applies to saints and sinners alike: 'As the just also may the sinners do Thy will, in order that they may be converted to Thee'; and hence God's name is hallowed in all the earth.[4] In relation to God's kingdom, Augustine says, if we 'take heaven and earth as signifying spirit and flesh', the resurrection, the perfection of God's heavenly will, means that 'as the [human] spirit does not resist God, following and doing his will, so also may the body not resist the spirit or soul, which is now harassed by the body's infirmities and is prone to fall in with the body's habits'.[5] The answer to the third supplication is complete personal alignment with the will of God for the individual. Augustine opted for what could be described as a *mimetic* view – when the earth mirrors the heavens. Yet, as we have already observed, there is only one individual in whom such alignment exists, because there is only one place on earth in which divine and creaturely life are *united* – in the Father's actions for salvation through the Messiah and in the Spirit. This is because, as Barth commented, 'The fulfilment of God's will is an accomplishment beyond our capacity. It is not we who do the will of God. To Him belongs the plan and execution, and its time of fulfilment.'[6]

Discerning the Father's will

We have observed that to receive the Father's name is to receive a promise: God's nature is essentially promissory in relation to his creation. The significance of this lies in the fact that God's promises are the means by which he reveals and establishes his will on earth. If YHWH promises that he *will be* the risen Messiah, Jesus, we must therefore assume he *wills* to be so: YHWH told Moses, 'I will be who I will be,' and Peter reveals the fulfilment of this as he proclaims 'Messiah Jesus is LORD.' In the context of eschatology the future (or the possibilities for the Spirit's perfecting work) is not absorption into God's essential nature so much as the perfection of his will for creation. At the same time, insight into the future is insight into God's will; for there will be no other future for creation apart from the hallowing of God's name in and through the lordship of Jesus. Therefore as we reflect on Messiah Jesus' exhortation to call on the Father to perfect his heavenly will on earth, we must do so with the expectation that the answer will be found in the enthronement of his Messiah and by his Holy Spirit.

We gain apostolic insight into God's will for creation through his Son in the divine promise that Paul expounds to the church in Ephesus:

> Praise the God and Father of our Lord Messiah Jesus who has blessed us with all spiritual blessing in the heavens, in Christ; he chose us in him before the foundation of the world so that we might be holy and blameless before him in love; he predetermined us for sonship in him according to his good pleasure and will for the praise of his glorious grace through Messiah Jesus, which he gave us freely in the beloved one. We have redemption in him through his blood, the forgiveness of sins, according to the riches of his grace which

139

he granted to us richly in all wisdom and understanding. He made known to us the mystery of his will according to his good pleasure that he intended in him for the management of the fullness of time: to sum up all things in the Messiah – the things in the heavens and the earth in him. (Eph. 1:3–10)

The hymn at the beginning of Ephesians is not obviously a promise – God does not say, 'I will do this or that.' Rather, the object of trust for the church is the apostolic insight into history as the span 'from before the foundations of the earth' to the exaltation of Jesus as Lord. The promise is that God's saving actions in Jesus are rooted in his eternal purposes; that is, they stem from the inner life of the triune God. In this configuration Paul draws our attention to at least three things concerning the Father's will for creation. His intention is discerned, first, in 'the choice of the divine will (good pleasure v.5), second in the mystery of divine will (v.9) and thirdly in the plan of divine will (v.11)'.[7] Thus to understand the divine will and how this might be perfected on earth as it is in heaven, we need to understand that *God's will for the earth is revealed in the choices he makes in order to perfect his plan – choices that are consistently mysterious.* Ephesians 1 proclaims that all three of these aspects of divine will come together in the person of the Lord Jesus (v. 10). The key term for understanding God's will in Ephesians 1 is *anakephalaiōsasthai* – 'to be brought together or summed up in'. According to O'Brien the verb is employed creatively by Paul 'to describe the magnificent goal of God's gracious purposes for the whole of creation'.[8] In this sense Jesus is the goal of God's will to be done on the earth as it is in heaven. More precisely, God's predestined will for creation (Eph. 1:4) is realized and perfected in and through the ministry of the royal and eternal Son, Jesus the Messiah. Central to this is his role as the spiritually designated *interpreter and executor* of the Father's will. We shall explore how Jesus the Christ is the perfection of the Father's often mysterious plan throughout the greater narrative of Scripture, as Calvin said was necessary. However, before we do that, we must pause to consider the significance of God's choice to reveal his will through Jesus of Nazareth for modern eschatology. Here, in conversation with Barth, we shall discover the importance of an explicitly trinitarian description of God's electing will in the economy of salvation before moving on to distinguish the purpose of election as the pattern of God's plan in the canonical story.

The Father's will in his planned and mysterious choices

One of the chief implications of Ephesians 1 is that all creation is designed for the glorification of Messiah Jesus and this was *God's will or choice* 'from before the foundation of the earth' (1:4). *The universe was created for the Lord Jesus Christ.* Paul writes a similar thing to the church in Colossae: 'all things have been created through Him *and for Him*' (Col. 1:16). This appears to fit well with the images from John's Apocalypse that anticipate *The End* with all creation gathered around 'the Lamb who was slain' (Rev. 5; cf. 13:6). Barth took these observations as warrant to reinterpret both the meaning and significance of the Christian doctrine of election. As he famously put it, 'God's eternal will is the election of Jesus Christ.'[9]

Barth's reconfiguration of the doctrine of election was one of his major contributions to Christian theology in the twentieth century and is the backbone of his eschatology. His position rests on the meaning of *en Christō* (in Christ) in passages like Ephesians 1. At the level of syntax the issue is the relationship between *hēmas*, 'us', as the object of the majority of the verbs in chapter 1:3–14, and to what extent *en Christō* should be employed as an instrumental dative.[10] Those who disagree with Barth draw attention to the fact that God's actions are directed towards the 'us' throughout the passage. It has been argued that 'we' – the church – are the objects of the verbs and therefore God's choice must be of particular persons.[11] Those who support Barth draw attention to the messianic flavour given to the 'in Christ' clause. Paul refers to Christ as 'the beloved' (1:6, *en tō ēgapēmenō*) and the one in whom God planned his good pleasure (1:9, *tēn eudokian autou . . . en autō*). Markus Barth points to the messianic significance that these phrases hold in the Synoptic Gospels in the context of Jesus' baptism, where God refers to Jesus as 'my beloved Son, in whom I delight' (*sy ei ho hyios mou agapētos, en soi eudokēsa*).[12] He contends that the Gospel narratives oblige us to understand the election of anyone as a consequence of

God's choice of Jesus in the first instance. The two aspects of God's choice ought not to be isolated by any means, but neither should a simple mechanism of syntax hold sway over a greater biblical theme.

In the last chapter I sought to highlight the theological significance of God's designating in the Spirit his choice of ruler and saviour of his people Israel. I pursued this as part of a wider attempt to describe the perfection of God's rule on earth as the temporal expression of the relationship between Father and Son in the Spirit. Karl Barth's contention is that this story should be viewed as a product of divine self-determination from within eternity (or the immanent life of God) prior to the creation of anything outside that life. However, Barth's own exposition of God's intentions is much less reliant on the *historical* YHWH, whose promissory nature we explored in chapter 3. This YHWH is the Lord, whom we come to know as the risen Messiah (Acts 2:36).[13] Instead, Barth opted for the Johannine Logos incarnate as the foundation for his understanding of God's choice.[14] If, as Barth contended, God's being is in his act, there is much more in the pages of the Bible concerning the acts of the *Lord* as distinct from the acts of Logos. Therefore, we must rely on the long story of YHWH of Israel in order to substantiate the identity of the Logos as the Lord Jesus Christ. The foundation upon which Barth insists ignores the long narrative 'from creation' in which the plan of YHWH unfolds – the lordly interventions that anticipate his coming kingdom. Furthermore, when Barth contends that the Lord Jesus is both the electing God and the man elected from the eternity that is God's life preceding creation, the result is a significant theological deconstruction of the Reformed tradition as we can see when we consider the opinion of classical Reformed theologians like Francis Turretin:

> It is one thing for Christ as *Logon* to be the efficient cause of election; another for him as God-man and Mediator to be its object and meritorious cause. The former is asserted by Christ [John 13:18; 15:16] but not the latter.[15]

While there is not sufficient space here to engage in a full treatment of Karl Barth's doctrine of election, we ought to examine it briefly if only to appreciate its consequences for eschatology, since we have already adopted Barth's suggestions regarding the promises of God and the parousia of Christ. In particular, we need to investigate the repercussions for Barth's more protological approach to eschatology in comparison with the more Spirit-driven portrait that we have established of Jesus Christ as the kinsman redeemer.

God's choice in Christ

The Reformed doctrines of election and predestination have had a significant effect on the way in which Christians understand the relationship between God's will and creaturely history. Proponents see the twin doctrines functioning to uphold both the doctrines of God's sovereignty over history and his grace within history (at the very least).[16] Those who oppose the doctrines, especially predestination, claim that such theology is indistinguishable from pagan (Hellenistic) ideas of determinism and, while they might uphold the sovereignty of God, ultimately they render both the grace of God and history meaningless.[17] The dialogue between Barth and Moltmann over the conceptual focus of eschatology represents the tension between the *now* and the *not-yet*: Moltmann being the advocate for the *not-yet* of an eschatology still to come, Barth, the advocate of the *now* or the present achievement of God awaiting revelation. The central issue is the nature of history and which of these two foci allows for the most credible and therefore liveable theological description of life in the Middle. As we have noted, Moltmann accused Barth's theology of Hellenistic tendencies that leave no place for creaturely history. He complained that Barth's stress on the self-revelation of God meant an 'eternal presence of God in time', a 'present without any future'.[18] One of the things that brought Barth to notoriety in the twentieth century was his attempt to reconfigure the Reformed description of election in order to produce a very different picture of the grace of God in history.

The source of Barth's contention with Reformed theology was its deeply held conviction that God makes a double decree of election to both salvation and perdition.[19] Barth reacted against this concept for a number of reasons but chiefly because, to him, it treated the Christian God in the abstract, 'determined by the fact that both quantities [the God who chooses and the humanity he chooses] are treated as unknown'.[20] Instead, Barth argued that God's will ought to be understood from the perspective of his free decision to become the man Jesus the Messiah:

> For how could we have said anything about the knowledge and reality of God had we not considered this positive attitude learning from it how God gives Himself to be known, and what He is both in Himself and in all His works?[21]

The positive attitude of God is his movement towards his creatures in the incarnate Son: 'The attitude or relation for which God has once and for all decided, to which He has committed us and wills us to be committed by us, is the relation or attitude to Jesus Christ.'[22] Since God has freely chosen to reveal himself in creation as the incarnate Son, this is the beginning, the middle and the end for understanding God and his will for it. If we are to heed Calvin's warning regarding the will of God, Barth claims, we must look to Messiah Jesus in the gospel. Consequently, we must understand creation, and humanity in particular, as the partner towards whom and for whom God has freely chosen to be:

> Election should serve at once to emphasize and explain what we have already said in the word grace, God in His love elects another to fellowship with Himself . . . He ordains that He should not be entirely self-sufficient as He might be.[23]

The human being exists in the context of God's choice to be the God of and for humanity in the man Jesus of Nazareth. This is the basis for the life of the human creature but it is also the very nature of the Christian God – the one who has freely chosen to be the God and Father of our Lord Messiah Jesus.

Once God has freely chosen to extend his eternal life to creation and to join in creaturely life, which is the meaning of created history,[24] the human creature is bound to respond as the recipient of God's grace: 'There is no grace without the lordship and claim of grace.'[25] God's decision to be with the creature leaves no room for an alternative existence for the creature; he/she/they live only in the light of God's gracious desire for fellowship with them. It is important to understand here that Barth proposes creation ought to be understood retrospectively on the basis of God's election in the Lord Jesus. That is, we start with the revelation of the risen Lord Jesus and then work backwards to consider God's intention in creating humanity in this light. This idea leads Barth directly into the Christian description of predestination or God's prior determining to unite eternal life with creaturely life in the Lord Messiah Jesus. In truth Barth prefers to talk only about God's election in grace rather than God's predetermining everything. Hence, and against the Reformed tradition, he declares of predestination:

> It is not a mere theorem whose content does not amount
> to anything more than instruction in, or the elucidation
> of, something which is quite unaffected by the distinction
> between right and wrong or good and evil. Its content is
> instruction and elucidation, but instruction and elucida-
> tion which are to us a proclamation of joy. It is not a
> mixed message of joy and terror, salvation and damnation
> . . . It does, of course, throw a shadow . . . In any case . . .
> the final word is never that of warning, of judgment, of
> punishment, of a barrier erected, of a grave opened.[26]

The doctrines of predestination and election are meant to be the 'most comfortable of doctrines'[27] because they describe God's free and loving decision to create humanity for fellowship with him – and nothing else: 'The divine election as such does not negate creation but affirms it.'[28] More to the point, for Barth, predestination is happening all the time as God moves in and from eternity above and beyond history to enable the creature to elect him. That is, God moves in time and space to enable the human creature to choose him – over and against the creature's sinful rejection of him: 'For the fulfillment of election involves the affirmation of the existence of elected man and its counter-part in man's election, in which God's election evokes and awakens faith, and meets and answers that faith as human decision.'[29]

So, instead of an allegedly mysterious divine fiat that predetermines creaturely existence as a prelude to the act of creation, Barth wants us to see that in the Lord Jesus God has revealed his eternal choice to have fellowship with human beings – despite knowing that they would reject him – and consequently acts towards humanity to ensure that they could and would have that fellowship.

Barth claims that the concept of God's choosing for creation became obscured when theologians spoke of 'the book of life' as having two columns – one for life and one for death.[30] The 'axioms of reason and/or the datum of experience'[31] led Reformed scholars to raise questions of the doctrine with the result that, 'Scripture [was] no longer able to say freely what it [willed] to say. It [could] only answer the questions put to it by man.'[32] Such questions 'put by men' included both election in view of 'God as omnipotent Will',[33] and election in view of

> what we observe to be the evident contrast between those who through the Church hear the Gospel ... obediently and with profit, and so to salvation, and those who hear with open hostility or without any result at all and so finally to condemnation.[34]

In terms of our discussion of time, the former represents a rational history predetermined by absolute coherence in the mind of God, with the latter representing an empirical history governed by correspondence with creaturely reality. Barth credits Aquinas with the development of the first view of election,[35] whereas the second view begins with Augustine and flows through Calvin and on into the Reformed tradition.[36] Against the latter tradition, and Calvin in particular as its architect, Barth argued that the 'facts' of election and/or divine decree could only be concretely determined by the gospel of the Lord, Messiah Jesus:[37] 'Its direct and proper object is not individuals generally, but one individual – and only in Him the people called and united by Him, and only in that people individuals in general in their private relationship with God.'[38]

Messiah Jesus is *the* elect man but, of course, he is also the God who elects:

> Who and what is the God who rules and feeds His people, creating and maintaining the whole world for its benefit, and guiding it according to His own good-pleasure? ... If in this way we ask further concerning the one point

146

upon which, according to Scripture, our attention and thoughts should and must be concentrated, then from first to last the Bible directs us to the name of Jesus Christ.[39]

Thus in Barth's view the Lord Jesus is both the electing God and the elected human. This is the clear and concrete teaching of Scripture on the subject and therefore the starting place for discerning both the will of God and the meaning of history. God is in no way compelled to be God in this way, and hence his decision for man is both free and loving. Nevertheless, 'in a free act of determination God has ordained concerning Himself . . . God has put Himself under obligation to man'.[40]

Of course, the humanity elected in Messiah Jesus is sinful – they are recalcitrant towards the promises of God, as we have seen specifically in Israel. This fact, according to Barth, is encapsulated in God's election to be the Lord Jesus. As the elect man, Jesus stands over and against every other human by virtue of his righteous relationship with the Father: 'The election of the man Jesus means, then, that a wrath is kindled, a sentence pronounced and finally executed, a rejection actualized.'[41] In the election of Jesus God rejects evil in his creation – in all its forms. Humanity, having succumbed to the power of Satan, follows the path laid out by Adam in Genesis 3: 'He stands under the wrath which is God's only answer to the creature which abuses and dishonours its creatureliness.'[42] Again and 'nevertheless',[43] in Jesus, the elect one who defeats Satan as in Matthew 4, the wrath which all humans have incurred is propitiated: 'God from all eternity ordains this obedient one in order that He might bear the suffering which the disobedient have deserved and which for the sake of God's righteousness must necessarily be borne.'[44] Election is the foundation of Christ's vicarious substitution – the Father has determined in eternity that Jesus must take the place of sinners under his wrath. Messiah Jesus is chosen to bear our alienation from God, and in this way Barth preserves the concept of a *double decree*. Yet in Messiah Jesus, God elects salvation for humanity even as he elects himself to the perdition, facing his own wrath against sin. He

> declared Himself guilty of the contradiction against Him in which man was involved . . . He took upon Himself

147

the rejection which man deserves . . . He tasted Himself the damnation, death and hell which ought to have
been the portion of fallen man.[45]

Strictly speaking, Barth's interpretation is not eschatological but,
in keeping with the Reformed tradition, soteriological. Hence
for many of his interpreters Barth's description of the cross is
oriented more towards the beginning than the end.[46] Barth's
reconfiguration of the traditional doctrine of predestination and
election seeks to articulate God's will entirely within the scope of
the gospel of the Lord Jesus: 'In Him God's plan for man is
disclosed, God's judgment on man fulfilled, God's deliverance of
man accomplished, God's gift to man present in fullness, God's
claim and promise to man declared.'[47]

The choice of God and the purpose of election

In sketching Barth's doctrine of election, our main concern is the
impact it might have for a Christian eschatology and our account
of life in the Middle. In so far as Barth is determined to interpret
Scripture in the light of the gospel of the Lord Jesus, it is easy to
share his concern that anything said about the will of God in the
world ought to start and finish there – Calvin said the same. In
addition, Barth's position places the focus of our attention at the
point where the eternal meets the historical – Messiah Jesus,
the Immanuel. In this way, both the desire to speculate on the
events of the transcendent and the temptation to read history as
the will of God are curbed. Whether or not Barth has appropriately read the Reformed tradition from which he saw himself
advancing is less of a concern for us here than whether his
innovation had a positive effect on eschatology – or not.[48] Even if
we were to accept Barth's account of the Augustinian/Calvinist
tradition regarding an eternal decree in favour of a minority that
is saved and against the reprobate,[49] would the virtual equation of
Messiah Jesus with the decree make that much difference to the
reality of history? When Barth writes 'He [Jesus] is the election of
God before which and without which and beside which God
cannot make any other choices . . . and He is the election . . . of
the free grace of God,'[50] the will of God seems to have been
hypostasized. In patristic terms the second hypostasis (the eternal
Son) of the Godhead is equated with the will of God. More than

this, if it is in the incarnate Son that the will of God to be God towards the creation has been revealed, then in what sense is there a genuine distinction between divine and creaturely time? Has not the eternity of divine life eclipsed the temporality of creaturely life from *the beginning* (creaturely life is but an accident of divine life)? Interpreters of Barth differ on the extent to which he might be guilty of this. So McCormack is quick to point out that for Barth, 'History is significant for the being of God in eternity; but it is significant only because God freely chooses that it should be so.'[51] Yet McCormack also considers Barth's position to require, theologically or at least logically, that the election of Messiah Jesus be understood on the same basis as we might understand the eternal Son to be generated from the Father.[52] The logicality here is a matter of speculating over whether God in his eternal life could somehow *find himself* in a given state of triunity or come to a consciousness of himself as triune as humans discover themselves – McCormack rightly contends that God is not like that. Hence to say that God 'chooses' to be triune is as much a matter of saying that he is absolutely self-determining even if there is no real *time* before and after such a decision – the triune God exists only and absolutely as he 'wills'. The difficulty is that McCormack takes this to its logical conclusion that the eternal Son 'is constituted by the anticipation of union with the humanity of Christ'.[53] Other Barth scholars think that McCormack's interpretation makes creation necessary for divine life, thereby negating divine freedom. Thus Hunsinger points to passages in Barth like the following:

> nothing would be lacking in his inward being as God in glory, as Father, Son and Holy Spirit, as the One who loves in freedom, if he did not show himself to the world, if he allowed it to complete its course to nothingness, just as nothing would be lacking to his glory if he had refrained from giving it being when he created it out of nothing.[54]

This passage (and others like it) indicates that Barth was sufficiently rigorous to ensure that his descriptions of God's triune freedom allowed for an appropriate freedom for creation and hence a genuine creaturely time in which and with which God freely and lovingly interacts.[55] God does not need creation at all, especially not for his immanent triune life. Hence creation is free to be a distinct, yet contingent, entity guided and governed by the loving grace of its creator.

Just as we do not need to be drawn into questions of Barth's understanding of Reformed history, neither do we need to get drawn into interpretations of Barth himself. When it comes to *eschatology* in either the greater Reformed tradition or Barth's revisions, Gunton observes a similar shortcoming:

> The common weakness of . . . formulations is to overweight the protological and underweight the eschatological determinants of the doctrine of election. Or rather: eschatology is so determined by protology that the end is effectively determined by the beginning, and history is, apparently, closed to the recreating work of the Spirit.[56]

The point here is that so much rests on what has been predetermined before the creation of the world that history, and our ability to give eschatology some of the complexity raised in the biblical narrative, seems to be something like 'going through the motions'.[57] More to the point, we are continually faced with the dilemma that the Bible itself reveals the essentially promissory nature of God's character in relationship to humanity – a nature that requires *time* for it to be understood and for God's sovereignty of history to be grasped.

Of course, we must affirm that in biblical terms, election is prevenient and particular – we shall explore this as we consider the mystery of God's will. The doctrine of grace demands that any person is chosen apart from his or her willing and before he or she has accepted that choice. Examples abound of God's electing particular people, including kings and prophets (Jer. 1:5). The New Testament makes explicit that such a call, especially in the case of Israel, is irrevocable: 'God did not reject his people whom he foreknew' (Rom. 11:2). However, presumably and at least logically, some creatures, humans in particular, are not included in God's intention for blessing (Deut. 7:7–8), any more than, as we shall see, the biblical portrait of the Lord Jesus *as Messiah* requires his vindication over the enemies of salvation – something of a minor key at best in Barth's theology.

From a systematic point of view, a key issue here is the relationship between time and eternity and the dynamics of eternal and historical divine action. Barth rightly identified a weakness in theologies which fail to give equal weight to the pre-temporality, supra-temporality and post-temporality of God, and these in turn fail to deal with the overall thrust of the Christian gospel.[58] Yet, as Gunton points out, the tendency towards an ahistorical eschatology is still present in Barth himself. So, the kind of eschatology that is present in Ephesians, Romans 8 – 11 or the Apocalypse disappears. In these passages we get a

> greater orientation to the destiny of this material creation as the context which is also inextricably bound up with the goal of the human; a consequently different conception of the way in which eschatology might be conceived to be realized; and, in sum, a more concrete pneumatology.[59]

So a biblically disciplined eschatology ought to entail explicit sensitivity to the material nature of the creation as the *place* in which God's promises are perfected by his Spirit – the realm of his reign. Hence an embodied human existence, transformed from the effects of sin, death and evil, ought to be expected in the new creation. I have already laid down the conditions for this possibility by upholding the physically embodied nature of Messiah Jesus' everlasting mediation of the Father in the new creation. In addition, I have established the dependency of the realized kingdom on the general resurrection in the Spirit. That is, the heavenly kingdom has not come to the earth before the resurrection of the dead. Finally, at Calvin's suggestion,[60] greater attention should be given to the historical calling of Israel *above and beyond* their being the people from whom Christ Jesus came. So, as Paul says, the descendants of Abraham 'were and are elect, and their rejection is not eternal like that of the traditional reprobate, but temporary and instrumental'.[61] Barth complained that the Reformed reading of the Israelite situation struggled to distinguish a theological description of election from the observable circumstances in which such a reading arose. Perhaps the experiential interpretation of election is the fruit of too much focus on the ultimate salvation of the individual in order to come to some conclusion on the numbers involved.[62] Gunton rightly argues, 'The proper interest served by the doctrine of election concerns not the numbers, but *the purpose* of the election of such quantities as there are.'[63] So the significance of the choice of Israel or the church is their *purpose* in the will of God before it is the fate of the individuals within them. The point of this long excursus into Barth's theology is so that we might understand better the purpose of God's choice in the history of promise. Below we shall explore *the principle of purpose* in the canonical story of election. Yet, following some of Barth's positions, we shall look back into the past of Jesus Christ in order to locate our description of eschatology in relation to God's will summed up in Messiah Jesus as his plan for creation.

The messianic purpose in the plan of the Father

As we explored the canonical significance of God's chosen leader/ Son we noted the importance of the Davidic Messiah as one taken *from* the Israelites. If the baptism of Jesus at the Jordan identifies Jesus as the Son of God through his sonship from David, then the wilderness episode can also be thought of as enriching his sonship of God through Israel. As we noted, in this episode the narrative identity of the Messiah is expanded as he assumes the sonship of Israel from God's word to them in Deuteronomy. In fact, when Jesus chose to 'live by the word of God' in the first temptation, the reference to Deuteronomy 8 implies his submission to the discipline of God as the Israelite son: 'Keep in mind that the LORD your God has been disciplining you just as a man disciplines his son' (Deut. 8:5). Israel, called 'my son' by YHWH in Exodus 4:22–23, was also led into the wilderness by the cloud and pillar of fire, which represented divine action (cf. Deut. 8:2)[64] – the cloud that was later to descend upon the tabernacle to fulfil the promise that God would dwell among his people (cf. Exod. 25:8).[65] The implication is that in recounting Jesus' temptation, Luke (note Matt. 4:1–11) is merging Israel's sonship of YHWH with the Davidic king's.[66] There is a re-constitution of Israel's sonship in the person of Messiah Jesus.[67]

Israel failed to obey YHWH during their desert sojourn, a failure that was to be repeated again and again throughout their history.[68] Barth comments, 'As [the crucified Messiah of Israel] He is the original hearer of the divine promise. As such He is the suffering inaugurator of the passing of the first human form of the community.'[69] In fact, in anticipation of the cross, in the Spirit, Jesus is empowered to succeed in his trials, preparing him to fulfil the expectations established for Israel.[70] As we noted in the previous chapter, he is the chosen kinsman redeemer who saves his people from their enemies. Yet within this narrative identity, or type, that we identified lies the kernel of the eschatological nature of election in the canonical story.

In terms of the will of God the relationship between the Messiah and Israel is that of *one for the many* because closer examination reveals that the term 'Messiah' represents a particular person in the history of God's dealing with a particular people – the nation of Israel.[71] For God to particularize Jesus as the Messiah in the power of the Spirit meant, for the early church, that the particular history of the chosen people had reached its fulfilment.[72] Yet it also implied that the God of Israel and creator of all had designated the boundaries and direction of the history of creation.[73] Messiah Jesus was the fulfilment of God's plan for all the earth. Barth's interpretation of election appears to establish this understanding on the basis of John's Gospel alone. However, if we look back further into the past we shall see a general anticipation of this kind of ministry for the Messiah throughout the Old Testament narrative.

A chosen king for Israel

That the lordship of Jesus should be constituted in relation to his people, and vice versa, is not really a *novum*, in the plan of God, to use Moltmann's phrase.[74] The connection between Jesus and Israel is prefigured in the relationship that the Davidic narratives establish between Israel and their Messiah. From a simple historical and political point of view, 'David is a point of unity for Israel as a whole.'[75] David's anointing (2 Sam. 5:1–3; 1 Chr. 11:1–3, 13–28), his victory over the Jebusites (1 Chr. 11:4) and the installation of the ark (2 Sam. 6; 1 Chr. 13; 15) each involve 'all Israel'. Going back to the royal covenant of 2 Samuel 7 we see that in verses 6–16 the fortunes of David are intertwined with the developing history of Israel, 'the promises are given to David as Israel's representative'.[76] Throughout the narrative to this point David has been the agent delivering the rest that the exodus deliverance anticipated. Hence the Davidic promise of 2 Samuel 7 also carries with it the flavour of the promises that YHWH made to Abraham in Genesis 12:1–3. According to 2 Samuel 7:9–11, YHWH will make David's name great (v. 9), provide a place for Israel (v. 10; note the description of the borders in comparison with Gen. 15:18) and will give David rest from his enemies (v. 11a) – no doubt eclipsing the rest that has already been provided (v. 1).[77] At the very least, as we have noted, the hope of the people lies in this relationship between God and the king:

> God, give Your justice to the king
> and Your righteousness to the king's son.
> He will judge Your people with righteousness
> and Your afflicted ones with justice.
> May the mountains bring prosperity to the people
> and the hills, righteousness.
> May he vindicate the afflicted among the people,
> help the poor,
> and crush the oppressor.
>
> (Ps. 72:1–4)

When YHWH delivers victory into the hands of the Messiah, the people and the land flourish. Furthermore, in so far as Psalm 110 anticipates a priestly role for the Messiah, we can see another instance in which the king of Israel embodies YHWH's expectation for Israel pronounced at Sinai: 'a kingdom of priests' (cf. Exod. 19:5–6). In short, the Messiah is the one chosen for the many and, as such, the one through whom God's intentions for his people are to be achieved.

There is, of course, an element of mystery in God's choice of David. David's entry into the greater narrative as Messiah continues a theme of God's favouring the younger over the older, as we see in 1 Samuel 16.[78] Samuel has been instructed by YHWH to go to Bethlehem and anoint Saul's successor. At a feast held to avert the king's suspicion the sons of Jesse are brought before Samuel for selection. At this point younger/older brother themes re-emerge as Samuel is drawn to the physical characteristics of the elder sons, but is told by the Lord (seven times), 'Do not look at his appearance or his stature, because I have rejected him. Man does not see what the LORD sees, for man sees what is visible, but the LORD sees the heart' (1 Sam. 16:7). While Samuel seems determined to follow the misguided trend of choosing the one 'head and shoulders taller' (cf. Saul in 1 Sam. 9:2),[79] the Lord has a characteristically different approach to the fulfilment of his will. YHWH chooses the youngest, who while good looking is also small: 'Anoint him, for he is the one' (1 Sam. 16:12), says YHWH. As Barth similarly observed:

> This is he. But why? We can only answer with the tradition: Just because he, Jesse's youngest, the little shepherd, is definitely not suitable to be the mighty king of Israel . . . just because he was so utterly incapable of doing justice to the necessary intentions of the human choice of a human king.[80]

Mention in the narrative that YHWH 'sees the heart' is popularly construed in English translations to mean that David is being chosen for his personality, of which the reader, as yet, knows nothing. In fact, if we contextualize this statement with Samuel's words to Saul in 1 Samuel 13:14, 'the LORD has sought out a man after his own heart and appointed him ruler of his people' (NIV 2011), then the anointing scene in Bethlehem contrasts two ways of choosing. Samuel, and humankind in general by association, chooses on the basis of superficial or circumstantial characteristics. In contrast YHWH chooses 'according to his own heart' – a better rendering of the Hebrew for both 13:14 and 16:7.[81] God chooses what is less impressive in the eyes of his human creatures in order to highlight the gracious character of his choice *for* his human creatures.

A chosen people for all the nations

Moving further back into the past of Jesus the Christ, the nation of Israel represents for Barth 'the people of the Jews which resists its divine election'. It is that form of the elected community that 'has to exhibit . . . the unwillingness, incapacity and unworthiness of man with respect to the love of God directed to him'.[82] A key issue for us will be whether or not there is anything prescriptive in the calling of Israel for our understanding of the Father's choice of the Messiah. Barth described the choice of community as 'the historical environment of the man Jesus Christ', or the 'special environment'.[83] The election of Israel was to provide the context from within which Messiah Jesus would emerge:

> It is *mediate*, that is, in so far as it is the middle point between the election of Jesus Christ and (included in this) the election of those who have believed, and do and will believe, in Him. It is *mediating* in so far as the relation between the election of Jesus Christ and that of all believers (and *vice versa*) is mediated and conditioned by it.[84]

In contrast to this I contest that, from the narrative perspective, it is the election of Israel that conditions the election of Messiah Jesus.

At several points in the Old Testament story we are told, 'there was a time when Israel did not exist. Israel came to exist because of the decisive, initiatory action of Yahweh'.[85] Never is any explanation given for this action beyond the will of YHWH. The most common manner in which this choice is expressed is through the language of love (e.g. Deut. 7:8; 23:5; Jer. 31:3; Isa. 43:3–4; Hos. 3:1; 11:1). At the heart of the covenant promises that YHWH makes with Israel are the words of Exodus 19:5–6. Here YHWH speaks of Israel's special distinction in relation to the rest of the nations, 'a kingdom of priests' and 'a holy nation'. At Sinai all that has been anticipated in the exodus narrative thus far has reached a point of fulfilment: 'Israel is to be transformed into a worshiping people of God enjoying the liberating power of her God.'[86] What is of special interest to us is the extent to which Israel enjoys the power of YHWH *for a purpose*.

The key term in the commissioning statement for Israel is the noun translated as his 'treasured possession'. While the majority of occurrences of this language are within a Sinai context (Deut. 7:6; 14:2; 26:18; Ps. 135:4; Mal. 3:17), two illuminating instances are not. In Ecclesiastes 2:8 and 1 Chronicles 29:3 the language used refers to the private property of the king.[87] The second reference is to the personal treasury of David that he intended to devote to the construction of the temple – the resting place of the name. Considering the importance of Israel as the bearers of the divine name, it is not hard to see a connection between YHWH's desire for Israel and their vocation in the world: 'Then all the peoples of the earth will see that you are called by Yahweh's name, and they will stand in awe of you' (Deut. 28:10; cf. Num. 6:27). *To be the treasured possession of YHWH in this circumstance is to be chosen for a particular purpose.* Hence the language of priesthood and rule that follows ought to be understood not only as a particular identity but also as a significant mediatorial relation for YHWH and with the world:[88] 'Israel has theological significance for the proper ordering and for the well-being of all of creation.'[89] Goldingay contends that 'describing Israel as a priesthood does not attribute to it a priestly role on behalf of the world or between God and the world'.[90] Yet at the same time he acknowledges the link between Exodus 19:3–8 and Genesis 12:1–3. He sees importance in the connection in terms of 'YHWH's lordship over the whole world' and thus the Sinai statement 'works towards the world's inclusion rather than its exclusion'.[91] Therefore as a holy nation Israel is to be both the people whom God promised to Abraham (Gen. 12:2) *and* the means through which the blessing to all nations (Gen. 12:3) is to come as she serves in priestly fashion – separated for and devoted to YHWH.[92] As Dumbrell notes, 'Israel's theocratic constitution is to be eventually, eschatologically, the world's constitution; the model of divine rule over Israel is to be the model of Yahweh's universal lordship.'[93] Even much later, during the exile, Isaiah (42:6 and 49:6) speaks of Israel as a 'covenant to the people' and 'light to the nations', indicating 'the well-being of the non-Jewish nations is entrusted to the life and work of Israel'.[94] Israel fulfil their purpose in the world as they keep YHWH's covenant (Isa. 49:5). The prophet is referring to the patriarchal covenant into which Israel has been incorporated ever since YHWH, in Exodus 3, revealed his name to Moses. Israel is to be for the nations what the Messiah will be for them – the one is chosen for the purpose of bringing blessing to the many.

As with the Messiah, the divine choice of Israel is revealed in mysterious circumstances. If it was not already obvious in the flow of the narrative from the beginning of Exodus, throughout the account and especially the 'forty years of wandering in the

157

wilderness', the Mosaic monologue in Deuteronomy makes explicit to Israel that there was nothing about them that warranted YHWH's choice:

> The LORD your God has chosen you to be His own possession out of all the peoples on the face of the earth. The LORD was devoted to you and chose you, not because you were more numerous than all peoples, for you were the fewest of all peoples. But because the LORD loved you and kept the oath He swore to your fathers. (Deut. 7:6–8)

Once again Israel are reminded that they are the 'treasured possession' of YHWH (cf. Exod. 19:5–6), but their status is qualified.[95] Israel are not treasured and hence chosen because of any worldly quality they might possess – here it is size. Even though they are a great multitude they are still considered the 'fewest of all peoples'. Ultimately, the gracious nature of God's intention is described in terms of love and fidelity. That is, YHWH loves Israel and wills to remain faithful to the promises that he has already made to their ancestors.[96]

It ought to be made explicit at this juncture that a key aspect of the mysterious will of God is that his choice and plan involves sinners – *God's will is mysterious because he chooses sinners in order to fulfil his promises to a humanity that is universally antagonistic to his plans for it.* For his part God ensures that the plans continue, leaving antagonistic humankind in a cursed state. As Barth notes:

> The tradition could not be clearer as to the continually operative principle of the distinguishing choice: the freedom with which this choice cuts across and contradicts all the distinctions that are humanly regulated or planned on the basis of human predilections, and the relativity of the distinctions actually made.[97]

In the exodus story we gain insight into the broader significance of YHWH's choice of Israel. To repeat Dumbrell's observation, 'Israel's theocratic constitution is to be eventually, eschatologically, the world's constitution; the model of divine rule over

Israel is to be the model of Yahweh's universal lordship.'[98] Israel's life with God will be programmatic for the rest of creation because their recalcitrance is the essence of humankind's antagonism towards God's plan.

Choosing Abraham as a blessing for all nations

So, from the perspective of the biblical story, the Father chooses one (or a few) for purposes involving the many. As we travel even further back into the past of the Messiah we see from Matthew's genealogy that the line of the Messiah is also the line of the greatest patriarch. Jesus is the son of David *and* he is the son of Abraham. If we look more closely at the context of Abraham's call, humanity has been scattered over the earth (Gen. 11:9). God calls the one man, Abram, and makes him promises regarding a place, a name, a vast progeny and the prospect of undoing the divisive scattering of Babel, as Abram is promised that 'all tribes/peoples will be blessed in/through you' (Gen. 12:3; cf. 22:18).[99] In so far as Abram is 'called' by YHWH, strictly speaking, he is summoned like a servant rather than commissioned like a prophet. Nevertheless, a servant serves his master, and, at the very least, God's desire expressed in a choice is a matter of recruitment (cf. Gen. 18:18–19).[100] *God's plan for all the nations will be put into effect through the one chosen servant* – Abraham. A prime example of Abraham's role as the mediator of blessing comes in the interchange with YHWH over Sodom (Gen. 18). Here, in the context of considering his intention to bless the world through Abraham, YHWH shares the purpose of his visit with his servant. YHWH expresses concern for justice in the light of reports about the city. Abraham, famously, enters into dialogue with YHWH over the nature and extent of this justice and what we observe is that 'he [Abraham] becomes a blessing to people by praying for them'.[101] As God's chosen one, Abraham plays a role both in discovering God's will and by taking part in the determination of that will for the earth – even in its most wretched and infamous state.

Abraham's commission is not without mystery either. The issue of progeny is one of the major themes of the patriarchal narratives,[102] especially the *difficulties* that the various families face when it comes to procreation. Being fruitful, multiplying and filling the earth has been basic to God's will for humanity since the garden (Gen. 1:28; cf. 9:1), and the Babel story finishes with humanity spreading out across the world. Here, then, is a more mysterious aspect of God's will for the patriarchs. For example, though the Lord promises Abram, 'I will make you into a great nation' (Gen. 12:2), 'I will make your offspring like the dust of the earth' (Gen. 13:16), 'Look at the sky and count the stars . . . Your offspring will be that numerous' (Gen. 15:5), Abraham and Sarah remain unable to have children (cf. Gen. 11:30). As Goldingay notes, 'God says "fill the earth" but closes the womb (Gen. 16:2).'[103] Although their trials take centre stage when it comes to God's promise of vast progeny, we also read that 'Isaac prayed to the LORD on behalf of his wife *because she was childless*' (Gen. 25:21; emphasis added). Likewise, we read, in the succeeding generation, 'When the LORD saw that Leah was unloved, He opened her womb; but *Rachel was unable to conceive*' (Gen. 29:31; emphasis added). Childlessness was considered 'an unmitigated disaster' in ancient Near Eastern times,[104] and the fact that each successive generation experiences the same challenge enables the reader to keep asking the question *How could this be God's heavenly will, given the promises he makes?*

The first clue to God's intentions for the fulfilment of the promise of progeny comes in the strange vision experience of Abram in Genesis 15. In the midst of conversation between YHWH and Abram concerning God's promise that Abraham would inherit the land, Abram is instructed to divide the carcasses of various animals into opposing halves. The exact rationale for this ritual is a matter of debate,[105] but the most prominent feature of Abram's subsequent vision is that only YHWH passes between the carcasses in his theophanic form (Gen. 15:17). In effect, what we may deduce here is that YHWH makes the covenant with himself for Abram – *God alone will be the means through which all his promises are to be fulfilled.*[106]

That the fulfilment of the promise will be a matter of divine achievement alone is confirmed in the ensuing story as the sign of circumcision is added to the covenant. Immediately following the evening theophany, we read in chapter 16 that Abram and Sarai have taken it upon themselves to solve the mystery of God's will concerning progeny through the hapless servant Hagar and her child Ishmael (Gen. 16). By way of contrast, in chapter 17 YHWH appears a third time to Abram, reiterating the progeny promise and giving him the practice of circumcision as a guarantee of the promise (17:9–14). Circumcision is to be an act of consecration on the part of Abraham and his descendants.[107] Furthermore, YHWH takes the opportunity to remind Abram that the promise will be fulfilled through Sarai, as if emphasizing that progeny according to the promise will be entirely due to the Lord's intervention. Even when Abram reoffers his earthly solution in the form of Ishmael to the seemingly unproductive and therefore mysterious heavenly will, God is resolute in the face of Abram's (possible) cynicism: 'God said, "No. Your wife Sarah will bear you a son, and you will name him Isaac. I will confirm My covenant with him as an everlasting covenant for his future offspring"' (Gen. 17:19).

The fulfilment of God's promises to Abram will be embodied in Isaac, the child of promise, even as they are engraved on Abram's body through circumcision.[108]

At this point we can appreciate something more of the mysterious nature of divine grace towards the promise recipients. Once again *the younger son is preferred over the older one*.[109] As Barth observed regarding God's grace in election:

> we might perhaps ask if Isaac was not after all chosen because of some merits of his own and Ishmael rejected because of some fault of his own. There was much to praise in the later nation Israel (and in Jacob too), and much to blame in Ishmael (and in Esau too). But whatever we may find to praise or blame, the election of the one and the rejection of the other certainly bear no relation to it.[110]

The story states quite plainly that Ishmael will share in Abram's blessing and Ishmael himself will be blessed in similar ways to Abram in terms of progeny (Gen. 17:20; cf. 16:10), yet the covenant will pass to Isaac. Simply having a lot of children is not evidence of divine blessing, or at least not the key to the fulfilment of divine will. The promise that through Abram 'all nations will be blessed', the promise that will return humankind to the plan of God, can come only through Isaac.[111] God himself will fulfil the covenant because Isaac is the child that only he can provide. The lordly intervention of YHWH will provide the fulfilment of the promise that is mysterious from an earthly perspective, but

161

an act of grace from the standpoint of God's will. In fact, to understand God's will as mysterious is to recognize that God's actions are a gracious provision in which he binds himself to his ultimate plan for his relationship to his rebellious creatures. These earthly events are God's will revealed in such a way that the promise recipient will know that only God can be their author and perfecter.

Choosing Noah and preserving the promise

Thus far we have concentrated on the pattern of God's choosing in the biblical narrative and how it forms the historical precedent for the Father's intention to consummate his will in Messiah Jesus. At the same time, we see the elements of God's will as a plan emerging in the greater narrative – the Father's intention is to spread his blessings to the nations. Of course, we already know that intrinsic to the name that is vindicated in the Lord Jesus is God's desire to be gracious and compassionate towards his recalcitrant people. As we look to the beginnings of the canonical story with Abraham, we see that this desire to be gracious and compassionate, in fact to save, is foundational to the blessings that God plans to pour out on the nations.

Going back past Abraham into the mists of biblical prehistory we arrive at the figure of Noah. Noah emerges from the godly line of Seth as one anticipated to 'bring us relief from the agonizing labor of our hands, caused by the ground the LORD has cursed' (Gen. 5:29).[112] He is the seventh in line from the first to 'call on the Name of the Lord', a line that represents YHWH's alternative path of fellowship compared to the rich and powerful line of Cain.[113] As such Noah appears to be a relatively obscure choice in YHWH's desire to *maintain* fellowship with a world that is taking all his blessings for granted and descending into depravity.[114] Noah finds 'grace' or 'favour' in God's sight (Gen. 6:8). He is not explicitly or verbally called. He appears, as Barth describes it, as an example of the 'mysterious freedom' that is 'the determination of the election of the individual in the Old Testament'.[115] Yet 'God Himself is the mystery of the elect.'[116] Hence, like Israel after him (Deut. 7:7–11), God chooses Noah and his family to be the one(s) through whom the Father's commitment to creation is maintained. Even before Israel, the *one* is preserved in keeping with the promise 'I will be your God and you shall be My people.'

162

The emphasis is entirely on YHWH's actions for 'the living' through Noah: 'Like the act of creation itself, it is an extraordinary commitment on God's part that emerges from God's own being.'[117] This personal element is recorded starkly as YHWH's reactions in the account change from regret and grief (Gen. 6:6) to pleasure (Gen. 8:21) and promise. Through the one man and his family the Lord's commitment to creation is upheld and renewed: 'despite the bad inclination of the human heart indeed because of it (Gen. 8:21) . . . God "guarantees the intactness of the cosmic cycle on earth forever"'.[118]

The context of Noah's story is quite important for determining the plan of God for the world. At a basic level Noah, one man, fits the pattern of God's choice that we have followed from the time of Messiah Jesus. However, in this case Noah more obviously serves the purpose of YHWH in *upholding his commitment to the creation*. In dialogue with Noah in both Genesis 6:17–18 and 9:8–17 mention is made of a covenant that exists between God and creation – one which will be 'caused to stand'.[119] Thus Noah as God's choice will serve as the means by which God's plan for fellowship with creation – especially all living things – will be upheld or *preserved*. The calling of Noah ensures that the divine plan for creation will be perpetuated despite the deplorable state into which it has fallen. The pattern of divine choice is that God the creator preserves the hope of the many through promises made to the one. Yet the many live in Noah's future – not his present. Noah is preserved *from* the many in his context. God acts against the forces of sin, death and evil in creation in the time of Noah, forces that take form in the attempts of creatures to thwart God's plan for the world. This is highly significant for Barth's depiction of God's will, for the Noah story makes it clear that God is quite prepared to dispense with his human creatures should the need arise: 'the LORD regretted that He had made man on the earth, and He was grieved in His heart' (Gen. 6:6). Barth goes to some length to argue that the famous dichotomies of choice – Cain and Abel, Isaac and Ishmael, Jacob and Esau – do not necessarily involve absolute rejection for some: 'Even its rejected members [of the race of Abraham] (just because of the separation which excludes them) are not forsaken, but after, as before, share in the special care and guidance of the electing God.'[120] In so far as Barth is discussing the descendants of

Abraham his argument has some merit. However, the Noah story offers the precedent for God's will to include the wholesale rejection of humankind: 'I will wipe off from the face of the earth mankind, whom I created' (Gen. 6:7). In his mysterious grace God determines to preserve humanity despite its recalcitrance, something that even the flood could not overcome (note Gen. 9:20–27). The choice of God is to preserve his plan for fellowship with humanity, a plan that begins with Christ Jesus' greatest ancestor: Adam.

Adam as the beginning of the plan

To describe Adam as *the one for the many* seems self-evident – unless like Moltmann we consider him to be a more mythical representative figure of YHWH's engagement with humankind.[121] Since we are reading the Messiah's story backwards, the role of Adam as the progenitor is important for the *kind* of beginning he represents. On the basis of Ephesians 1:10 we must consider Adam to be the beginning of that which is summed up in the Lord Jesus. In highly significant passages like Romans 5 and 1 Corinthians 15 Paul compares Adam and Messiah Jesus in terms of sin and righteousness or death and resurrection. In both instances the relationship between the two is asymmetric, not just because the achievements of Messiah Jesus far surpass the failures of Adam, but because Adam was 'a type of the one to come', as Paul uses the phrase in Romans 5:14. YHWH begins with Adam in order to set in motion a plan that will come to fruition in Messiah Jesus. Hence Adam is one through whom many are to come as humanity is 'fruitful, multiplying and filling the earth' (Gen. 1:28), but he is only the beginning of a plan that will be perfected in the holy one who reigns over all. We get a sense of Adam as the beginning of a project in the creation accounts in two distinct ways.

First, there is the concept of humankind as the image of God. Among all the living things the human being is particularized as the creature that bears God's image in the world. God makes human beings with the intention that they will mediate him to the rest of creation by 'holding sway' over the other living things (Gen. 1:26–28).[122] However, we note the element of qualification in the description of human beings as the image of God:

164

The inclusion of the phrase 'in our likeness' seems designed to exclude any notion of an exact copy, while conveying the idea of some resemblance in either nature or function. Juxtaposing the words image and likeness avoids the potentially idolatrous idea of humankind being made without qualification in the image of God.[123]

From the beginning the man and the woman are *a likeness of the image* of God because, 'in times past it was *said* that man was made in the image of God, but not *shown*, [since] the Word, in whose image man was made, was still invisible'.[124] Nevertheless, 'an image is the visible representation of something, which suggests that God's image lies in the human body. That would fit with Genesis 1's portrayal of God as speaking, looking, making, setting – and creating.'[125] In fact, the Old Testament is full of depictions of YHWH's bodily engagement with creation; hence the phenomenon of people seeing him (e.g. Exod. 24:9–11). The Christian tradition is filled with attempts to prove that these anthropomorphisms could not mean what they seem to suggest. However, if we are allowed to reread the Genesis account through the lens of Ephesians 1, a simple and ancient solution to the issue is the one offered by Irenaeus of Lyons:

> This is why St Paul calls Adam the 'type of the One who was to come' (cf. Rom. 5:14) because the Word, the maker of all things, did a preliminary sketch in Adam of what, in God's plan, was to come to the human race through the Son of God.[126]

The human being is made, from the beginning, in the likeness of the image of God because before the creation of the world God intended to be incarnate in the Lord Jesus – 'who *is* the image of God' (Col. 1:15). While Barth's attempt to reconfigure the Reformed tradition of election might be considered novel, the practice of understanding the plan of God for creation through Messiah Jesus is not.[127]

The possibilities for the human being to prefigure the Messiah expand in chapter 2 of Genesis, where their embodiment is especially important for their relationship with God and the world. Humanity is like the ground but different because, like other living things, human beings have 'the breath of life' (Gen. 2:7). Unlike other living things, though (at least in this account), human beings are commissioned to form or fashion the earth as they 'till it and watch over it' (Gen. 2:15).[128] In this way they are like God, who 'separates the waters', and so on, in chapter 1. Most importantly, and most like God, human beings speak to and about creation (Gen. 2:19–20) and their speech is likewise an image of divine action, since God 'speaks and it is so' all through chapter 1.[129] Furthermore, human beings evince both a royal and priestly aspect in their relations with the garden. The language of Genesis 1:26–28 and 2:15 reflects both the descriptions given to the Canaan conquest and the work of the Levites in the tabernacle.[130] They have both a royal and a priestly character to their life before God and in the world. This then is to be the pattern with which human beings will 'fill the earth and subdue it' (Gen. 1:28).[131] Furthermore, this priestlike rule prefigures both Israel and the Messiah who were to succeed Adam.[132]

The second way in which the Genesis account indicates the possibilities of God's plan moving forward concerns the initial extent of human influence in creation. Humans are commissioned to image God to the whole earth, yet their beginning is in a distinct space within creation, the garden where YHWH places them. Traditionally the state of creation or the world was held to be universally perfect, a point from which everything *fell*.[133] However, the descriptions of 'good' and 'very good' need not be static or equated with more Hellenistic concepts of perfection.[134] It is more appropriate to read the Genesis account as describing a creation that was 'fit for purpose', with the prospect of change and development coming from the exercise of human commission.[135] The emphasis in Genesis 1:31 ('it was very good') is on a correspondence between divine intention and the universe that is 'ready to begin'.[136] The peace within which the man and the woman live with the Lord is confined to the garden that is clearly *distinct from the rest of the earth*. There is, therefore, every reason to expect that the human being is given the role of spreading an Eden-like shalom over the rest of the land in order to fulfil the divine intention for creation. The plan of God for the earth (his will) was for his image bearers to prepare the world for his coming at the appropriate time. Again Irenaeus suggests the scope of the divine plan:

> God has the power to give man perfection from the
> beginning, but man was incapable of receiving it,
> because he was an infant . . . It was for this reason that
> the Word of God, though perfect, became a child in
> solidarity with mankind. He did not do this for His own
> sake but because of the state of childhood in which man
> then existed. He wanted to be received in a way that
> suited man's capacity to receive.[137]

Irenaeus argued, against the Gnostics, that the God who made
the heavens and the earth was perfectly capable of creating
perfectly.[138] Nevertheless, through the lens of Ephesians 1 with its
testimony to Messiah Jesus, the universe was made and set on a
trajectory towards his coming. Human beings were made in his
likeness in anticipation of this coming and the work given to
them was preparatory towards that end. From this perspective
time and history are an integral aspect of God's will for the earth
as the record of God's lordly dealings with his creatures in order
to bring his plans to perfection in Messiah Jesus. Creation is not
necessary for the triune life of God, but neither is its existence
arbitrary.[139] It is part of the Father's intention to glorify his
incarnate Son in the Spirit.

A further advantage of understanding the plan of God in this
fashion relates to the comment that God's commitment to
creation is grounded on his own being. We may agree with Barth
that the covenant revealed to Noah (Gen. 9:14) represents a self-
committal 'characterised (no matter what time-concepts may be
presupposed) as a relationship which is not haphazard and
transitory, but which derives its necessity from God Himself'.[140]
When we understand the plan of God for creation in terms of the
relationship between the Father and his royal and eternal Son we
have a concrete focus for the Father's heavenly will in creation, for
creatureliness. It is a tenacious adherence to a creation that exists
for his beloved Son, in whom he delights – his namesake. The
Father wills to be gracious and compassionate towards this
creation for the sake of his Son, and therefore he steadfastly
resolves to preserve creatures made in the likeness of his Son in
the power of his Spirit over whom his Messiah will reign. The
Father steadfastly returns the antagonistic creation to his plan
throughout the greater narrative by invoking a principle for the

purpose in the form of electing one/few for the sake of the many. It belongs to the crucified Messiah to reveal the depths of that steadfastness, though it is previewed in the long story of YHWH's indomitable plan.

Our Father, your will be done

On earth

Thus far in this chapter we have explored the idea that the Father's heavenly will in the history created by his promises is perfected in the glorification of Jesus the Christ as the Lord of all creation. Guided by the third petition of the Lord's Prayer and reading the Bible through the lens of Ephesians 1 I have argued that God's will is revealed in his plans to bring blessing to the many through his choice of the one/few. This choice was frequently mysterious in its execution, but it was ultimately perfected in the risen Jesus of Nazareth as the Messiah. Of course, the lordship of Jesus was not simply the last of God's choices. On the contrary the Father's choice *in, through and for* his royal and eternal Son is the pre-eminent reason for creation and the goal to which the Spirit perfects all things. It would be a mistake, however, to assume that this reading of the biblical narrative was not explicitly informed by the ministry of Christ Jesus himself. Hence, as this chapter nears completion, we should attend, albeit briefly, to the gospel's portrait of Messiah Jesus as the chief interpreter of God's will for the earth while he was on the earth.

Christ Jesus as the interpreter of the Father's will

We have identified a number of ways in which the coming of the kingdom of God through Messiah Jesus was different from what was expected. The salvation this king would bring for his kinsmen was 'from their sins' in the first instance – not from Gentile overlords. Second, the enemy against whom the Messiah would battle was the ancient enemy of the sons of Adam: Satan and his minions. The chief of these in the Gospel narratives turns out to be neither the unclean spirits nor the Romans, but the leaders of the chosen people.[141] Considering that the nature of God's presence in and with Jesus was a mystery, it is not surprising, perhaps, that YHWH's salvation through Jesus the son of David

168

is counter-intuitive. For this reason and explicitly in the case of God's rule over the earth, Jesus as the spiritually empowered Messiah acts as the chief *interpreter* of God's will. His subsequent ministry is characterized by *word* and deed for the sake of teaching the promise recipients what it means for God's will to be perfected on the earth through Jesus.

In the previous chapter we noted that the triumphant Messiah emerges from the wilderness in his hometown to speak in the local synagogue in the power of the Spirit (Matt. 13:54; Mark 6:1; Luke 4:16). Among other things this incident marks the inauguration of Jesus' ministry as a prophet, if for no other reason than in the ensuing conflict with his brethren Jesus refers to himself as such (Matt. 13:57; Mark 6:4; Luke 4:24). Jesus goes further than others (e.g. John the Baptizer) by teaching itinerantly, extensively and with greater urgency and with frequent signs of supernatural endorsement by way of miracles. In the words of Luke 24:19, 'he was a prophet mighty in word and deed'. As the prophetic ministry of the Messiah progresses, Jesus' exposition of the will of God focuses on the intervention of the kingdom of God. In the previous chapter we established that Jesus of Nazareth is the long-promised messianic son of David and Servant of YHWH who is empowered by God's Spirit to mediate the heavenly reign of God to the earth. However, the dynamics of this campaign are counter-intuitive at a number of levels, and hence Jesus interprets the kingdom as 'mysterious or secret' (Matt. 13:11; Mark 4:11; Luke 8:10). There is one passing reference to the desire of the people to 'make Jesus king by force' (John 6:15) apart from this: 'That there should be a coming of God's kingdom in the way Jesus proclaimed, in a hidden, secret form, working quietly among men, was utterly novel to Jesus' contemporaries.'[142] A significant characteristic of Jesus' interpretation of the kingdom comes in the form of parables. These stories, drawing as they do on everyday life experiences, 'do not merely talk about the divine offer of mercy; they both make the offer, and defend Jesus' right to make it'.[143] Messiah Jesus not only tells stories that explain the nature of the kingdom of God, but in telling them Jesus is mediating God's reign and thus bringing in the kingdom and fulfilling the Father's will for salvation:[144] 'The kingdom is characterised by what happens in the story.'[145] The chief reason for this is the frequency with which Christ Jesus is not just the storyteller but also *a central character* in the particular kingdom vignette.

An additional and distinctive characteristic of Jesus' interpretive mission is the way he refers to himself by using the mysterious 'Son of Man' title. While there is some history behind this title, recent biblical scholarship has come to focus on Daniel 7 as the Old Testament background to it.[146] Of particular interest to us is the fact that Jesus favours this term for himself, especially as he approaches Jerusalem and articulates his imminent death there in terms of the will of God. As Barth observed, 'The [apocalyptic] discourse of Mark 13 is a repetition of the three prophecies of the passion and resurrection of Jesus elevated to a cosmic scale.'[147] In the apocalyptic language of Daniel 7 the seer represents the crisis for Israel as she suffers oppression at the hands of various empires before, during and after the exile (Dan. 7:1–11).[148] In this passage YHWH vindicates the Son of Man figure who represents humanity and is given the role of Adam/Israel – 'dominion' over the earth in the form of authority to pronounce the judgment of God (Dan. 7:12–14).[149] We have already examined in various ways the theological significance of the relationship between Jesus as Messiah and the temple in the Gospel narratives. It is within this context that we ought to approach the apocalyptic element in Jesus' Olivet discourse just prior to the triumphal entry. Recorded variously in Matthew 24, Mark 13 and Luke 21, Jesus uses 'apocalyptic metaphor and symbol to evoke the full resonances of Old Testament prophecy and to invest the coming events with their full theological significance'.[150]

The details of Jesus' pronouncements are hotly contested among New Testament commentators and millennial theologians.[151] However, these analyses persistently overlook the way that the Gospel writers interweave the respective fates of the Messiah and the temple. As Bolt notes, 'Jesus alerts his disciples to watch out for something that will be destructive and sacrilegious.'[152] From early on in the Gospel accounts (at least in John) the destruction of the temple is bound up with the person of Jesus.[153] In addition and as noted in the previous chapter, Jesus will arrive in the temple in a matter of days to the acclamation of the crowd as Messiah, while in the shadows the sons of Satan will plot his destruction. In the week that follows, Jesus as Messiah will play the role of executing the will of God, first by cleansing the temple and then by denouncing the Jerusalem establishment for their idolatrous behaviour towards the temple. They respond at his trial by continually referring to Jesus' remarks about the temple and its destruction, while Jesus depicts himself as 'the Son of Man' destined for 'the right hand of power with the clouds of heaven'. The issue of sacrilege concerning the temple and Jesus' claims about himself pervades the entire scene. Subsequently, Jesus is executed as the King of the Jews, crowned with thorns and enthroned on a cross while the temple is decommissioned, or even desecrated (Matt. 27:51; Mark 15:38; Luke 23:45), since the glory of the Lord has departed the city for the hill of Golgotha.

Thus in terms of Jesus' apocalyptic interpretation of his death as the Son of Man (Matt. 24; Mark 13), 'could there be a greater act of sacrilege than the destruction of God's Son in such a horrendous way?'[154] What greater *abomination* could there be than for God's plan to include the people of promise (the 'treasured possession') banding together with the pagans to execute as a mere 'insurrectionist' (Acts 4:25–28) the one to whom the royal covenant belongs? What greater *tribulation* (Matt. 24:29) could there be for the chosen 'beloved Son' than to 'drink the cup' of God's wrath (Matt. 26:39; Mark 14:36; Luke 22:42)? What deeper mystery could there be in the will of the Father than that the Messiah of God, empowered by his Spirit (cf. Heb. 9:14), should utter such a cry of *desolation* (Matt. 27:46; Mark 15:34)? All this takes place while *the sun is darkened*, the *moon sheds no light* and the earth *shakes* (Matt. 27:45, 51; Mark 15:33; Luke 23:44) and 'the Lamb of God' (John 1:29) endures his last Passover. As Barth surmised, 'God . . . really [is] the hidden God and [is] manifest in this very hiddenness, where God himself has hidden himself, in the way He was hidden here'.[155] In the Olivet discourse Jesus foreshadows the mystery of God's will, the Father's heavenly will for the Messiah's death, in the only mode appropriate for circumstances that should otherwise obliterate the promises that Jesus seeks to fulfil. For surely at Golgotha, the disciples of Jesus must have been compelled to ask, 'How could this be God's heavenly will for the earth?' (Luke 24:21).

The church in the plan of God

In keeping with Daniel's vision that Jesus invoked on the Mount of Olives, the Son of Man is vindicated when raised to the right

171

hand of God, as the Pentecost testimony reveals. More than this, the kinsman redeemer suffered the ultimate antagonism of the sons of Adam and in God's plan, to save them (Acts 2:23). Hence as the prophet foretold:

> He Himself bore our sicknesses,
> and He carried our pains;
> but we in turn regarded Him stricken,
> *struck down by God*, and afflicted.
> But He was pierced because of our transgressions,
> crushed because of our iniquities;
> punishment for our peace was on Him,
> and we are healed by His wounds . . .
> Yet the LORD was pleased to crush Him severely.
>
> (Isa. 53:4–5, 10; emphasis added)

This reading of the messianic crisis becomes basic to the church's testimony from the very beginning as seen in the interactions between Philip and the Ethiopian Eunuch: 'beginning from *these writings* [Philip] proclaimed to him the good news of Jesus' (Acts 8:31–35).

We have already established that the ascended Messiah mediates the reign of the Father to the earth in the power of his Spirit. In one of his final interpretive acts of the Father's will Christ Jesus indicated as much to his disciples as they gathered for the last Passover meal together. At that time Jesus spoke of the Spirit's convicting the world 'about sin, righteousness and judgment'. The consequence of this activity will be that the general notion of sin according to the Law will be superseded by antagonism towards Christ Jesus: 'they do not believe in me' (John 16:9). In complementary terms the concept of righteousness is now bound up in the relationship between the Father and the Son.[156] Finally, the judgment of God has fallen on 'the father of lies' (John 8:44) or 'the ruler of this world' (John 16:11), as death is defeated along with the 'strong man' who wields its power, first against the royal Son and consequently the sons of Adam (cf. Heb. 2:14).

Subsequently, a primary aspect of the risen Messiah's reign during life in the Middle is the time when his Spirit will speak generally through members of the community and at the same time distinguish a new community of promise. Both Jeremiah and Isaiah heralded the advent of a new covenant to be established between YHWH and his new people.[157] The Spirit is the agent in whom God gives himself through his Messiah to his new people in order to empower this community to 'call upon the name of the Lord', Jesus. At the same time, and having received salvation in that name, the church reveals the mystery of the Father's will for his Son and the scope of the salvation that the Father achieves through him.

As we have noted, recognizing the agency of the Spirit in constituting the church avoids certain problems involved when the church claims, 'God is with us.' One of these problems was that too much attention was being given to the divine nature of Christ at the expense of his humanity. Gunton identified this problem with Barth's doctrine of election in so far as it is difficult not to read the latter as claiming that all humanity is ultimately the church of Christ.[158] In addition, and in terms of God's choice, Gunton was keen to remind us that in discussions of eschatology both initiation and *continuance* of faith are a gift from God. In the more protologically focused discussions of God's choice Gunton notes a movement away from 'grace mediated communally'; that is, away from church as communion (that spatial sense of life in the Middle[159]) towards an individual, inward experience of grace, on the one hand, and, on the other, a movement away from the eschatological enabling of humans by the Spirit towards a 'conception of grace as a semisubstantial force either assisting or determining human perseverance causally'.[160] What is lost here is the sense in which 'the Lord who is the Spirit' personally mediates the will of God in the economy of salvation (2 Cor. 3:17–18). In line with what we have been exploring, Gunton suggests, against Barth, that we ought to understand the Spirit as the electing God. For it is the Spirit who 'gathers the Church to the Father through Christ and in order that his will be done on earth'.[161] In this way we might distinguish the Spirit's creating work, which is universal, from the Spirit's perfecting work, which though it achieves a universal end as all things being summed up in Christ Jesus (Eph. 1:9–10), is achieved through the particulars of the election of Israel and the resurrection of Christ Jesus from the dead. Calvin draws out this distinction in his commentary on Romans 8:14:

But it is right to observe, that the working of the Spirit is various: for there is that which is universal, by which all creatures are sustained and preserved; there is that also which is peculiar to men, and varying in its character: but what Paul means here is sanctification, with which the Lord favours none but his own elect, and by which he separates them for sons to himself.[162]

At the risk of contradicting Calvin, what we have observed in the plan of God is that, in eschatological terms, 'the elect are not *primarily* those chosen for a unique destiny out from the whole, but are chosen out of the whole as the community with whom the destiny of the whole is in some way bound up'.[163] This position is reflected in the New Testament application of Israel as God's possession, language taken from Exodus 19:5 and Deuteronomy 7:6 and applied to the church:

But you are a chosen race, a royal priesthood, a holy nation, a people for His possession, so that you may proclaim the praises of the one who called you out of darkness into His marvellous light. Once you were not a people, but now you are God's people; you had not received mercy, but now you have received mercy. (1 Peter 2:9–10)[164]

The Spirit constitutes the church for proclamation both passively and actively in obedience to the messianic commission (Matt. 28:18–20; cf. Acts 1:8). This divine achievement is revealed in the human activity of gospel testimony.

Furthermore, in the Ephesian letter Paul adds that, from a Jewish perspective, the 'mystery of the Father's will' is the fact that the blessings of salvation are made available to the Gentiles. They too are 'co-inheritors, co-body-members and having a share in the promises of Messiah Jesus through the gospel' (cf. 2:11–22, the reference to Christ as 'one new man').[165] Those who were 'strangers to the covenants of promise' (2:12) have been granted 'access to the Father (through the Messiah) in the one Spirit' (2:18). From the standpoint of the plan of God that we examined above, what is revealed in the Father's messianic achievement is consistent with his actions throughout the history of promise

– that the promises were for the many through a chosen one. However, apart from the possible scope of God's plan being mysterious, there is also the mysterious manner in which the plan is managed (*hē oikonomia*): 'so that through the church, the extraordinarily varied wisdom of God might now be known by the heavenly rulers and authorities' (3:10).

The Spirit-constituted church reveals the counter-intuitive nature of the Father's wisdom because it is the spiritual body of the crucified Messiah who is, in the Spirit, both 'the power of God and the wisdom of God' (1 Cor. 1:24). So as Christ Jesus is present in the church by the Spirit, the mysterious nature of the Father's will is made accessible even to non-terrestrial creatures: 'the preaching of the gospel exhibits the manifold grace of God, with which, till now, the heavenly angels themselves were unacquainted'.[166] The appearance of the church in the Father's will is a further testimony to the Father's mysterious government of history because the story of God's designs is that he

> chose the foolish things of the world to shame the wise; God chose the weak things of the world to shame the strong. God chose the lowly things of this world and the despised things – and the things that are not – to nullify the things that are. (1 Cor. 1:27–28)

As the Father's testament to the coming kingdom of the Messiah, the life of the church should be governed by the character of her Lord and Saviour. In terms of the larger issues in Barth's discussion of election however, namely the ultimate scope of salvation for humanity through Christ, we shall defer a decision until we consider the eschatological nature of God's forgiveness. In the meantime, we must, briefly, consider that part of God's will for the earth that was never addressed by Barth is the ultimate revelation of his heavenly will at the final judgment.

As it is in heaven

Jesus as the executor of the Father's will

During his earthly ministry Jesus, as the Spirit-anointed messianic prophet, reveals the will of God as an 'immanent' (*engys*) kingdom (cf. Matt. 3:2; Mark 1:15; Luke 10:9). The immanence of this kingdom is directly proportional to the scope of Jesus' own ministry; that is, Jesus is not simply the interpreter of the Father's will *but also the executor*. Unlike his predecessors, Jesus as prophetic Messiah not only spoke of the will of God, but 'His authority [also] consisted in the power to accomplish what he proclaimed.'[167] *In the person of Messiah Jesus the divine achievement* is *a human activity* – as Isaiah and Ezekiel foresaw (cf. Isa. 7; Ezek. 34). Divine and creaturely life have come together in such a way that the coming of God or the right ordering of creation could take place as Barth described it.

As we explored the Old Testament *past* of Jesus as the son of David we observed that kingship grew out of the prior reign of judges in Israel. From here judgment and carrying out God's judgment is a key theme in the description of the king of God's kingdom (cf. 1 Kgs 3:16ff.). The Messiah is renowned for his ability to bring wise judgments. According to Isaiah 11 this is because he has been anointed with God's Spirit:

> The Spirit of the LORD will rest on Him . . .
> His delight will be in the fear of the LORD.
> He will not judge
> by what He sees with His eyes,
> He will not execute justice
> by what He hears with His ears,
> but He will judge the poor righteously
> and execute justice for the oppressed of the land.
>
> (Isa. 11:2–4)

Here we see that God will empower his king to judge and bring justice upon the earth, especially for his oppressed people. Judgment is the rectification of moral order, the bringing about of justice, and, in terms of the kingdom of God, the issues of justice repeatedly come down to an attitude towards God's king. So in Psalm 2:

> So now, kings, be wise;
> receive instruction, you judges of the earth.
> Serve the LORD with reverential awe
> and rejoice with trembling.

176

> Pay homage to the Son or He will be angry
> and you will perish in your rebellion,
> for His anger may ignite at any moment.
> All those who take refuge in Him are happy.
>
> (Ps. 2:10–12)

In the Gospel accounts, and in John's Gospel in particular, Jesus speaks of himself as mediator through whom the judgment of God will come in a fashion highly allusive to the apocalyptic scenes of Daniel 7:10–14.[168] Thus 'the Father . . . has given all judgment to the Son' and this as the expected vindication of the Son mentioned above in chapter 3, 'so that all people will honour the Son just as they honour the Father' (John 5:21). The right of judgment, we are told, belongs to Jesus because 'he is the Son of Man', and, furthermore, 'the time is coming when all who are in the graves will hear his voice and come out – those who have done good things, to the resurrection of life, but those who have done evil things, to the resurrection of judgment' (John 5:29; cf. Dan. 12:2). The scenario of the risen Christ's presiding over a final judgment was a consistent, though not especially prominent, element of apostolic testimony (Acts 10:42; 17:31; cf. 1 Peter 4:5; 2 Tim. 4:1). Thus the perfection of the heavenly will of the Father for the earth will occur when his Messiah executes his will, bringing peace and prosecuting justice upon the antagonistic humanity in general and the recalcitrant recipients of his promises in particular. Modern commentators, like Moltmann, who laud the sympathy of Jesus the Christ for the godless and godforsaken must also recognize the divine right of judgment for Jesus the Lord in calling sinners to repent. What remains now is to consider the basis upon which such a verdict is passed.

Vindicating the Son: blessing and curse

Since the time of entry into the land of promise, the judgment of YHWH upon the recipients of the promise was delineated in terms of blessing and cursing (Deut. 27 – 30). With the fulfilment of the Law through the ministry of Christ Jesus the new covenant revolves entirely around fealty to the Father's chosen king: 'whoever believes in the Son has life, whoever does not believe in the Son will not have life' (John 3:36). Hence, in keeping with the Father's plan to glorify himself by the vindication of his royal Son

177

(John 1) and the economic resolution of the immanent relationship between Father and eternal Son (John 2), the revelation of the Father's perfected will for the earth will be 'summed up' (Eph. 1:9–10) as the glorified Messiah is worshipped as Lord (Phil. 2:11).

We have already aligned the perfected arrival of the kingdom of God on the earth with the return of the king and the resurrection of the dead. At this point the words of the prophet Zechariah, incorporated into John's passion account, will achieve their perfect significance: 'they will look on . . . the one they have pierced' (Zech. 12:10 TNIV; cf. John 19:37). John's subsequent vision of the 'heavenly session' in Revelation 5 has the vast throng gathered before the 'one standing as a lamb who had been slain' (5:6). As I have consistently maintained, the risen Jesus will be vindicated everlastingly as the *crucified* kinsman redeemer. More particularly, in discussing the kingdom we noted, over and against Moltmann, concerning the importance of resurrection in determining the significance of Jesus' paschal sacrifice, that it is essential to the Father's vindication of his Messiah that the crucified Jesus be recognized as the ascended Christ of God. Hence I drew attention to the abiding theological significance of the death scars of the risen Christ. There I commented that the continued reference to them in both the Gospel accounts and the Revelation held greater importance than merely acting as a phenomenal indicator – that the same Jesus who died was now alive. Rather, I argued that the death scars indicate the messianic victory over sin *as well as death* and this victory is similarly preserved as part of his victorious kingship. At that point, my argument with Moltmann sought to establish the theological necessity of an ongoing paschal mediation of the risen Christ before the Father for those baptized into Jesus' name.

In the context of a final judgment and with the prospect of the Father's vindicating his triumphant Son against his enemies, the death scars take on an additional layer of theological significance. In contending with Moltmann I mentioned the incredulity of Calvin towards the prospect of the returning Christ being identified as the crucified saviour.[169] Yet, as I argued, the risen Messiah remains 'the crucified one' even in John's apocalyptic vision in Revelation 5. Hence it seems reasonable to infer that the anticipated Messiah of Psalm 110, who awaits the subjugation of

178

his enemies, is the same crucified king – it is in this manner that he serves as 'a priest forever in the order of Melchizedek' (Heb. 5:6–10; 7:17).[170] Thus the refrain of the vast multitude gathered before the Lamb consists of 'You were slaughtered, and you redeemed for God by your blood . . . a kingdom and priests to our God' (Rev. 5:9–10). What the church anticipates for this final judgment is the promise that through the crucified and now glorified Christ the blessing of redemption for God's service will be mediated and perfected everlastingly for those elected in the Spirit of sonship (cf. Rom. 8:14–16). Since 'the holy one and the ones made holy all have the one Father' (Heb. 2:11), the passion of those baptized into the name of the Messiah rests on their incorporation into his worship, according to Psalm 22:22:

> I will proclaim Your name to my brothers [and sisters];
> I will praise You in the congregation.
>
> (Ps. 22:22; cf. Heb. 2:12)

The perfection of the Father's plan to celebrate his beloved Son is the congregation (the many) constituted everlastingly in the power of his Spirit for the acclamation of the Messiah's paschal sacrifice.

At the same time, since the Father mediates blessing through the person of the glorified Christ as an everlasting act of vindication of the latter, we must hold that the Father will likewise everlastingly mediate his curse against those who blaspheme the Holy Spirit by refusing the gracious activity of the Son for them.[171] Paul indicates as much when assuring the Thessalonian Christians that Christ will vindicate them against their oppressors, 'imposing vengeance upon those who do not know God and do not listen to the gospel of our Lord Jesus' (2 Thess. 1:8). Similarly, the writer to the Hebrews promises severe punishment for those who 'trampled the Son of God and profaned the blood of the covenant . . . and insulted the Spirit of grace' (Heb. 10:29). More floridly, John's Apocalypse foresees wrath 'in the sight of the Lamb' (Rev. 14:10) for those who have given allegiance to minions of the evil one. From this perspective, the death scars of the glorified Messiah become, for the sons of Satan, the everlasting medium for the wrath of God towards their antagonism, their envy and their collusion in the schemes of 'their father'.

179

My broad-brush portrait of the fatherhood of God on the earth as it is in heaven is now complete. We have explored the hallowing of his name, the coming of his kingdom and the perfection of his will. In this way, we have addressed the *what*, *how* and *why* of eschatology through the Son and in the Spirit. What remains is for us to clarify this theological vision for the sake of a meaningful account of a way of life in the Middle. We shall pursue this through the second batch of three petitions of the Lord's prayer calling on our heavenly Father to preserve, forgive and deliver us.

6

GOOD LORD, PRESERVE US

Thus far we have been working on the premise that the balance between individual and universal eschatology can only be found in a theological exposition of the topic.[1] Following the advice of Volf, we have pursued an exposition of eschatology that seeks not only 'a plausible intellectual vision but more importantly, a compelling account of a way of life'.[2] Consequently, in the opening chapters of this book we cast our vision in terms of praying for the fatherhood of God to be perfected on earth as it is in heaven. We established that the Christian hope stands on God's promise to authenticate his saving presence in Jesus the Christ. We looked forward to a future in which Christ Jesus will be universally acclaimed as the Lord, and in his name we baptize people for the forgiveness of sins as his Spirit constitutes his church. The risen Jesus is the ruler through whom and in the power of whose Spirit the church proclaims the coming kingdom of God. We remember his victory over sin, death and evil each time we celebrate the Lord's Supper. In the power of God's Spirit Christians are directed towards this perfection of the Father's plan for all of creation as we wait for the return of the king, the resurrection of the dead and the final judgment. In effect, I have marked out the broadest possible context in which to place life in the Middle. Now I shall make more explicit what Volf has called 'the compelling account of a way of life' by expounding the final three petitions of the Lord's Prayer.

Our aim now is to fill in the contours of life in the Middle or, to quote Calvin, 'come down to ourselves, and connect with those former petitions, which look to God alone, solicitude about our own salvation'.[3] We shall reflect on what we know, on what we must do and for what we can hope. As we do this, we shall continue to converse with Barth and Moltmann in the areas where their contribution to modern eschatology has been most significant.

Preserved by the word of promise

There is some debate as to exactly what it is that the Lord Jesus exhorts us to ask for when we cry, 'Father, give us today our daily [*ton epiousion*] bread' (Matt. 6:11; Luke 11:3). *From an eschatological point of view I shall argue that the Lord is exhorting us to look to him to preserve us throughout life in the Middle and into the new creation.* Nevertheless, it certainly bothered Calvin to think that Messiah Jesus had put our bodies before our souls in our requests:

> Though the forgiveness of sins is to be preferred to food, as far as the soul is more valuable than the body, yet our Lord commenced with bread and the supports of an earthly life, that from such a beginning he might carry us higher. We do not ask that our daily bread may be given to us before we ask that we may be reconciled to God, as if the perishing food of the belly were to be considered more valuable than the eternal salvation of the soul: but we do so that we may ascend, as it were by steps, from earth to heaven.[4]

Calvin appears to adopt a kind of retrieval ethic whereby we pray for relief from hunger in order that we might better understand the need for relief from condemnation of the soul. In eschatological terms Calvin's response reflects a rather unfortunate tendency to separate soul and body in the plans of God. This was nothing new. Earlier church fathers shared Calvin's discomfort and also preferred a spiritual interpretation of the Lord's exhortation: 'we are asking that we should perpetually be in Christ and that we should not be separated from his body'.[5] Gregory of Nyssa understood the exhortation as guidance on how to ensure that everyday life remained open to spiritual pursuits: 'we are commanded to ask for our daily bread . . . [because] the nature that is temperate and content with little according to the idea of *apatheia* should be made equal to the nature that has no material needs at all [like angels]'.[6] Gregory's asceticism comes to the fore here and stands in contrast to the pragmatism of Calvin. Augustine for his part struggled to reconcile the exhortation to pray for 'all that is necessary to sustain this life' with the instruction 'Do not worry about tomorrow' (Matt. 6:34). Surely we must have a concern for that for which we pray? But Gregory's spiritual interpretation of the petition suggests the opposite.[7]

In relatively recent times Brown gave the traditional 'spiritual sense' a more appropriately eschatological focus by suggesting that *ton epiousion* refers to 'the bread for the coming day, for the future'.[8] From this perspective Jesus encourages us to pray for 'God's final intervention and for that bread which would be given at the heavenly table'.[9] The petition is to be given a place at the Father's table in the new creation. Brown finds this interpretation embedded in YHWH's promise to Israel in Exodus 16:4, 'I am going to rain bread from heaven for you. The people are to go out each day and gather enough for that day'. The promise is repeated in Psalm 78:24 but, most importantly, is taken up by Jesus in John 6, where Jesus refers to himself as the 'Bread of Life'.[10] The connection with Christ as the Bread of Life has, from at least Augustine's time on, led many (including Brown) to assume that the Lord's Supper is somehow the answer to the prayer. Hence Augustine queried, 'was it said of the Sacrament of Christ's Body which we receive daily?'[11] The bishop decides that the Lord's injunction ought not to be confused with local practices since one would be unable to pray the Lord's Prayer after celebrating the Lord's Supper: 'we should no longer be able to say *Give us this day* with regard to something we have already received!'[12]

To see the Lord's Supper as an eschatological practice is certainly in keeping with what Paul tells the church in Corinth (1 Cor. 11:26) and, as I pointed out in chapter 4, this plays an important role in distinguishing the church from the coming

183

kingdom of God. In addition, we would hardly want to stray from the promise that life in the Spirit comes through trust in the body of Jesus given for the world (John 6:51). Furthermore, it is only appropriate to long for a place at the wedding feast of the Lamb – granted that we do expect that to be on the new earth! (Rev. 19:9). However, it is not self-evident that the Lord had these specific things in mind when he encouraged us to pray for 'our daily bread'. From a purely linguistic point of view it is equally valid to suggest that Jesus was encouraging us to call on God to sustain us each day, as in the words of Psalm 104:27–28:

> All of them [Your creatures] wait for You
> to give them their food at the right time.
> When You give it to them,
> they gather it;
> when You open Your hand,
> they are satisfied with good things.

Still, and particularly given what we have established concerning God's will for creation, any request for sustenance from God must be made with an ear to the future perfected in the glorified Christ. Augustine also points us towards an important truth when he says that the 'daily bread' we are to ask for is 'the divine precepts which we are to think over and put into practice each day'.[13] The source or foundation for sustaining life in the Middle is the promises of God – *this is what we know*. We have already observed a strong scriptural precedent for seeing a reference to bread from the Lord as being symbolic of his sustaining us by his word – *this is what the Messiah himself did* (Matt. 4; Luke 4). *To clarify our hope* I shall begin with John 6, as Brown suggested, but we shall see that there is much more than a suggestion of the church's commemorative practices. We shall refine our passion for the possibilities of God's perfecting work by focusing on his promise to raise the dead in a manner fit to worship Jesus as Lord and to vindicate his victory over death. We have already seen the importance of resurrection for Moltmann, particularly in the first chapter when we explored the significance for the concept of promise in establishing a Christian eschatology. In the last chapter, where we explored the will of God in and for Christ Jesus, we engaged in an extended dialogue with Barth, particularly with what some critics referred to as his reduction of Christ to a principle of election.[14] In this chapter we shall see that Moltmann's future-oriented eschatology tends to reduce Christ to a resurrection principle that ultimately displaces Christ as the focus of divine will.

Preserved by the resurrected one

The Gospel accounts anticipate that the Messiah will be the Lord of the resurrection. In John 6 the question of how God the Father preserves human life runs through the narrative with a mixture of material and spiritual alternatives being examined along the way. Ultimately, though, the fundamental scenario in which preservation is required (throughout the passage) is in the face of death. At the same time, the ultimate preservation of life in the face of death is promised in the person and work of the Lord Jesus. Considering what we have seen of the kinsman redeemer's commission to save God's people from their enemy, death, we ought not to be surprised.

In John 6:25 we read that within 24 hours of the miraculous feeding of the crowds we find the Lord Jesus in dispute with the Jews over how they might 'do the works of God' and so 'gain eternal life' (John 6:25ff.). On the one hand, Jesus chastises them for fixating on the merely material:

> I tell you truly, you are seeking me not because you saw a sign but because you ate the loaves and were filled. Do not work for the food that perishes but the food that remains for life eternal, which the Son of Man will give you, for God the Father has sealed Him. (John 6:26–27)

The Jews' practice of looking to God to deliver basic sustenance (their daily bread) is by no means a fault, considering the words of the psalmist mentioned above (cf. Ps. 104:27). Nevertheless, it is the superficial nature of such provision to which Jesus objects since, by the Father's mandate, the Son of Man has far more durable sustenance to offer. On the other hand, the crowds do seem prepared to consider a spiritual source of food from God, albeit over and against what Jesus offers: 'What sign are you going to do so that we might see and believe in you? . . . Our fathers ate

185

manna in the wilderness; as it is written, "He gave them bread from heaven to eat"' (John 6:30–31; cf. Exod. 16:4–5; Ps. 78:24). The crowds test Jesus' authority with appeals to their heritage but their claim is countered by Jesus' sharp challenge 'Your fathers ate the manna in the wilderness and they died' (6:49). The only means of preservation beyond death, according to Jesus, is 'the true bread from heaven' (6:32), which is the flesh of Jesus himself, given for the world (6:51). Furthermore, Jesus claims a particular authority in the face of death for those who partake of *the* 'bread from heaven', namely 'I will raise him up on the last day' (John 6:39–40, 44, 54; cf. 5:28–29). The Lord Jesus promises repeatedly in this discourse to 'raise up' his followers with the added assurance that he gives his body and blood to secure this end (v. 54). It is through his paschal sacrifice that Jesus becomes their 'Bread of Life' and in this way their petition to the Father to be preserved takes on an everlasting character in its fulfilment. The significance of this promise deepens later on when Jesus confronts the Jews over their aspirations for this 'last day'.

We need only to move on in John's Gospel to the events of chapter 11 and the dialogue between Jesus and Martha over the question of 'the last day'. Here we find an explicit connection between Jewish expectations of a general resurrection of the dead (John 11:24) and the ministry of Jesus the Christ. Jesus' absolute statement of identification with this eschatological event indicates more than a 'You have heard it said, but I say' rhetorical move such as we might associate with Matthew's account of the Sermon on the Mount.[15] In keeping with the style of the other *egō eimi* statements in the Fourth Gospel, Jesus is again deconstructing contemporary Jewish theology, in this case of the general resurrection.[16] Jesus has already indicated in both John 5 and 6 that he is the one who will 'raise up the dead' on the last day, and now in John 11 he proclaims himself to be both the source of life for that resurrection and the manner of creaturely life before God in that resurrection. In so doing, Jesus eclipses Israelite expectations of life in the face of death and deconstructs his audience's aspirations concerning the actions of God 'on the last day'.

Resurrection in the prefigurative tradition

The idea of resurrection appears late in the story of Israel and only rarely.[17] In the context of YHWH's judgment upon Judah,

Isaiah encourages the remnant with anticipation of a corporate rising from the dead:

> Your dead will live; their bodies will rise.
> Awake and sing, you who dwell in the dust!
> For you will be covered with the morning dew,
> and the earth will bring forth the departed spirits.
>
> (Isa. 26:19)

Goldingay notes a degree of ambiguity here as contextually YHWH is bringing peace for the nations (Isa. 25:7–8) by destroying the power of death in the world.[18] The Job story gives a similar hint albeit from an individual perspective:

> But I know my living Redeemer,
> and He will stand on the dust at last.
> Even after my skin has been destroyed,
> yet I will see God in my flesh.
> I will see Him myself;
> my eyes will look at Him, and not as a stranger.
> My heart longs within me.
>
> (Job 19:25–27)

Significantly in this reference there is some prospect of the dead being in bodily proximity with God, although the context speaks more of the sufferer having an opportunity to confront God with his circumstances.

The most influential reference, particularly in the first century AD, comes from Daniel 12:[19]

> At that time
> Michael the great prince
> who stands watch over your people will rise up.
> There will be a time of distress
> such as never has occurred
> since nations came into being until that time.
> But at that time all your people
> who are found written in the book will escape.
> Many of those who sleep in the dust
> of the earth will awake,

187

some to eternal life,
and some to shame and eternal contempt.

(Dan. 12:1–2)

The context portrays Israel's God's reversing the actions of
wicked pagans through resurrection of those who sought to lead
Israel in the ways of righteousness. Notable in this vision is the
qualification of the raised – 'many' as distinct from all those who
have died: 'The rest – the great majority of humans, and indeed
of Israelites – are simply not mentioned.'[20] Regardless of what
immediate historical detail can be connected with this vision,
there is a definite anticipation of the righteous, if not all the dead,
being raised bodily in the circumstances of God's judgment.
Taken altogether, these references offer the possibility that at a
certain point in the history of the cosmos (some/most/all of?)
those who were dead will be brought back to life in God's presence.

The Messiah and the resurrection

In his dialogue with Martha Jesus states explicitly that faith in
him will result in a life that transcends the experience of death:
'the one who believes in me even if he dies, he will live' (John
11:25). In fact, the one who lives in Messiah Jesus, trusting by
implication in his resurrection, will never die (John 6:50; 8:51).
The subsequent raising of Lazarus from the tomb both confirms
the authority that the Father has given the Son to command the
dead to live (cf. John 5:21–25) and reiterates Jesus' claims to be
both the heavenly source of life for humans and the one who
will command them to rise from the dead 'on the last day' (6:39,
44, 54).

As with the other instances we have considered, the *egō eimi* in
John 11:25 is metaphorical in the sense that confession of faith
in Jesus as the Messiah, as the one who already possesses the life
of the age to come, will result in possession in the Spirit of such
life for the believer before God in the present age.[21] In fact, commentators tend to focus exclusively on this consequence of Jesus'
assertion: 'the believer now possesses, already, a divinely given
immortal life which will survive death and be re-embodied, in
the final resurrection'.[22] Taken within the whole of the New
Testament's teaching about salvation, it is not difficult to agree

with such remarks. However, such a reading of Christ Jesus' absolute claim in John 11 fails to consider *the eschatological significance* of Jesus' words. Even Calvin, when commentating on John 11:25, writes only that Jesus' assertion refers to Christian discipleship prior to the event of death: 'Because by his Spirit he regenerates the children of Adam, who had been alienated from God by sin, so that they begin to live a new life.'[23] While this is no doubt an accurate description of divine activity in the life of the believer, the context of John 11 has the Lord's standing at the entrance of a new tomb debating with the bereaved about their understanding of a general resurrection and their proximity to 'the last day'. Before we consider God's act of regeneration in the Spirit for the believer, we need to see that the meaning of Jesus' words to Martha rests on the life that Jesus has in himself (John 1:4; 5:26) that is mediated to the believer through 'his flesh and blood' (John 6:53–58). The challenge that Jesus makes to the mourners is that the Father has appropriated the meaning and the reality of resurrection to Jesus the Son. As Bonhoeffer might have said,[24] Christ Jesus has become the limit that stands between his audience and God's will for humanity in the shadow of death, and their collective speculation regarding *life after death*. That life might exist for humanity beyond death can only be understood by faith in Jesus Christ, who is 'the resurrection and the life'. The *egō eimi* construction introduces an asymmetry in favour of the risen Jesus when it comes to understanding the manner in which God preserves creaturely life in general and humanity in particular in the face of death, and relegates all other conceptions to a combination of aspiration, speculation and superstition.

The 'life that will never die' is the unique possession of the resurrected Messiah who in the Spirit mediates a promise of participation in that life to his followers even though they are separated from his experience by their own death and a general resurrection. As the unfolding narrative will make explicit, unlike Lazarus, Jesus of Nazareth will undergo death but will be redeemed from its ultimate curse – he does not see decay (Acts 2:27; cf. Ps. 16:10). Though, as the crucifixion accounts make explicit, Christ was genuinely dead, in the power of the Spirit (Rom. 1:4) he was transformed by his resurrection in such a way that he was spared the effects of Adam's curse, and did not 'return

189

to dust' (Gen. 3:19). When Jesus speaks to Martha at the tomb of her brother, he makes himself, his person and history the object of faith for anyone who might otherwise look forward to resurrection from death on 'the last day'. Their hope in the face of death and its apocalyptic future is the person of Jesus, who, by the power of the Spirit, will conquer death and its annihilating effects when he is raised to life himself, transformed by resurrection.

Resurrection in person or in principle?

If the resurrection of Jesus the Christ is God's supreme intervention in history, does this somehow reduce Jesus' I AM statement to a kind of divinely revealed endorsement of life in the face of death? Modern theology certainly gives that impression, as we can observe in the writings of Moltmann.[25] In *Theology of Hope* the resurrection appearances of Jesus are expounded 'in terms of earlier promises, and this exposition in turn takes place in the form of prophetic proclamation of, and eschatological outlook towards, the future of Christ'.[26] The exaltation of Jesus as Lord serves the final goal 'of the sole lordship of God, in which all things become new'.[27] So far, so good; but it is ironic, then, that in his mature Christology, *The Way of Jesus Christ*, his discussion of the resurrection as a historical event is remarkably muted when it comes to the *embodiment* of Jesus the Christ. Moltmann takes Paul's Damascus road encounter as standard for all the other resurrection appearances, and so the apostolic exposition mentioned above is reduced to an interpretation of 'visionary phenomena' or a 'resurrection experience'.[28] This is hardly uncommon, particularly in the work of nineteenth- and twentieth-century liberal theologians. Some of these writers manifest an outwardly pious reservation regarding the possibility of the risen Jesus being able to re-renter the creation:

> Through his risen bodiliness matter has been elevated to a final destiny which goes far beyond the bodiliness we experience in this world. 'Exalted at the right hand of God' (Acts 2:33), Christ was revealed as sharing in the divine mystery and not to be manipulated, weighed, measured or in other ways treated like an ordinary object in this world. He appears where and to whom he wills (for example, Luke 24:31).[29]

If the temple symbolism invoked by Jesus himself meant that the 'divine presence' dwelt in him, it is not self-evident why the power of the Creator should be limited by Jesus' perfected creaturely state. Other moderns fixate on the way that the Gospel Easter stories attribute properties to the risen Jesus 'that are not properties of a physical body as we know it, e.g. the ability to appear in a room whose doors are closed'[30] or 'to move from one place to another with incredible rapidity, and to appear suddenly'.[31] Certainly, as we have observed, the creatureliness of the risen Jesus was transformed through the experience of death by the power of God's Spirit. Nevertheless, the activities of the risen Jesus among his disciples are relatively trivial compared to those *before his death*, whether it was the resuscitation of Lazarus or walking on water (Matt. 14:25; Mark 6:48–49; John 6:19–20). Furthermore, the risen Jesus is by no means the only person recorded in Scripture as having moved 'from one place to another with incredible rapidity'. Elijah in 1 Kings 18:46 and Philip in Acts 8:39 perform similar feats and both possess physical bodies as we know them.

We might say that Moltmann '*argues historically* for the validity of the appearances and so of the Resurrection, rather than merely accepting them as certainly "given" because of Scriptural assertions about them'.[32] Yet, even here, this would be to misunderstand the way that the concept of promise features in his theology: 'The resurrection of Jesus from the dead by God does not speak the "language of facts," but only the language of faith and hope, that is, the "language of promise."'[33] This language of promise involves the disciples employing apocalyptic symbols from their prefigurative tradition to make sense of an event 'that has no congruence with actuality, being rather a contradiction to what is that is based on imagination's idea of what could be'.[34] Once again, the future determines the present since resurrection life belongs only to the future of creation. Despite having been committed to the historical importance of Christ Jesus' resurrection when defining hope, Moltmann favours a symbolic interpretation of the resurrection,[35] which is the complement of his understanding of the crucifixion. We noted in chapter 1 that for Moltmann the God who saves is the Father who forsakes his Son for *all godlessness and godforsakenness*. Thus with Jesus' cry of dereliction 'all disaster, forsakenness by

191

God, absolute death, the infinite curse of damnation and sinking into nothingness is in God himself'.[36] Consequently, for Moltmann it follows that

> his resurrection must then be understood . . . as a conquest of the deadliness of death, as a conquest of godforsakenness, as a conquest of judgment and of the curse, as a beginning of the fulfilment of the promised life, and thus as a conquest of all that is dead in death, as a negation of the negative (Hegel), as a negation of the negation of God.[37]

God's actions for life in the resurrection of Christ Jesus, mentioned above, become for Moltmann the object of Christian faith above and beyond faith in the Messiah as the resurrected one. Christ's resurrection is paradigmatic: 'But that is only the basis for . . . rebirth, not as yet the goal.'[38] Instead, Moltmann refers to 'the process of resurrection' initiated through Christ Jesus:[39] 'Belief in resurrection is not summed up by assent to a dogma and the registering of a historical fact. It means participating in this creative act of God.'[40] He describes this process in concentric circles that begin with Christ and spread to the whole cosmos: 'A coherent process issues from the rebirth of Christ through the Spirit, by way of rebirth of mortal human beings through the Spirit, to the universal rebirth of the cosmos through the Spirit.'[41] Our participation or faith in resurrection 'is itself a living force which raises people up and frees them . . . because their eyes are now turned towards the future of life'.[42] The shift in focus here is subtle but significant. Resurrection in the Spirit as God's action for life eclipses the resurrection of Jesus Christ, the one through whom God's actions are mediated. In fact, there appears to be a complete absence of the ascension and heavenly session in Moltmann's account of Christ's resurrection. Admittedly, as Farrow has pointed out, '[in modern theology] both exegetically and theologically the ascension is quickly assimilated to the resurrection'.[43] Be that as it may, the assimilation seems to be all too complete in Moltmann's theology, particularly considering that by far the focus of the messianic narrative was not resurrection per se but the rule of the Son of God in the Spirit. Tragically, it seems 'the mediatorial function of the Son, Jesus Christ, passes back to the Spirit, from whence it came'.[44]

The claim of Jesus the Christ to *be* 'the resurrection' must be understood in terms of his pre-eminent place in the will of God for creation. In his glorified person 'all things hold together' not in the abstract but rather as a prescription for understanding creatureliness in the will of God. The rest of the New Testament confirms the prescriptive nature of Christ's resurrection for our understanding of what the Lord meant when he said, 'I am the resurrection.' So for example Paul writes:

> But now Christ has been raised from the dead, the first fruits of those who have fallen asleep. (1 Cor. 15:20)

> And he [Christ] is the head of the body, the church; he is the beginning and the firstborn from among the dead, so that in everything he might have the supremacy. (Col. 1:18)

From these verses we may conclude, with Moltmann, that Christ's resurrection forms a precedent for the resurrection of others, at least in terms of the phenomenon. As Paul again states in 1 Corinthians 15:13, 'If there is no resurrection of the dead, then not even Christ has been raised.' Now since Jesus has been raised to life from the dead it is possible for the dead to be raised to life. However, this is the perfect point at which to grasp the significance of Jesus' claim in John 11 to be '*the* resurrection'. The Lord is not just the first example of resurrection – the resurrection of Christ is more than a divine act to clarify an otherwise generally held belief or to set in train an expanding process. Despite the notable anticipations and visions of such an event in the Old Testament, the possibility of the dead being raised to life again apart from the Spirit's intervention for Christ Jesus is largely a matter of aspiration in response to the curse of death. Instead, for Jesus Christ to claim to be 'the resurrection' means that any subsequent resurrection of the dead is dependent upon and must be understood in relation to his own. The prospect of any continuity between this age and the one to come rests entirely on the person of Jesus the resurrected Christ of God.

We see this elsewhere in the New Testament as we get indications that the resurrection of Christ shows how the rest of those who die will be raised: 'If we have been united with him like this in his death, we will certainly also be united with him in his resurrection' (Rom. 6:5).

Of course, it could be argued that the association made here between the experience of the risen Jesus and that of the ordinary individual is purely metaphorical. Can we expect to be raised from the dead if we are not crucified as Jesus was? Later in Romans 8 Paul adds, 'if the Spirit of him who raised Jesus from the dead is living in you, he who raised Christ from the dead will also give life to your mortal bodies through his Spirit, who lives in you' (Rom. 8:11).

Even if this verse is meant to be a reference to the way that God regenerates us in the power of the Holy Spirit, it states quite explicitly that the phenomenon of resurrection in the power of the Spirit that was experienced by Jesus Christ is open to all who have died during 'life in the Spirit'. The resurrection of Jesus the Messiah from the dead is the revelation of what the God who made the heavens and the earth wills for his creation in general and for the human being in particular.

What we know about God's promise to preserve human life is that God's royal and eternal Son, Christ Jesus, will execute his Father's desire to perfect his relationship with his human creatures by raising them to life on 'the last day'. This is the hope of all who live in the face of death and the future of all that have died. The resurrected Christ Jesus *is himself* the continuity between this age and the new creation. The bodily resurrection of Jesus the Christ is divine confirmation of the significance of material creaturely existence, yet the Christian hope is in the resurrection of Christ Jesus, *not resurrection in abstract*. The new creation exists entirely in the person of the risen and ascended Jesus Christ as a promise for his future. He alone is the continuity between this age and the age to come. As he is the resurrection, he is the source of life for a general resurrection and the promised creaturely life on the last day of this age and beyond into the future of God's acts to create the world anew: 'God's supreme act of new creation' has 'only [one] real prototype – other than the first creation – [which is] the resurrection of Jesus'.[45] This is what we know from the gospel of the risen Jesus the Christ, so how should we understand the preview of resurrection life given us in the risen Messiah?

Life in the Middle as resurrection life

According to Moltmann, 'If we ask about the praxis of resurrection hope, we are asking about the way of life and the experience of life of the people who are animate – "ensouled" – by this hope.'[46] From what we have established thus far we should say that the electing Spirit animates the church by blessing individuals with life from the Father's promises through Jesus Christ. Or, as Paul writes, 'the love of God has been poured into our hearts through the Holy Spirit who was given to us' (Rom. 5:5). It is the Spirit of 'sonship in whom we cry Abba Father' in the likeness of the image of God, the royal and eternal Son (Rom. 8:14; Gal. 4:6; cf. Mark 14:36). The life and hope of these regenerated children of the Father (Titus 3:5) are revealed in their first act as they call upon the name of the risen Jesus to receive forgiveness for their sins, a response that is embodied and celebrated in the practices of baptism and the Lord's Supper. The behaviour of this new people of promise is manifested in the fruit of the Spirit: 'love, joy, peace, patience, kindness, gentleness, faithfulness and self-control' (Gal. 5:22–23). Broadly speaking, Moltmann depicts resurrection life in the Middle as the divine process characterized by 'the uniting of what has been separated'.[47] To the extent that such a description pertains to union with Christ in the Spirit, there is much here that we can agree with.

Moltmann begins with the unification of body and soul for the individual by noting the persistent tendency in the Western tradition, particularly since the Enlightenment, of not simply distinguishing body and soul within the human person, but pitting one against the other.[48] Whether it is the classic division of *divine* spirit and *evil* matter that sees the soul seeking redemption from the body in eternity with God, or the modern variant of the ego having a body in need of control as a metaphor for attaining Godlike control of the world, 'in the Spirit of the resurrection soul and body find the way to their wholeness even *before* death'.[49] Death need no longer be feared, nor be merely accepted, and therefore wholeness of the human person 'is a unity which absorbs into itself differentiations and disunions, and heals them'.[50] There is more to say regarding personal wholeness in relation to death, but prior to that eventuality the New Testament is certainly explicit about the importance of our embodied actions in the world. As Gunton observed, there is a necessary eschatological tension in, for example, Paul's exhortations to the church in Corinth: 'we are what we do and yet we are what we shall be'.[51] The discussions between Paul and the church cover many issues but most, if not all, centre on the consequences of embodied existence in the light of the resurrection – whether it is eating and drinking or the sexual and conjugal aspects of personal relation-ships. All of these require a definite coherence between mind/soul and body as a consequence of being 'member[s] of Christ and the place of the Spirit's activity'.[52] Moltmann goes further. For him the promise of wholeness in the Spirit for the individual includes being able to 'identify himself with himself in the transmutations of the time of his life'.[53] Hope in the resurrection gives value to every stage of human life, even back to the womb: 'it is a hope for all the hours of human life from first to last'.[54] Accordingly, any embodied self needs to recognize the dignity of every stage of her life in the sight of God. While Moltmann would no doubt disagree, we could add that the point he is trying to make is reflected in the various household codes recorded in the epistles to Ephesus and Colossae or in 1 Peter.[55] Here the various stages of life are reappropriated and redeemed in Christ and by the Spirit.

Of course, the wholeness of any person is dependent upon his or her life in human community: 'The horizon of the "resurrection of the body" spans not merely bodiliness of the individual person but sociality too.'[56] In Moltmann's view the Western tradition of focusing on the disembodied soul has led to competitive indi-vidualism which can only be healed through the renewed sociality that the Spirit of resurrection brings.[57] The temporal aspects of personhood are affected by the resurrection, but in this instance Moltmann has the concept of intergenerational connection in mind: 'Human beings are not merely personal and social beings. They are generation beings too.'[58] Human community works across time as people emerge within community and eventually take their place as custodians of community for the sake of the coming generation: 'Since everyone lives in the sequence of gener-ations and owed his life to it, everyone is also duty bound to care

for the older and the younger generations.'[59] Hope in the resurrection enables generations to play their part in the sequence
without fear, allowing a just distribution of resources without
exploitation: 'this hope challenges and resists the power of death
in the midst of life'.[60] Going further than Moltmann we could
point to the role that the Spirit plays in creating a dynamically
and mutually constitutive life for sons and daughters in *the family
of Abraham* (1 Cor. 12:12–13; cf. Gal. 3:14–29). In a similar
fashion, the writer to the Hebrews recounts the history of the Old
Testament and encourages his readers to see themselves among 'a
great cloud of witnesses surrounding us' (Heb. 12:1). In this way
the Spirit creates church history as believers are given the gift of
self-understanding that facilitates the fellowship of the Spirit
throughout time.

Finally, in Moltmann's view, resurrection hope can address the
growing alienation of humanity from the natural world: 'human
beings *are* nature and they *have* nature'.[61] Instead of following
the path of 'humanising nature' or attempting to exert ever-
exploitative control over nature, resurrection hope offers the
possibility of humans living in harmony with nature again: 'Just
as soul and body interpenetrate one another, so human beings
and nature find one another in mutual *perichoresis*.'[62] The Spirit
of resurrection fosters a 'reverence for life' in all its forms that
results in a renewed desire for wholeness throughout life.[63]

Two things should be noted in response to this brief summary
of Moltmann's position. First, although Moltmann expects
the Spirit to be the agent bringing the above described unity in the
cosmos, and uses the language of process so consistently, he does
not expect the resurrection to be anything other than a divine
achievement. While resurrection hope is by no means a retreat
into quietism on the part of the church, Moltmann envisages the
divine energy of resurrection hope as motivating the church to
live towards the coming future of God: 'we become active when
we hope'.[64] Despite the optimistic feel of Moltmann's account,
there is no suggestion of the Spirit's equipping 'humans to help in
the work of getting the project [of creation] back on track'.[65]
Neither is there any sense of the kind of activism that sees the
church laying the foundation for the coming kingdom of God.[66]
Instead, living in resurrection hope becomes a protest against a
world bound by godlessness and godforsakenness: 'the ability to

wait [for God's future] also means not conforming to the conditions of this world of injustice and violence'.[67]

The second issue worth noting in Moltmann's approach to God's preserving life, however, flows out of the first and gives us some insight into Moltmann's particular protological concerns. Moltmann's desire for a theology that affirms life in the face of death has consistently moved away from the traditional absolute distinction between God and creation: 'the centre of this [ecological] thinking is no longer the distinction between God and the world'.[68] Instead, Moltmann prefers what he refers to as 'panentheism',[69] where God is present in the world even as the world is present in God: '[the] triune God . . . unremittingly breathes the Spirit into his creation'.[70] In fact, he portrays the Spirit as the principle of evolution; he is the designer of creativity on all levels. The Spirit is the designer of the organic nature of creation that brings harmony and perichoresis within ecosystems at every level (including between God and creation).[71] Thus the Spirit of God *is the cosmic spirit*, the life of the universe,[72] and

> he [God] gives himself away to the beings he has created, he suffers with their sufferings, he goes with them through the misery of the foreign land. The God who in the Spirit dwells in his creation is present to every one of his creatures and remains bound to them.[73]

Consequently, a basic concern of Moltmann's entire project is theodicy, articulating the activity of God's Spirit in order to explain the presence of evil in the world. For Moltmann Christian theology becomes relevant only when it takes the theodicy question as an 'absolute presupposition', only 'when it accepts this solidarity with present suffering'.[74] Since human suffering is 'the central problem in most religions',[75] resurrection hope is articulated in terms of the self-justification of God in the light of such suffering. God's answer to this predicament is the victory of life over death, hope, and freedom in the face of tyranny and despair. Through the resurrection of Christ *in the Spirit* a way emerges for those trapped in death and evil to escape into the broad and open future of God's life, which is characterized by joy and freedom.[76]

Against Moltmann I contend that when we pray for God to preserve us in the face of death we do so, as argued above, on the basis that *Jesus the Christ* was raised from the dead. This was a peculiar and penultimate intervention in the history of promise that served the Father's will for Christ Jesus, *the only one* in whom divine and creaturely life overlap. When we insist that the Father's actions in the Spirit are mediated through the risen Christ, we not only hold closer to testimony of the Scriptures; we also avoid losing hope for a genuinely distinct creaturely life without death. Modern theologians like Moltmann have mistakenly dispensed with this theological necessity out of a desire to rescue us from an allegedly monistic, distant and even tyrannous doctrine of God.[77] However, as Gunton observes:

> Rightly rejecting monist forms of belief, the modern world has simply displaced them into immanence, where they are more monistic, more heteronomous in their outworking . . . An immanent deity, because it leaves no space between persons and between persons and the world, is the most heteronomous of all.[78]

In modern Romantic theology the Spirit of resurrection overcomes death, but at the cost of a genuinely distinct creaturely life. The process of making whole that Moltmann described above is the homogenizing of creation in the Spirit, not its particularizing. Furthermore, any description of God's relationship with the world that diminishes the ontological distance between God and the world proportionally diminishes the character of God's grace towards the world.[79] During life in the Middle we live in the power of the perfecting work of the Spirit *of Christ* (Phil. 1:19; 1 Peter 1:11). This is what we know and pray for, but what can we hope for it as we do?

Raised up on the last day by and for the Christ

The Lord Jesus Christ is the chief executor of the divine will and therefore it has been given to him to raise the dead at the beginning of the new creation: 'just as the Father raises the dead and gives life; in the same way the Son gives life to whomever he wills' (John 5:21). The hope of resurrection for the dead rests on the Messiah's own resurrection in the power of God's Spirit (cf. Rom. 1:4). Furthermore, in order to understand this great promise theologically as opposed to merely phenomenologically, we must attend to the true *purpose* for which the dead are raised. We may discern this purpose by reconsidering what we have learned about the Father's intention to make his name holy and to perfect his kingdom on the earth.

The dead are raised to worship the Christ

We observed in Philippians 2:9–11 that Paul foresees all creation will be brought to worship before the ascended Christ Jesus in order that he might be exalted as Lord to the glory of God the Father. God the Father gives the name (Lord) that is his alone to the exalted Christ in order that the Messiah Jesus may be acclaimed and proclaimed as Lord. What is explicit in the passage is God the Father's desire to exalt his Messiah via all creatures, throughout all creation, being brought before the Messiah to worship him as Lord. When commenting on Philippians Calvin helpfully observes that Paul makes another appeal to Isaiah 45 in Romans 14:11, where he describes 'the day of judgement' more explicitly.[80] Hence whatever the events of 'the last day' may be, they cannot be less than what appears in Philippians, since the Apocalypse of John contains a similar portrait in Revelation 5:13: 'every creature that is in heaven and on the earth and under the earth and in the sea and all things in them I heard say, "Blessing and honour and glory and dominion . . . to the Lamb"'. In so far as Philippians 2 is echoing Peter's words from Pentecost we might say that the Philippian portrait contains a graphic depiction of what Psalm 110:1 looks like when fulfilled – the bowed knees and confessing tongues of his enemies are the footstool for the Messiah's feet. Paul is here confirming the continuity of the resurrected dead with the glorified Jesus in so far as *they are raised in a manner fit to worship* the exalted Christ of God as Lord. Mention of knees and mouths suggests an embodied experience for all creatures but, more importantly, all creatures are brought before the Christ of God in his risen and glorified state – they are brought to his resurrection life. As a window into the 'last day' or even the new creation we can anticipate a necessary continuity for creaturely existence for the glorification of the crucified and risen Christ of God.

200

The dead are raised to vindicate Christ's victory

When we considered how the kingdom is realized in 1 Corinthians 15:24–28, we saw that a central feature of it was the ultimate defeat of death – 'the last enemy'. Through the lens of this passage we observed the apostolic configuration of the risen Christ as the Spirit-empowered and triumphant kinsman redeemer of YHWH, who has defeated the enemies of God's people once and for all. In fact, the royal and eternal Son is the victor over Satan, the strong man who wields the power of death (Heb. 2:14–15). It is only fitting that those who lived in fear of death should be raised again to life *as vindication of the messianic victory*.

Death is the universal human problem, as Paul notes in 1 Corinthians 15:22: 'as in Adam all die'. Everyone who belongs with Adam will die. Death is the malignant evil that makes wombs barren and sucks the breath from infants as they sleep, that hateful shadow that snuffs out the light of youth and steals dignity from the aged, that vicious adversary that reduces the fleet of foot to hobbling, that hideous strength that turns sharp wits to doddering fools, that relentless tide that sweeps away rich and poor alike. But for the kingdom of God death is even worse than this, because of the promise that God made to David and his sons about kingship. We read in 2 Samuel 7:16, 'Your house and kingdom will endure before Me *forever*, and your throne will be established *forever*' (emphasis added). No kingdom can endure if the king is dead, no throne can stand when the king is laid in a tomb; worst of all, God's promises to make the king's enemies a footstool beneath his feet are nothing when the king breathes his last. Death is not just the enemy of humanity; it is the enemy of God's chosen king. And, what is more, death is *the enemy of God's promises* to and through the king. Hence the significance of what Peter preached on the day of Pentecost: 'God raised [Jesus] from the dead, freeing him from the agony of death, because it was impossible for death to keep its hold on him' (Acts 2:24). It was impossible for death to keep its hold on him because God had promised that he would rule everlastingly. When God raised Jesus to life his promise was vindicated: God's word was proved to be true, 'For we know that since Christ was raised from the dead, he cannot die again; death no longer has mastery over him' (Rom. 6:9). However, the events of Easter Sunday are a hint, a sneak preview, of the ultimate revelation. When 'the trumpet sounds, the dead will be raised . . . and death will be swallowed up in victory' (1 Cor. 15:52–54), the victory of God the Father through his spiritually empowered king. At this point the royal and eternal Son will exercise the promised authority given him by the Father, mentioned in John 5:21, 25, 28, and command 'the sea . . . Death . . . and Hades' to 'give up their dead' (Rev. 20:13) as vindication of his universal kingdom.

The dead are raised transformed

The promise in response to our prayer for preservation is that the dead are raised in a fit state to acclaim and proclaim the crucified and risen Messiah as Lord. In keeping with the Father's will, they are raised into his resurrection life 'to sum up all things' in the royal and eternal Son. As I hinted when considering Christ himself, this is human life transformed or perfected beyond the effects of sin, death and evil. In 1 Corinthians 15:35ff. Paul discusses the 'kind of body' that is raised or the nature of resurrected embodiment through a number of related creaturely metaphors to explain the transformation between our earthly bodies now and the bodies of the resurrected dead.

Despite appealing to various creaturely parallels, Paul's description is essentially theological: 'it is God who gives the body' (1 Cor. 15:38). Nevertheless, when the dead are put into the grave they are 'sown like a seed', which makes dying the beginning of a process of *transformation*.[81] God's Spirit is the agent throughout this process of transformation, but the Corinthians must keep in mind that the transformation takes place entirely within the realm of the creaturely. Within this sphere of existence there can be either 'heavenly or earthly' bodies: 'There are . . . heavenly bodies and there are earthly bodies; but there is a glory of the heavenly bodies, and there is a glory of the earthly bodies' (1 Cor. 15:40). The key thing to note is that everything to which Paul appeals in making his point, everything mentioned in these few verses, belongs to what we might call the *old* or original/current creation prior to the general resurrection. A simple principle is being invoked that God creates varieties of embodiment and that principle applies to the distinction between the 'natural' body that we receive when we are born and the 'spiritual' body we receive at the resurrection of the dead.[82] The bodies have the same creaturely substance but they have different characteristics and are separated by the principle of fulfilment/perfection.

The most important comparison between a natural body and a spiritual body rests on the distinction between Adam and Christ Jesus, to which Paul appeals twice in a kind of bookend fashion:

> For as in Adam all die, so in Christ all will be made alive. (1 Cor. 15:22)

> Just as it is written, 'The first man, Adam, became a living being'; the last Adam [Jesus Christ], a life-giving spirit. (1 Cor. 15:45)

In between those verses Paul describes with a number of pairs the difference between our bodies before and after we are resurrected: 'perishable/imperishable; dishonour/glory; weakness/power; natural/spiritual' (1 Cor. 15:42–44). None of the pairs listed requires that the first kind be material but the second somehow be immaterial, and the reason lies in the second comparison between Adam and the Christ (v. 45). The difference between the first man, Adam, and the risen Lord Jesus is *how they come to be alive*: 'The first man was of the dust of the earth, the second man from heaven' (v. 47). Where Paul compares Adam as a 'living being' with the man Jesus as a 'life-giving spirit' in 15:45, it is not necessary to assert that the man Jesus of Nazareth has become something unnatural or non-creaturely with his ascension.[83] Instead, the distinction is between being animated in the ordinary sense of all living things and being animated entirely by the Holy Spirit. Hence in Genesis 2:7 we read that God 'breathed . . . into his [Adam's] nostrils, and the man became a living being', whereas in Romans 1:4 we read that Jesus Christ '*through the Spirit of holiness* was declared with power to be the Son of God by his resurrection from the dead'. In all, the comparison between Adam and the Lord Jesus serves to expand what we have observed above, that the person of Jesus the Christ is both the resurrection and the life: he is the continuity between the old and the new creation.

As we might expect, Moltmann's failure convincingly to affirm the bodily resurrection and ascension of Christ Jesus carries over into his description of the raising of the dead. Critics have complained that for Moltmann Jesus Christ is simply a divine mechanism whereby God can take on human suffering for the sake of taking humanity into the Trinity. The cost for a gospel-shaped Christian hope is that 'humanity no longer lives in unity with Christ now, in hope of fulfilment of humanity through Christ to come'.[84] Instead, Moltmann's focus rests on the fact that the

> resurrection hope makes people ready to live their lives in love wholly, and to say a full and entire Yes to a life that leads to death. We throw ourselves into this life and empty ourselves into the deadly realm of non-identity by virtue of the hope that God will find us in death and will raise us and gather us.[85]

Beyond these realized aspects of resurrection hope Moltmann is much more interested in the 'cosmic Shekinah of God',[86] the cosmic indwelling of God in creation, to the point where 'he almost forgets to mention the last things'.[87]

The dead are raised in Christ Jesus

Finally, understanding the purpose of the general resurrection gives us an appropriately theological perspective from which to view our own, especially when that involves death prior to Christ's return. We pray to our heavenly Father for preservation in the context of mortality, confident that on the last day the dead are called to life and their mortality is transformed into immortality to be perfected in the image of their creator, the Lord Jesus Christ (Col. 3:10; cf. Col. 1:16–17). As I have argued repeatedly, the person of Jesus the Christ is the promise of continuity for the creation, and especially for humanity, which is otherwise marred by sin, death and evil. What is also significant for life in the Middle is the fact that the risen Messiah Jesus is the creaturely *discontinuity* between the events of Easter Sunday and the general resurrection, since he alone is 'the firstborn from among the dead' (Col. 1:18; cf. 1 Cor. 15:20). Christ Jesus is himself the promise and hope of God the Father for all who have died and so the apostles encouraged the churches, 'your life is hidden *in Christ* with God. When the Messiah, *who is your life*, is revealed, then you also will be revealed with him in glory' (Col. 3:3–4; cf. 1 John 2:28). Thus, from a theological point of view, the Christian hope founded on

204

a gospel-focused reading of the Bible must understand Jesus the Christ as *the intermediate state* of creaturely life in the overlap between this age and the age to come.

Whether it was because of the paucity of reflection in the Christian tradition on the ascension of the Christ,[88] or, more likely, the near universal human fear of and fascination with ghosts and the spirit world or just the fear of death plain and simple, human beings have speculated and prognosticated about a somehow immaterial, disembodied human existence beyond death from time immemorial.[89] In addition, traditional Eastern and Western cosmologies entertain either a general conflict between spirit and matter and/or a more particular anthropological dualism that divides the human being into body and mind/spirit/soul.[90] When we add to this portrait the variety of resurrection beliefs or reincarnation narratives in the religions of the ancient world, it becomes all the more important for Christians to distinguish what the Bible *teaches* about the Father's acts to preserve us through the experience of death from the various pagan beliefs which the Bible *records*. As Moltmann wryly observes, 'The immortal soul is an opinion – the resurrection of the dead is a hope.'[91]

In the history of Western thought Plato's theory of the immortal soul that exists prior to birth and after death has been influential for Christian theology at various times and in different ways. So Origen (AD 185–254), Christianity's first systematic theologian, wrote in his *De principiis*:

> The soul, having a substance and life of its own, shall after its departure from the world, be rewarded according to its deserts, being destined to obtain either an inheritance of eternal life and blessedness, if its actions shall have procured this for it, or to be delivered up to eternal fire and punishments, if the guilt of its crimes shall have brought it down to this.[92]

Much later Augustine of Hippo (AD 354–430) wrote in *The City of God*:

> [The soul] is therefore called immortal, because in a sense, it does not cease to live and to feel; while the body

> is called mortal because it can be forsaken of all life, and
> cannot by itself live at all. The death, then, of the soul,
> takes place when God forsakes it, as the death of the
> body when the soul forsakes it.[93]

Both of these theologians moved away from Platonic thought in terms of whether humans existed as souls before birth.[94] However, they both believed that the soul created by God was nevertheless immortal and could exist even without a human body *post mortem* until it was re-embodied at the general resurrection.[95] It was an idea that was deeply embedded in the Christian tradition aided and abetted in subsequent Christian culture by works like Dante's *Divine Comedy*. Calvin's first tract, 'Psychopannychia', was written to oppose the idea that disembodied souls somehow sleep (or disintegrate) between death and the general resurrection, as Luther and the Anabaptists believed in their different ways.[96] Instead, he reasserted a fairly traditional account of the immortality of the soul that survives the body in death and awaits a resurrection body.

The historical legacy of Origen and Augustine prompted subsequent generations of Christian scholars, especially modern Protestant ones, to search for a supposedly non-Hellenized or exclusively Hebraic view of biblical material on this issue.[97] Consequently, some argued that the ancient Israelites had an entirely holistic view of human beings, that humans do not have discrete souls but are ensouled or alive in a way distinct from other animals since they are made in the image of God.[98] Old Testament occurrences of concepts like 'resting with his fathers' or Sheol as the place of the dead were viewed as euphemisms for death:

> It is not the dead who praise the LORD,
> nor any of those descending into the silence of death.
> (Ps. 115:17)

And 'the dead don't know anything' (Eccl. 9:5).[99] Subsequent works on ancient Hellenistic philosophy and ancient Hebrew anthropology questioned the existence of a sharp divide between Greek and Hebrew cultures over the soul–body relationship *and* the likelihood of either culture being completely monolithic on the subject. A variety of views on the relationship between body and soul are prominent in Greek thought[100] – even Plato's – and evidence has been put forward that ancient Hebrews considered it possible to consult the spirits/souls of the dead long before the Hebrews had any recorded interactions with the Greeks.[101] Thus when passing references are made in the New Testament to a human soul separate from the body, especially in the context of death, the reader ought to be circumspect before asserting whether it is Greek or Hebrew thought at work or some combination of both. Either way, scholars remain divided as to whether the Bible supports the traditional doctrine of the 'intermediate' state and/or the concept of a soul somehow separate from the human body.

When viewing this issue from the perspective of Christian hope, all these various anthropologies or cosmologies represent attempts to answer phenomenological or, at least, non-theological questions: Where are the dead? What happens to us when we die? Holy Scripture has been inductively explored to a greater or lesser extent in an, at times, empirical or scientific manner in order to establish on the basis of stronger or weaker inference what the biblical writers thought on the topic within the context of various reconstructions of the historical world-behind-the-text. The fact that such thinking appears in the Spirit-generated testimony of the prophets and apostles is then taken to be what 'the Bible teaches' on the subject of death, the intermediate state and the resurrection. Unfortunately, even these doctrines of the church are not the hope of the Christian gospel. When a more explicitly theological question is posed – for example: Where/how do the dead feature in the will of God revealed in Christ Jesus? What hope is there for the dead? Or, what hope can we hold out for them? – the consistent focus of the New Testament, or what the apostolic tradition *prescribes* for Christian hope, is the bodily resurrection of Jesus the Christ.

Even if passing references to the *possibility* of our souls leaving our bodies in death, to continue existing somehow with the ascended Christ, can be found in the New Testament (e.g. Phil. 1:20–24; 2 Cor. 5:6–9), they are of relatively trivial significance for the Christian hope compared to explicitly prescriptive passages focusing on the dead in relation to the risen Christ. In fact, when the Lord himself makes mention, in passing, of such possibilities prior to his resurrection (e.g. Matt. 10:28; Luke 16:19–31), we

207

must relativize their importance in relation to his prescriptive statements examined above from John 11. Thus in the case of 1 Corinthians 15, examined briefly above, Paul's exclusive focus is on possibilities for our embodied state once it is freed from the effects of sin, death and evil by the resurrection of the Lord Jesus. All of those possibilities are grounded on the reality and experience of the risen Christ Jesus without any mention of an intermediate state as inferred by the tradition either prior to or contemporaneous with Paul. Next, the only explicit 'word from the Lord' given by Paul to a church is found in 1 Thessalonians 4:14–16: 'For since we believe that Jesus Christ died and rose, in the same way God, *through Jesus Christ*, will bring the sleeping ones with him . . . then the dead *in Christ* will rise first.' Since all Christians make up the body of Christ, who is the head, as noted above, those who die before his return are not lost because they have already been incorporated by the electing Spirit into the promise of Christ Jesus for the resurrection life of the new creation. They have been raised in Christ and will be revealed in glory by Christ when God the Father sends him at the last day. Finally, Paul seeks to encourage the church in Rome to endure 'the sufferings of the present time' (Rom. 8:18) in anticipation of the return of Messiah Jesus (8:19; see parallel references in 1 Cor. 1:7; Col. 3:4; 1 Peter 1:7, 13; 1 John 3:2). The passage rises to a glorious crescendo as Paul reminds them that the risen Christ 'intercedes for them at the right hand of God' so that '[nothing] can separate them from the love of Christ'. As he says, 'not even death nor life . . . can separate us from the love of God that is in Christ Jesus our Lord' (Rom. 8:39). The glory of the messianic vision of Psalm 110 is the hope of Christians for God's preservation from death and there is no mention of an intermediate stage in the process.

The heavenly session of Jesus the Christ is more readily the focus of Christian hope in the area of eschatological forgiveness, the theme to which we turn next. It is in that context that we shall consider how Christ represents the living and the dead before God the Father as our great high priest. When in the power of God's Spirit we cry, 'Good Lord, preserve us,' the answer is 'yes, and everlastingly yes' in the person of the glorified Messiah Jesus, who is the resurrection and the life.

7

GOOD LORD, FORGIVE US

The hope promised by the Father to those who live in the shadow
of death that characterizes life in the Middle is the ascended
Messiah Jesus. He is the triumphant, Spirit-empowered kinsman
redeemer for those made in his image who are oppressed by
Satan. The dead will be raised, to vindicate both Jesus' triumph
and the mode of his triumph, which was his sacrificial death for
the forgiveness of sins. Every knee will bow, and every tongue will
confess that Jesus the Christ is the Lord. At this point we must
clarify our hope in the light of God's covenantal promise to
perfect his relationship with his creatures, principally those made
in the likeness of his image. While the resurrection of the dead
will vindicate the triumph of the universal king, as the perfected
executor of the Father's will, the Messiah must also sit in judgment
against his enemies, those who blasphemed at the instigation
of the strong man and whose actions constitute the history of
rebellion against God's plan to consummate all things in Christ
Jesus.

It is in the light of the coming judgment by the royal and
eternal Son that we call out to our heavenly Father for forgiveness,
as the fifth petition of the Lord's Prayer reminds us. Calvin noted

that the presence of this request reveals both our need for forgiveness and the possibility of finding it from our heavenly Father.[1] The language of indebtedness is used in the Matthean form of the Prayer (Matt. 6:12). However, as both Gregory of Nyssa and Barth observed, our very lives are a gift from God the Father and for this we are indebted to him. The debt only increases when we consider the antagonistic manner in which we resist his grace:[2] 'the human race is insolvent, and has no right to claim remission of its debt'.[3] In fact, our indebtedness is made all the more explicit because of the actions of the Father through his Son:

> The passage enjoins . . . [us] . . . to call to mind the common debt of human nature in which everyone including himself has a share, because he participates in the common lot of human nature, and to beseech the Judge to grant forgiveness of sins.[4]

The triumphant Messiah of Psalm 110 is the executor of the Father's will to 'judge the world in righteousness. He has given proof of this to all by raising him from the dead' (Acts 17:31). Nevertheless, the Judge is also our kinsman redeemer empowered by the Spirit to be our saviour. Even more than this, the Messiah is also our great high priest in the order of Melchizedek (Ps. 110:4). As we consider the Father's promise of forgiveness in the light of this eschatological judgment and the promise's consequences for life in the Middle, we shall explore the possibilities of the Spirit's perfecting work through the one who pleads for us with the Father, the ascended Jesus Christ. We shall start with his high-priestly ministry, and go on from there to consider what we should do in response to the forgiveness he makes available and what we can hope for in terms of the last judgment. We shall also re-engage with Barth on the issue of the will of God in Christ and, in particular, examine the scope of the eschatological forgiveness that comes through the Father's choice of the royal and eternal Son. I shall contend that Barth was *insufficiently* Christological in his attempt to explain the will of God the Father in, through and for his royal and eternal Son. Barth's unfinished work on redemption left too much ambiguity concerning the Father's promise of everlasting mercy for those who serve the

210

Messiah as his inheritance *and* an everlasting curse of wrath for those who were the enemies of his saving actions.

Forgiveness through the crucified one

The degree to which forgiveness for sin is available during life in the Middle is encapsulated in John's words:

> If we say that we do not have sin, we are deceiving ourselves and the truth is not in us. If we confess our sins, he is faithful and just and will forgive our sins and cleanse us from all unrighteousness. My children, I write these things to you so that you will not sin but if anyone does sin we have an advocate before the Father, Jesus Christ the righteous one. He is the propitiation for our sins; not for ours only but for the sins of the whole world. (1 John 1:8 – 2:2)

We call out to our heavenly Father for forgiveness, knowing that Jesus the Christ, the 'righteous one', pleads for us with the Father on the basis of his atoning work. As we observed in chapter 3, the Messiah personally eclipses the significance of the temple as the dwelling place of God, the point at which heaven and earth meet. By the death of Jesus Christ the temple in Jerusalem is decommissioned in favour of the cross at Golgotha as the place where the divine name dwells. Hence the electing Spirit constitutes the church by moving individuals to call on the name of the Lord Jesus for the forgiveness of sins (cf. Acts 4:10–12). In chapter 4 I argued that it was inherent in the duties of the Messiah to establish the conditions for the right worship of YHWH to be possible. Thus the Messiah not only takes charge of the temple, but also confirms its place in the Levitical cult. In his exposition of 1 John Calvin recognized that the legal concept of advocacy must be interpreted in the reference to 'righteousness' and 'propitiation': 'Propitiation is added, because no one is fit to be a high priest without a sacrifice.'[5] Barth, however, considered Christ Jesus' judicial mediation as 'the same thing' as 'the Priest who represented us'. Barth's decision to focus almost exclusively on the forensic aspect of reconciliation means, however, that the logic of sacrifice – whether an offering is sufficient for atonement – is lost.

Instead, his exposition of atonement relies entirely on the forensic logic of 'the punishment matching the crime'. In the Reformed tradition such an exclusively forensic account limits our understanding of Christ's priestly work to a strictly limited atonement – Christ dies exclusively for the elect. Alternatively, in Barth's case, atonement must inevitably be universal due to the exactitude of the match between Christ's righteousness and the sin of humanity.

In the Gospel narratives the nature and extent of that mediation is explained by Jesus during the Passover meal. He assumes the practice of propitiating YHWH's wrath through substitutionary sacrifice and expounds his own narrative of the expiation of sin. As the pre-eminent interpreter of the Father's will, Christ Jesus proceeds to appropriate both these cultic symbols as an exposition of his impending death. The royal and eternal Son will 'drink the cup' of wrath, mentioned in Gethsemane, on the cross while his 'blood of the covenant [will be] poured out for many, for the forgiveness of sins' (Matt. 26:28). We can understand this further by considering the priestly aspect of the heavenly session.

Forgiveness through the great high priest

From Jesus' own interpretation, and from the subsequent apostolic preaching, his sacrificial death is as the priest in the order of Melchizedek (Ps. 110:4). The writer to the Hebrews understood it: 'The one who said to him, "You are my son, today I have begotten you," also said in another place, "You are a priest for ever, according to the order of Melchizedek"' (Heb. 5:5–6). God the Father not only vindicates the sacrifice of Jesus Christ through resurrection in the Spirit, but also designates him as the inheritor of the Old Testament cultic system and mediator of forgiveness from heaven to earth. The reality of this mediation is captured in Hebrews by an appeal to the ancient king of Salem to whom Abraham had shown deference. The order of Melchizedek is subsequently proclaimed to be superior even to God's ordained priesthood in the line of Aaron (Heb. 7:1–2, 9, 15–22). The eternal priesthood of Melchizedek, 'king of righteousness', is the typological prefiguration of Jesus,[6] since 'He [Jesus Christ] is . . . the King of righteousness, because of what he effects in diffusing righteousness on all his people.'[7] Furthermore, having been confirmed by the Spirit in his resurrection, Messiah Jesus 'became a source of eternal salvation' since 'he is able to save completely those who come to God through him, since he always lives to intercede for them' (Heb. 5:9; 7:25). As I argued in chapter 2, the glorified Lord Jesus Christ is the eternal mediator between God the Father and creation. He mediates the blessing of forgiveness everlastingly because he is, *in himself*, the sufficient offering: 'through *his own blood*, he went once and for all, into the [heavenly] sanctuary, securing an eternal redemption' (Heb. 9:12). As the everlasting priest the ascended Christ Jesus has 'entered into heaven itself so that he might now appear in the presence of God for us . . . now at the perfection of the ages he appeared once, for the removal of sin *through the sacrifice of himself*' (Heb. 9:24–26). As Calvin recognized:

> he is performing his office as a priest; for it belongs to a priest to intercede for the people, that they may obtain favour with God. This is what Christ is ever doing, for it was for this purpose that he rose again from the dead.[8]

Jesus the Christ is the everlasting mediator of forgiveness for sin. It is a forgiveness mediated through the sufficiency of the sacrifice – himself – and is immortalized *in his person*. In fact, it is immortalized in the death scars preserved in his resurrected body, as I contended against Moltmann in chapter 4. He complained that ideas of an expiatory death by Christ Jesus for sin cut off Christ's death from his resurrection.[9] On the contrary, what we know from the testimony of Hebrews concerning the Melchizedek priesthood ensures that the ascended and *crucified* Messiah presents his paschal sacrifice – memorialized in his death scars – to the Father *now* and *for ever*.

The true witness to forgiveness?

Unlike Moltmann, as observed in the previous chapter, for Barth the resurrection of Jesus the Christ is more than a theological principle and therefore the ascension has a central and prescriptive role in Barth's theology.[10] Barth's emphasis on the ascension and on its prescriptive importance for Christian theology can be seen at the most basic level of the ascension's historical and systematic significance. The ascension does

213

not mean . . . that he ceased to be a creature, man. What it does mean is that he showed himself to be the creature, the man, who in provisional distinction from all other men lives on the God-ward side of the universe, sharing His throne, existing and acting in the mode of God, and therefore to be remembered as such, to be known once for all as the exalted creature, this exalted man, and henceforth to be accepted as the One who exists in this to all eternity.[11]

The bodily resurrection of Jesus Christ is included in his subsequent ascension to the Father's right hand. Thus his humanity, and therefore our essential creatureliness, is preserved in a way that is peculiar to him. It is what we call 'resurrection life'. The chief difference between him and us as humans is that the ascension also means that Christ's humanity has been transferred to the presence of God. Christ's humanity is otherwise invisible to us but represented through biblical metaphor at 'the right hand of God's throne' (cf. Ps. 110:1).

The ascension is immediately located in the context of Barth's consideration of 'the man reconciled with God in Jesus Christ . . . the covenant man who faces the covenant God in the reconstitution and renewal of the covenant'.[12] Hence the humanity of Messiah Jesus fulfils the complementary half of God's covenantal promise 'I will be your God'; that is, 'you shall be my people'. More broadly, in *Church Dogmatics* Barth explores the risen Christ Jesus

without ceasing to be human, but assumed and accepted in His creatureliness and corruption by the Son of God . . . this one Son of Man – returned home to where He belonged, to His place as true man, to fellowship with God.[13]

Thus Barth concludes his theological interpretation of the incarnation as the Son of God going into the 'far country' with 'the homecoming of the Son of Man'.[14] He prefers this more apocalyptic title – Son of Man – because the returned Son of Man is 'the true and new man in virtue of this exaltation, the second Adam in whom there has taken place, and is actualised, the sanctification of all men'.[15] Barth's exposition of the ascension is broader still, though it is in keeping with his doctrine of election.[16] The ascended Jesus Christ is the man with whom and through whom God wills to have fellowship with us his human creatures.

This account of the exalted Son of Man is strengthened by calling

> Him the 'royal man' in recollection of the fact that we are now dealing with the . . . 'kingly office' of Jesus Christ: . . . with that man who has not only declared and inaugurated, but in his own person was and is and will be the kingdom and lordship of the God who reconciles the world with Himself.[17]

In keeping with his doctrine of election Barth understands Jesus the Christ as the purpose and goal of all God's activity in creation – especially in a creation that resists his lordship. Finally, as a culmination, Barth presents his theological justification for

> the meaning, or better, the power, of the existence of the one man Jesus Christ for those among whom and for whom, as the Reconciler, He, the Son of God, became also the Son of Man and one of them, their Brother.[18]

The other, and perhaps more fundamental, pillar of Barth's approach – Revelation – is the broadest context for the ascension. In keeping with the tenor of his work from his commentary on Romans Barth pushes his readers to reflect on God's free and lordly confrontation with them in his self-revelation to them as creatures and, what is more, sinners. This revelation comes only in and through the God-man, Jesus Christ. In Barth's thinking the exaltation of the Son of Man is the theological complement of the humiliation of the Son of God,[19] and it is necessary to ensure that the revelation of God in the gospel is consistent. That is, the God who submitted himself to humiliation on the cross for us is raised and glorified as such in his ascension. Alternatively, Barth asks:

> How do we really know . . . that Jesus Christ was and is and will be the eternal Word of God in our flesh . . . , in

215

whom . . . our human essence is exalted to fellowship with God?[20]

It is because, writes Barth, 'Revelation takes place in and with reconciliation. Indeed, the latter is also revelation. As God acts in it, He also speaks.'[21] It is the free and lordly act of God through his Son, who humbles himself to the point of death on the cross and then ascends back into heaven as the exalted Son of Man. As God acts in this twofold movement he also reveals the truth of reconciliation that it

> is God's active Yes to man as it is the fulfilment of the eternal decision in which God has determined, determines and will determine himself for man to be his God, and man for himself to be his man . . . 'Reconciliation' in the Christian sense of the word . . . is the history in which God concludes and confirms his covenant with man, maintaining and carrying it to its goal in spite of every threat.[22]

The objective reality of fallen but forgiven humanity is revealed in the ascended Christ Jesus in a way that reveals God's will for his relationship to humanity as its Creator and Reconciler. Jesus Christ is the 'true witness' to the being and act of God in and towards the world, even as he is the true witness to the present and future state of humanity.[23]

Forgiveness through the priest-king

Barth understood his exposition of the ascension within the doctrine of reconciliation as establishing a thoroughly threefold office for the Lord Jesus – prophet, priest and king. He outlines the historical progress of the doctrine beginning with Revelation 5:5–6, where Christ Jesus is depicted as '"the lion of the tribe of Judah that hath prevailed" yet also as "the Lamb as it had been slain"'.[24] From the sub-apostolic age through the patristic era and into the Middle Ages Christ Jesus is 'related to Aaron on the one side, and David, Solomon and even Joshua on the other, as the One who fulfils their prophetic existence'.[25] The Reformation, with the possible exception of Calvin, whose interpretation, in Barth's estimation, was closest to his own exposition in the *Church*

Dogmatics, followed the tradition. Barth thinks that Calvin favoured the kingly office above the priestly, at least in *Institutes* II.15, where the latter receives only cursory attention at the end of the chapter, while the prophetic and the kingly offices absorb the bulk of his attention. Overall, however, Barth claims that his own discussion is the only truly threefold theological reflection on the offices of Christ.

It is here that Barth is most vulnerable to criticism, especially in the context of the forgiveness of sin. Despite the volume of words in the *Church Dogmatics* devoted to the heavenly session, the significance of the priestly aspect of Messiah Jesus' mediation, not unlike Calvin's exposition, is less than that of the kingly and prophetic aspects of the descent and ascent of the God-man.[26] In Barth's case it was because he considered the cultic aspects of the New Testament portrayal of Jesus the Christ to be too far removed from the understanding of his audience and, more importantly, he felt better able to expand the significance of Christ Jesus' work in reconciliation by focusing on the forensic aspects of the New Testament portrayal.[27]

The Messiah as the Melchizedek priest does feature in Barth's examination of the material from Hebrews, which establishes the superiority of the high-priestly ministry of the Messiah over that of any priest in the line of Aaron:

> At the point to which the existence of the Old Testament
> priest, the human priest called by God, points and can
> only point, there now stands the acts of Jesus Christ in
> a way that is different to every other human priest, even
> the priest and the high-priest from the Old Testament.[28]

This acknowledgment notwithstanding, the context in Barth's account of reconciliation is the humiliation of the Son of God at the cross and, in particular, his obedience to the will of God. The focus of the priestly office is the messianic self-sacrificial *act* at Golgotha as distinct from his heavenly session.

The most explicit reference to the heavenly session occurs in the *Church Dogmatics* IV/3, §70.1, where Barth discusses the God-man as the 'true witness'. Barth recognizes that 'It is as this One, Suffering and Afflicted' that Messiah Jesus now makes intercession for those who come to God (cf. Heb. 7:24–25).[29]

Further, he recognizes the risen Christ Jesus as 'the Lamb slain' who '*still stands* between the throne of God and the heavenly and earthly cosmos' (cf. Rev. 5:6). However, the reader's attention is diverted towards the prophetic nature of Christ's 'insurpassable and definitive rather than provisional and relative . . . suffering . . . Jesus Christ [is] victorious in [this] suffering'.[30] For Barth, this is the ultimate revelation that God is on our side (*pro nobis*) as sinners: 'In His mercy God's own mercy is present and active. God Himself suffers with us as He suffers.'[31] Barth's focus here, in keeping with the Protestant tradition, is on the repeated refrain of 'he sat down' in the letter to the Hebrews (1:3; 8:1; 10:12; 12:2) as signification that the sacrificial act of Christ at the cross, the nexus of his high-priestly duties, has *achieved* the conditions for the possibility of forgiveness 'once and for all'.[32] We may indeed pray that the Father will forgive our sin in the name of Jesus the Christ because his self-sacrifice is always sufficient to turn away God's wrath from us and has met the just penalty due to us for rejecting God's promises. This act of the Messiah's is the sole means by which forgiveness may be attained.

Barth's eschatology is incomplete, but, even so, there are elements of his exposition that could or, at least, should, have been taken further. Against the Reformed tradition, Barth wanted Jesus the Christ to be the revelation of the electing God and the elect man. He followed this through in the doctrine of reconciliation, with the Messiah as the Son of God descending to the cross and ascending into glory as the Son of Man. I distinguished my exposition of God's will from Barth's in chapter 5 by turning the focus of our attention to the Spirit as the electing God who constitutes the church in and through the risen Christ, who is the Father's chosen one. We may now take this further as we start to consider the forgiveness of sin eschatologically. We can welcome elements of Barth's position on both election and revelation. In terms of election I have argued that it is in the person of Jesus the Melchizedek priest that everlasting forgiveness is available, since he is the living sacrifice for sin. However, and here we could argue that Barth was *insufficiently* Christological, the risen Messiah himself becomes the 'true (and everlasting) witness' to the wrath of God against sin. His immortalized scars have been taken 'into the [heavenly] sanctuary securing an eternal redemption' (cf. Heb. 9:12). Yet they are an everlasting testimony to *both* mercy *and* wrath, since it is not simply the office or order of Christ's priesthood that reveals the will of the Father but also the offering of his person. As Barth himself wrote, 'He is the atonement as the fulfilment of the covenant.'[33] We shall consider the significance of the dual nature of his offering further when we turn to our hope.

Life in the Middle as forgiven life

I have maintained all along that the first act of those regenerated by the electing Spirit is to call upon our heavenly Father for the forgiveness of sins, an act that is grounded on the Father's promise to mediate forgiveness through the person and work of our great high priest. We respond to the Father's promise in hope and that hope is embodied in our prayers. However, our hope is not merely embodied in prayer for ourselves; it must lead inevitably to forgiveness, which is an ordinary characteristic of life in the Middle.

That our hope of forgiveness is embodied in our practice of it is made explicit in the fifth petition of the Lord's Prayer (Matt. 6:12; Luke 11:4). From the very beginning the Lord himself had so interpreted the Father's will: 'For if you forgive people their trespasses, your heavenly Father will also forgive you but if you do not forgive people neither will your Father forgive you your trespasses' (Matt. 6:14–15; cf. Mark 11:25–26). The act of forgiving transgressors is directly linked to receiving forgiveness: 'the one who is forgiven little, loves little' (Luke 7:47; cf. Matt. 18:21–35) or, as Barth commented, 'For those who know that they are cast upon the mercy of God, that they cannot exist without the divine forgiveness . . . cannot do otherwise than to forgive their fellow human beings.'[34] Forgiving others is basic to the 'charity and brotherly love' that Calvin understood as 'the third advantage of the Sacrament [Lord's Supper]' and essential for holy life in the church.[35]

Since the practice of forgiveness is founded on God's initiative towards sinners in Christ Jesus, the right to judge sin and therefore potentially to forgive sin belongs to God alone. Barth described it thus: 'By the fact that God commands us to forgive our debtors, He reminds us that we must not arrogate to ourselves what is His privilege – to judge.'[36] Before God the Father we are not in the position to forgive another 'the fact of [their] guilt'.[37] Rather, we make God's forgiveness, offered to them in Christ Jesus, our own.

219

Barth turned this around to reflect on the importance of the neighbour that we meet in Christ, in whom we meet Christ, to point out that our neighbour is the reminder and barrier who keeps us in the forgiveness offered through Christ Jesus:

> The neighbour cannot forgive me my sin. But if my sin is forgiven, my neighbour can say to me that I need this forgiveness, that I cannot choose between a life of forgiveness and some other life which will perhaps illumine me better. The neighbour can keep me to the fact that a choice and decision has already been made concerning me in this respect. The neighbour can speak to me about my own confession of sin.[38]

As I have maintained from the beginning, the church is the spatial aspect of life in the Middle and the place within which our lives are shaped by the promises of God, the forgiveness of sin in particular. The practice of forgiveness involves a variety of relationship dynamics for forgiven sinners, and throughout his exposition of divine reconciliation Barth acknowledges these to a greater or lesser extent.[39] The ethical vision of the *Church Dogmatics* and Barth's theology in general has been the subject of much debate and, since the project was unfinished, Barth did not give the same attention to ethical issues that we find in works devoted to moral theology.[40] Nevertheless, recent scholarship has highlighted the ethical nature of Barth's work, which rests on his 'theological epistemology, anthropology and eschatology'.[41] We shall draw on that scholarship and briefly examine the practice of forgiveness in Barth's theology.

The practice of forgiveness

If Moltmann's resurrection hope that I discussed in the previous chapter is to have the kind of holistic and socially reconstructive effects that I proposed, then life in the Middle will involve sinners forgiving one another as they have been forgiven. More importantly, in the modern age of tolerance we must first recognize the distinction between 'surmounting the indecipherable complexities of difference' and 'confronting and overcoming discernible wrong'.[42] That is, the Christian practice of forgiveness is much more than finding ways to alleviate conflict by relativizing guilt.

220

Kant's moralism was the context for Barth's[43] reflections on ethical questions, and his approach to forgiveness was similar – for him, there is no 'weak overlooking and pardoning of human wrong'.[44] Nevertheless, following the example of our heavenly Father's patience (Rom. 2:4),[45] Christians are called upon to be patient with their transgressors, and in Barth's thinking the distinction between *forbearance* and forgiveness is similar to the distinction between love for the neighbour and a general congeniality or 'friendliness' towards others:[46]

> It is the position of readiness of the Christian as he looks and moves to the neighbour or brother of to-morrow in each of his fellows, even including the 'enemy' of the people and the community. Those who themselves exist in this context of the history of salvation . . . must be ready and on the way to love for all, even in relationships in which its realisation is at the moment impossible.[47]

The existence shaped by God's promises during life in the Middle means that the Christian lives in anticipation of restoration with his or her transgressor, 'bearing with them' on the way to forgiveness (Col. 3:13). Forbearance out of love for Christ Jesus, in the first instance, and the transgressor, in the second, accords with Paul's injunctions in Ephesians 4 to 'walk according to their calling' (Eph. 4:1) and allows the disciple to be more than passive as he or she waits upon full repentance from his or her transgressors. Because the disciple's life is shaped by the Father's promises made through our Lord and Messiah, however, those who forbear with their transgressors do so on the implicit understanding that Jesus the Christ will judge: 'He who has acted there as Judge will also judge', *even if it is* 'He and not I [who] will judge others.'[48] Mercy towards those who sin against us may only triumph in the face of judgment, not without it.[49]

Ordinarily, as Coutts notes, the practice of forgiveness involves *confrontation*, at the very least in so far as a wrong is identified even as it is forgiven.[50] Especially in a church, conflict avoidance in the name of 'love and peace' undermines genuine unity since '[when] the question of truth is sacrificed to that of love and peace, we are not on the way to one Church'.[51] It must be noted at this point, however, that Barth is concerned mainly with confrontation that may arise when fundamental aspects of Christian truth are contested as distinct from more mundane examples of interpersonal conflict. So, while it may be possible to draw principles from doctrinal disputes and apply them to any relationship breakdown, as Coutts does, Barth's focus is 'the glorious divine Yes' that encloses 'the No' which 'radically [challenges] and [overthrows] their existence'.[52] This circumstance is not the same as the interpersonal grievances involved when the Lord Jesus encourages a believer to 'take two or three witnesses' (Matt. 18:16) to contest with the brother who has sinned against them – even if the church is subsequently involved.

Confession is an essential milestone in the reconciliation process and, as Coutts notes, it involves both parties.[53] Confrontation requires an element of confession on the part of the aggrieved, who must confess that they have been wronged in some way. For forgiveness to proceed, there must also be a complementary confession on the part of the wrongdoer – owning up to his or her offence and recognizing it as offensive. Coutts rightly observes that such an event may well require varying degrees of forbearance from either party until, in the power of the Spirit that constitutes the church, estranged Christians 'honestly and seriously try to hear and perhaps hear the voice of the Lord . . . and then try to hear, and perhaps actually hear, the voice of the others'.[54] The basic assumption for both must be that Christ Jesus not only mediates *for* each of them before God, but also *between* each of them before God the Father. Only the Spirit who prompts us to 'cry Abba Father' and confess our dependence upon his forgiveness can overcome the divisions that sinners create between themselves (cf. Eph. 2:14–22).

The forbearance that has nevertheless confronted sin, confessing that it is wrong, in anticipation of a similar recognition/confession on the part of the wrongdoer, has taken a step towards forgiveness and reconciliation, following the divine example. From Barth's perspective, forgiveness is a gift given in freedom but that also means that forgiveness, or the offer of it, precedes repentance: 'repentance does not cause but relies on forgiveness'.[55] Repentance, for Barth, 'is the first natural breath in the air of the forgiveness which has already come to pass and which is already present to men. Repentance itself can now be called a gift of God

(Ac. 5:31; 11:18).'[56] The gifts of forgiveness and repentance may well be refused, and without confession repentance is meaningless in the face of the aggrieved party's gracious initiative. Therefore the gift of forgiveness has been disdained – such is the typical behaviour of the perennial abuser who has, in fact, willed to remain unreconciled: 'unwillingness to repent is the constant renewal of [his or her] sin'.[57] The one who forbears in freedom, even with a persistent abuser, does so in the light of the coming judgment mentioned above. His or her persistent offer of forgiveness adds to the condemnation of the unrepentant in the light of this judgment 'whatever you did not do for the least of these, you did not do for me either' (Matt. 25:45).

The burden of those who forbear with their antagonists, in the face of varying degrees of confession/repentance, is not one that should be borne alone. The church into which forgiven sinners are admitted can and should play a role in the process of reconciliation. Thus the Lord Jesus outlines the process of *correction* in passages like Matthew 18, which begins with a private confrontation and ends not just with 'tell the church' but also 'if he also refuses to listen to the church, he will be to you like an outsider/unbeliever [*ethnikos*] and a tax collector' (Matt. 18:17; cf. 1 Cor. 5:9–13). That is, the church as the body into which both the aggrieved and the wrongdoer have been incorporated by the Spirit may appropriate the conflict to the point at which the church rules for the aggrieved: 'The children of God who are liberated for invocation of God as their Father exist in responsibility to him and therefore to his people and therefore to each of its many members.'[58] However, in Barth's thinking and in keeping with the idea of forbearance, the disciplinary act of separation is likewise in anticipation of subsequent reconciliation: 'Temporary separation may be necessary in order that new and better fellowship may be possible – but only for this reason.'[59] The intervention of the church is at the point where reconciliation has failed to proceed as distinct from the weight of the offence and the 'two or three witnesses' act as a counterbalance between the one and the many for both the aggrieved and the accused.[60] Yet all this is to keep the process of reconciliation moving forward towards complete forgiveness.

Finally, both the aggrieved and the accused have free access to the forgiveness that is mediated through the great high priest,

Jesus the Christ. Because of this, the desire for revenge and the felt need to make reparation must be limited for interpersonal forgiveness to mirror the divine act as it ought to. As we shall see in the next section, the Father's act to glorify Jesus as Lord ought not to reduce the Messiah's final judgment to an act of *self*-vindication. Similarly, while the Scriptures urge disciples 'to offer your bodies as a living sacrifice, holy and pleasing to God' (Rom. 12:1), this could never compensate for the self-sacrifice of the great high priest. Consequently, during life in the Middle forgiveness between sinners and even reconciliation may well only be provisional, or even promissory, particularly where no real reparation can be made for the grievance. As Coutts observes, it may well be at this point that the sacrament of the Lord's Supper can be most powerful.[61] The rhythm of remembrance and anticipation essential to this corporate activity revolves around proclaiming the Father's gracious acts towards us in Christ Jesus. As a church identifies the universal need for God's forgiveness and the blessing of receiving it together, it has a great levelling effect on the community. On the level playing field of the Father's gift of forgiveness through Christ Jesus and in the power of his Spirit, space is created for the aggrieved to forbear with the accused and to offer forgiveness as a gift, while perpetrators are given the hope of release from the consequences of their sin, '[when] he comes' (1 Cor. 11:26). Until then, the difficult task of living with memories may need to accept that 'rather than being deleted [memories], [they] will simply fail to surface in one's consciousness – they will not come to mind'.[62]

We cannot pursue the delicacies and intricacies of interpersonal forgiveness in the light of the coming judgment, for we must now turn our attention to the event itself and ask what we may hope for in terms of forgiveness of sin.

Forgiveness of sin and the day of judgment

As we explored the perfection of the Father's will in and through Jesus the Christ, we observed that an aspect of his everlasting vindication was his authority and right to act as the executor of the Father's heavenly will for the earth. The glorified Messiah will be the judge of all the earth at the time of the Father's choosing (Acts 17:31). In the last chapter I gave a theological account of this future time as that of the general resurrection, when the Son of Man will command the dead to live in the perfection of the new creation. Through his everlasting mediator, God the Father will then enter into judgment in order that his will be perfected everlastingly. It has long been argued that Barth's exposition of the doctrine of election must inevitably lead to a universal verdict of blessing for humankind, that the perfection of God's relationship with his creatures must entail universal forgiveness of sin. In what follows I shall again attempt a theological exposition of the final judgment as I did of the general resurrection, by reconsidering the promises of God the Father concerning his name, his reign and his will. In particular, we shall seek an eschatological answer to the question 'Why does God ultimately judge creation?'

The final judgment vindicates Messiah Jesus as Lord

To begin with, let us return to the conclusion of chapter 3. God the Father has promised that he will be glorified when all of creation – living and dead – is brought together to confess Messiah Jesus as the Lord (Phil. 2:11). On that day the self-sacrifice of Jesus the Christ will be vindicated as the Father's act of salvation in fulfilment of his promises to Abraham, Isaac and Jacob. As we observed in chapter 3 this is both a vindication of God's promissory name – to be present as the saving one – and the fact that YHWH was active in Jesus of Nazareth for the forgiveness of sin at the cross. Joseph was told to give the son of Mary the name Jesus, 'for he will save his people from their sins' (Matt. 1:21), and this son of a virgin would be called Immanuel – 'God with us' – in fulfilment of Isaiah's prophecy (Matt. 1:22–23; cf. Isa. 7:14). In addition, as we explored in chapter 3, the universal acclamation and proclamation of Messiah Jesus as Lord is the hallowing of that name. It is the universal recognition that Messiah Jesus is the holy one of Israel who acts in the power of the Holy Spirit as the angel promised (Luke 1:35). In him and through him the Father's promise to be 'the compassionate and gracious God, slow to anger, abounding in love and faithfulness, maintaining love . . . and forgiving wickedness, rebellion and sin' is perfected. 'Yet . . . not leav[ing] the guilty unpunished' (Exod. 34:7). In the final judgment, God forgives sin in order to vindicate Jesus the Christ as *this* Lord.

225

If, therefore, we anticipate the universal acclamation and proc-lamation of Christ Jesus as the Lord, should we also, and necessarily, anticipate that the forgiveness of sins will be, corres-pondingly, universal? After all, Paul encourages the church in Rome by saying, 'If you *confess* with your mouth *that Jesus is Lord* and believe in your heart that God raised him from the dead, you will be saved' (Rom. 10:9). Universal proclamation of lordship ought therefore to equate with universal forgiveness and salvation in the final judgment. In addition, in the same letter, Paul tells the church, 'So then, just as through one trespass there is *condem-nation for all people*, so also through one righteous act there is *justification of life for everyone*' (Rom. 5:18). From what Paul writes of sin in Romans 3 of the letter there can be no doubt that the condemnation is universal (cf. Rom. 3:10–12, 23). Should we therefore assume, according to Romans 5:18, that forgiveness in the final judgment will also be universal? This conclusion, as we saw in chapter 5, was an almost irresistible outcome for Barth's exposition of the doctrine of election and one to which Barth him-self was not completely averse: 'One thing is sure, that there is no theological justification for setting any limits on our side to the friendliness of God towards man which appeared in Jesus Christ.'[63]

To be fair, Barth's interaction with the Reformed tradition was determined to uphold both the New Testament witness to the universal scope of God's reconciling actions *and* the irresistible nature of God's grace in those actions.[64] In contrast, most modern descriptions of universal salvation, particularly those that argue for universal forgiveness of sin, tend to fall into two categories:[65] one in which the emphasis is placed on the indomitable nature of God's love for creation over against his wrath towards sin, death and evil, with the result that no one can be lost if God's love is ultimately and genuinely victorious;[66] and the other in which God's justice rests on exclusively restorative or therapeutic foundations, so that eventually all human creatures will abandon their rebellion (even *post mortem*) and accept God's forgiveness.[67] The possibility that some will be cursed with God's wrath at the final judgment exists only if God's love is somehow powerless against his wrath or human freedom is able to resist the divine intent. Barth rejected both these alternatives along with the ancient doctrine of *apokatastasis* ('restoration of all things'; cf. Acts 3:21) proposed by Origen.[68]

226

It is from an optimistic estimate of man in conjunction with this postulate of the infinite potentiality of the divine being that the assertion of a final redemption of each and all, known as the doctrine of the *apokatastasis*, usually draws its inspiration and power.[69]

Against this, Barth argued, 'God does not owe eternal patience and therefore deliverance' to sinners.[70] More importantly Barth also recognized that wrath was the action of God's *holy love* towards sin, death and evil as distinct from wrath, by definition, being opposed to love.

God's wrath in his holy love
In order to understand the forgiveness of sin both theologically and eschatologically we must understand the complementary relationship between God's love and his wrath. Ironically, Barth's contribution to this topic is most useful. In keeping with the Christian tradition, Barth understood God's life in himself as simple. Yet Barth's determination to understand God's life in himself only through his acts means that God's various and distinct attributes or perfections[71] are both 'the form of love in which God is free, [and] a form of freedom in which God loves'.[72] God is simple because all his attributes revealed in his acts are nothing but God himself. A further critical feature of Barth's description is the act of fellowship in which God freely and lovingly engages with creation: 'God is He who, without having to do so, seeks and creates fellowship between Himself and us.'[73] The fellowship that God initiates with creation he already enjoys in himself eternally as Father, Son and Holy Spirit, and so Barth uses the term 'overflow'. It is an

overflow which is not demanded or presupposed by any necessity, constraint, or obligation, least of all from the outside, from our side, or by any law by which God himself is bound and obliged. On the contrary, in itself and as such it is again rooted in Himself alone.[74]

As an internally generated act of God the overflow is free and the character of fellowship which overflows is one of love. Therefore the overflow of God to everything that is not God is at once

227

loving and free in equal measure and absolutely grounded on his essence. This is of critical importance when it comes to locating sin, death and evil in the fellowship arising from the overflow of God's eternal life:

> [The overflow] establishes and embraces the antithesis between Creator and His creatures. It establishes and embraces necessarily too, God's anger and struggle against sin, God's separation from sinners, God's judgement hanging over them and consummated on them. There is death and hell and eternal damnation in the scope of this relationship of His.[75]

In this context wrath is God's anger at sin in the creation that he loves and his actions against it. But this wrath is not independent or isolated from his love and is therefore an aspect of the one fellowship that arises from the overflow that brings God's eternal life to creation. God acts in wrath towards sin, death and evil in creation *generated entirely from his holy love* for creation.

In the context of God's holy love towards creation grace is, for Barth, God's action both towards that which is not God and therefore 'not worthy' of fellowship but also, and most importantly, towards that which is 'utterly unworthy'; that is, the overflow of God for fellowship is 'unimpeded even by sin, by the resistance with which the creature faces Him'.[76] Nevertheless, God 'neither compromises with his [man's] resistance, nor ignores it, still less calls it good'.[77] Rather, *the revelation of God's grace results in the recipients experiencing God in opposition to them*, 'his opposition to the opposition in which man exists over and against him'.[78] Here is where we find God's wrath. Just as

> the tables of the Law with their annihilating commands and threats were hidden in the ark of the covenant and so placed under the throne of grace besprinkled with the blood of atoning sacrifice. But again this covenant cannot stand without the revelation of the Law of God in all its holiness, and therefore not without the revelation of the divine opposition and judgement of the wrath of God from heaven against all the ungodliness and unrighteousness of men (Rom. 1:18).[79]

The overflow of God's inner fellowship is graciously revealed as a holy opposition to humankind's persistent and consistent antagonism towards fellowship with God as revealed in his promises. Hence 'the holiness of God is not side by side but with His grace, and His wrath is not separate from but in His love'.[80] In fact (and reflecting on the confrontation between the thrice-holy God and the prophet Isaiah, in Isa. 6), Barth remarks that the holy love of God that rejects man's rejection of him means that wrath is integral to the perfection of holy fellowship between God and the human being: 'To accept God's grace it necessarily means therefore, to respect God's holiness, and therefore to accept, heed and keep His laws, to fear His threats, to experience His wrath and to suffer His punishment.'[81] To distance God's wrath from his love would be to alienate the holiness of God's love from his grace.

At the final judgment, and in the first instance, the Holy Spirit of God gathers creation, which he loves, to substantiate once and for all that the holy name of Lord belongs to Jesus the Christ. In the long story of God's name that we explored, the holy opposition that Barth described included God's activity to vindicate his name even against his covenant people without compromising his name in his determination to save them from exile:

> It is not for your sake that I will act, house of Israel, but for My holy name . . . I will honor the holiness of My great name . . . The nations will know that I am Yahweh . . . when I demonstrate My holiness through you in their sight.
>
> For I will take you from the nations and gather you from all the countries, and will bring you into your own land. (Ezek. 36:22–24)

In the power of the Holy Spirit, Messiah Jesus was acknowledged as holy by angels, demons and sinners during his ministry (Luke 1:35; 4:34; Mark 1:24; John 6:69). As the royal *and* eternal Son, when Jesus the Christ loves, we willingly accept this as the love of God in action. However, as Gunton observed, we ought also to accept that Christ Jesus' 'anger at the sickness which disfigures the creation is the wrath of God against evil' (cf. John 11:33–38).[82] To this we should add Jesus' angry reaction to the unbelief of the Jewish leaders (cf. Mark 3:35). When the Father exalts the royal and eternal Son before every bowed knee 'in heaven, on the earth and under the earth' it will be, in the first instance, to confess him as Lord, *the holy one of the Israel story* (Phil. 2:10). At the same time, therefore, it is not theologically necessary to assume that all those so gathered will experience the holy love of the Father mediated through his holy one in the same manner. The issue can be further clarified as we reconsider the perfection of God's kingdom through the glorified Jesus Christ.

The final judgment vindicates the Lord Jesus as the Christ

As we explored the promise of the coming kingdom of God we observed that the long story of divine reign is encapsulated in the economic resolution of the relationship between the Father and his royal and eternal Son in the power of the Spirit. From 1 Corinthians 15:24–25 we noted that *The End* or the kingdom comes at the perfection of the history created by God's promises, particularly the royal covenant as captured in Psalm 110:1:

> Sit at My right hand
> until I make Your enemies Your footstool.

Thus, in the second instance, the final judgment is for the purpose of delivering justice to God's Messiah, that *he* is vindicated against *his* enemies (see also Pss 18:48; 45:5; 72:9; 89:10; 110:2). Alternatively, in Barth's language, having said *No* to the Messiah in Gethsemane in order to achieve his plan, in judgment the Father says *Yes* to his Son in order to perfect his plan:

> I will make the nations Your inheritance
> and the ends of the earth Your possession.
>
> (Ps. 2:8)

The Gospel narratives are quite explicit about the presence of various agents that seek to thwart or oppose the mission of the royal and eternal Son and, as we observed in chapter 4, are encapsulated in the 'strong man' parable that Jesus himself tells (Matt. 12:25–31; Mark 3:23–30; Luke 11:17–23). The most obvious is, of course, Satan and the various demons or evil/ unclean spirits that confront the Messiah directly. Mention of the devil's opposition towards the Spirit's perfecting work continues throughout the New Testament (1 Cor. 7:5; 2 Cor. 2:11; 11:14; 12:7; Eph. 4:27; 6:11; 1 Thess. 2:18; 1 Tim. 3:6; 5:15; Jas 4:7; 1 Peter 5:8; Rev. 2:10), despite the presence of the Messiah at 'the right hand of God', and having 'disarmed and disgraced the principalities and powers at the cross' (Col. 2:15). The only, albeit figurative, description of an end to the contest comes in Revelation 20:10 with the devil being consigned to an everlasting 'lake of fire and sulphur'. Therefore, at the very least, this cohort of darkness must be considered the enemies against whom the royal and eternal Son is vindicated at the final judgment. For these enemies of the Messiah the holy love of God for his creatures is mediated exclusively as wrath to vindicate the Father as righteous in his promise to his Son.

A greater challenge to the universalist position, as we observed in chapter 4, is the fact that the strong man's minions include more than exclusively supernatural agents. As the narratives advance we reach the point where the Messiah names, quite shockingly, the people of promise as 'sons of Satan'.[83] Initially confined to the leaders, the opposition spreads throughout the crowds who echo Satan's challenges at the foot of the cross 'if you are the Son of God' (Matt. 27:40; cf. Luke 23:37) and ultimately includes the Roman overlords as 'The kings of the earth took their stand and the rulers assembled together against the Lord and against his Messiah' (Acts 4:26; cf. Ps. 2:2).

In addition, and again in the context of the strong-man parable (Matt. 12:29; Mark 3:27; Luke 11:21), the Messiah nominates a particular sin as unforgivable: 'whoever speaks against the Holy Spirit will not be forgiven, neither in this age nor in the age to come' (Matt. 12:31; Mark 3:29; Luke 12:10). Calvin considers the weight of this statement to rest on the fact that

> those persons sin and blaspheme against the Holy Spirit, who maliciously turn to his dishonour the perfections of God, which have been revealed to him by the Spirit, in which his glory ought to be celebrated, and who, with Satan, their leader, are avowed enemies of the glory of God.[84]

It is quite possible, therefore, for human beings to be so closed to the mission of the Messiah that they perceive that which is truly good *to be evil* (cf. Rom. 1:28–32). In fact, Mark's account makes specific reference to the attitude of the scribes: 'they were saying he [Jesus] had an unclean spirit' (Mark 3:30). Hence the enmity in question here towards the royal and eternal Son has passed beyond contesting the validity of the Messiah's person and work, to specific enmity towards, or rejection of, his person and work as *a source of goodness.*[85]

The reformer went on to speculate that such behaviour 'is a token of reprobation, and hence it follows, that whoever have fallen into it, have been delivered over to a reprobate mind'.[86] Barth, in comparison, treats 'the famous hard saying'[87] as more a hypothetical possibility than a likely response.[88] Between these two extremes we should acknowledge that satanically inspired enmity towards the Spirit is distinguished from simple contest with the Son (Matt. 12:31; Luke 12:10) as unforgivable. This is seen most starkly in Jesus' rebuke ('Get behind me, Satan' [Matt. 16:23; Mark 8:33]) to Peter's rather more obviously naive opposition to the former's death and hence failure to grasp the plan of God the Father. Later, even Peter's thrice-repeated denial of Jesus does not result in a 'satanic sifting' (Luke 22:31) of him.

On the other hand, until the perfecting Spirit intervenes in the lives of human creatures they '[walk] according . . . to the ruler who exercises authority over the lower heavens, the spirit now working in the disobedient'. In fact, all living in 'fleshly desires, carrying out the inclinations of [their] flesh and thoughts . . . [are] by nature children under wrath' (Eph. 2:1–3). They are 'storing up wrath for [themselves] on the day of wrath' (Rom. 2:5; cf. Jude 6). Such persons, as Barth observed, experience the holy love of God as wrath because they are considered 'alienated and *enemies* in [their] minds by their evil works' (Col. 1:21). We noted in chapter 5 that Barth's exposition of election left little or no space for various New Testament aspects of eschatology that allow the history of creation to be significant for the revelation of the will of God for creation after the resurrection. Though a highly qualified theological version of universalism, Barth's exposition of the doctrines of election and reconciliation leaves only hypothetical space for enemies of the Messiah, since at the cross the

> wrath of God which is the fire of His love has taken him
> [the enemy] away and all his transgressions and offences

and errors and follies and lies and faults and crimes against God and his fellowmen and himself, just as a whole burnt offering is consumed on the altar with the flesh and skin and bones and hoofs and horns, rising up as fire to heaven and disappearing. That is how God has dealt with the man who broke covenant with Himself, God has vindicated Himself in relation to this man.[89]

The enemy of the Christ, one deemed guilty of blasphemy against the Holy Spirit, has been totally eclipsed by the Lord Jesus as the rebellious human from Barth's perspective.[90] What the above quotes evidence is the *sufficiency* of Christ's sacrifice for sin in keeping with the cultic language of atonement. If, perhaps, Barth had maintained equilibrium between this cultic language of sufficiency and the forensic language of equity (the punishment fits the crime), there would be more conceptual space to discuss God's reconciling work in a way that includes his righteous vindication of the royal and eternal Son.[91] The absence of Christ Jesus as the priestly king in Barth's ascension theology diminishes the possibility of maintaining the necessary harmony even on his own terms.[92] Furthermore, there is no reflection on Psalm 110:1 in the *Church Dogmatics* and therefore little acknowledgment that the righteousness of *any and all* of the Father's promises rests on the complete vindication of his royal and eternal Son. The prospect of the final judgment for the sake of the glorified Messiah is absent, which may be an aspect of what some have referred to as Barth's 'holy silence' on the matter of wrath at the final judgment.[93] Yet from the perspective of the New Testament judgment is dreadful and explicit. The psalmist warned the people of Israel:

> Pay homage to the Son or He will be angry
> and you will perish in your rebellion,
> for His anger may ignite at any moment.
> All those who take refuge in Him are happy.
> (Ps. 2:12)

The Lord Jesus will be vindicated as Messiah against his enemies when he is revealed 'from heaven with his mighty, fiery angels, inflicting vengeance on those who do not know God and on those

233

who do not obey the gospel of our Lord Jesus' (2 Thess. 1:7–8). The vindication takes the form of God's holy love mediated as wrath through the death scars of the glorified Messiah who sacrificed himself on the cross since he is and remains 'the Lamb who was slain' (Rev. 5:6–13). In his person God preserves an everlasting memorial of the antagonism of humanity towards the promises of the Father in general and the grace of the Lord Jesus in particular. Consequently, there is a curse for those resurrected as enemies since 'they will look at the one they have pierced' (Zech. 12:10; cf. John 19:37). Commensurate with the reign of the royal and eternal Son, the curse is an everlasting, personal retribution of *subjugated* confession 'that Jesus *Christ* is Lord, to the glory of God the Father'. The terror of this retribution is anticipated in apocalyptic imagery throughout the New Testament and especially in Revelation. While the tradition has strayed in its attention towards the geography of hell, or more accurately Gehenna, in the Gospel narratives,[94] it is essential nevertheless that Christian eschatology take seriously *the personal commitment* of the Father to vindicate his royal and eternal Son in the power of his Holy Spirit at his return. Therefore we ought to heed the explicit warnings of Scripture, '[Do not] despise the riches of his kindness, restraint, and patience, [by] not recognizing that God's kindness is intended to lead you to repentance' (Rom. 2:4).

If, however, 'the gift is not like the trespass' (Rom. 5:15), how much more is the blessing unlike the curse and therefore the hope of forgiveness at the final judgment? I bring this chapter to a close by returning to the Father's will summed up in Messiah Jesus as the Lord, and the mercy mediated through the great high priest.

The final judgment vindicates the inheritance of the Lord Jesus Christ

The ultimate hope for forgiveness at the final judgment rests on the Father's plan from before the creation of the world to 'sum up all things in Christ Jesus' (Eph. 1:9–10). The perfection of the plan set in motion through the first man in the garden is expressed in the Apocalypse using the Immanuel and covenant promises: 'Look, the dwelling of God is with humanity, he will dwell with them, they will be his people and he himself will be their God' (Rev. 21:3). The perfecting work of the Spirit reaches its goal with 'the redemption of the possession to the praise of [the Father's] glory' (Eph. 1:14). That is, at the final judgment, and, as we observed in chapter 5, the perfect king Jesus' personal treasury, devoted to the establishment of the *new* temple (Eccl. 2:8; 1 Chr. 29:3; cf. Eph. 2:21–22), will finally be presented in the form of the bride of the Christ, 'splendid . . . without spot or wrinkle . . . but holy and blameless' (Eph. 5:27; cf. Rev. 21:2). At long last the blessing 'to all nations' promised through Abraham of offspring 'as numerous as the stars of the sky and the sand on the seashore' (Gen. 22:17) is fulfilled in the power of the Holy Spirit (Gal. 3:14). These children of God, adopted through the royal and eternal Son (Eph. 1:5; cf. John 1:12), are the 'vast multitude from every nation, tribe, people and language, which no one could number, standing before the throne and before the Lamb' (Rev. 7:9). On them is bestowed confirmation of 'redemption through his [the Messiah's] blood, forgiveness of [their] trespasses' (Eph. 1:7).

At the perfection of the Father's will, when every creature is brought together in the power of the Spirit in a new creation, it is the Lord Jesus Christ who 'wins'. Of him will be sung, 'You are worthy to take the scroll and to open its seals, because You were slaughtered, and You redeemed people for God by Your blood from every tribe and language and people and nation' (Rev. 5:9). Jesus the Christ is acclaimed and proclaimed everlastingly as the victor, and not by abstract attributes of God like grace or mercy, or even love. Instead, as Barth himself preferred:

> 'Triumph of Grace' might at any rate give rise to the impression that what is meant to be indicated is the victory of one principle, that of grace, over another which is to be described as evil, sin, the devil or death. But we are not concerned here with the precedence, victory or triumph of a principle, even though the principle be that of grace. We are concerned with the living person of Jesus Christ.[95]

Barth's point here, in different language, is that the perfection of the Father's will is much more than an account of divine conflict resolution with universally therapeutic application as preferred by Romantic universalists.[96] Even concepts like grace, as central to the gospel message and the attributes of God as they may be, are descriptions of God's action in and through the person of

Jesus the Christ: 'He Himself [is] its Bearer, Bringer and Revealer, [He] is the Victory.'[97] More importantly, perhaps, the summing up of all things in Christ Jesus is the ultimate act of the love of the Father in the Spirit for *the royal and eternal Son*. First and foremost, the Christian hope rests on the revelation that 'the Father loves the [incarnate] Son' (John 3:35; 5:20; 10:17) since 'all things are for him' (Col. 1:16). In this light the eschatological church is the people whom the royal and eternal Son has 'redeemed for God', and to whom the love that the Father has for the Son is mediated everlastingly through the priest in the order of Melchizedek *as mercy* and forgiveness.

8

GOOD LORD, DELIVER US

My description of eschatology, shaped by the fourth, fifth and sixth petitions of the Lord's Prayer, was intended to deepen the account of life in the Middle experienced by God's people. Accordingly, we reflected on the effects of resurrection hope for believers who have been brought by the Spirit into the church. In dialogue with Moltmann we considered the possibilities of the Father's perfecting work for his children in terms of a life characterized by the fruit of the Spirit as well as their personal, social and temporal integration into the body of Christ. The resurrection life of believers in the Spirit is, of course, founded on the resurrection life of Jesus the Christ, which was unique in itself but also intended for us.

In addition, and in conversation with Barth, we paid particular attention to the dynamics of forgiveness within the newly integrated relationships believers have as members of Christ's body. Since the Spirit integrates individuals into the body of Christ on the basis of the forgiveness that Christ has won for them, the kind of reintegration that Moltmann favours can occur only among sinners who have experienced forgiveness. In the shadow of the cross and in the light of the final judgment the proclamation of

237

the Father's forgiveness is demonstrated in baptism and the Lord's Supper, in order to create a culture of forbearance and release from the failures that sinners regularly fall into. In this final chapter I shall complete the description of our passion for the possibilities of God's perfecting work that characterizes life in the Middle.

In chapter 1 we worked with a Christocentric form of passion – 'taking up [our] cross and following' the crucified Christ (Matt. 16:24; Mark 8:34; Luke 9:23). The context for this experience of our hope is captured for us in the last petition of the Lord's Prayer, 'do not bring us into temptation but deliver us from the evil one' (Matt. 6:13). As has been my practice throughout the book, I shall briefly investigate the eschatological dimension of this request before moving on to consider *what we know* of the ascended Christ's reign on the earth prior to his return, *what we should do* as we wait for his arrival and *what we can hope for* when the Father consummates all things in his royal and eternal Son and by his Holy Spirit.

The Middle as a time of trial

Ultimate deliverance from the attacks of Satan will come when the royal Son does the Father's will by pouring out his wrath on his enemies. Until that time the effects of sin, death and evil during life in the Middle are real, whether they arise from within or without, even though Jesus the Christ rules from the 'right hand' of God's throne (cf. Ps. 110:1). The Middle, shaped as it is by remembrance and anticipation, is still a time of trial. Traditionally, the temptations that afflict us were viewed by some to be synonymous with evil since one cannot suffer the former without being caught up in the latter:[1] temptation itself was an evil. Christians of a more ascetic persuasion, like Gregory of Nyssa, therefore urged their readers to separate themselves from the world or, at least, to pray they would be removed from such trials. In contrast, Augustine recognized that God does not tempt us: 'God is not tempted by evil and God tempts no one' (Jas 1:13). Nevertheless, he may test us and therefore *allow* us to be tempted so that we may learn just how dependent we are on him. So the sixth petition is a prayer for deliverance from being *overwhelmed* by trials. People who are subject to fire cannot but be touched by it, but nevertheless they try not to be destroyed by it.[2] As the story of Job makes clear, Satan may ask permission to tempt humans and, Augustine reminds us, God may permit it either as punishment or as a trial of our faith.[3] Yet even here different tests must be distinguished; for example, between the experience of Judas and Peter in relation to the devil. Augustine wanted us to pray for deliverance from the evil into which we have already been led.[4]

Calvin, for his part, understood the sixth petition as an echo of the law engraved upon the heart (Prov. 3:3; 2 Cor. 3:3). The Lord's leading throughout life in the Middle may include periods or seasons of trial, which may involve either riches or poverty that beguile or discourage us in turn. These seasons are periods of training in righteousness. Yet Calvin made an important distinction between temptations that arise from our own desires and those which are the product of the devil's guile. In other words, there is a difference between trials from within and tests from without. God does allow temptation as a test to make our faith stronger or 'exercised', but Satan seeks only to destroy: 'God, along with the temptation, makes a way of escape, that his own may be able patiently to bear all that he imposes upon them [1 Cor. 10:13; 2 Peter 2:9].'[5] Calvin was keen to point out that we do not pray in order to be able to challenge the evil one but so that when we are faced with his attacks we may not be vanquished. Barth similarly recognizes that 'blessed is the man who endures trials' (Jas 1:12). They will even be a source from which God can bring good as Paul encourages the Romans (8:28). Against the materialism of liberal Protestantism in the twentieth century Barth was determined to recapture the metaphysical reality of evil during life in the Middle: *Das Nichts* he called it.[6] The form in which evil comes is sin and death but most of all, it is as the devil. As with the saviour, so with his followers – the evil one will persistently seek to derail our efforts to follow the saviour even though he has no ultimate power over us. We pray to be led in such a way as 'to avoid this limit on the left, the pernicious boundary'.[7]

Since 'no slave is greater than his/her master' (John 13:16; 15:20) opposition to the Messiah or enmity towards him will be experienced by those who follow him. The Lord's own words to the gathered disciples were if the world hates you, know that it hated me beforehand. If you were of the world, the world would love you as its own. You are not of the world, but I have chosen you out of the world; because of this, the world hates you. (John 15:18–19)

The final petition of the Lord's Prayer is the cry of God's children for guidance through the trials of life in the Middle and, ultimately, redemption from the consequences of sin, death and evil. More generally, perhaps, it is a version of Niebuhr's serenity prayer, 'God grant me the serenity to accept the things I cannot change, the courage to change the things I can, and the wisdom to know the difference.'[8] The sixth petition invokes the dialectic between human activity and divine intervention, or that which we can and should do for ourselves, guided by the perfecting Spirit, and that which only God can do for us. We considered similar concepts when evaluating Moltmann's work on resurrection hope in chapter 1. Therefore, to understand the Father's answer to this petition theologically, we must re-engage with modern discussions about God's relationship to history and, in particular, with the ways in which the promises of God that underwrite our prayers shape the events through which we need guidance, and the antagonism to these promises from which we need deliverance. In short, we must return to the Father's perfecting work in the power of his Spirit.

Deliverance and the perfecting work of the Spirit

In chapter 1 I outlined the perfecting work of the Father in and for creation. The Holy Spirit moves all of creation towards its consummation in Jesus the Christ, which has been the Father's will since before there was a creation. There we focused on the mediation of God in the Spirit that enables the universe to be completely different from the nature of its Creator and yet, at the same time, remain absolutely dependent on the will of God in Jesus the Christ. In the subsequent chapters I drew attention to the work of the Spirit in, through and for the Messiah Jesus, who is Lord, in fulfilment of the Father's will. In this chapter we shall concentrate on the electing Spirit's work of leading those who belong to the church towards their ultimate deliverance. Chapter 8 of Paul's letter to the Romans will be our starting point:

240

> I consider the sufferings of the present time not worth comparing to the glory about to be revealed to us. For the creation longingly awaits the revelation of the children of God. The creation was subjected to futility, not willingly, but through the subjecting one, in hope that the creation itself will be released from the bondage of corruption into the glorious freedom of the children of God. For we know that all creation has been groaning together, suffering as with the pangs of childbirth until now. We also, who have the first fruits of the Spirit, we ourselves groan inwardly eagerly awaiting our adoption, the redemption of our bodies. For in this hope we were saved and hope that is seen is no hope at all. If we hope for what is not seen, we wait for it patiently. (Rom. 8:18–25)

Paul describes life in the Middle as 'the present time'. It is a period characterized by 'groaning' both for the church, those 'who have the first fruits of the Spirit', and for 'the creation in general'. Moltmann reads this as 'an apocalyptic pressure of affliction, for everything that wants to live has to die'.[9] We may expound this more precisely by focusing on three things. First, we note that the 'futility' to which creation has been subjected is not just mortality but the consequence of divine fiat, as the vague passive suggests – 'the subjecting one'.[10] The present time of trial is no accident but rather a consequence of God's holy love for a world afflicted by human antagonism towards God's promises; as Calvin put it, 'in the sad disorder which followed the fall of Adam, the whole machinery of the world would have instantly become deranged'.[11] Second, the ability to perceive the Middle as a time of trial depends upon the electing (and therefore revelatory) work of the Spirit. More specifically perhaps, the groaning *of the children of God* is what accompanies the perfecting work of the Spirit – as distinct from the mere pressure of mortality suggested by Moltmann, which affects all the living. This is because, third, the sufferings of God's children result from their hope for 'the redemption of our bodies'. This redemption is more than the general resurrection that we looked at in chapter 6, since it includes what Paul describes as 'the glorious freedom of the children of God'. Understanding 'the present time' as a time of 'groaning' has been, and will no doubt remain, a trial for God's people as we struggle with the 'now' of God's achievements in Christ Jesus and await the 'not-yet' of their perfection in the Spirit. In the modern period, though not exclusively, the experience of the church during life in the Middle has frequently been discussed in the context of the millennium, the thousand-year reign of Christ and the saints prior to the new creation. As we explore what it means for the Father to lead and deliver us throughout life in the Middle we ought to consider the contribution of millennial theology.

The Middle and the millennium

The New Testament constantly draws attention to the fact that we are 'in the last days' and since the resurrection of Jesus his followers have longed to know when *The End* will come (cf. Acts 1:6). It was a particular concern of proponents of millennial theology in the nineteenth and twentieth centuries to chart the course for when the Middle will finally be over and the general resurrection and final judgment will take place. They sought to determine how the Father might be leading the church towards ultimate delivery from 'the world, the flesh and the devil'. We shall consider some of the options in millennial theology for interpreting the Father's leading on the way to confirming what I have already said about the kingdom of God in history.

The millennial family

Millennialism represents a broad range of (often conflicting) beliefs that are primarily concerned with 'a period of peace and righteousness on the earth associated with the Second Coming of Christ'.[12] Although millennial thought rests on a number of biblical texts, the most important one is Revelation 20:1–10, which specifically mentions the imprisonment of the devil 'for a thousand years' and the subsequent reign of the martyrs with Christ for 'a thousand years' (Rev. 20:3–4). Millennialists divide along three main lines of interpretation of what is meant by Christ Jesus and the martyrs reigning for a thousand years. The three lines are defined as 'premillennialism', 'postmillennialism' and 'amillennialism'. They are distinguished from one another according to *where* adherents place the millennium in relation to the second coming of the Lord Jesus. Premillennialists place the parousia before the start of the millennium and postmillennialists place it afterwards. Amillennialists generally hold that the 'millennium is the period of time between the two advents of our Lord [the earthly career of the Lord Jesus and his second coming] with the thousand years of Revelation 20 being *symbolic* of the entire [intervening] age'.[13]

Premillennialists claim that the millennium will be 'dramatically or cataclysmically inaugurated by the second coming'.[14] They look for a 'great tribulation'[15] to occur immediately before the millennium involving signs of the times – 'cosmic phenomena, persecution and great suffering'.[16] Christ's return will result in the binding of Satan and his minions, bringing peace for the 'thousand years'. The exact timing of the great tribulation is a cause for further division among premillennialists. The pre-tribulationists hold that the church will be removed from the earth just before the cataclysms, whereas the post-tribulationists maintain that it will suffer the events that lead to the second coming. This idea that the church will be removed prior to the tribulation – 'the rapture' – is a feature of dispensational pre-millennialism that emerged in the nineteenth century through the work of J. N. Darby, founder of the Plymouth Brethren.[17] The rapture occurs when 'the saints meet the Lord in the air, before his manifestation on the earth'.[18] This follows from Paul's remarks in 1 Thessalonians 4:17 concerning those alive at the return of Christ Jesus, 'we . . . will be snatched away in the clouds to meet the Lord in the air'. Darby incorporated these ideas into his 'dispensational' system of theology. A dispensation referred to a period in history that was characterized by God's relating to people in a particular way:

1. *Age of Innocence* – Pre law and pre fall
2. *Age of Conscience* – Pre law post fall
3. *Age of Human Government* – The new economy after the Noahic flood
4. *Age of Promise* – From the call of Abraham to Moses
5. *Age of Law* – From Moses to Christ
6. *Age of Church/Grace* – Post ascension to second advent
7. *Age of the Kingdom/Millennium* – From second advent to new-creation.[19]

243

Darby's system of dispensational premillennialism gained significant popular media and political support (due to the prominence of Israel in the system) in America towards the end of the twentieth century.[20]

Postmillennialists look for the second coming of the Lord Jesus after a long period of gradual success in terms of the conversion of men and women. They see the rule of God as primarily in the spiritual and moral reform of individuals.[21] As the human activity of evangelism spreads throughout the world, God will achieve his rule in human hearts. Consequently, there will be a long period of peace symbolized by the millennium. At the end of this period the Lord Jesus will return, the dead will be raised for judgment and, after a brief period of conflict, Satan and his minions will be destroyed before the inauguration of the new creation.

One thing that both these types of millennialism have in common is a futurist perspective on life in the Middle. Their view of the present is affected in various ways by their expectations for the future.

The millennium as a source of hope

Millennialism in the modern era has been a distinctive feature of Anglo-American theology, and Moltmann's engagement with it is unusual considering his continental, academic and liberal Protestant tendencies.[22] Millennialism is more at home among various forms of fundamentalist and subsequently, at times, anti-intellectual Christian theology, and the topic scarcely rates a mention in the *Church Dogmatics*.[23] But Moltmann offers a broad survey of Christian millennialism and defines it thus: 'Christian eschatology – eschatology, that is, which is messianic, healing and saving – is millenarian eschatology.'[24] His survey of the last two thousand years of Western history draws attention to what he calls a distinction between 'historical' and 'eschatological' millenarianism:

> Historical millenarianism . . . is a religious theory used to legitimate political or ecclesiastical power, and is exposed to acts of messianic violence and the disappointments of history. Eschatological millenarianism . . . is a necessary picture of hope in resistance, in suffering and in the exiles of this world.[25]

For Moltmann, *historical* millenarianism covers both *premillennial* and *postmillennial* theology (as defined above) with the distinction, at least in political terms, resting on the proponent's experience of political power throughout Western history. A major consequence of this experience is the effect of such power on the group in question's exegesis of Scripture in the light of history.[26]

> Every historical epoch serves to prepare that final con-
> dition which is supposed to be history's goal, and as an
> intermediate stage acquires its meaning in the light of
> that goal. World history is then a giant, purposeful,
> providential sequence, and a tremendous realisation of a
> divine master plan.[27]

Millennialism or millenarianism is a way of seeing God's hand in history with the purpose of discerning the arrival of the kingdom of God. Alternatively, we might say it is a matter of reading history to discern how God is leading us in anticipation of his deliverance. Millennialism for those who experience persecution, or who have a political minority status, tends to be more pre-millennial, as traditionally defined, while those who enjoy political power, even if it is simply peace and prosperity, reflect a more postmillennial view. Biblical concepts, particularly Old Testament ideas of a coming Messiah or apocalyptic crisis, may even be appropriated by secular movements. Those on the rise, according to Moltmann, have a messianic tone to their proclamation, while those on the margins view history as a downward spiral anticipating an apocalyptic interruption of history. Constantinian Rome[28] in the fourth century is the prime *political* millenarianism for Moltmann. The newly converted emperor claimed the role as the mediator of Christ's rule to the world for 'a thousand years'. The United States of America is the modern counterpart to Constantine's Rome: 'From being a refuge for the persecuted saints and an experiment in freedom and democratic self-government, America turned into a world power with a world mission.'[29] The rise of the Roman Church in the medieval period is, for Moltmann, a particularly *ecclesial* form of historical mil-lennialism. The Holy Church, as opposed to the Holy Empire, was the organization to bring salvation to the nations. The church ceased to be a struggling and suffering community, and became instead the triumphant kingdom of God on the earth, reaching a high point at Vatican I.[30] Moltmann lays blame for this development on Augustine and his 'City of God' with its priestly orders and structure. In addition, Mariology appropriated the apocalyptic symbolism of the 'woman and the dragon' (cf. Rev. 12:4, 13, 16). Moltmann also describes the West's Enlightenment culture as *epochal* millenarianism. As mentioned above and in chapter 1, modern philosophies (especially Hegel, as in the case of Marxism) have appropriated certain Christian concepts from the culture they rejected on the way to justifying colonialism, economic imperialism and environmental exploitation as signs of progress, be it in the form of permanent revolution or endless economic growth:

> Only millenarianism makes it possible to understand the kingdom of God not apocalyptically but teleologically, and allows it to be viewed, no longer as the catastrophic end of this world, but as a moral and political ideal which human beings can approach by working unremittingly on themselves and the world.[31]

Millenarianism, then, is the way of reading history in order to determine when it has, or will, come to its expected, if not inevitable, end – some form of, or secular variation on, the reign of Christ and the saints.[32]

The result of these kinds of historical millenarianism is, in Moltmann's view, an overrealized and frequently triumphalist view of God's activity in history in the case of political or ecclesial millenarianism, or, for the secular millenarians, the evolutionary end of history. In regard to the Christian forms of millennialism Moltmann surmises, 'It is not the disappointment that was for two thousand years Christianity's chief problem, it was the fulfilment.'[33] He is particularly critical of the view that has been traditionally labelled amillennialism. Since the time of Augustine the majority view in the Western church was that passages like Revelation 20 are simply symbolic of the whole period between the resurrection of Christ and the perfection of all things in the Spirit.[34] From Moltmann's perspective this 'denial of any millennium at all'[35] serves only to perpetuate the political status quo, rendering calls for eschatological millenarianism subversive and heretical. Since the future goal of history has already been realized, calls for a radical future change are viewed as a threat to the prevailing orders.

For Moltmann, the appropriate theological alternative to historical millennialism is *eschatological* millenarianism. His attention is drawn to those in both Revelation 7 and 20 who die because of their faith: 'the millenarian hope *is hope for martyrs*. This hope is realised in resistance to the godless kingdoms of the world, and the refusal to conform to their idol worship and cults of power.'[36] My working definition of hope, shaped by interaction with Moltmann, has been a Christlike passion for the possibilities of God's work of perfection. In keeping with this, a millennial hope is as follows:

> the end of this world-time of sin and death is foreseeable by the people who believe, and who struggle against the power of this world with 'the power of the world to come,' and who thus enter into Christ's struggle.[37]

The concept of the millennium, when viewed eschatologically, ought to generate in God's people the kind of hope that will preserve them for the coming kingdom of Christ Jesus as they resist the opportunity to settle for the lesser alternatives of a world that is passing away. Of course, even this hope may be deformed, and Moltmann is critical of dispensational millenarianism for what he views as escapism:

> If the call is no longer to resistance against the powers and their idols, but . . . instead escapades into religious dream worlds are offered in the face of a world destined for downfall . . . the meaning of the millenarian hope is turned upside down.[38]

Resurrection hope looks to the renewal of the earth into which the cross of Christ was driven, not to release from the mundane into a netherworld freed from material constraint.

Our goal in this chapter is to understand the 'leading' and 'deliverance' we can expect from our heavenly Father during life in the Middle. Therefore my response to Moltmann on the issue of the millennium is confined to whether his reading of the last two millennia supports my view or not. While there is much to welcome in Moltmann's sketch of eschatological millenarianism – and I shall discuss this further in the next section – there are several problems with it as well.

First, Moltmann's decision to lump all the traditional categories together as historical or 'presentative'[39] millenarianism detracts from the coherence of his position in so far as he still wishes to engage the tradition.[40] Without accepting all of Moltmann's hermeneutics of suspicion, we can agree that, from a world-view perspective, postmillennialism has an extremely optimistic view of life in the Middle.[41] To the extent that it rests its confidence on the power of God's Spirit 'to give life to our mortal bodies' through the proclamation of God's word, it is to be taken seriously, but only if it is distinct from political messianism, as Moltmann cautions. Otherwise, the pessimism of premillennialism has some impact where life in the Middle is 'subject to frustration . . . groaning as in the pains of childbirth', which we observed from Scripture above. Yet even here the apocalyptic crisis that precedes the reign of God should be equally visible in bourgeois consumerism, as in the decline of family values and the progressive liberal agenda of 'the left'.

A second problem with homogenizing the various traditional definitions of millennialism relates to the relationship between divine sovereignty and human freedom. Despite having identified the significance of messianism and apocalypticism for millennialism, Moltmann does not recognize the extent to which the pessimism of premillennialism refers to the inability of humans, including Christians, to do anything about history (whether or not they have political power) and hence the necessity of apocalyptic divine intervention. In contrast, postmillenarians are relatively positive about human contributions to the arrival of the millennium and are therefore more likely to view its arrival as a natural historical process.[42] Even so, as traditionally defined, both of these positions are *futurist*, a point which Moltmann does not always seem to appreciate.[43]

The third reservation I would have about Moltmann's account of the millennium relates to a question that he poses, which is whether millennialism is theologically necessary at all.

As noted in chapter 1, from early on Moltmann has been dedicated to furthering an eschatological transformation of *this* world. At the same time, he has always been opposed to 'the idea of a Christian society in which the church is coterminous with civil society'.[44] Hence the main thrust of his futurist eschatology has been to show either political, ecclesial or epochal historical millenarianism as presumptuous or hubristic in comparison with the actual kingdom of God in Jesus Christ. Yet, as Bauckham argues, it is not explicit in Moltmann's account why eschatological millenarianism can provide the necessary theological support for resistance or perseverance as distinct from the traditional hope for the new creation, much of which Moltmann seems to support, albeit in his own fashion. Similarly, Bauckham raises the possibility that Christians resisting the world and working towards the kind of millennial hope that Moltmann espouses may also become politically oppressive.[45] To be fair, Moltmann sees the millennium as a necessary *transition* to mediate between history and eternity. As we saw in the previous chapter, the Spirit does his work of renewing creation with consequences of resurrection hope but if 'we leave out this transition [the millennium], as non-millenarian eschatologies do, then world history will end – according to modern fantasy – with an abrupt *Big Bang*'.[46] Again, it is not immediately obvious as to why such a transition is necessary considering that even with the dramatic images of the Apocalypse or 2 Peter that Moltmann describes rather manipulatively as 'Hiroshima images' and 'catastrophe', what comes after is still the blessed new creation of the kingdom of God.[47]

It could be argued that Moltmann is simply seeking to preserve some kind of genuine concrete goal for the course of this world prior to being 'consumed by the perfection of nature'.[48] Hence the millennium is that period in which human activity is still meaningfully effective in creation under the rule of Christ before the Messiah himself 'hands everything over to the Father, so that God may be all in all' (1 Cor. 15:28). We noted in chapter 6 that Moltmann's portrait of the new creation left the ontological distinction between God and creation unacceptably ambiguous, so in that light it is easier to see why human acts of resistance need a concrete goal *within history*. More importantly, we also noted that the Western tradition itself, as presented by Bauckham, neglected the central place of the glorified royal and eternal Son in the new creation, especially in relation to God the Father. The beatific vision of an unmediated presence of the Father in the new creation marginalizes the glorified Christ and *especially his creaturely humanity*. From that perspective it is possible to sympathize with Moltmann's claim that otherworldly views of the consummation of creation leave little or nothing for the church to live for.

Perhaps the critical question to put to Moltmann, and to any exponent of millennial theology, is more specifically exegetical or hermeneutical. I established in chapter 2 a theological purpose for apocalyptic writings in relation to the provisional nature of God's promises – even in their fulfilment through Jesus the Christ. Apocalyptic portraits, like Revelation 20, are revealed to the people of God in the power of the Spirit at points in the history of his promises when their content seems to be most removed from everyday experience. In addition, these elaborate portraits attempt to convey to their original hearers a divine perspective, metaphorically and thematically, on the creaturely history that God's promises have created. As I argued in chapter 4, this includes the original audiences the Lord himself addressed in relation to the temple and Jerusalem. Therefore what John depicts in the reign of Christ and his martyrs is a contextually necessary variation on the 'until' of Psalm 110:1. The apostolic interpretation of David's prophecy in relation to Jesus the Christ is central to our understanding of the Father's promise to and for the kinsman redeemer that we explored in chapter 4. Christ Jesus, having defeated Satan, the enemy of God's people, who otherwise 'held the power of death' (cf. Heb. 2:14; Rev. 20:4) over humanity, has ascended to the 'right hand' of the Father. Yet even the ascended Messiah waits for the residue of Satan's power to be eradicated at the general resurrection (cf. 1 Cor. 15:26). At this point in the history of the Father's promises the ultimate enemy of God's royal and eternal Son, the strong man, will be cursed everlastingly as a consequence of the final judgment (cf. Rev. 20:14). Since the Apocalypse is written to encourage Christians to 'overcome' or 'be victorious' (see Rev. 2:7, 11, 17, 26; 3:5, 12, 21; 21:7) in the face of Roman persecution,[49] it is essential that those who have died faithful to Christ Jesus be depicted as such, victorious and not ultimately vanquished by the dragon and his minions. So the Apocalypse is a more elaborate metaphor but similar in purpose to the words that Paul wrote to the Thessalonian and Colossian churches. The faithful departed are 'hidden in Christ' (1 Thess. 4:14; Col. 3:3) and therefore reign with him,[50] as will be revealed at his return. Far from being the foundation for political obduracy, as Moltmann implies, the amillennial position outlined above makes for a much easier alignment of apocalyptic imagery with the greater biblical narrative. More importantly, in terms of our expectation for God's leading and deliverance, the amillennial position grounds our understanding of life in the Middle on the victory of the ascended Christ and the promise that even if we perish we shall nevertheless be vindicated and hence delivered.

Life in the Middle as waiting for the kingdom

On the basis of Romans 8 we expect life in the Middle to be characterized by anticipation in the form of 'groaning'. We should expect this reaction as we live through the 'until' of the ascended Christ's reign, described as the millennium, until he returns in glory. The correlate of 'groaning' according to Romans 8 is 'waiting' (Rom. 8:25). The 'until' of Christ's heavenly reign means that our hope is 'unseen' (vv. 24–25). Since the Christian hope of the coming kingdom of God is invisible we 'wait for it patiently'. Throughout the New Testament we are encouraged, and even exhorted, to 'wait' for the return of the Lord Jesus as the Christ. This can be expressed objectively or subjectively.

From the subjective point of view we await 'the redemption of our bodies' or resurrection (Rom. 8:23–25); we await 'the hope of righteousness' (Gal. 5:5) or the final verdict of justification before the judgment seat of the Christ; in the same way we await ultimate salvation from wrath (Heb. 9:28; 1 Thess. 1:10). As we wait we are encouraged to live 'at peace with him without spot or blemish' (2 Peter 3:14).

The more objective perspective of waiting is focused on the return of the king, since 'He is now waiting until His enemies are made His footstool' (Heb. 10:13). At such a time he will 'be revealed' (1 Cor. 1:7), 'appearing [in] glory' (Titus 2:13) 'from heaven' (Phil. 3:20; 1 Thess. 1:10) on the day of God: 'The heavens will be on fire and be dissolved because of it, and the elements will melt with the heat. But based on his promise, we wait for the new heavens and a new earth, where righteousness

251

will dwell' (2 Peter 3:12). The 'redemption of our bodies' mentioned in Romans 8 coincides, according to 2 Peter, with a general transformation of the creation. We await both a personal and a cosmic transformation of creatureliness, a 'new heaven' and a 'new earth' or, more generally, the new creation (cf. Rev. 21:1).

The perfecting work of the Spirit throughout life in the Middle

From a theological perspective it is those who have 'the first fruits of the Spirit' who groan in anticipation of the return of the king. They have been 'sealed with . . . the down payment' (Eph. 1:13–14) of the Spirit, the 'deposit in our hearts' (2 Cor. 1:22). When the Father acts in this way the perfecting work of the Spirit becomes an individual and/or personal reality for an otherwise antagonistic human being (Eph. 2:3). Earlier in Romans 8 Paul describes the experience as having 'the mindset of the Spirit' and it is the key means by which the Father answers our prayers for guidance during life in the Middle. In chapter 6 we examined Moltmann's description of the effects of the resurrection hope at the personal, social and cosmic levels. As we meditate on what we should do, in the light of what we know about the millennium, we shall reflect on the Spirit's role in fashioning a new mindset for the Christian and therefore leading us through this present time of groaning, empowering us to wait patiently and moving us (and the whole creation) towards the ultimate deliverance in the coming kingdom of God.

The work of the Spirit during the millennium has become a matter of special concern during the modern period. Whether as part of a response to the decline of Christendom in the West or the blossoming of the Pentecostal movement in the Global South,[51] across the planet Christians from a wide collection of cultural and ethnic backgrounds have expressed 'a hunger for a concrete, lived experience of [God's] life-giving Spirit'.[52] As the proclamation of the gospel message spreads internationally, hundreds of millions of Christians want 'an awareness of God in, with and beneath the experience of life, which gives us assurance of God's fellowship, friendship and love'.[53] That is, when Christians pray for God's leading, they want God's Spirit to deliver them to show that God is with and for them.[54] Whether it is the experience of life as threatened and endangered or as liberated and delivered, as Welker catalogued:

> A people are threatened with annihilation. A political system collapses or is abruptly reshaped. The moral network of a community is rent asunder. The sun sets on an historical world. People receive a new identity. A dispersed people are led together again. People who are strange or even hostile to each other open God's reality for each other. A disintegrated world grows together.[55]

The modern period has been a time of great upheaval, or 'revolution' in more Romantic terms.[56] So, in order to distinguish the perfecting work of the Spirit from the 'spirit of the times', which appears to be a perennial millenarian problem, we need an explicitly triune description of divine mediation to ensure that it is the *Holy* Spirit from whom we seek God's leading. To this end let us recall Calvin's description of God's triune action in the world:

> It is not fitting to suppress the distinction that we observe to be expressed in Scripture. It is this: to the Father is attributed the beginning of activity, and the fountain and wellspring of all things; to the Son, wisdom, counsel, and the ordered disposition of all things; but to the Spirit is assigned the power and efficacy of that activity.[57]

Of special interest to us here is the interaction between the Son and the Spirit in the Father's activities: the Spirit effects 'the wisdom, counsel and ordered disposition' that comes through the Son. We must keep these two aspects of divine activity in mind as we return to Romans 8.

The mindset of the Spirit

At the beginning of Romans 8 Paul describes life in the last days by way of a contrast between those who live with the mindset of the flesh and those with the mindset of the Spirit (8:6). From a purely lexical level the term 'mindset' describes our 'intention, aim, aspiration or striving'.[58] It is a person's basic disposition that guides and/or governs his or her actions and reactions within the network of relationships that make up creaturely life. In the context of Romans 8 the difference between the mindset of the Spirit and the mindset of the flesh is the direction in which they lead a person – 'the mindset of the flesh is death, but the mindset of the Spirit is life and peace' (Rom. 8:6).

In terms of the perfecting work of the Spirit for an individual, the mindset of the Spirit could equally be described as regeneration.[59] As Calvin remarked, the mindset of the Spirit is 'the secret energy of the Spirit by which we come to enjoy Christ and all his benefits'.[60] More precisely, and in relation to Moltmann's description of generic wholeness in chapter 6, the work of the Spirit is to lead the 'intentions, aims, aspirations or strivings' of an individual according to 'the wisdom, counsel and ordered disposition' of the royal and eternal Son. Thus in Romans 8:15 we read, 'you received the Spirit of sonship in whom we cry *Abba*, Father'. This act of redirection towards the Father in heaven is the Spirit's testimony 'together with our spirit that we are God's children' (8:16). Paul grasps the essential nature of that disposition by way of reference to the experience of the Lord Jesus in the Garden of Gethsemane (cf. esp. Mark 14:36). The electing work of the Spirit is made explicit as the disposition of the royal and eternal Son towards the Father in God's children. As explored at length in chapter 1, the perfection of the royal and eternal Son's righteousness towards God is revealed in the words 'not my will, but yours be done'.[61] In the same way that the Spirit perfected the incarnate Son in self-sacrificial submission towards the Father, the Spirit of sonship perfects the disposition of the Son in the sons and daughters of God, who hear the promises of God, respond in hope and embody that hope in prayer.

The Father's answer to our request for leading and deliverance is revealed as the Spirit mediates to us the disposition of the royal and eternal Son. Through the perfecting work of the Spirit, the children of God join with the Son in submitting to the Father, join in his passion for the possibilities of God's perfecting work and, therefore, 'we suffer with him' (Rom. 8:17). In the first instance this is made manifest in our lives as Paul describes it in the flow from Romans 7 to 8. The chief struggle of the mindset of the flesh is, 'For I do not do the good that I want to do, but I practise the evil that I do not want to do' (Rom. 7:15). This mindset of the flesh that leads to death is that from which Paul seeks deliverance (7:24). The Spirit's mindset enables the children of God to sacrifice self to the will of God and experience the sufferings of Christ Jesus in that event along with the benefits of forgiveness that come through his paschal sacrifice – the fruit of his high-priestly intercession. Hence, they, and all creation, groan in the Spirit as they seek to resist the futility of the world, marred as it is by sin, death and evil (8:20), in anticipation of the redemption of their bodies and the freedom of justification. The Spirit leads them towards the summing up of all things in Christ Jesus in such a way as to 'deliver us from the evil one' or, as Calvin described it, 'the Spirit takes on himself a part of the burden, by which our weakness is oppressed; so that he not only helps and succours us but lifts us up'.[62] In fact, the Spirit's mindset leads us to long for that which has been achieved in the Lord Jesus to be perfected in all creation (Rom. 8:23).

Life in the Spirit and in the body

So, with the mindset of the Spirit, we wait for the return of Christ when he will take up his inheritance. Our waiting, however, is active since 'the love of God has been poured into our hearts through the Spirit who was given to us' (Rom. 5:5). In the power of the Spirit this is the same love that the Father has for the royal and eternal Son (John 17:26), and, of course, it is the same love that the Father had for the world in sending his Son as its saviour (John 3:16). Hence to the faith and hope of Christ Jesus we add love as the means by which we embody the passion of Christ for the possibilities of God's perfecting work. The concept of embodiment, furthermore, is paramount for understanding how we are to be led in the context of temptation in the hope of deliverance from evil. We may reflect on this in two ways, both of which involve the work of the Spirit, the presence of God in the body, and the significance of Christ Jesus in relation to the temple – a consistent feature of our explorations of the Gospel narratives.

'Your body is a temple of the Holy Spirit'

In chapter 6 I discussed Moltmann's view of the effects of resurrection hope in the power of the Spirit, the chief consequence of which was the renewed possibility of wholeness for life in the

Middle. In the first instance this was geared to the individual, the right alignment of body and mind: 'we are what we do in the body and what our bodies are eschatologically'.[63] The establishment of the spiritual mindset in a Christian by the Father results, as Paul remarks, in our being renewed in the image of the Lord who created us (Col. 3:10). Hence, just as the Spirit empowered Jesus to eclipse the temple as the presence of God in the world, and to establish the conditions for right worship of God the Father on the earth, '[our] bod[ies] [are] a temple of the Holy Spirit . . . [We] are not [our] own; [we] were bought with a price. Therefore [we] honour God with [our] bodies' (1 Cor. 6:17, 19–20). In context Paul is exhorting Christians to 'flee sexual immorality' (6:18) on the way to discussing the righteous expression of physical relations between husbands and wives in marriage as a union of bodies (1 Cor. 7). However, throughout the Corinthian correspondence the most basic activities done in and with the body (eating, drinking, loving, learning) ought to be led by 'the Spirit who comes from God' as distinct from 'the spirit of the world' (1 Cor. 2:12). Thus Christians live toward the coming kingdom renouncing their former embodied activities as immoral (idolatry, adultery, same-sex practices, theft, greed, etc.; see 1 Cor. 6:9–11), since 'the body . . . is for the Lord' (6:13). Instead, 'justified in the name of the Lord Jesus Christ and by the Spirit of our God' (1 Cor. 6:11) the Christian anticipates 'being transformed into the . . . image [of the Lord] . . . this is from the Lord who is the Spirit' (2 Cor. 3:18–19). More generally still, while keeping the cultic tone, Paul encourages the Christians in Rome to 'offer [their] bodies as living sacrifices, holy and pleasing to God . . . [as an] act of spiritual worship' (Rom. 12:1). Our modern Romantic culture is marked by a self-love consisting of self-determination and self-actualization and, invariably, as Moltmann observed, separating the mind from the body.[64] By way of contrast, the mindset of the Spirit produces a love of one's whole self, born from adoption by the God and Father of our Lord Jesus Christ:

> The new birth is neither a conversion to our authentic inner self nor a migration . . . of the soul into a heavenly realm, but a translation of a person into the house of God . . . erected in the midst of the world.[65]

Eschatological confusion about the millennium affects the individual in similar ways as it plagues the church, especially when we
talk of the Spirit's perfecting work in the believer. In a kind of
personal postmillennialism, for some Christians perfection before
the resurrection is a real expectation. The perfect child of God is
one in

> 'Whom is the mind which is in Christ,' and who so
> 'walketh as Christ also walked;' a man 'that hath clean
> hands and a pure heart,' or that is 'cleansed from all
> filthiness of flesh and spirit;' one in whom is 'no occasion
> of stumbling' and who accordingly 'does not commit
> sin' . . . one in whom God hath fulfilled His faithful
> word 'From all your filthiness and from all your idols I
> will cleanse you.'[66]

Such perfection need not imply 'a dispensation from doing good
and attending to all the ordinances of God' nor 'a freedom from
ignorance, mistake, temptation, and a thousand infirmities necessarily connected with flesh and blood'.[67] The work of the Spirit in
the believer should ensure 'pure love reigning alone in the heart
and life',[68] and should keep the children of God from sinning
voluntarily. Among Pentecostal Christians it is anticipated that
this moment of perfection may come upon the Christian sometime
after justification. Hence the emergence of belief in a second
blessing of the Holy Spirit: 'None therefore ought to believe that
the work is done, 'til there is added the testimony of the Spirit
witnessing his entire sanctification as clearly as his justification'.[69]
    There are important eschatological issues to address when
distinguishing the perfecting work of the Spirit from the concept
of sinless perfection described above. In Romans 8:11 Paul
established the connection between the archetypal event of the
Spirit's perfecting Messiah Jesus and the Spirit's subsequent and
derivative actions in the experience of God's adopted children:
'the one who raised Christ from the dead [by his Spirit] will bring
to life your mortal bodies via the indwelling of his Spirit in you'.
By the same means as the Father raised Christ Jesus from the
dead, he will also regenerate our mortal bodies – his perfecting
Spirit. Yet, as Calvin commented, 'in the person of Christ was
exhibited a *specimen* of the power which belongs to the whole

body of the Church'.[70] It is the quality of the power at work in the believer that counts, not the quantity. As noted above, the Spirit's activity prior to the resurrection is a 'first fruits' or 'deposit'. In reality, the life that is given to our mortal bodies through the Spirit is, in the first instance, a specimen of the everlasting life enjoyed by the resurrected Lord Jesus that I described in chapter 6. Therefore our experience is one of struggle, knowing the truth about sin, death and evil, yet, at the same time, not being ultimately delivered from it:

> That is to say, the end of this world-time of sin and death is foreseeable by the people who believe, and who struggle against the power of this world with 'the power of the world to come,' and who thus enter into Christ's struggle.[71]

Hence the great promise of Romans 8 that the 'Spirit intercedes for us' when 'we do not know what to pray as we ought' (Rom. 8:26). Since it is the Spirit of Christ, 'who ever lives to intercede for us' (Heb. 7:25), that is at work in us, we are not abandoned in our trials. Instead, we are delivered: 'He who searches the hearts knows the Spirit's mindset because he intercedes for holy ones according to the will of God' (Rom. 8:27). Of course, as I have maintained from the beginning, the space of life in the Middle is not an individual sphere but the Spirit-constituted body of Christ, the church.

'You are . . . God's dwelling in the Spirit'

I have maintained throughout this book that through the gift of his Spirit among the people, YHWH's heavenly glory is mediated to the earth through Messiah Jesus when 'all the peoples of the earth will see that you are called by Yahweh's name' (Deut. 28:10; cf. Num. 6:27), *the name of Jesus*. In fact, those who bear the name of the Lord Jesus on the earth are a new temple in the Spirit (Eph. 2:22). During life in the Middle the rule of the king in the Spirit is revealed in the church's acts of confession, done in the name of the king, but not as the king himself. This is because the first activity of the Spirit in constituting the church for the risen Christ is to vindicate Christ's reign over the church even as the Spirit distinguishes him from it. The church as a temple in the Spirit is constituted from the many 'temples of the Spirit' discussed in the previous section since 'by the one Spirit all were baptized into the one body' (1 Cor. 12:13). Hence the mindset of the Spirit is manifested in the one body of Christ (Phil. 2:2; cf. 1 Cor. 2:16), even though the body is 'made up of many members' (1 Cor. 12:14). The mindset of the Spirit that guides the church is therefore the same Christlike passion: 'He was crucified in weakness, but he lives by God's power. For *we also are weak* in him, yet toward the world we shall live with him by God's power' (2 Cor. 13:4). In the context of the millennium the power of God's Spirit means that churches live 'beautiful lives' as 'aliens and strangers' in order that should the nations misinterpret their deeds as evil, they will nevertheless give glory to God on the 'last day' (1 Peter 2:12; cf. Isa. 10:3; Jer. 6:15). Thus, as argued in chapter 3, the extent to which church or churches could be thought of as *Christ towards the world*, and therefore the extent to which the church exercises any kind of *authority in the world*, is theologically defined and confined. As Gunton remarked:

> In all life, and especially in the life of the church, eschato-logical reserve should be the hallmark of thought and action: a recollection of the limits of our possibilities, given at once both human finitude and the sin that continues to hold back even, sometimes especially, those who are on the way to final redemption.[72]

As observed in my discussion of millenarianism, Christians ought to exercise the greatest eschatological reserve when making proposals about the political status of the church or the churches in relation to the rest of the world. In chapter 5, and following Gunton, I argued that 'the elect are not *primarily* those chosen for a unique destiny out from the whole, but are chosen out of the whole as the community with whom the destiny of the whole is in some way bound up'.[73] Hence the church assumes the place in the plan of God as his special possession (Exod. 19:5; Deut. 7:6; cf. 1 Peter 2:9) and both passively and actively testifies to the messianic victory in so far as the divine achievement is revealed in human activity (cf. John 13:35). However, the Spirit-constituted church reveals the counter-intuitive nature of the Father's wisdom, because, as the spiritual body of the Messiah crucified in the Spirit, it is testimony to the Father's mysterious government of history in which he

> chose the foolish things of the world to shame the wise; God chose the weak things of the world to shame the strong. God chose the lowly things of this world and the despised things – and the things that are not – to nullify the things that are. (1 Cor. 1:27–28)

The church is the new people of promise belonging to the one for whom 'the nations are an inheritance' and 'the ends of the earth Your possession' (Ps. 2:8). It is therefore already a political entity albeit mysterious and despicable to the world. In fact, it is (or should be) the church's polity as encapsulated in the mindset of the Spirit that distinguishes the church from the world even as he sends the church into the world (Matt. 28:18–20; cf. Acts 1:8). The church's polity is governed by eschatological virtues since 'these three remain: faith, hope and love' (1 Cor. 13:13). As such, it exists as a counter-testimony to the homogenizing forces of globalization as a community whose membership is not a matter of 'Jew or Greek, male or female, slave or free', for any who exhibit the mindset of the Spirit are constituted as 'one in Christ' (Gal. 3:28). Likewise, the church must exist in contrast to the segregating powers of consumerism, where the rich are given priority over the poor (Jas 2:5–6), considering, 'the grace of our Lord Jesus was to become poor because of you, even though he was rich, so that in his poverty you might become rich' (2 Cor. 8:9). Furthermore, the evidence of the Spirit's mindset among the body of Christ means that 'no one can say' that a member is not necessary; or equally, 'no one can say' that they have nothing to contribute (1 Cor. 12:15–17, 21). Hence the passion for the possibilities of God's perfecting work in the church is for a genuine, common unity instituted *in Christ*, on the one hand, and, on the other, a concrete diversity constituted *by the Spirit*. In the Spirit, Christ Jesus, the head, gives freedom to his members to live and be who and what he has made them to be, for where 'the Spirit is, there is freedom' (2 Cor. 3:17).

Even so, until the resurrection, the body of Christ is no more perfect than the bodies that make it up and so we pray, 'lead us not into temptation'. Accordingly, 'while it may be necessary in particular cases to exclude from fellowship those who commit serious offences and remain unrepentant, the body of Christ remains those very people who are doing the things he deplores'.[74] What distinguishes the culture of the church from the Romantic society around it is the Spirit's virtue of 'self-control' (Gal. 5:23; 1 Tim. 3:2, 11; Titus 1:8; 2:5–6; 2 Peter 1:6) as opposed to the desire for self-expression and the discipline of 'submitting yourselves to one another out of reverence for Christ' (Eph. 5:21) over and against self-determination. In all, the church is a temple in the Spirit to the name of Jesus the Christ when it hears his address to forgiven sinners and which, therefore, groans along with all creation in anticipation of the revelation of the children of God. In this way, and only this way, is the church both 'the power of God and the wisdom of God' (1 Cor. 1:24). This is what we should do with the eschatological time and space of life in the Middle but what can we hope for at the end of time?

Delivering the earth to the heavenly fatherhood of God

I conclude our exploration of the coming of God's heavenly fatherhood to the earth by using the same themes that have led us throughout – the hallowing of his name and the coming of his kingdom as the perfection of his will. Yet we do so mindful of the themes of history and polity discussed in this chapter. On the day of the Father's choosing the children of God will be revealed in glory, the waiting and groaning will come to an end and, in the words of Revelation 21:1–2:

> I saw a new heaven and a new earth, for the first heaven and the first earth had gone and the sea no longer existed. I saw the holy city, a new Jerusalem, coming down out of heaven from God prepared as a bride for her husband.

We can give some concrete substance to this metaphor as we rehearse the basic promises of God that we have investigated throughout, promises regarding the covenant, Immanuel and the Messiah.

261

Delivered according to God's faithfulness

In chapter 3 we explored the canonical significance of the name of the Lord when bestowed upon the ascended Messiah Jesus. There we focused on the fact that when the Father confers the name of the Lord upon his glorified Son, he vindicates both that name and his saving actions in the cross of Christ. More specifically, the Father vindicates the self-sacrificial death of Christ Jesus on the cross as the long-promised saving action of the God of Israel. In short, God the Father ensures once and for all time that the promissory name he gave to Moses 'I will be who I will be' is fulfilled in the risen Jesus, who is both Lord and Messiah.

By vindicating the crucified Christ Jesus with the name of the Lord, the Father reveals to his children the depths with which he is 'the compassionate and gracious God, slow to anger, abounding in love and faithfulness, maintaining love to thousands, and forgiving wickedness, rebellion and sin' (Exod. 34:6–7 TNIV). In the power of God's Spirit, 'everyone who calls upon the name of the Lord will be saved' (Acts 2:21; cf. Joel 2:32). Through the sacrifice of Christ Jesus there is forgiveness of sin in his name as well as compassion for God's children who groan in anticipation of the redemption of their bodies as they struggle to live according to the Spirit and not the flesh. The mercy of God is mediated through Christ to his body as they struggle against 'the rulers, against the authorities, against the world powers of this darkness, against the spiritual forces of evil in the heavens' (Eph. 6:12). Most of all, the promise of the Father is that he will vindicate the churches who wait patiently yet labour with the Spirit's mindset to be the body of Christ. As Paul wrote to the church in Rome, 'If God is for us, who can be against us? . . . Who will bring a charge against the elect of God? It is God who justifies' (Rom. 8:31–34). The hope of the church during the trials of life in the Middle is the faithfulness of the God who vindicates his name as saviour.

Delivered according to God's intervention

The faithfulness of the Father to his promises was further explored as we investigated the theme of his kingdom in the greater biblical narrative. In chapter 4 I charted the course of God's actions in the power of his Spirit to save his people from their enemies through a kinsman redeemer. This spiritually anointed agent, the

Christ, is the one through whom the Father exercises his rule over the history that is shaped by his promises. In fact, the fulfilment of God's promises depends upon the royal covenant made with the kinsman redeemer who is revealed to be the eternal Son of God by the resurrection of the Lord Jesus. Through his royal and eternal Son, God the Father intervenes in the history of creaturely antagonism to his promises in order to defeat humanity's greatest enemy, Satan. Through his sacrificial death, Christ Jesus removed the sting of sin from human flesh and made the Law which gave sin its power redundant. Thus the kinsman redeemer disempowers death, destroying Satan, who wielded his power over the sons of Adam, those living in the fear of death (Heb. 2:14–15).

Of course, as John's Apocalypse graphically depicts, though the evil one has been defeated he is still active in creation, albeit bound by the Lord Jesus' own 'until' (Rev. 12; 20). What is more, in keeping with apocalyptic writings in general, the earthly powers of history are neither independent from nor neutral to the church but are servants of the evil one. They persistently seek to divert the church's worship of the God and Father of our Lord Jesus Christ towards their idols of prosperity, immorality and power. Even so, the power of God at work in the church to overcome the world is the mindset of the Spirit. As John writes, 'this is the victory that overcomes the world – our faith' (1 John 5:4). Faith and hope in the power of the Spirit and the gospel of the Lord Jesus Christ are equally proportional and mutually constitutive. Therefore the church's chief means of political resistance in the world is the rhythm of remembrance and anticipation. That is, the church maintains her own polity, with its various disciplines, as a counter-testimony against the state, in submission to the resurrected and enthroned Messiah of God in whose Spirit she is constituted. The church lives patiently yet expectantly in the world, towards the revelation of the true sovereign of the world, who will redeem her from the powers that work against her – both within and without. At the Messiah's return the Lord Jesus will prosecute the justice of God and establish an everlasting reign of righteousness and peace. Again, as Paul encourages the church in Rome, 'Who can separate us from the love of Christ? Can oppression or distress or persecution or hunger or destitution or danger or sword? . . . No, in all these things we prevail completely through him who loved us' (Rom. 8:35–37). The hope of the church for deliverance from the trials of life in the Middle rests on the victory of the Father through his royal and eternal Son in the power of his Spirit against the evil one and his minions.

Delivered according to God's intention

In chapter 5 we drew on a third thread in the history of the Father's promises, namely his mysterious choice to consummate his plan for creation in the Lord Jesus Christ. We discovered an essential pattern to the Father's plan in terms of his choice of the one/few for the sake of showing mercy to the many. Furthermore, we established that the mysterious or counter-intuitive pattern of choosing was to ensure, at all times, that God's actions flowed out of his benevolence towards creation, a creation that not only need not have existed, but also conspicuously resisted his plan for it. Ultimately, though, I argued that the purpose of this plan was the glorification of the royal and eternal Son by the Father in the Spirit. I highlighted the Bible's account of the Son as the Spirit-empowered interpreter and executor of the Father's will for creation, who, in his grace, 'did not come to be served but to serve and give his life as a ransom for many' (Mark 10:45).

When the Father releases the creation from the futility to which it has been subjected and the children of God have been revealed at the resurrection of the dead, the electing work of the Spirit will be perfected. The steadfast love of the Father will have returned the creation to his plan to sum up all things in Christ Jesus, the Lord. Because of his love for the Father, the church will be presented as his bride, his inheritance and his treasured possession. The children of God will enjoy an everlasting life of freedom in service to their God and Father as, in the power of the Spirit, they join in worship of the Father with their great high priest in the order of Melchizedek. Without the afflictions of sin, death and evil, those created in the likeness of God's image will engage in the redeemed civilization of God (Rev. 21). As the inhabitants of God's new metropolis, they will govern the new creation in holiness, righteousness and love. The hope of the church for deliverance from the trials of life in the Middle rests on the mysterious choices that perfect God's plan for creation, bringing it to his full glory, in Christ Jesus, the Lord.

Notes

Introduction

[1] Robert B. Pippen, *Modernism as a Philosophical Problem*, 2nd edn (Oxford: Blackwell, 1999), p. 22.

[2] See Tim Blanning, *The Romantic Revolution* (New York: Modern Library Chronicles, 2010), p. ix. While Romanticism as a movement has previously been confined to the study of certain forms of art (poetry, music, etc.), a growing body of literature has identified various characteristics of the modern era that can be collated under the heading of Romanticism, starting with Isaiah Berlin, *The Roots of Romanticism* (London: Pimlico, 2000). See also Fredrick C. Beiser, *The Romantic Imperative* (Cambridge, Mass.: Harvard University Press, 2003). For the relationship between Romanticism and science see Richard Holmes, *The Age of Wonder: How the Romantic Generation Discovered the Beauty and Terror of Science* (New York: Vintage, 2008).

[3] William J. Dumbrell, *The Search for Order: Biblical Eschatology in Focus* (Grand Rapids: Baker, 1994), p. 9.

[4] See Kevin J. Vanhoozer and Daniel Treier, *Theology and the Mirror of Scripture: A Mere Evangelical Account* (Downers Grove: IVP Academic; Nottingham: Apollos, 2015).

[5] See Graeme Goldsworthy, *Gospel-Centred Hermeneutics: Biblical-Theological Foundations and Principles* (Nottingham: Apollos, 2006).

[6] With the possible exception of Wolfhart Pannenberg.

[7] Moltmann's attitude towards the Bible in theology can be captured in his own words: 'I take Scripture as a stimulus to my own theological thinking, not as an authoritative blueprint and confining boundary' (*Experiences in Theology: Ways and Forms of Christian Theology* [London: SCM, 2000], p. xxii).

[8] Friedrich D. E. Schleiermacher, *On Religion: Speeches to Its Cultured Despisers*, tr. John Oman (New York: Harper, 1958), p. 15.

Chapter 1: Life in the Middle?

[1] Dietrich Bonhoeffer, *Creation and Fall*, ed. John W. De Gruchy, tr. Douglas Stephen Bax, Dietrich Bonhoeffer Works English, vol. 3 (Minneapolis: Fortress, 1997), p. 28.

[2] John D. Barrow, 'The Far, Far Future', in George F. R. Ellis (ed.), *The Far-Future Universe* (London: Templeton Foundation, 2002), p. 23.

[3] Yuval Noah Harari, *Homo Deus: A Brief History of Tomorrow* (London: Vintage, 2017), p. 2.

[4] Dietrich Bonhoeffer, *Ethik*, ed. Eberhard Bethge, 2nd rev. edn, Dietrich Bonhöffer Werke, vol. 6 (Munich: Chr. Kaiser, 1998), p. 40.

[5] Dietrich Bonhoeffer, *Akt und Sein: Tranzendentalphilosophie und Ontologie in der Systematischen Theologie*, ed. Eberhard Bethge, Dietrich Bonhöffer Werke, vol. 2 (Munich: Chr. Kaiser, 1988), p. 118.

[6] Miroslav Volf, 'Theology for a Way of Life', in Miroslav Volf and Dorothy C. Bass (eds.), *Practicing Theology* (Grand Rapids: Eerdmans, 2002), p. 247.

[7] Joseph Ratzinger, *Eschatology: Death and Eternal Life*, 2nd edn (Washington D.C: Catholic University of America, 1988), p. 1.

[8] Douglas H. Knight, *The Eschatological Economy: Time and the Hospitality of God* (Grand Rapids: Eerdmans, 2006), p. x/2.

[9] Wolfhart Pannenberg, 'Modernity, History and Eschatology', in Jerry L. Walls (ed.), *The Oxford Handbook of Eschatology* (Oxford: Oxford University Press, 2008), p. 494.

[10] Pannenberg, 'Modernity', p. 494.

[11] Pannenberg, 'Modernity', p. 495.

[12] Robert B. Pippin, *Modernism as a Philosophical Problem: On the Dissatisfactions of European High Culture*, 2nd edn (Oxford: Blackwell, 1999), p. 4.

[13] Wolfhart Pannenberg, *Systematic Theology*, vol. 3 (Edinburgh: T&T Clark, 1998), p. 533.

[14] Pannenberg, *Systematic Theology*, vol. 3, p. 533.

[15] Johannes Weiss, *Jesus' Proclamation of the Kingdom of God*, tr. Richard Hiers and David Holland (London: SCM, 1971), p. 135.

[16] Weiss, *Jesus' Proclamation*, p. 130.

[17] Albert Schweitzer, *The Quest for the Historical Jesus*, 3rd edn (London: Adam and Charles Black, 1954), p. 400.

[18] Schweitzer, *Quest*, p. 239.

[19] Christoph Schwöbel, 'The Last Things First', in David Fergusson, Marcel Sarot and Anthony C. Thistleton (eds.), *The Future as God's Gift* (London: T&T Clark, 2000), p. 223.

[20] Karl Barth, *The Epistle to the Romans*, tr. Edwyn Hoskins, 6th edn (Oxford: Oxford University Press, 1933), p. 288.

[21] Barth, *Romans*, p. 314.

[22] Barth, *Romans*, p. 314.

[23] Reviews appeared in *Newsweek* plus the *New York Times* and *Los Angeles Times*. See Jürgen Moltmann, *A Broad Place: An Autobiography* (Minneapolis: Fortress, 2008), p. 98.

[24] Jürgen Moltmann, *Theology of Hope: On the Ground and the Implications of a Christian Eschatology* (London: SCM, 1967), p. 2.

[25] Moltmann does concede that Barth had changed his emphases even by the time of *Church Dogmatics* II/1; cited in Moltmann, *Theology of Hope*, p. 44.

[26] Barth, *Church Dogmatics* I/2, pp. 114–115; cited in Moltmann, *Theology of Hope*, p. 44.

[27] Moltmann, *Theology of Hope*, p. 44.

[28] Moltmann, *Theology of Hope*, p. 5.

[29] Schwöbel, 'Last Things', p. 232.

[30] John Calvin, *Institutes of the Christian Religion*, ed. J. T. McNeil, tr. F. L. Battles, Library of Christian Classics, vols. 20–21 (Philadelphia: Westminster, 1969), III.20.13.

[31] Richard J. Middleton, *A New Heaven and a New Earth* (Grand Rapids: Baker Academic, 2014), p. 15.

[32] Karl Barth, *Church Dogmatics* IV/1, ed. G. W. Bromiley and T. F. Torrance (Edinburgh: T&T Clark, 1956), §57.51.

[33] Barth, *Church Dogmatics* IV/1, p. 4.

[34] John Calvin, 'Harmony of the Gospels', in *Biblical Commentaries* (Albany, Ore.: AGES Software, 1997), pp. 107–108.

[35] Walter Brueggemann, *Theology of the Old Testament* (Minneapolis: Fortress, 1997), p. 171.

[36] Barth, *Church Dogmatics* IV/1, p. 7.

[37] Barth, *Church Dogmatics* IV/1, p. 6.

[38] See William J. Dumbrell, *The Search for Order: Biblical Eschatology in Focus* (Grand Rapids: Baker, 1994), pp. 39ff.

[39] Note esp. Ps. 119:57 in the context of a psalm all about the benefits of possessing the Word of the Lord. See also Ps. 142:5; Jer. 10:16; 51:19.

[40] Cf. Isa. 44:3, 'I will pour out My Spirit on your [Jacob's] descendants.'

[41] Barth, *Church Dogmatics* IV/1, p. 22. See also Dumbrell, *Search*, p. 104.

[42] Barth, *Church Dogmatics* IV/1, p. 43.

[43] Peter T. O'Brien, *The Letter to the Hebrews*, Pillar New Testament Commentary (Grand Rapids: Eerdmans, 2010), p. 299.

[44] Moltmann, *Theology of Hope*, p. 94.

[45] Moltmann, *Theology of Hope*, pp. 94–95.

[46] Moltmann, *Theology of Hope*, p. 6.

[47] Calvin, *Institutes* III.2.16.

[48] Moltmann, *Theology of Hope*, p. 6.

[49] Paul Ricoeur, 'Freedom in the Light of Hope', in *The Conflict of Interpretations* (Evanston: Northwestern University Press, 1974), pp. 402–424.

[50] Moltmann, *Theology of Hope*, p. 6.

[51] The phrase originated with Kierkegaard (Ricoeur, 'Freedom', p. 407), and Moltmann similarly invoked the expression throughout (Moltmann, *Theology of Hope*, pp. 5, 20, 144).

[52] Ricoeur, 'Freedom', p. 410.

[53] Paul S. Fiddes, *The Promised End: Eschatology in Theology and Literature* (Oxford: Blackwell, 2000), p. 46.

[54] Moltmann, *Theology of Hope*, p. 72.

[55] Moltmann, *Theology of Hope*, p. 72.

[56] Moltmann, *Theology of Hope*, p. 72.

[57] Moltmann, *Theology of Hope*, p. 201.

[58] Moltmann, *Theology of Hope*, p. 198.

[59] Moltmann, *Theology of Hope*, p. 198.

[60] Frederick C. Beiser, *The Romantic Imperative* (Cambridge, Mass.: Harvard University Press, 2003), p. 54.

[61] Beiser, *Romantic Imperative*, p. 61.

[62] Moltmann, *Theology of Hope*, p. 166.

[63] Eberhard Jüngel, 'The World as Possibility and Actuality', in John Webster (ed.), *Theological Essays* (Edinburgh: T&T Clark, 1989), p. 97.

[64] Jüngel, 'World', p. 99.

[65] Jüngel, 'World', p. 103.

[66] Jüngel, 'World', p. 106.

[67] Jüngel, 'World', p. 107.

[68] Jüngel, 'World', p. 108.

[69] Jüngel, 'World', p. 110. Original emphasis.

[70] Jüngel, 'World', p. 111.

[71] Jüngel, 'World', p. 114.

[72] Moltmann, *Theology of Hope*, pp. 94–95.

[73] Karl Rahner, 'The Hermeneutics of Eschatological Assertion', in *Theological Investigations*, vol. 23 (London: Darton, Longman & Todd, 1961–92), p. 331.

[74] Brueggemann, *Theology*, p. 172.

[75] Brueggemann, *Theology*, p. 172.

[76] Brueggemann, *Theology*, p. 172.

[77] Karl Barth, *Church Dogmatics* I/2, ed. T. F. Torrance and G. W. Bromiley (Edinburgh: T&T Clark, 1956), p. 95.

[78] Adrio König, *The Eclipse of Christ in Eschatology* (Grand Rapids: Eerdmans, 1989), pp. 11–12.

[79] Dumbrell, *Search*, p. 108.

[80] David G. Peterson, *The Acts of the Apostles*, Pillar New Testament Commentary (Grand Rapids: Eerdmans, 2009), p. 141.

[81] Dumbrell, *Search*, p. 108.

[82] Barth, *Church Dogmatics* I/2, p. 94.

[83] Calvin, *Institutes* II.10.12.

[84] Calvin draws the reader's attention to Rom. 1:2–3; 3:21.

[85] Calvin, *Institutes* II.10.13.

[86] Moltmann, *Theology of Hope*, p. 99.

[87] Moltmann, *Theology of Hope*, p. 106.

[88] Calvin, *Institutes* III.1.1.

[89] Moltmann, *Theology of Hope*, p. 147.

[90] Irenaeus of Lyons developed the useful analogy for creation by 'Hands of God, that is, the Son and the Spirit'. See Irenaeus, 'Against Heresies', in Robert M. Grant (ed.), *Irenaeus of Lyons* (London: Routledge, 1997), V.28.24.

[91] Calvin, *Institutes* II.2.16.

[92] Basil of Caesarea, *Sur le Saint-Esprit*, tr. Benoît Pruche, 2nd edn (Paris: Cerf, 1968), 16.38.15. My translation is of the Greek text in this volume.

[93] Colin E. Gunton, *Intellect and Action* (Edinburgh: T&T Clark, 2000), p. 104.

[94] Colin E. Gunton, *Father, Son and Holy Spirit* (Edinburgh: T&T Clark, 2003), p. 117.

[95] Calvin, *Institutes* III.20.22.

[96] Kevin J. Vanhoozer comments, 'Embedded in [our] theodramatic practices are implicit metaphysical beliefs' ('On the Very Idea of a Theological System: An Essay in Aid of Triangulating Scripture, Church and World', in A. T. B. McGowan [ed.], *Always Reforming: Explorations in Systematic Theology* [Leicester: Apollos, 2006], p. 175).

[97] Calvin, *Institutes* III.20.25.

[98] See esp. Ricoeur, 'Freedom', §§II.411ff.

[99] Ricoeur, 'Freedom', p. 402.

[100] Calvin comments, 'if we are ashamed that Christ should experience fear and sorrow, our redemption will perish and be lost' ('Harmony of the Gospels', p. 175).

[101] God speaks these words to him at his baptism (Matt. 3:17; Mark 1:11; Luke 3:22; cf. Ps. 2:7; Isa. 42:1; 2 Sam. 7:14), and similarly at the transfiguration (Matt. 17:5; Mark 9:7; Luke 9:35). Note also Luke's record of Jesus' youthful awareness of a particular relationship with God as Father (Luke 2:49).

[102] Calvin, 'Harmony of the Gospels', p. 176.

[103] The Gospel configurations themselves become the fulfilment of what was promised beforehand: 'Record my misery; list my tears on your scroll – are they not in your record?' (Ps. 56:8 TNIV).

[104] Colin E. Gunton, *Enlightenment and Alienation: An Essay Towards a Trinitarian Theology* (Eugene, Ore.: Wipf & Stock, 2006), p. 92.

[105] Colin E. Gunton, 'Authority and Freedom', in *Theology Through the Theologians* (Edinburgh: T&T Clark, 1996), p. 224.

[106] David A. Höhne, *Spirit and Sonship: Colin Gunton's Theology of Particularity and the Holy Spirit* (Farnham: Ashgate, 2010), pp. 101ff.

[107] While the Greek word *pneuma* is not employed in any of these Gospel accounts, it is not necessary to conclude that Jesus here, or anywhere, acts without the ministry of God's Spirit. See William H. Shepherd, *The Narrative Function of the Holy Spirit as a Character in Luke-Acts*, Society of Biblical Literature Dissertation, vol. 147 (Atlanta: Scholars Press, 1994). See also Calvin on Messiah Jesus' temptation: 'We know, that Christ was fortified by the Spirit with such power, that the darts of Satan could not pierce him' ('Harmony of the Gospels', p. 188).

[108] Jürgen Moltmann, *The Spirit of Life: A Universal Affirmation* (London: SCM, 1992), p. 64.

[109] Moltmann, *Spirit of Life*, p. 65.

[110] Jürgen Moltmann, *The Crucified God: The Cross of Christ as the Foundation and Criticism of Christian Theology* (London: SCM, 1974).

[111] Jürgen Moltmann, *The Way of Jesus Christ: Christology in Messianic Dimensions* (London: SCM, 1989), p. 167.

[112] Moltmann, *Crucified God*, p. 246.

[113] Peter G. Bolt, *The Cross from a Distance*, New Studies in Biblical Theology, vol. 18 (Leicester: Apollos; Downers Grove: InterVarsity Press, 2004), p. 110.

[114] We might even pause to consider Satan's challenge on 'the highest point of the temple' (Matt. 4:5; Luke 4:9). Jesus here resists the temptation to put God's salvation to the test. Yet perhaps this was also because simply his dying, like all sinners are cursed to do, was not God's will for him. Rather, Jesus was to die a cursed death for all sinners.

[115] Calvin, 'Harmony of the Gospels', Mark 8:31, p. 221.

[116] John Calvin, *Commentary on the Letter to the Hebrews* (Albany, Ore.: AGES Software, 1997), p. 153.

Chapter 2: Praying for the perfection of life in the Middle

[1] John Calvin, *Institutes of the Christian Religion*, ed. J. T. McNeil, tr. F. L. Battles, Library of Christian Classics, vols. 20–21 (Philadelphia: Westminster, 1969), III.20.34.

[2] Calvin, *Institutes* III.20.34.

[3] Kenneth Stevenson, *The Lord's Prayer: A Text in Tradition* (London: SCM, 2004), pp. 3ff.

[4] Raymond E. Brown, 'The *Pater Noster* as an Eschatological Prayer', in *New Testament Essays* (London: Geoffrey Chapman, 1965), p. 217.

[5] Jürgen Moltmann, *The Coming of God: Christian Eschatology* (London: SCM, 1996), p. xv.

[6] See B. A. Gerrish, *Christian Faith: Dogmatics in Outline* (Louisville, Ky.: Westminster John Knox, 2015), p. 317.

[7] Moltmann, *Coming of God*, p. xv.

[8] Whether we take the form found in Matthew's or Luke's Gospel (and for the sake of familiarity I shall follow the former), the present study will follow Calvin's exegesis of six divisions, with additional attention given to the importance of God's heavenly fatherhood on the earth that will be expounded in this chapter.

[9] Ernst Lohmeyer, *The Lord's Prayer*, tr. John Bowden (London: Collins, 1965), p. 13.

[10] Gregory of Nyssa, *The Lord's Prayer, the Beatitudes*, tr. Hilda C. Graef, Ancient Christian Writers, vol. 18 (New York: Newman, 1954), p. 36.

[11] T. H. L. Parker, *John Calvin* (Sydney: Lion, 1975), p. 42.

[12] Brown, '*Pater Noster*', p. 228.

[13] Kevin J. Vanhoozer, *The Drama of Doctrine: A Canonical Linguistic Approach to Christian Theology* (Louisville, Ky.: Westminster John Knox, 2005), p. 213.

[14] Vanhoozer, *Drama*, p. 177.

[15] See Daniel Treier, *Introducing Theological Interpretation of Scripture* (Grand Rapids: Baker Academic, 2008).

[16] Kevin J. Vanhoozer and Daniel J. Treier, *Theology and the Mirror of Scripture* (Downers Grove: IVP Academic, 2015), pp. 159ff.

[17] D. E. Aune, T. J. Geddert and C. A. Evans, 'Apocalypticism', in C. A. Evans and S. E. Porter (eds.), *Dictionary of New Testament Background* (Leicester: Inter-Varsity Press, 2000), p. 46.

[18] Paul Ricoeur, *Time and Narrative*, tr. Kathleen McLaughlin and David Pellauer, vol. 1 (Chicago: University of Chicago Press, 1984), p. 54.

[19] Klaus Koch, *The Rediscovery of Apocalyptic*, Studies in Biblical Theology, vol. 22 (London: SCM, 1972), pp. 24ff.

[20] Leon Morris, *Apocalyptic* (London: Inter-Varsity Press, 1972), p. 43.

[21] D. S. Russell, *Apocalyptic: Ancient and Modern* (London: SCM, 1978), pp. 1ff.

[22] Andre Lacocque, 'Apocalyptic Symbolism: A Ricoeurian Hermeneutical Approach', *Biblical Studies* 26 (1981), p. 7.

[23] Lacocque, 'Apocalyptic Symbolism', p. 11.

[24] Richard Bauckham, *The Climax of Prophecy: Studies on the Book of Revelation* (Edinburgh: T&T Clark, 1993), p. xi.

[25] Richard Bauckham and Trevor Hart, *Hope Against Hope* (London: Darton, Longman & Todd, 1999), p. 73.

[26] Alan Bandy, 'The Hermeneutics of Symbolism: How to Interpret the Symbols of John's Apocalypse', *Southern Baptist Journal of Theology* 14.1 (2010), p. 47.

[27] See Paul Ricoeur, *The Rule of Metaphor*, tr. R. Czerny, K. McLaughlin and J. Costello SJ, Routledge Classics (London: Routledge, 2003).

[28] Karl Barth, *Church Dogmatics* I/1, ed. G. W. Bromiley and T. F. Torrance, 2nd edn (Edinburgh: T&T Clark, 1975), pp. 243–244.

[29] Bauckham and Hart, *Hope Against Hope*, p. 74.

[30] Bauckham and Hart, *Hope Against Hope*, p. 74.

[31] See section above, 'God's promises for the Middle', p. 8.

[32] Jürgen Moltmann, *Theology of Hope: On the Ground and the Implications of a Christian Eschatology* (London: SCM, 1967), p. 124.

[33] Moltmann, *Theology of Hope*, p. 124.

[34] Moltmann, *Theology of Hope*, p. 167.

[35] Colin E. Gunton, 'A Rose by Any Other Name? From "Christian Doctrine" to "Systematic Theology"', in *Intellect and Action* (Edinburgh: T&T Clark, 2000), p. 43.

[36] Augustine, *The Lord's Sermon on the Mount*, tr. John J. Jepson, Ancient Christian Writers, vol. 5 (New York: Newman, 1948), p. 104.

[37] Gerald Bray, *Yours Is the Kingdom: A Systematic Theology of the Lord's Prayer* (Nottingham: Inter-Varsity Press, 2007), p. 19. For prophetic allusions Augustine points to Isa. 1:2; Ps. 82:6; Mal. 1:6 (*Sermon on the Mount*, p. 104).

[38] Barth, *Church Dogmatics* I/1, p. 386.

[39] Barth, *Church Dogmatics* I/1, p. 388.

[40] 'Against the Heathen', in *St. Athanasius: Selected Works*, Nicene and Post-Nicene Fathers of the Christian Church, ed. Philip Schaff, vol. 4 (Edinburgh: T&T Clark, 1991), pp. 24–25 (§§39–40). See also in the same volume, 'Against the Heathen', pp. 6–7 (§§6–7); also 'Defence of the Nicene Council/[Definition]', pp. 167–172 (§§26, 30–31).

[41] See the chapter 'The Paradox of Romantic Metaphysics' in Fredrick C. Beiser, *The Romantic Imperative* (Cambridge, Mass.: Harvard University Press, 2003), pp. 131–152.

[42] Jürgen Moltmann, *The Trinity and the Kingdom of God* (London: SCM, 1981), p. 106.

[43] Karl Barth, *Church Dogmatics* II/1, ed. G. W. Bromiley and T. F. Torrance (Edinburgh: T&T Clark, 1957), p. 635.

[44] Barth, *Church Dogmatics* II/1, p. 635.

[45] Barth, *Church Dogmatics* II/1, p. 636.

[46] Barth, *Church Dogmatics* II/1, p. 636.

[47] Moltmann, *Coming of God*, p. 18.

[48] Barth, *Church Dogmatics* II/1, p. 629.

[49] John Webster, 'Trinity and Creation', *International Journal of Systematic Theology* 12.1 (2010), p. 5.

[50] Barth, *Church Dogmatics* II/1, p. 615.

[51] Barth, *Church Dogmatics* II/1, p. 615.

[52] Barth, *Church Dogmatics* II/1, p. 616.

[53] Colin E. Gunton, *The One, the Three and the Many* (Cambridge: Cambridge University Press, 1993), pp. 155ff.

[54] Karl Barth, *Church Dogmatics* III/2, ed. G. W. Bromiley and T. F. Torrance (Edinburgh: T&T Clark, 1960), p. 441.

[55] Barth, *Church Dogmatics* III/2, p. 442.

[56] Barth, *Church Dogmatics* III/2, p. 455.

[57] Barth, *Church Dogmatics* III/2, p. 467.

[58] Barth, *Church Dogmatics* III/2, p. 475.

[59] Barth, *Church Dogmatics* III/2, p. 477.

[60] Bruce L. McCormack, 'The Actuality of God', in Bruce L. McCormack (ed.), *Engaging the Doctrine of God* (Grand Rapids: Baker Academic, 2008), p. 222. Emphasis added.

[61] Barth, *Church Dogmatics* III/2, p. 487.

[62] Barth, *Church Dogmatics* III/2, p. 487.

[63] Barth, *Church Dogmatics* III/2, p. 490.

[64] Barth, *Church Dogmatics* III/2, p. 490.

[65] Barth, *Church Dogmatics* III/2, p. 496.

[66] Karl Barth, *Church Dogmatics* IV/3.1, ed. T. F. Torrance and G. W. Bromiley (Edinburgh: T&T Clark, 1961), p. 294.

[67] Moltmann, *Theology of Hope*, p. 2.

[68] Barth, *Church Dogmatics* II/1, p. 616.

[69] 'Barth's vision of the fulfilment of history is profoundly open to history . . . it is [therefore] profoundly historical' (Mike Higton, 'The Fulfilment of History in Barth, Frei, Auerbach and Dante', in John C. McDowell and Mike Higton [eds.], *Conversing with Barth* [Aldershot: Ashgate, 2004], p. 120).

[70] Moltmann, *Coming of God*, p. 25.

[71] Moltmann, *Coming of God*, p. 26.

[72] Moltmann, *Coming of God*, p. 26.

[73] Moltmann, *Coming of God*, pp. 28–29.

[74] Gerhard Sauter, 'Why Is Karl Barth's Church Dogmatics Not a "Theology of Hope?"', *Scottish Journal of Theology* 52.4 (1999), p. 415. Moltmann adds the notion of *novum* to advent to emphasize the newness of that which is coming (*Coming of God*, pp. 265–266).

[75] Moltmann, *Coming of God*, p. 294.

[76] Moltmann, *Trinity and the Kingdom*, p. 109. Moltmann borrowed this notion of divine self-restriction (*zimzum*) from Kabbalism. 'Zimzum means concentration and contraction, and signifies a withdrawing of oneself into oneself' (Jürgen Moltmann, *God in Creation*, tr. Margaret Kohl [London: SCM, 1985], p. 87).

[77] See Brian J. Walsh, 'Theology of Hope and the Doctrine of Creation: An Appraisal of Jürgen Moltmann', *Evangelical Quarterly* 59.1 (1987), p. 53.

[78] Moltmann, *God in Creation*, p. 102.

[79] See e.g. Douglas Farrow, 'In the End Is the Beginning: A Review of Jürgen Moltmann's Systematic Contributions', *Modern Theology* 14.3 (1998), pp. 425–447.

[80] Jürgen Moltmann, *The Crucified God: The Cross of Christ as the Foundation and Criticism of Christian Theology* (London: SCM, 1974), p. 277.

[81] Moltmann, *Trinity and the Kingdom*, p. 168.

[82] Moltmann, *Trinity and the Kingdom*, p. 161.

[83] Moltmann, *Coming of God*, p. 182. Emphasis added.

[84] Moltmann, *Theology of Hope*, p. 2.

[85] Adolph von Harnack, *The History of Christian Dogma* (London: Williams & Norgate, 1897), p. 63.

[86] Harnack, *History of Christian Dogma*, p. 68.

[87] Barth, *Church Dogmatics* I/1, p. 386.

[88] Barth, *Church Dogmatics* III/1, ed. G. W. Bromiley and T. F. Torrance (Edinburgh: T&T Clark, 1986), p. 44.

[89] Karl Barth, *Prayer*, ed. Don E. Saliers, tr. Sally F. Terrien, 50th Anniversary edn (Louisville, Ky.: Westminster John Knox, 2002), p. 24.

[90] Brown, '*Pater Noster*', p. 238. Stevenson observes that Origen took up this option in his exposition of the prayer, but few later commentators followed him (*Lord's Prayer*, p. 14).

[91] Christopher Morse, *The Difference Heaven Makes* (Edinburgh: T&T Clark, 2010), p. 6.

[92] William J. Dumbrell, *The End of the Beginning: Revelation 21–22 and the Old Testament* (Eugene, Ore.: Wipf & Stock, 2001), p. 166.

[93] Dumbrell, *End of the Beginning*, p. 167.

[94] Rev. 21:16 has Jerusalem as a cube 1,367 miles (2,200 km) on the side.

[95] Ezek. 47:3ff. has water flowing out of the temple for a distance of 1 mile (1.5 km).

[96] Rev. 4 – 5 has winged creatures, ancient elders, millions of angels, etc.

[97] Isa. 11 foresees a messianic era with wolves and lambs, leopards and goats, lions and yearlings, all led by children.

[98] Paul S. Fiddes, *The Promised End: Eschatology in Theology and Literature* (Oxford: Blackwell, 2000), p. 27.

[99] N. T. Wright, *The Resurrection of the Son of God*, Christian Origins and the Question of God, vol. 3 (London: SPCK, 2003), p. 204; cf. Acts 26:3–8.

[100] Gregory Nazianzen, 'Epistle 101', Nicene and Post-Nicene Fathers of the Christian Church, ed. Philip Schaff, vol. 7 (Edinburgh: T&T Clark, 1989), p. 440.

[101] Colin E. Gunton, *The Triune Creator*, Edinburgh Studies in Constructive Theology (Grand Rapids: Eerdmans, 1998), p. 59.

[102] Robert C. Doyle, *Eschatology and the Shape of the Christian Life* (London: Paternoster, 1999), p. 112.

Chapter 3: The name above all names

[1] Augustine, *The Lord's Sermon on the Mount*, tr. John J. Jepson, Ancient Christian Writers, vol. 5 (New York: Newman, 1948), p. 108. Emphasis added.

[2] Karl Barth, *Prayer*, ed. Don E. Saliers, tr. Sally F. Terrien, 50th Anniversary edn (Louisville, Ky.: Westminster John Knox, 2002), p. 32.

[3] Karl Barth, *Church Dogmatics* IV/4, tr. Geoffrey Bromiley (Grand Rapids: Eerdmans, 1981), p. 120.

[4] John Calvin, *Institutes of the Christian Religion*, ed. J. T. McNeil, tr. F. L. Battles, Library of Christian Classics, vols. 20–21 (Philadelphia: Westminster, 1969), III.20.41.

[5] Barth, *Church Dogmatics* IV/4, p. 120.

[6] Barth, *Prayer*, p. 33.

[7] John Calvin, *Commentary on Philippians* (Eugene, Ore.: AGES Software, 1997), p. 50.

[8] Peter T. O'Brien, *Commentary on Philippians*, New International Greek Testament Commentary (Grand Rapids: Eerdmans, 1991), p. 238.

[9] Karl Barth, *Church Dogmatics* IV/2, ed. G. W. Bromiley and T. F. Torrance (Edinburgh: T&T Clark, 1958), p. 151.

[10] O'Brien, *Philippians*, p. 239.

[11] Barth, *Church Dogmatics* IV/2, p. 151.

[12] Brevard S. Childs, *Exodus* (London: SCM, 1974), p. 71.

[13] HCSB adapted.

[14] Childs, *Exodus*, pp. 76–77. See also Robert Alter, *The Five Books of Moses* (New York: Norton, 2004), p. 321.

[15] Colin E. Gunton, *Act and Being* (London: SCM, 2002), p. 11.

[16] John Goldingay, *Israel's Gospel*, Old Testament Theology, vol. 1 (Downers Grove: IVP Academic, 2003), p. 336.

[17] John Calvin, 'Exodus', in *Biblical Commentaries* (Albany, Ore.: AGES Software, 1997), p. 56.

[18] John Goldingay, *Israel's Faith*, Old Testament Theology, vol. 2 (Downers Grove: IVP Academic, 2006), p. 107.

[19] See Karl Rahner, 'The Hermeneutics of Eschatological Assertion', in *Theological Investigations*, vol. 23 (London: Darton, Longman & Todd, 1961–92), p. 331.

[20] See Jürgen Moltmann, *Theology of Hope* (London: SCM, 1967), p. 86.

[21] Goldingay, *Israel's Gospel*, p. 299.

[22] Walter Brueggemann, *Theology of the Old Testament* (Minneapolis: Fortress, 1997), p. 174.

[23] Contra Paul Ricoeur, 'Naming God', *Union Seminary Quarterly Review* 34.4 (1979), p. 222.

[24] William J. Dumbrell, *The Search for Order: Biblical Eschatology in Focus* (Grand Rapids: Baker, 1994), p. 40.

[25] Goldingay, *Israel's Gospel*, p. 311.

[26] Brueggemann, *Theology*, pp. 177–178; cf. Ps. 23; Ezek. 34.

[27] Karl Barth, *Church Dogmatics* II/1, ed. G. W. Bromiley and T. F. Torrance (Edinburgh: T&T Clark, 1957), p. 47.

[28] R. W. L. Moberly, *At the Mountain of God: Story and Theology in Exodus 32–34*, Journal for the Study of the Old Testament: Supplements, vol. 22 (Sheffield: JSOT Press, 1983), pp. 60ff.

[29] John Calvin, 'Exodus', in *Harmony of the Law*, vol. 3 (Albany, Ore.: AGES Software, 1998), p. 269.

[30] Brueggemann, *Theology*, p. 214. Dumbrell draws attention to the importance of Moses as the mediator of this covenant (*Search*, pp. 49–52).

[31] Calvin, 'Exodus', p. 275.

[32] Calvin, 'Exodus', p. 275.

[33] Goldingay, *Israel's Gospel*, p. 403.

[34] Barth, *Church Dogmatics* IV/4, p. 92.

[35] Barth, *Church Dogmatics* IV/4, p. 92.

[36] Brueggemann, *Theology*, p. 216.

[37] Calvin, 'Exodus', p. 284.

[38] Calvin, 'Exodus', p. 284.

[39] Brueggemann, *Theology*, p. 270.

[40] Calvin, 'Exodus', p. 285.

[41] Moltmann, *Theology of Hope*, p. 94.

[42] Barth, *Church Dogmatics* IV/4, p. 93.

[43] Moltmann, *Theology of Hope*, p. 86.

[44] Moltmann, *Theology of Hope*, p. 93.

[45] Childs resists attempts to reread this reference in the light of later Jerusalem temple theology, claiming that the Exodus reference allows for multiple places for God's name to dwell (*Exodus*, p. 466).

[46] Yves M. J. Congar, *The Mystery of the Temple: Or the Manner of God's Presence to His Creatures from Genesis to the Apocalypse* (Westminster, Md.: Newman, 1962), p. 12.

[47] Brueggemann, *Theology*, pp. 662–663.

[48] Moshe Weinfeld, *Deuteronomy and the Deuteronomic School* (Oxford: Oxford University Press, 1972), pp. 191ff.

[49] Gregory K. Beale, *The Temple and the Church's Mission*, New Studies in Biblical Theology, vol. 17 (Leicester: Apollos; Downers Grove: InterVarsity Press, 2004), pp. 34ff.

[50] Dumbrell, *Search*, pp. 47–48. See also Craig R. Koester, *The Dwelling of God*, Catholic Bible Quarterly Monograph, vol. 22 (Washington: CBAA, 1989).

[51] Brueggemann, *Theology*, p. 669.

[52] Beale, *Temple*, pp. 50–51.

[53] C. T. R. Hayward, *The Jewish Temple* (London: Routledge, 1996), p. 6.

[54] Dumbrell, *Search*, p. 75.

[55] Brueggemann, *Theology*, pp. 654–655.

[56] Dumbrell, *Search*, p. 98.

[57] Robert W. Jenson, *The Triune Identity* (Philadelphia: Fortress, 1982), p. 38.

[58] Goldingay, *Israel's Faith*, p. 286.

[59] Brueggemann, *Theology*, p. 400.

[60] Karl Barth, *Church Dogmatics* III/2, ed. G. W. Bromiley and T. F. Torrance (Edinburgh: T&T Clark, 1960), p. 475.

[61] Goldingay, *Israel's Faith*, p. 287.

[62] Daniel J. Hays, *The Temple and the Tabernacle* (Edinburgh: T&T Clark, 2016), p. 130.

[63] N. T. Wright, *The New Testament and the People of God*, vol. 1 (London: SPCK, 1992), p. 268.

[64] John Calvin, 'Harmony of the Gospels', in *Biblical Commentaries* (Albany, Ore.: AGES Software, 1997), p. 101.

[65] Colin E. Gunton, 'Christology: Two Dogmas Revisited. Edward Irving's Christology', in *Theology Through the Theologians* (Edinburgh: T&T Clark, 1996), p. 156.

[66] Colin E. Gunton, *Act and Being* (London: SCM, 2003), p. 136. Emphasis added.

[67] Herman Ridderbos, *The Gospel of John*, tr. John Vriend (Grand Rapids: Eerdmans, 1997), p. 25.

[68] See Colin E. Gunton, *Christ and Creation*, The Didsbury Lectures (Grand Rapids: Eerdmans, 1992), pp. 35ff.

[69] William J. Dumbrell, 'Law and Grace: The Nature of the Contrast in John 1:17', *Evangelical Quarterly* 58.1 (1986), p. 25.

[70] Raymond E. Brown, *The Gospel According to John*, Anchor Bible, vol. 1 (Garden City, N.Y.: Doubleday, 1966), pp. 32–33. See also Dumbrell, 'Law and Grace'.

[71] Dumbrell, *Search*, p. 238.

[72] Dumbrell, *Search*, pp. 47–48.

[73] Fernando Segovia, 'The Journey(s) of the Word of God: A Reading of the Plot of the Fourth Gospel', *Semeia* 55 (1991), p. 36.

[74] John Nolland, *Luke 1–9:20*, Word Biblical Commentary, vol. 35a (Dallas: Word, 1989), p. 54.

[75] Raymond Brown, *Birth of the Messiah*, Anchor Bible Reference Library (New York: Doubleday, 1993), p. 328.

[76] Brown, *Birth of the Messiah*, p. 314.

[77] Nolland, *Luke 1–9:20*, p. 54. See also Joseph A. Fitzmyer, *The Gospel According to Luke 1–9*, Anchor Bible 28 (Garden City, N.Y.: Doubleday, 1981), p. 338.

[78] John Calvin, 'Harmony of the Gospels', in *Biblical Commentaries* (Albany, Ore.: AGES Software, 1997), p. 51.

[79] Nahum M. Sarna, *Exodus*, Jewish Publication Society Torah (Philadelphia: JPS 1990), p. 237; Childs, *Exodus*, p. 638.

[80] Andreas J. Köstenberger, *A Theology of John's Gospel and Letters*, Biblical Theology of the New Testament (Grand Rapids: Zondervan, 2009), p. 428.

[81] For a full discussion of Jesus' likely intentions see N. T. Wright, *Jesus and the Victory of God*, Christian Origins and the Question of God, vol. 2 (London: SPCK, 1996), pp. 413ff.

[82] Cf. Beale, *Temple*, p. 178.

[83] John Calvin, 'The Gospel of John', in *Biblical Commentaries* (Albany, Ore.: AGES Software, 1998), p. 81.

[84] See Köstenberger, *John's Gospel and Letters*, pp. 425ff. For an extensive treatment of the significance of temple symbolism in the Synoptic Gospels see Beale, *Temple*, pp. 169–200.

[85] Following Shepherd, I have taken it as a given that the Spirit continues to work in and for the Messiah even when not named in the text (William H. Shepherd, *The Narrative Function of the Holy Spirit as a Character in Luke-Acts*, Society of Biblical Literature Dissertation, vol. 147 [Atlanta: Scholars Press, 1994], p. 137).

[86] John Nolland, *Luke 9:21–18:34*, Word Biblical Commentary, vol. 35b (Dallas: Word, 1993), p. 498.

[87] Nolland, *Luke 9:21–18:34*, p. 501.

[88] Rudolph Schnackenburg, *The Gospel According to St. John*, vol. 2 (London: Burns & Oates, 1980): the bread of life (6:35, p. 48); the living bread (6:51); the bread which has come down from heaven (6:41); the light of the world (8:12); the door (10:7, 9); the good shepherd (10:11, 14); the resurrection and the life (11:25); the way, the truth and the life (14:6); the vine (15:1, p. 5).

[89] Schnackenburg, *John*, vol. 2, p. 80.

[90] Schnackenburg, *John*, vol. 2, p. 80.

[91] R. Alan Culpepper, *Anatomy of the Fourth Gospel* (Philadelphia: Fortress, 1983).

[92] David Mark Ball, *I Am in John's Gospel*, Journal for the Study of the New Testament: Supplements, vol. 124 (Sheffield: Sheffield Academic Press, 1996), p. 204.

[93] Ball, *I Am*, pp. 205ff.; C. K. Barrett, *The Gospel According to St John*, 2nd edn (London: SPCK, 1978); D. A. Carson, *The Gospel According to John* (Leicester: Inter-Varsity Press, 1991).

[94] Ball, *I Am*, p. 224.

[95] John Calvin, *Commentary on the Gospel According to John* (Albany, Ore.: AGES Software, 1998), p. 370.

[96] Carson, *John*, pp. 381–338; Ridderbos, *John*, pp. 359ff.

[97] Barth, *Church Dogmatics* IV/2, p. 168.

[98] See Schnackenburg, *John*, vol. 2, pp. 80ff.

[99] Jürgen Moltmann, *The Crucified God: The Cross of Christ as the Foundation and Criticism of Christian Theology* (London: SCM, 1974), p. 243. The reference to Paul here is in conjunction with a meditation on the words of 2 Cor. 5:21 ('He made him sin for us') and Gal. 3:13 ('He became as a curse for us'). See also Jürgen Moltmann, *The Way of Jesus Christ: Christology in Messianic Dimensions* (London: SCM, 1989), p. 173.

[100] Moltmann, *Way of Jesus Christ*, p. 167.

[101] Moltmann, *Way of Jesus Christ*, p. 167. Original emphasis.

[102] Jürgen Moltmann, *The Spirit of Life: A Universal Affirmation* (London: SCM, 1992), p. 63.

[103] Moltmann, *Spirit of Life*, p. 64.

[104] Moltmann, *Way of Jesus Christ*, pp. 94–95.

[105] See David A. Höhne, *Spirit and Sonship: Colin Gunton's Theology of Particularity and the Holy Spirit* (Farnham: Ashgate, 2010).

[106] Shepherd, *Spirit as a Character*, p. 137.

[107] Wright, *Jesus*, p. 405.

[108] Wright, *Jesus*, p. 417.

[109] John Calvin, 'Harmony of the Gospels', in *Biblical Commentaries* (Albany, Ore.: AGES Software, 1997), p. 5.

[110] Calvin, 'Harmony of the Gospels', p. 251.

[111] Beale, *Temple*, p. 190.

[112] Mark L. Strauss, *The Davidic Messiah in Luke-Acts: The Promise and Its Fulfilment in Lukan Christology*, Journal for the Study of the New Testament: Supplement Series, vol. 110 (Sheffield: Sheffield Academic Press, 1995), p. 140.

[113] John Calvin, 'Acts of the Apostles', in *Biblical Commentaries* (Albany, Ore.: AGES Software, 1998), p. 92.

[114] O'Brien, *Philippians*, p. 239.

[115] Colin E. Gunton, *The Promise of Trinitarian Theology*, 2nd edn (Edinburgh: T&T Clark, 1997), p. 66. Gunton associates the former problem with the way Barth's doctrine of election is interpreted as universalist: 'God is none other than the One who in His Son or Word elects Himself, and in and with Himself elects His people' (Karl Barth, *Church Dogmatics* II/2, ed. G. W. Bromiley and T. F. Torrance [Edinburgh: T&T Clark, 1957], p. 67). The latter problem Gunton recognizes, with elements of the Second Vatican Council's

ecclesiology, 'As the assumed nature . . . serves the Word as a living organ of salvation, so in somewhat similar way . . . does the social structure of the church serve the Spirit of Christ' (*Vatican II, The Conciliar and Post Conciliar Documents* [Grand Rapids: Eerdmans, 1994], p. 357).

[116] 'That Jesus is without sin does not imply that he is omniscient, or even infallible' (Gunton, *Trinitarian Theology*, p. 66). Gunton quotes Jesus' ignorance of 'the Day' in Mark 13:32 as support for this remark. Instead, Gunton argues for a configuration of the human Jesus' freely accepting the Spirit's guidance in the face of temptation as opposed to 'some inbuilt divine programming' (p. 66).

[117] Gunton, *Trinitarian Theology*, p. 67.

[118] Miroslav Volf, 'Soft Difference: Theological Reflections on the Relation Between Church and Culture in 1 Peter', *Ex auditu* 10 (1994), p. 17.

[119] Volf, 'Soft Difference', p. 18.

[120] Dumbrell, *Search*, p. 334.

[121] G. K. Beale, *The Book of Revelation*, New International Greek Testament Commentary (Grand Rapids: Eerdmans, 1999), p. 311.

[122] William J. Dumbrell, *Revelation: Visions for Today* (Sydney: Redeemer Baptist, 2011), p. 80. See also Beale, *Revelation*, p. 312.

[123] Dumbrell, *Search*, p. 335.

[124] Augustine, 'Letter 92', Nicene and Post-Nicene Fathers of the Christian Church, ed. Philip Schaff (Albany, Ore.: AGES Software, 1997), pp. 741–745.

[125] Augustine, 'Letter 92', p. 743.

[126] Richard Bauckham and Trevor Hart, *Hope Against Hope* (London: Darton, Longman & Todd, 1999), p. 172.

[127] Beale, *Revelation*, p. 320.

[128] Beale, *Temple*, p. 330.

Chapter 4: God's kingdom all in all

[1] Karl Rahner, 'Experiences of a Catholic Theologian', *Theological Studies* 61.1 (2000), p. 8.

[2] Rahner, 'Experiences', p. 10. Original emphasis.

[3] Gregory of Nyssa, *The Lord's Prayer, the Beatitudes*, tr. Hilda C. Graef, Ancient Christian Writers, vol. 18 (New York: Newman, 1954), p. 50.

[4] Gregory, *Lord's Prayer*, p. 51.

[5] John Calvin, *Institutes of the Christian Religion*, ed. J. T. McNeil, tr. F. L. Battles, Library of Christian Classics, vols. 20–21 (Philadelphia: Westminster, 1969), III.20.42.

[6] Adolf von Harnack, *The History of Christian Dogma* (London: Williams & Norgate, 1897), p. 63.

[7] Karl Barth, *Church Dogmatics* IV/4, tr. Geoffrey Bromiley (Grand Rapids: Eerdmans, 1981), p. 236. Original emphasis.

[8] Barth, *Church Dogmatics* IV/4, p. 237.

[9] Barth, *Church Dogmatics* IV/4, p. 242.

[10] Anthony C. Thiselton, *The First Epistle to the Corinthians*, New International Greek Testament Commentary (Grand Rapids: Eerdmans, 2000), p. 1230.

[11] Raymond E. Brown, 'The *Pater Noster* as an Eschatological Prayer', in *New Testament Essays* (London: Geoffrey Chapman, 1965), p. 233. See also George E. Ladd, *The Presence of the Future* (Grand Rapids: Eerdmans, 1974).

[12] Brown, '*Pater Noster*', p. 233.

[13] Brown, '*Pater Noster*', p. 233.

[14] Colin E. Gunton, 'Christology: Two Dogmas Revisited. Edward Irving's Christology', in *Theology Through the Theologians* (Edinburgh: T&T Clark, 1996), p. 156.

[15] Colin E. Gunton, *Act and Being* (London: SCM, 2002), p. 136.

[16] John Goldingay, *Israel's Faith*, Old Testament Theology, vol. 2 (Downers Grove: IVP Academic, 2006), p. 209.

[17] William J. Dumbrell, *Covenant and Creation* (Exeter: Paternoster, 1984), pp. 93–104.

[18] William J. Dumbrell, *The Search for Order: Biblical Eschatology in Focus* (Grand Rapids: Baker, 1994), pp. 53–54.

[19] Barry Webb, *The Book of Judges: An Integrated Reading* (Eugene, Ore.: Wipf & Stock, 2008), p. 61.

[20] John Goldingay, *Israel's Life*, Old Testament Theology, vol. 3 (Downers Grove: IVP Academic, 2009), p. 719.

[21] Dumbrell, *Search*, p. 58.

[22] See Michael S. Moore, 'To King or Not to King: A Canonical-Historical Approach to Ruth', *Bulletin for Biblical Research* 11.1 (2001), pp. 27–41.

[23] Victor H. Matthews, *Judges and Ruth*, New Cambridge Bible Commentary (Cambridge: Cambridge University Press, 2004), p. 242.

[24] Murray D. Gow, *The Book of Ruth: Its Structure, Theme and Purpose* (Leicester: Apollos, 1990), p. 132.

[25] See Matthews, *Judges and Ruth*, p. 242.

[26] Walter Brueggemann, *Theology of the Old Testament* (Minneapolis: Fortress, 1997), p. 602.

[27] William J. Dumbrell, *The Faith of Israel*, 2nd edn (Grand Rapids: Baker Academic, 2002), p. 84.

[28] Brueggemann, *Theology*, p. 605.

[29] Karl Barth, *Church Dogmatics* IV/2, ed. G. W. Bromiley and T. F. Torrance (Edinburgh: T&T Clark, 1958), p. 24.

[30] Brueggemann, *Theology*, p. 606.

[31] Goldingay, *Israel's Life*, p. 732.

[32] Robert Alter, *The Book of the Psalms* (New York: Norton, 2007), p. 397.

[33] Dumbrell, *Faith of Israel*, p. 174.

[34] Alter, *Psalms*, p. 52.

[35] Robert Alter, *The David Story: A Translation with Commentary of 1 and 2 Samuel* (New York: Norton, 1999), p. 109.

[36] Alter, *David Story*, p. 233.

[37] Brueggemann, *Theology*, p. 658.

[38] Brueggemann, *Theology*, p. 615.

[39] John Goldingay, *Israel's Gospel*, Old Testament Theology, vol. 1 (Downers Grove: IVP Academic, 2003).

[40] Brueggemann, *Theology*, pp. 602ff.

[41] Goldingay, *Israel's Gospel*, p. 552.

[42] Dumbrell, *Search*, p. 88.

[43] As Wright points out, the intertestamental literature maintains a messianic hope. See N. T. Wright, *Jesus and the Victory of God*, Christian Origins and the Question of God, vol. 2 (London: SPCK, 1996), p. 151.

[44] Karl Barth, *Church Dogmatics* III/2, ed. G. W. Bromiley and T. F. Torrance (Edinburgh: T&T Clark, 1960), p. 475.

[45] John Calvin, 'Harmony of the Gospels', in *Biblical Commentaries* (Albany, Ore.: AGES Software, 1997), p. 50.

[46] Wright, *Jesus*, pp. 451ff.

[47] George E. Ladd, *The Presence of the Future* (Grand Rapids: Eerdmans, 1974), p. 118.

[48] Kilian McDonnell reminds us that up to this point Jesus came to the Jordan 'without fame, an anonymous face in the crowd' (*The Baptism of Jesus in the Jordan: The Trinitarian and Cosmic Order of Salvation* [Collegeville: Glazier, 1996], p. 4).

[49] William J. Dumbrell, 'Spirit and Kingdom of God in the Old Testament', *Reformed Theological Review* 33 (January–April 1974), p. 5.

[50] The LXX has been cited here because of the presence of this text throughout Luke's Gospel.

[51] Karl Barth, *Church Dogmatics* IV/1, ed. G. W. Bromiley and T. F. Torrance (Edinburgh: T&T Clark, 1956), p. 260.

[52] Barth, *Church Dogmatics* IV/1, p. 260.

[53] Colin E. Gunton, *Enlightenment and Alienation: An Essay Towards a Trinitarian Theology* (Eugene, Ore.: Wipf & Stock, 2006), p. 92.

[54] Walter Brueggemann comments, 'The wilderness memory [for Israel] is one of vulnerable dependence, the shattering of illusions of adequacy' (*Deuteronomy*, ed. Patrick D. Miller, Abingdon Old Testament Commentary [Nashville: Abingdon, 2001], p. 103).

[55] Charles A. Kimball, quoting France, points to the importance of the concentration on Deuteronomy throughout this confrontation: 'the fact that the choice was in all three cases made from this single small section of the Old Testament suggests that . . . he not only wished to be seen, but saw himself, as Israel, tested and taught in the desert as God's "son" Israel had been' (*Jesus'*

Exposition of the Old Testament in Luke's Gospel, ed. Stanley E. Porter, Journal for the Study of the New Testament: Supplement Series, vol. 94 [Sheffield: Sheffield Academic Press, 1994], p. 90).

56 Barth, *Church Dogmatics* IV/1, p. 261.

57 Moshe Weinfeld, *Deuteronomy 1–11*, ed. W. F. Albright, Anchor Bible Commentary, vol. 5 (Garden City, N.Y.: Doubleday, 1991), p. 344.

58 Barth, *Church Dogmatics* IV/1, p. 262.

59 Barth, *Church Dogmatics* IV/1, p. 263.

60 Barth, *Church Dogmatics* IV/1, p. 26.

61 Alter, *Psalms*, p. 47.

62 We note that upon receipt of the Spirit Saul joined in with the prophets (1 Sam. 10:10–12). David's prophetic ministry is not explicitly recognized during his reign but is frequently mentioned in the New Testament – particularly by Jesus Christ himself.

63 See Wright, *Jesus*, pp. 451–454.

64 Calvin, 'Harmony of the Gospels', p. 59.

65 Wright, *Jesus*, p. 454.

66 Jürgen Moltmann, *The Way of Jesus Christ: Christology in Messianic Dimensions* (London: SCM, 1989), p. 99.

67 The social/political structures are also the instruments which those at the time would have called 'angels and demons'. Moltmann recognizes these in the original stories but moves away from acknowledging them in the present in favour of a more materialist description (*Way of Jesus Christ*, pp. 105–110).

68 Moltmann, *Way of Jesus Christ*, p. 99.

69 Moltmann, *Way of Jesus Christ*, pp. 8ff.

70 Moltmann, *Way of Jesus Christ*, p. 99.

71 Moltmann, *Way of Jesus Christ*, p. 101. Original emphases.

72 Moltmann, *Way of Jesus Christ*, p. 102.

73 Richard A. Burridge, *What Are the Gospels? A Comparison with Graeco-Roman Biography*, 2nd edn (Grand Rapids: Eerdmans, 2004).

74 Willis H. Salier, 'Deliverance Without Exorcisms? Jesus and Satan in John's Gospel', in Peter G. Bolt (ed.), *Christ's Victory Over Evil* (Nottingham: Apollos, 2009), pp. 82–103.

75 John Calvin, *Commentary on the Gospel According to John* (Albany, Ore.: AGES Software, 1998), p. 312.

76 Rudolph Schnackenburg, *The Gospel According to St. John*, vol. 2 (London: Burns & Oates, 1980), p. 213. Schnackenburg points also to 1 John 3:8, 'Whoever commits sin is of the devil.'

77 Calvin, *John*, p. 313.

78 Moltmann, *Way of Jesus Christ*, p. 106.

79 Moltmann, *Way of Jesus Christ*, p. 106.

80 Dumbrell, *Search*, p. 174. Dumbrell adds intertestamental sources referring to Judas Maccabeus in 1 Maccabees 4.36–59 and 2 Maccabees 10.1–8.

81 David Seccombe, *The King of God's Kingdom* (Carlisle: Paternoster, 2002), p. 504.

82 Dumbrell, *Search*, p. 174.

83 Seccombe, *King*, pp. 506–509.

84 Wright, *Jesus*, p. 508.

85 Wright, *Jesus*, pp. 497–502.

86 Ladd, *Presence of the Future*, p. 266.

87 Goldingay, *Israel's Life*, p. 162.

88 Goldingay, *Israel's Life*, p. 163.

89 Wright, *Jesus*, p. 557.

90 Goldingay, *Israel's Life*, p. 162.

91 John Calvin, 'Exodus', in *Biblical Commentaries* (Albany, Ore.: AGES Software, 1997), p. 285.

92 Calvin, 'Harmony of the Gospels', p. 249.

93 Note, the original Passover plague happens under the cover of darkness in Exod. 12.

94 Jürgen Moltmann, *The Spirit of Life: A Universal Affirmation* (London: SCM, 1992), p. 89.

95 Moltmann, *Way of Jesus Christ*, p. 188.

96 Moltmann, *Way of Jesus Christ*, p. 188.

97 Moltmann, *Way of Jesus Christ*, p. 188.

98 Calvin, 'Harmony of the Gospels', p. 304.

99 Calvin, 'Harmony of the Gospels', p. 305. Emphasis added.

100 Moltmann, *Way of Jesus Christ*, p. 97. Original emphasis. I noted a similar tone in Barth's insistence on God's kingdom as his coming but noted his restriction to the coming of the Word to that which was his own.

101 Moltmann, *Way of Jesus Christ*, p. 97.

102 Jürgen Moltmann, *The Church in the Power of the Holy Spirit* (London: SCM, 1977), p. 190.

103 Moltmann, *Church*, p. 190.

104 Moltmann, *Way of Jesus Christ*, p. 97.

105 Moltmann, *Way of Jesus Christ*, p. 98. Original emphasis.

106 Jürgen Moltmann, *The Trinity and the Kingdom of God* (London: SCM, 1981), p. 209.

107 Ladd, *Presence of the Future*, p. 138.

108 Charles H. Talbert observes, 'It would . . . be a mistake to think of Pentecost as a once-for-all event for the evangelist. In Acts the outpouring of the Holy Spirit is depicted as repeatable in the life of the church (e.g. 4:31; 8:17; 10:1–11, 19; 19:1–6)' (*Reading Acts: A Literary and Theological Commentary on the Acts of the Apostles*, Reading the New Testament [New York: Crossroad, 1997], p. 50).

109 Dumbrell, *Search*, pp. 98–99.

[110] Gregory K. Beale, *The Temple and the Church's Mission*, New Studies in Biblical Theology, vol. 17 (Leicester: Apollos; Downers Grove: InterVarsity Press, 2004), p. 204.

[111] Beale, *Temple*, p. 205.

[112] Dumbrell, *Search*, pp. 223–224.

[113] Robert C. Tannehill, *The Narrative Unity of Luke-Acts: A Literary Interpretation*, vol. 2 (Minneapolis: Augsburg Fortress, 1990).

[114] Jürgen Moltmann, *Theology of Hope* (London: SCM, 1967), p. 209.

[115] A concept that was later articulated through the various instances of Paul's Christ/head/body metaphor: Rom. 12:4; 1 Cor. 10:17; 12:12–13; Eph. 5:23; Col. 1:18.

[116] Mark L. Strauss, *The Davidic Messiah in Luke-Acts: The Promise and Its Fulfilment in Lukan Christology*, Journal for the Study of the New Testament: Supplement Series, vol. 110 (Sheffield: Sheffield Academic Press, 1995), p. 140.

[117] Calvin, *Institutes* III.1.1.

[118] Colin E. Gunton, 'The Church: John Owen and John Zizioulas on the Church', in *Theology Through the Theologians* (Edinburgh: T&T Clark, 1996), p. 201. Emphasis added.

[119] John Calvin, '1 John', in *Biblical Commentaries* (Albany, Ore.: AGES Software, 1997), p. 16.

[120] See James Gleick, *Chaos: Making a New Science* (London: Penguin, 2008).

[121] Dietrich Bonhoeffer, *Ethics*, tr. Reinhard Krauss, Dietrich Bonhöffer Works English, vol. 6 (Minneapolis: Fortress, 2005), p. 63.

[122] Barth, *Church Dogmatics* IV/4, p. 120.

[123] N. T. Wright, *The Resurrection of the Son of God*, Christian Origins and the Question of God, vol. 3 (London: SPCK, 2003), pp. 343–344. Considering the constant comparison Paul makes between Messiah Jesus and Adam in 1 Cor. 15 it seems fair to read this as God's Messiah perfecting the rule over creation that God originally gave Adam.

[124] Calvin, '1 Corinthians', in *Biblical Commentaries* (Albany, Ore.: AGES Software, 1997), p. 413.

Chapter 5: The Father's will for one and all

[1] John Calvin, 'On Election and Reprobation', in *Sermons* (Albany, Ore.: AGES Software, 1997), p. 57.

[2] Augustine, *The Lord's Sermon on the Mount*, tr. John J. Jepson, Ancient Christian Writers, vol. 5 (New York: Newman, 1948), p. 110.

[3] Augustine, *Sermon on the Mount*, p. 111.

[4] Augustine, *Sermon on the Mount*, p. 111.

[5] Augustine, *Sermon on the Mount*, p. 111.

[6] Karl Barth, *Prayer*, ed. Don E. Saliers, tr. Sally F. Terrien, 50th Anniversary edn (Louisville, Ky.: Westminster John Knox, 2002), p. 42.

[7] Raymond E. Brown, 'The *Pater Noster* as an Eschatological Prayer', in *New Testament Essays* (London: Geoffrey Chapman, 1965), p. 236.

[8] Peter T. O'Brien, 'The Summing up of All Things', in P. J. Williams (ed.), *The New Testament in Its First Century Setting* (Grand Rapids: Eerdmans, 2004), p. 218.

[9] Karl Barth, *Church Dogmatics* II/2, ed. G. W. Bromiley and T. F. Torrance (Edinburgh: T&T Clark, 1957), p. 146.

[10] See Constantine Campbell, *Paul and Union with Christ* (Grand Rapids: Zondervan, 2012).

[11] Peter T. O'Brien, *The Letter to the Ephesians*, Pillar New Testament Commentary (Grand Rapids: Eerdmans, 1999), p. 97, n. 49.

[12] Markus Barth, *Ephesians*, Anchor Bible, vols. 34, 34A (Garden City, N.Y.: Doubleday, 1974), p. 107.

[13] There is, of course, the lengthy exposition of Rom. 9 – 11 in *Church Dogmatics* II/2, §34 that interprets parts of the larger canonical story.

[14] See esp. Barth, *Church Dogmatics* II/2, pp. 117–120.

[15] Francis Turretin, *Institutes of Elenctic Theology*, tr. George Giger, vol. 1 (Phillipsburg: P&R, 1992), p. 354.

[16] John Calvin, 'A Defence of the Secret Providence of God', in *Calvin's Calvinism* (Grand Rapids: Reformed Free, 1987), pp. 223–350.

[17] E.g. see Clark H. Pinnock, *Flame of Love: A Theology of the Holy Spirit* (Downers Grove: InterVarsity Press, 1996).

[18] Barth, *Church Dogmatics* I/2, pp. 114–115; cited in Jürgen Moltmann, *Theology of Hope: On the Ground and the Implications of a Christian Eschatology* (London: SCM, 1967), p. 44.

[19] For a classic articulation of the Reformed Scholastic tradition see Turretin, *Institutes*, pp. 311–431.

[20] Barth, *Church Dogmatics* II/2, p. 146.

[21] Barth, *Church Dogmatics* II/2, p. 6.

[22] Barth, *Church Dogmatics* II/2, p. 8.

[23] Barth, *Church Dogmatics* II/2, p. 10.

[24] Bruce L. McCormack, 'The Actuality of God', in Bruce L. McCormack (ed.), *Engaging the Doctrine of God* (Grand Rapids: Baker Academic, 2008), p. 222.

[25] Barth, *Church Dogmatics* II/2, p. 12.

[26] Barth, *Church Dogmatics* II/2, pp. 12–13.

[27] See Book of Common Prayer, Article 17.

[28] Barth, *Church Dogmatics* II/2, p. 27.

[29] Barth, *Church Dogmatics* II/2, p. 177.

[30] Barth, *Church Dogmatics* II/2, p. 16.

[31] Barth, *Church Dogmatics* II/2, p. 3.

[32] Barth, *Church Dogmatics* II/2, p. 41.

[33] Barth, *Church Dogmatics* II/2, p. 44.

[34] Barth, *Church Dogmatics* II/2, p. 38.

[35] Barth, *Church Dogmatics* II/2, p. 45.

[36] Barth, *Church Dogmatics* II/2, p. 39. To be fair, Barth acknowledges that Calvin did not base his doctrine of predestination on experience: 'But he [Calvin] did buttress his doctrine so emphatically by the appeal to it that we can hardly fail to recognise that much of the pathos and emotional power with which he defended it . . . was determined by his experience' (*Church Dogmatics* II/2, p. 39).

[37] Barth's refiguring of the tradition has been hotly contested, particularly his reading of Calvin. See Richard Muller, 'The Place and Importance of Karl Barth in the Twentieth Century: A Review Essay', *Westminster Theological Journal* 50.1 (1988), pp. 127–156. See also Richard Muller, 'A Note on "Christocentrism" and the Imprudent Use of Such Terminology', *Westminster Theological Journal* 68.2 (2006), pp. 254–260.

[38] Barth, *Church Dogmatics* II/2, p. 43.

[39] Barth, *Church Dogmatics* II/2, p. 53.

[40] Barth, *Church Dogmatics* II/2, p. 101.

[41] Barth, *Church Dogmatics* II/2, p. 122.

[42] Barth, *Church Dogmatics* II/2, p. 123.

[43] Barth writes, 'Against our No He places His own *Nevertheless*. He is free in the very fact that His creatures' opposition to His love cannot be an obstacle to Him' (*Church Dogmatics* II/2, p. 28; emphasis added).

[44] Barth, *Church Dogmatics* II/2, p. 123.

[45] Barth, *Church Dogmatics* II/2, p. 164.

[46] Colin E. Gunton, *The Barth Lectures*, ed. P. H. Brazier (Edinburgh: T&T Clark, 2007), p. 115.

[47] Barth, *Church Dogmatics* II/2, p. 94.

[48] For a strong critique of Barth see Richard Muller, 'What I Haven't Learned from Karl Barth', *Reformed Journal* 37.3 (1987), p. 17.

[49] This interpretation is somewhat in contrast to the original stance of the Princeton men typified in Warfield. See B. B. Warfield, 'Are They Few That Be Saved?', in S. G. Craig (ed.), *Biblical and Theological Studies* (Philadelphia: P&R, 1952), p. 349.

[50] Barth, *Church Dogmatics* II/2, p. 94.

[51] Bruce L. McCormack, 'Grace and Being: The Role of God's Gracious Election in Karl Barth's Theological Ontology', in John Webster (ed.), *The Cambridge Companion to Karl Barth* (Cambridge: Cambridge University Press, 2000), p. 100.

[52] McCormack, 'Grace and Being', p. 103.

[53] McCormack, 'Grace and Being', p. 104.

[54] Karl Barth, *Church Dogmatics* IV/1, ed. G. W. Bromiley and T. F. Torrance (Edinburgh: T&T Clark, 1956), p. 213.

[55] George Hunsinger, 'Election and the Trinity: Twenty-Five Theses on the Theology of Karl Barth', *Modern Theology* 24.2 (2008), p. 182.

[56] Colin E. Gunton, 'Election and Ecclesiology in the Post-Constantinian Age', in *Intellect and Action* (Edinburgh: T&T Clark, 2000), p. 141.

[57] Gunton, 'Election and Ecclesiology', p. 141.

[58] Karl Barth, *Church Dogmatics* II/1, ed. G. W. Bromiley and T. F. Torrance (Edinburgh: T&T Clark, 1957), p. 615.

[59] Gunton, 'Election and Ecclesiology', p. 144.

[60] John Calvin, *Institutes of the Christian Religion*, ed. J. T. McNeil, tr. F. L. Battles, Library of Christian Classics, vols. 20–21 (Philadelphia: Westminster, 1969), II.10.12. See Rom. 11:25–26.

[61] Gunton, 'Election and Ecclesiology', p. 145.

[62] See Barth, *Church Dogmatics* II/2, pp. 318ff.

[63] Gunton, 'Election and Ecclesiology', p. 145. Emphasis added.

[64] See Matthias Wenk, *Community-Forming Power: The Socio-Ethical Role of the Spirit in Luke-Acts*, Journal of Pentecostal Theology Supplementary Series 19 (Sheffield: Sheffield Academic Press, 2000), p. 196.

[65] See John Nolland, *Luke 1–9:20*, Word Bible Commentary 35a (Dallas: Word, 1989), p. 178. At the same time Messiah Jesus is, as we have seen, the Immanuel who personally embodies all that was expected for the tabernacle. By the Spirit Jesus is the Lord present in the wilderness vindicating his name as was promised through Ezekiel; esp. Ezek. 36:22–24.

[66] See Wenk, *Community-Forming Power*, p. 197.

[67] N. T. Wright, 'Jesus, Israel and the Cross', *Society of Biblical Literature Seminar Papers* 24 (1985), p. 84.

[68] Mark L. Strauss, *The Davidic Messiah in Luke-Acts: The Promise and Its Fulfillment in Lukan Christology*, Journal for the Study of the New Testament: Supplement Series, vol. 110 (Sheffield: Sheffield Academic Press, 1995), pp. 215–216.

[69] Barth, *Church Dogmatics* II/2, p. 198.

[70] I. Howard Marshall, *The Gospel of Luke: A Commentary on the Greek Text* (Grand Rapids: Eerdmans, 1978), p. 166.

[71] N. T. Wright, *Jesus and the Victory of God*, Christian Origins and the Question of God, vol. 2 (London: SPCK, 1996), pp. 481ff.

[72] N. T. Wright, 'The Letter to the Romans', in L. E. Keck (ed.), *The New Interpreter's Bible* (Nashville: Abingdon, 2002), p. 416.

[73] N. T. Wright, *The Resurrection of the Son of God*, Christian Origins and the Question of God, vol. 3 (London: SPCK, 2003), p. 724.

[74] Jürgen Moltmann, *The Coming of God: Christian Eschatology* (London: SCM, 1996), pp. 27ff.

[75] John Goldingay, *Israel's Gospel*, Old Testament Theology, vol. 1 (Downers Grove: IVP Academic, 2003), p. 555.

[76] William J. Dumbrell, *The Search for Order: Biblical Eschatology in Focus* (Grand Rapids: Baker, 1994), p. 71.

[77] Dumbrell, *Search*, p. 70.

[78] Goldingay, *Israel's Gospel*, p. 149.

[79] Robert Alter, *The David Story: A Translation with Commentary of 1 and 2 Samuel* (New York: Norton, 1999), p. 96.

[80] Barth, *Church Dogmatics* II/2, p. 373.

[81] John Woodhouse, *1 Samuel: Looking for a Leader*, ed. R. Kent Hughes, Preaching the Word (Wheaton: Crossway, 2008), p. 286. See also Goldingay, *Israel's Gospel*, p. 557.

[82] Barth, *Church Dogmatics* II/2, p. 198.

[83] Barth, *Church Dogmatics* II/2, p. 196.

[84] Barth, *Church Dogmatics* II/2, p. 196. Original emphasis.

[85] Walter Brueggemann, *Theology of the Old Testament* (Minneapolis: Fortress, 1997), p. 414.

[86] Dumbrell, *Search*, p. 44.

[87] Dumbrell, *Search*, p. 44. See also Robert Alter, *The Five Books of Moses* (New York: Norton, 2004), p. 423.

[88] Dumbrell, *Search*, p. 45.

[89] Brueggemann, *Theology*, p. 431.

[90] Goldingay, *Israel's Gospel*, p. 374.

[91] Goldingay, *Israel's Gospel*, p. 374.

[92] Dumbrell notes that the language of blessing from Gen. 12:3 indicates that the nations will come to Israel in order to receive blessing from YHWH as opposed to Israel's going out to them (*Search*, p. 35).

[93] Dumbrell, *Search*, p. 46. See also William J. Dumbrell, *Covenant and Creation* (Exeter: Paternoster, 1984), pp. 84–90.

[94] Brueggemann, *Theology*, p. 433.

[95] Alter, *Five Books*, p. 917.

[96] R. W. L. Moberly, *Old Testament Theology: Reading the Hebrew Bible as Christian Scripture* (Grand Rapids: Baker, 2013), p. 45.

[97] Barth, *Church Dogmatics* II/2, p. 356.

[98] Dumbrell, *Search*, p. 46.

[99] Dumbrell, *Search*, p. 33.

[100] Goldingay, *Israel's Gospel*, p. 216.

[101] Goldingay, *Israel's Gospel*, p. 219.

[102] David J. A. Clines, *The Theme of the Pentateuch*, Journal for the Study of the Old Testament: Supplements, vol. 10 (Sheffield: JSOT Press, 1978), pp. 32–33.

[103] Goldingay, *Israel's Gospel*, p. 273.

[104] Gordon J. Wenham, *Genesis 1–15*, Word Biblical Commentary, vol. 1 (Waco: Word, 1987), p. 334.

[105] Nahum Sarna, *Genesis*, Jewish Publication Society Torah Commentary (Philadelphia: JPS, 1989), p. 126. See also Gerhard von Rad, *Genesis*, Old Testament Library (London: SCM, 1961), p. 188.

[106] Wenham, *Genesis 1–15*, p. 332.

[107] Dumbrell, *Covenant and Creation*, p. 74.

[108] Alter, *Five Books*, p. 84.

[109] Goldingay, *Israel's Gospel*, p. 149.

[110] Barth, *Church Dogmatics* II/2, p. 216.

[111] Brueggemann, *Theology*, p. 167.

[112] Alter notes that the language used here, 'pain', is used in the Bible exclusively of Adam and Eve and suggests a further strengthening of the possibility that Noah will somehow reverse the effects of the fall (*Five Books*, p. 37).

[113] Goldingay, *Israel's Gospel*, p. 160.

[114] See Goldingay, *Israel's Gospel*, p. 161.

[115] Barth, *Church Dogmatics* II/2, p. 342.

[116] Barth, *Church Dogmatics* II/2, p. 343.

[117] Goldingay, *Israel's Gospel*, p. 173.

[118] Rolf Knierim, *The Task of Old Testament Theology*, p. 207; cited in Goldingay, *Israel's Gospel*, p. 177.

[119] Dumbrell, *Search*, p. 31. See also Dumbrell, *Covenant and Creation*, pp. 24–25.

[120] Barth, *Church Dogmatics* II/2, p. 217.

[121] 'The myth about Paradise and the Fall never played as fundamental a role in Judaism as in Christianity' (Jürgen Moltmann, *The Spirit of Life: A Universal Affirmation* [London: SCM, 1992], p. 126). For ample evidence to the contrary see N. T. Wright, *Paul and the Faithfulness of God* (Minneapolis: Fortress, 2013).

[122] Alter, *Five Books*, p. 8.

[123] Dumbrell, *Search*, p. 18.

[124] Irenaeus, *The Scandal of the Incarnation*, ed. Hans Urs von Balthasar, tr. John Saward (San Francisco: Ignatius, 1981), V.16.12. Original emphasis.

[125] Goldingay, *Israel's Gospel*, p. 102.

[126] Irenaeus, *Scandal* III.22.23.

[127] Barth recognized the similarity of his approach to Irenaeus in §47, 'Man in His Time', *Church Dogmatics* III/2, ed. G. W. Bromiley and T. F. Torrance (Edinburgh: T&T Clark, 1960), p. 483.

[128] Alter, *Five Books*, p. 21.

[129] Walter Zimmerli, 'The Place and Limit of Wisdom in the Framework of Old Testament Theology', *Scottish Journal of Theology* 17.2 (1964), pp. 146–158.

[130] Dumbrell, *Search*, p. 19.

[131] Goldingay, *Israel's Gospel*, p. 111.

[132] N. T. Wright, *The New Testament and the People of God*, vol. 1 (London: SPCK, 1992), pp. 262ff.

[133] See e.g. Augustine's *City of God*, bk. XIV.

[134] Francis Watson, *Text and Truth* (Edinburgh: T&T Clark, 1997), p. 289.

[135] Dumbrell, *Search*, p. 22.

[136] Dumbrell, *Search*, p. 20.

[137] Irenaeus, *Scandal* IV.38.31–32.

[138] Eric Osborn, *Irenaeus of Lyons* (Cambridge: Cambridge University Press, 2001), ch. 3.

[139] Colin E. Gunton, *The Triune Creator* (Grand Rapids: Eerdmans, 1998).

[140] Barth, *Church Dogmatics* II/2, p. 102.

[141] Wright, *Jesus*, p. 451.

[142] George E. Ladd, *The Presence of the Future* (Grand Rapids: Eerdmans, 1974), p. 224.

[143] Wright, *Jesus*, p. 176.

[144] Ladd, *Presence of the Future*, p. 166.

[145] Paul Ricoeur, '"The Kingdom" in the Parables of Jesus', *Anglican Theological Review* 58.2 (1981), p. 166.

[146] Wright, *New Testament*, ch. 10.

[147] Barth, *Church Dogmatics* III/2, p. 501.

[148] See John Goldingay, *Israel's Life*, Old Testament Theology, vol. 3 (Downers Grove: InterVarsity Press, 2009), pp. 540–542.

[149] Wright, *Jesus*, pp. 360–365.

[150] Wright, *Jesus*, p. 340.

[151] Wright makes an elegantly simple case for understanding Jesus' teaching as culturally relevant and prophetically/historically accurate. See Wright, *Jesus*, pp. 339–368. See also Wright, *New Testament*, ch. 10. That said, as straightforward as this explanation may appear in terms of allowing the text of the Gospel *narratives* to address their first *hearers*, there are some issues from within the narratives themselves that prompt us to ask for more. For one thing, 'If Jesus' discourse is just before the passion, is it [not] in fact an apocalyptic for the passion?' (Peter G. Bolt, *The Cross from a Distance*, New Studies in Biblical Theology, vol. 18 [Leicester: Apollos; Downers Grove: InterVarsity Press, 2004], p. 85).

[152] Bolt, *Cross*, p. 101.

[153] Andreas J. Köstenberger, *A Theology of John's Gospel and Letters*, Biblical Theology of the New Testament (Grand Rapids: Zondervan, 2009), pp. 425ff.

[154] Bolt, *Cross*, p. 101.

[155] Barth, *Church Dogmatics* II/1, p. 89.

[156] Andreas J. Köstenberger, *John*, ed. R. Yarbrough and R. Stein, Baker Exegetical Commentary on the New Testament (Grand Rapids: Baker Academic, 2007), p. 472.

[157] Dumbrell, *Search*, pp. 98ff.

[158] Colin E. Gunton, *The Promise of Trinitarian Theology*, 2nd edn (Edinburgh: T&T Clark, 1997), p. 66. Gunton cites Barth, *Church Dogmatics* II/2, p. 67.

[159] See above ch. 1; see also Dietrich Bonhoeffer, *Act and Being*, ed. Wayne Whitson Floyd, tr. Martin Rumscheidt, Dietrich Bonhöffer Works English, vol. 2 (Minneapolis: Fortress, 1996), p. 121.

[160] Gunton, 'Election and Ecclesiology', p. 146.

[161] Gunton, 'Election and Ecclesiology', p. 129.

[162] John Calvin, 'Romans', in *Biblical Commentaries* (Albany, Ore.: AGES Software, 1998), pp. 227–228.

[163] Gunton, 'Election and Ecclesiology', p. 149. Emphasis added.

[164] Strictly speaking, Peter's language of possession, to which he alludes, is not an exact match with Exod. 19:5 and Deut. 7:6. In the LXX Deut. 7:6 and Exod. 19:5 have *periousios*, whereas Peter uses *peripoiēsis*, 'that which is acquired as a possession' (Walter Bauer, William F. Arndt, Wilbur Gingrich and Frederick W. Danker, *A Greek–English Lexicon of the New Testament*, 2nd edn [Chicago: University of Chicago Press, 1979], p. 648). Significantly, however, in Titus 2:14 Paul uses the LXX terminology in reference to the church as that which God redeemed for himself.

[165] O'Brien, *Ephesians*, p. 34.

[166] Calvin, 'Ephesians', in *Biblical Commentaries* (Albany, Ore.: AGES Software, 1998), p. 62.

[167] Ladd, *Presence of the Future*, p. 166.

[168] Herman Ridderbos, *The Gospel of John*, tr. John Vriend (Grand Rapids: Eerdmans, 1997), pp. 200–201.

[169] John Calvin, 'Harmony of the Gospels', in *Biblical Commentaries* (Albany, Ore.: AGES Software, 1997), p. 305.

[170] The reference to Ps. 110:4 in Heb. 5, 7 follows the LXX and therefore differs from the HCSB version.

[171] Charles A. Wanamaker, *The Epistles to the Thessalonians*, New International Greek Testament Commentary (Grand Rapids: Eerdmans, 1990).

Chapter 6: Good Lord, preserve us

[1] Jürgen Moltmann, *The Coming of God: Christian Eschatology* (London: SCM, 1996), p. xv.

[2] Miroslav Volf, 'Theology for a Way of Life', in Miroslav Volf and Dorothy C. Bass (eds.), *Practicing Theology* (Grand Rapids: Eerdmans, 2002), p. 247.

[3] John Calvin, 'Harmony of the Gospels', in *Biblical Commentaries* (Albany, Ore.: AGES Software, 1997), p. 271.

[4] Calvin, 'Harmony of the Gospels', p. 270.

[5] Tertullian, 'Tertullian on Prayer', in *Tertullian, Cyprian, Origen on the Lord's Prayer*, Popular Patristics (New York: St Vladimir's Press, 2004), p. 90.

[6] Gregory of Nyssa, *The Lord's Prayer, the Beatitudes*, tr. Hilda C. Graef, Ancient Christian Writers, vol. 18 (New York: Newman, 1954), p. 63.

[7] Augustine, *The Lord's Sermon on the Mount*, tr. John J. Jepson, Ancient Christian Writers, vol. 5 (New York: Newman, 1948), p. 113.

[8] Raymond E. Brown, 'The *Pater Noster* as an Eschatological Prayer', in *New Testament Essays* (London: Geoffrey Chapman, 1965), p. 240. Brown's interpretation depends on *ton epiousion* deriving from *epi* plus *einai*, the verb 'to go, come'.

[9] Brown, '*Pater Noster*', p. 241. Brown supports this with references to Luke 6:21 (satisfaction for the hungry), 14:15 (eating bread in the kingdom); Luke 22:29–30 (eating at the table of the kingdom); Matt. 8:11 (eating with the patriarchs at table in the kingdom).

[10] Brown, '*Pater Noster*', p. 242.

[11] Augustine, *Sermon on the Mount*, p. 113.

[12] Augustine, *Sermon on the Mount*, p. 114.

[13] Augustine, *Sermon on the Mount*, p. 114.

[14] See G. C. Berkouwer, *The Triumph of Grace in the Theology of Karl Barth* (London: Paternoster, 1956).

[15] Matt. 5 *passim*.

[16] Jesus' claim is, in the text of John, without reference or allusion either to the various hints of resurrection in the Old Testament (Isa. 26:19; Job 19:25; Dan. 12:1ff.) or the more general rabbinic speculations as discussed by N. T. Wright, *The Resurrection of the Son of God* (London: SPCK, 2003), pt. 1.

[17] John Goldingay, *Israel's Faith*, vol. 2 (Downers Grove: IVP Academic, 2006), p. 646.

[18] Goldingay, *Israel's Faith*, p. 826.

[19] Wright, *Resurrection*, p. 109.

[20] Wright, *Resurrection*, p. 114.

[21] Wright, *Resurrection*, p. 444.

[22] Wright, *Resurrection*, p. 444.

[23] John Calvin, *The Gospel According to John* (Albany, Ore.: AGES Software, 1998), p. 392.

[24] Dietrich Bonhoeffer, 'Christologie', in Eberhard Bethge (ed.), *Berlin 1932–1933*, Dietrich Bonhöffer Werke (Munich: Chr. Kaiser, 1997), p. 286.

[25] Jürgen Moltmann, *Hope and Planning* (London: SCM, 1971), p. 44; 'The Lordship of Christ and Human Society', in J. Moltmann and J. Weissbach, *Two Studies in the Theology of Bonhoeffer* (New York: Scribner's, 1967), p. 66; 'Messianic Hope: Christianity, Christians and Jews', *Concilium* 98 (1974), p. 66.

[26] Jürgen Moltmann, *The Theology of Hope* (London: SCM, 1967), p. 178.

[27] Moltmann, *Theology of Hope*, p. 208.

[28] Jürgen Moltmann, *The Way of Jesus Christ* (London: SCM, 1989), p. 218.

[29] Gerald O'Collins, *Jesus Risen* (Mahwah: Paulist Press, 1987), p. 119.

[30] Joseph J. Smith SJ, 'N. T. Wright's Understanding of the Nature of Jesus' Risen Body', *Heythrop Journal* 57 (2016), p. 30.

[31] Raymond E. Brown, *Responses to 101 Questions on the Bible* (Mahwah: Paulist Press, 1990), p. 75.

[32] Langdon Gilkey, *Religion and the Scientific Future Reflections on Myth, Science, and Theology* (New York: Harper, 1970), p. 150. Original emphasis.

[33] Moltmann, *Coming of God*, p. 173.

[34] Randall Otto, 'The Resurrection in Jürgen Moltmann', *Journal of the Evangelical Theological Society* 35 (March 1992), p. 86.

[35] Otto, 'Resurrection', p. 81.

[36] Moltmann, *Coming of God*, p. 246.

[37] Moltmann, *Theology of Hope*, p. 211.

[38] Jürgen Moltmann, *The Spirit of Life* (London: SCM, 1992), p. 151.

[39] Moltmann, *Way of Jesus Christ*, p. 240.

[40] Moltmann, *Way of Jesus Christ*, p. 241.

[41] Moltmann, *Spirit of Life*, p. 153.

[42] Moltmann, *Way of Jesus Christ*, p. 241.

[43] Douglas Farrow, *Ascension and Ecclesia* (Edinburgh: T&T Clark, 1999), p. 8.

[44] Douglas Farrow, 'In the End Is the Beginning: A Review of Jürgen Moltmann's Systematic Contributions', *Modern Theology* 14.3 (1998), p. 439.

[45] N. T. Wright, *Surprised by Hope* (London: SPCK, 2007), p. 219.

[46] Moltmann, *Way of Jesus Christ*, p. 263.

[47] Moltmann, *Way of Jesus Christ*, p. 263.

[48] Moltmann, *Way of Jesus Christ*, pp. 265ff.

[49] Moltmann, *Way of Jesus Christ*, p. 266. Original emphasis.

[50] Moltmann, *Way of Jesus Christ*, p. 266.

[51] Colin E. Gunton, '"Until He Comes": Towards an Eschatology of Church Membership', *International Journal of Systematic Theology* 3.2 (2001), p. 192.

[52] Gunton, 'Until He Comes', p. 193.

[53] Moltmann, *Way of Jesus Christ*, p. 266.

[54] Moltmann, *Way of Jesus Christ*, p. 266.

[55] Moltmann has consistently maintained an egalitarian stance on the relationships between men and women, especially in marriage, and therefore, along with many modern commentators, views the household codes as another aspect of the primitive church that can be relaxed. See Sarah Coakley, 'The Trinity and Gender Reconsidered', in M. Volf and M. Welker (eds.), *God's Life in Trinity* (Minneapolis: Fortress, 2006), pp. 132–145.

[56] Moltmann, *Way of Jesus Christ*, p. 268.

[57] Daniel Bell Jr makes a similar case in *The Economy of Desire: Christianity and Capitalism in a Postmodern World* (Grand Rapids: Baker, 2012). See esp. ch. 4, 'Capitalist Theology'.

[58] Moltmann, *Way of Jesus Christ*, p. 269.

[59] Moltmann, *Way of Jesus Christ*, p. 270.

[60] Moltmann, *Way of Jesus Christ*, p. 270.

[61] Moltmann, *Way of Jesus Christ*, p. 271. Original emphasis.

[62] Moltmann, *Way of Jesus Christ*, p. 272.

[63] Moltmann, *Spirit of Life*, p. 172.

[64] Jürgen Moltmann, *The Ethics of Hope* (London: SCM, 2012), p. 3.

[65] Contra Wright, *Surprised by Hope*, p. 218.

[66] Contra Tim Keller, *Every Good Endeavour* (London: Hodder & Stoughton, 2012), pp. 156ff.

[67] Moltmann, *Ethics of Hope*, p. 7.

[68] Jürgen Moltmann, *God in Creation* (London: SCM, 1985), p. 13.

[69] Moltmann describes the relationship between God and creation as *panentheistic* such that 'The one-sided stress on God's transcendence in relation to the world led to deism, as with Newton. The one-sided stress on God's immanence in the world led to pantheism, as with Spinoza. The trinitarian concept of creation integrates the elements of truth in monotheism and pantheism. In the panentheistic view, God, having created the world, also dwells in it, and conversely the world, which he created, exists in him' (*God in Creation*, p. 98).

[70] Moltmann, *God in Creation*, p. 9.

[71] Moltmann, *God in Creation*, p. 100.

[72] See Jürgen Moltmann, *The Source of Life* (Minneapolis: Fortress, 1997).

[73] Moltmann, *God in Creation*, p. 15.

[74] Moltmann, *Hope and Planning*, p. 35.

[75] Jürgen Moltmann, *The Church in the Power of the Holy Spirit* (London: SCM, 1977), p. 161.

[76] Moltmann, *Spirit of Life*, pp. 153ff.

[77] Moltmann, *God in Creation*, p. 9.

[78] Colin E. Gunton, *The One, the Three and the Many* (Cambridge: Cambridge University Press, 1993), pp. 38–39.

[79] John Webster, 'Trinity and Creation', *International Journal of Systematic Theology* 12.1 (2010), pp. 4–19.

[80] John Calvin, 'Philippians', in *Biblical Commentaries* (Albany, Ore.: AGES Software, 1997), p. 51.

[81] Wright, *Resurrection*, pp. 315–316.

[82] Wright, *Resurrection*, p. 318.

[83] See Smith, 'Wright's Understanding', p. 32.

[84] Margaret B. Adam, *Our Only Hope* (Eugene, Ore.: Pickwick, 2013), p. 96.

[85] Moltmann, *Coming of God*, p. 66.

[86] Moltmann, *Coming of God*, p. xiii.

[87] Hans Schwarz, *Eschatology* (Grand Rapids: Eerdmans, 2000), p. 149.

[88] Farrow, *Ascension and Ecclesia*, p. 9.

[89] Israel in various periods was exposed to concepts of resurrection from Egypt and Babylon. See e.g. Kathryn M. Cooney, 'Gender Transformation in Death: A Case Study of Coffins from Ramesside Period Egypt', *Near Eastern Archaeology* 73.4 (2010), pp. 224–236. See also Roger Walsh, 'Experiences of

"Soul Journeys" in World's Religions: The Journeys of Mohammed, Saints Paul and John, Jewish Chariot Mysticism, Taoism's Highest Clarity School and Shamanism', *Journal of Theological Studies* 31.2 (2012), pp. 103–110.

[90] Plato's *Phaedo* and *The Republic* are the archetypal source for much of Western thought. See Peter W. Martens, 'Embodiment, Heresy, and the Hellenization of Christianity: The Descent of the Soul in Plato and Origen', *Harvard Theological Review* 108.4 (October 2015), pp. 594–620.

[91] Moltmann, *Coming of God*, p. 66.

[92] See Origen, *De principiis*, Ante-Nicene Fathers, vol. 4 (Edinburgh: T&T Clark, 1995), p. 240.

[93] See Augustine, Nicene and Post-Nicene Fathers, vol. 2 (Edinburgh: T&T Clark, 1993), p. 245.

[94] Origen, *De principiis* 1.7.1; 2.6.3–4; Augustine, *On Genesis*, tr. Edmund Hill (New York: New City, 2002), 3.19.29.

[95] Dera Sipe, 'Struggling with Flesh: Soul/Body Dualism in Porphyry and Augustine', *Concept* 29 (2006), pp. 2–38.

[96] John Calvin, 'Psychopannychia', in *Selected Works of John Calvin*, vol. 3.3 (Albany, Ore.: AGES Software, 1998), pp. 378–451.

[97] See esp. Adolf von Harnack, *The History of Christian Dogma* (London: Williams & Norgate, 1897). Martens helpfully identifies the following most pertinent section: '1:46–47 (on the antagonistic model Harnack uses for Jewish and Hellenistic cultures), 1:56–57 (on the irreconcilability of Paul's theology with the Greek world), and 2:333 (on the "dangerous" atmosphere in which Origen lived as a Christian and philosopher). On the "Hellenic spirit", 1:49' ('Embodiment, Heresy', p. 595, n. 2).

[98] See esp. Hans W. Wolff, *Anthropology of the Old Testament* (Philadelphia: Fortress, 1974).

[99] R. L. Harris, 'The Meaning of the Word *Sheol* as Shown by Parallels in Poetic Tests', *Bulletin of the Evangelical Theological Society* 4 (1961), pp. 129–135; 'Why Hebrew *Sheol* Was Translated Grave', in K. L. Barker (ed.), *The NIV: The Making of a Contemporary Translation* (London: Hodder & Stoughton, 1987), pp. 58–71.

[100] See Joel B. Green, *Body, Soul, and Human Life* (Grand Rapids: Baker, 2008), pp. 51ff.

[101] Paul Williamson, *Death and the Afterlife*, New Studies in Biblical Theology, vol. 44 (London: Apollos; Downers Grove: InterVarsity Press, 2017), p. 48.

Chapter 7: Good Lord, forgive us

[1] John Calvin, *Institutes of the Christian Religion*, ed. J. T. McNeil, tr. F. L. Battles, Library of Christian Classics, vols. 20–21 (Philadelphia: Westminster, 1969), III.20.45.

[2] Gregory Nazianzen, *The Lord's Prayer, The Beatitudes*, Ancient Christian Writers (New York: Newman, 1954), p. 78.

[3] Karl Barth, *Prayer*, ed. Don E. Saliers, tr. Sally F. Terrien, 50th Anniversary edn (Louisville, Ky.: Westminster John Knox, 2002), p. 54.

[4] Barth, *Prayer*, p. 54.

[5] John Calvin, '1 John', in *Biblical Commentaries* (Albany, Ore.: AGES Software, 1997), p. 17.

[6] Douglas Farrow, 'Melchizedek and Modernity', in Richard Bauckham, Daniel R. Driver, Trevor A. Hart and Nathan McDonald (eds.), *The Epistle to the Hebrews and Christian Theology* (Grand Rapids: Eerdmans, 2009), p. 287.

[7] John Calvin, 'Hebrews', in *Biblical Commentaries* (Albany, Ore.: AGES Software, 1997), p. 135.

[8] Calvin, 'Hebrews', p. 153.

[9] Jürgen Moltmann, *The Way of Jesus Christ* (London: SCM, 1996), p. 188.

[10] Andrew Burgess, *The Ascension in Karl Barth* (Aldershot: Ashgate, 2004), p. 24.

[11] Karl Barth, *Church Dogmatics* III/2, ed. G. W. Bromiley and T. F. Torrance (Edinburgh: T&T Clark, 1960), p. 454.

[12] Karl Barth, *Church Dogmatics* IV/1, ed. G. W. Bromiley and T. F. Torrance (Edinburgh: T&T Clark, 1956), pp. 4–5.

[13] Karl Barth, *Church Dogmatics* IV/2, ed. G. W. Bromiley and T. F. Torrance (Edinburgh: T&T Clark, 1958), p. 20.

[14] Barth, *Church Dogmatics* IV/2, §64.2.

[15] Barth, *Church Dogmatics* IV/2, p. 155.

[16] Barth, *Church Dogmatics* IV/2, p. 31.

[17] Barth, *Church Dogmatics* IV/2, p. 155.

[18] Barth, *Church Dogmatics* IV/2, p. 264.

[19] Cf. *Church Dogmatics* IV/1, §59.3.

[20] Barth, *Church Dogmatics* IV/2, p. 118.

[21] Karl Barth, *Church Dogmatics* IV/3, ed. T. F. Torrance and G. W. Bromiley (Edinburgh: T&T Clark, 1961), p. 8.

[22] Barth, *Church Dogmatics* IV/3, pp. 3ff.

[23] Barth, *Church Dogmatics* IV/3.1, §69.

[24] Barth, *Church Dogmatics* IV/3, p. 5.

[25] Barth, *Church Dogmatics* IV/3, p. 5.

[26] Douglas Farrow, 'Karl Barth on the Ascension: An Appreciation and Critique', *International Journal of Systematic Theology* 2.2 (2000), p. 143.

[27] Barth, *Church Dogmatics* IV/1, p. 275. McCormack considers Barth's exposition as the most forensic of the Reformed tradition. See Bruce L. McCormack, 'So That He May Be Merciful to All: Karl Barth and the Problem of Universalism', in Clifford B. Anderson (ed.), *Karl Barth and American Evangelicalism* (Grand Rapids: Eerdmans, 2011), pp. 227–249.

[28] Barth, *Church Dogmatics* IV/1, p. 276. See also Karl Barth, *Church Dogmatics* II/2, ed. G. W. Bromiley and T. F. Torrance (Edinburgh: T&T Clark, 1957), pp. 561–562.

[29] Barth, *Church Dogmatics* IV/3, p. 397.

[30] Barth, *Church Dogmatics* IV/3, p. 397. Emphasis added.

[31] Barth, *Church Dogmatics* IV/3, p. 397.

[32] Farrow, 'Melchizedek and Modernity', p. 292.

[33] Barth, *Church Dogmatics* IV/1, p. 122.

[34] Barth, *Prayer*, p. 54.

[35] John Calvin, 'Short Treatise on the Holy Supper of Our Lord Jesus Christ', in *Treatises on the Sacraments*, tr. Henry Beveridge (Grand Rapids: Christian Focus, 2002), p. 74.

[36] Karl Barth, *Church Dogmatics* II/1, ed. G. W. Bromiley and T. F. Torrance (Edinburgh: T&T Clark, 1957), p. 380.

[37] Miroslav Volf, *Free of Charge* (Grand Rapids: Zondervan, 2005), p. 196.

[38] Karl Barth, *Church Dogmatics* I/2, ed. T. F. Torrance and G. W. Bromiley (Edinburgh: T&T Clark, 1956), p. 435.

[39] John Coutts, *A Shared Mercy: Karl Barth on Forgiveness and the Church* (Downers Grove: IVP Academic, 2016), pp. 131ff. What follows is largely dependent upon Coutts's excellent constructive work in conversation with Barth on forgiveness.

[40] Nigel Biggar, 'Barth's Trinitarian Ethic', in John Webster (ed.), *The Cambridge Companion to Karl Barth* (Cambridge: Cambridge University Press, 2000), p. 227.

[41] Barth, *Church Dogmatics* II/2, p. 518. See Paul Nimmo, *Being in Action* (Edinburgh: T&T Clark, 2007), p. 4. See also John Webster, *Barth's Moral Theology* (Grand Rapids: Eerdmans, 1998), p. 80.

[42] Coutts, *Shared Mercy*, p. 132.

[43] Biggar, 'Barth's Trinitarian Ethic', p. 212.

[44] Barth, *Church Dogmatics* IV/1, p. 563.

[45] We note that patience is for Barth a divine perfection; e.g. see *Church Dogmatics* II/1, pp. 406–422. Adam J. Johnson subsequently suggests that Barth's doctrine of atonement could be constructively qualified as 'The Patient One Patient in Our Place', *God's Being in Reconciliation* (Edinburgh: T&T Clark, 2012), pp. 127ff.

[46] Coutts, *Shared Mercy*, p. 135.

[47] Barth, *Church Dogmatics* IV/2, p. 809.

[48] Barth, *Church Dogmatics* IV/1, p. 233.

[49] Coutts, *Shared Mercy*, p. 139.

[50] Volf, *Free of Charge*, p. 196.

[51] Barth, *Church Dogmatics* IV/1, p. 680.

[52] Barth, *Church Dogmatics* IV/3, p. 267.

[53] Coutts, *Shared Mercy*, p. 144.

54 Barth, *Church Dogmatics* IV/1, p. 684.

55 Coutts, *Shared Mercy*, p. 153.

56 Karl Barth, *Church Dogmatics* IV/4, tr. Geoffrey Bromiley (Grand Rapids: Eerdmans, 1981), p. 83.

57 Barth, *Church Dogmatics* IV/1, p. 258.

58 Barth, *Church Dogmatics* IV/4, p. 83.

59 Barth, *Church Dogmatics* IV/4, p. 83.

60 Coutts, *Shared Mercy*, p. 161.

61 Coutts, *Shared Mercy*, p. 168.

62 Miroslav Volf, *The End of Memory* (Grand Rapids: Eerdmans, 2006), p. 145.

63 'The Humanity of God', in *God, Grace and Gospel*, pp. 49–50; cited in Tom Greggs, 'Jesus Is Victor: Passing the Impasse of Barth on Universalism', *Scottish Journal of Theology* 60.2 (2007), p. 199.

64 McCormack, 'Merciful to All', p. 227.

65 Tom Greggs, 'Pessimistic Universalism: Rethinking the Wider Hope with Bonhoeffer and Barth', *Modern Theology* 26.4 (October 2010), p. 496.

66 See Rob Bell, *Love Wins* (New York: HarperCollins, 2007), and Gregory MacDonald, *The Evangelical Universalist*, 2nd edn (London: SPCK, 2012), p. 198.

67 Clark H. Pinnock, *Flame of Love* (Downers Grove: InterVarsity Press, 1996), p. 190. Significantly for the ongoing dialogue in the book, Moltmann is firmly in the universal salvation camp as a by-product of his largely therapeutic articulation of theodicy. See my 'Moltmann and Salvation', in Soon Wook Chung (ed.), *Jürgen Moltmann and Evangelical Theology* (Eugene, Ore.: Pickwick, 2012), pp. 152–173.

68 *On First Principles* 1.6.3.

69 Barth, *Church Dogmatics* I/2, p. 295.

70 Barth, *Church Dogmatics* IV/3, p. 477.

71 Barth preferred the term over attributes, since, '[Perfections] points at once to the thing itself instead of merely to its formal aspect, and because instead of something general it expresses at once that which is clearly distinctive. The fact that God's being has attributes is something which it has in common with the being of others. But that it is identical with a multitude of perfections – if the term is taken strictly – is something which is the "attribute" of God and God alone' (*Church Dogmatics* II/1, p. 322).

72 Barth, *Church Dogmatics* II/1, p. 322.

73 Barth, *Church Dogmatics* II/1, p. 273.

74 Barth, *Church Dogmatics* II/1, p. 273.

75 Barth, *Church Dogmatics* II/1, p. 274. Evil exists in the conceptual space that Barth leaves between the decretal will of God and the permissive will of God. See John McDowell, 'Much Ado About Nothing: Karl Barth's Being Unable to Do Nothing About Nothingness', *International Journal of Systematic Theology* 4.3 (2002), pp. 319–335.

[76] Barth, *Church Dogmatics* II/1, p. 355.

[77] Barth, *Church Dogmatics* II/1, p. 361.

[78] Barth, *Church Dogmatics* II/1, p. 362.

[79] Barth, *Church Dogmatics* II/1, p. 362.

[80] Barth, *Church Dogmatics* II/1, p. 363.

[81] Barth, *Church Dogmatics* II/1, p. 367.

[82] Colin Gunton, *Act and Being* (London: SCM, 2002), p. 70.

[83] Not surprisingly therefore Christ Jesus himself, in challenging the Pharisees during the various confrontations at the temple with them in the last week of his ministry before the crucifixion, quotes Ps. 110:1 (Matt. 22:44; Mark 12:36; Luke 20:42).

[84] John Calvin, 'Harmony of the Gospels', in *Biblical Commentaries* (Albany, Ore.: AGES Software, 1997), p. 55.

[85] The prime example of this situation comes when the serpent lies to the woman in Gen. 3:5 regarding God's intention to prevent her from knowing good and evil. As Calvin commented, 'When he [the serpent] says, God does know, he censures God as being moved by jealousy: and as having given the command concerning the tree, for the purpose of keeping man in an inferior rank' (*Commentary on Genesis* [Albany, Ore.: AGES Software, 1998], p. 86).

[86] John Calvin, 'Harmony of the Gospels', in *Biblical Commentaries* (Albany, Ore.: AGES Software, 1997), p. 56.

[87] Barth, *Church Dogmatics* IV/3, p. 358.

[88] Barth, *Church Dogmatics* IV/2, p. 159.

[89] Barth, *Church Dogmatics* IV/1, pp. 93–94.

[90] See David Lauber, *Barth on the Descent into Hell* (Aldershot: Ashgate, 2004).

[91] Barth, *Church Dogmatics* IV/1, p. 273. See Johnson, *God's Being in Reconciliation*, pp. 93ff.

[92] Barth was determined to articulate reconciliation in the person of Jesus Christ at the cross and resurrection, even to the point of describing the cross as eclipsing the 'second death' (Rev. 20:14). Of course, in the context of the Apostles' Creed even Calvin considered the 'descent into hell' as a reference to the cross and, whatever we make of the divine curse of wrath at the final judgment, it must be analogous of the cross as opposed to the cross being merely analogous of hell. See Lauber, *Descent into Hell*, esp. pp. 1–41.

[93] George Hunsinger, 'Hellfire and Damnation: Four Ancient and Modern Views', *Scottish Journal of Theology* 51.4 (1998), p. 426.

[94] See Michael Jensen, 'The Genesis of Hell: Eternal Torment in the Conciousness of Early Christians', *Reformed Theological Review* 65.2 (2006), pp. 132–148.

[95] Barth, *Church Dogmatics* IV/3, p. 173. The phrase 'Triumph of Grace' belongs to the work of Berkouwer (see above, ch. 6, p. 293, n. 14), against

whom Barth was contesting. Berkouwer claimed that the ultimate triumph of Grace was the rationale for Barth's work that led to universalism.

[96] See Friedrich D. E. Schleiermacher's aesthetic scepticism of the joy of the blessed in the light of the suffering of the cursed (*The Christian Faith* [Edinburgh: T&T Clark, 1968], §158, pp. 698ff.). See also Murray Rae, 'Salvation in Community', in *'All Shall Be Well': Explorations in Universalism and Christian Theology from Origen to Moltmann* (Eugene, Ore.: Cascade, 2001), pp. 171–197.

[97] Barth, *Church Dogmatics* IV/3, p. 173.

Chapter 8: Good Lord, deliver us

[1] Gregory of Nyssa, *The Lord's Prayer, The Beatitudes*, Ancient Christian Writers (New York: Newman, 1954), p. 83.

[2] Augustine, *The Lord's Sermon on the Mount*, Ancient Christian Writers (New York: Newman, 1948), p. 119.

[3] Augustine, *Sermon on the Mount*, p. 122.

[4] Augustine, *Sermon on the Mount*, p. 123.

[5] John Calvin, *Institutes of the Christian Religion*, tr. F. L. Battles, Library of Christian Classics, vols. 21–22 (Philadelphia: Westminster, 1969), III.20.46.

[6] See John McDowell, 'Much Ado About Nothing: Karl Barth's Being Unable to Do Nothing About Nothingness', *International Journal of Systematic Theology* 4.3 (2002), pp. 319–335.

[7] Karl Barth, *Prayer*, 50th Anniversary edn (Louisville, Ky.: Westminster John Knox, 2002), p. 61.

[8] Fred R. Shapiro, 'Who Wrote the Serenity Prayer', <https://www.chronicle.com/article/Who-Wrote-the-Serenity-Prayer-/146159>, accessed 7 November 2018.

[9] Jürgen Moltmann, *The Future of Creation* (London: SCM, 1979), p. 164.

[10] William J. Dumbrell, 'Genesis 1–3, Ecology, and the Dominion of Man', *Crux* 21 (1985), p. 24.

[11] John Calvin, 'Romans', in *Biblical Commentaries* (Albany, Ore.: AGES Software, 1997), p. 235.

[12] Timothy P. Weber, 'Millennialism', in Jerry L. Walls (ed.), *The Oxford Handbook of Eschatology* (Oxford: Oxford University Press, 2008), p. 365. The focus of the section will be on millennialism as it has appeared in the mainline Anglo-American Christian churches from the nineteenth and twentieth centuries onwards. Millennialism has been an issue throughout the history of the church and, for that matter, in Western civilization. See Fredric J. Baumgartner, *Longing for the End: A History of Millennialism in Western Civilisation* (New York: St Martin's, 1999).

[13] Kim Riddlebarger, *A Case for Amillennialism* (Grand Rapids: Baker, 2003), p. 31. Emphasis added.

14 Millard J. Erickson, *A Basic Guide to Eschatology: Making Sense of the Millennium*, rev. edn (Grand Rapids: Baker, 1998), p. 92.

15 J. N. Darby, 'What Saints Will Be in the Tribulation', in William Kelly (ed.), *The Collected Writings of J. N. Darby* (Oak Park, Ill.: Bible Truth, 1972), pp. 110–117.

16 Erickson, *Making Sense of the Millennium*, p. 92.

17 Robert C. Doyle, *Eschatology and the Shape of Christian Belief* (London: Paternoster, 1999), p. 331.

18 J. N. Darby, 'The Rapture of the Saints and the Character of the Jewish Remnant', in Darby, *Collected Writings*, p. 118.

19 The list comes from Doyle, *Eschatology*, p. 331.

20 See Gary DeMar, *End Times Fiction: A Biblical Consideration of the Left Behind Theology* (Nashville: Thomas Nelson, 2001). See also Baumgartner, *End*, pp. 240–242.

21 Erickson, *Making Sense of the Millennium*, p. 55.

22 Richard Bauckham, 'The Millennium', in *God Will Be All in All* (Edinburgh: T&T Clark, 1999), p. 123.

23 There is a single reference to Rev. 20 in Karl Barth, *Church Dogmatics* III/2, ed. G. W. Bromiley and T. F. Torrance (Edinburgh: T&T Clark, 1960), p. 167, and no mention of millennialism or millenarianism.

24 Jürgen Moltmann, *The Coming of God: Christian Eschatology* (London: SCM, 1996), p. 202.

25 Moltmann, *Coming of God*, p. 192.

26 Moltmann, *Coming of God*, p. 134.

27 Moltmann, *Coming of God*, p. 137.

28 Moltmann, *Coming of God*, pp. 161ff.

29 Moltmann, *Coming of God*, p. 174.

30 Moltmann, *Coming of God*, p. 179.

31 Moltmann, *Coming of God*, p. 186.

32 Moltmann, 'Is the World Coming to an End?', in *The Future as God's Gift* (Edinburgh: T&T Clark, 2000), p. 135.

33 Moltmann, *Coming of God*, p. 148.

34 Weber, 'Millennialism', p. 368.

35 Moltmann, *Coming of God*, p. 147.

36 Moltmann, *Coming of God*, p. 152. Original emphasis.

37 Moltmann, *Coming of God*, p. 194.

38 Moltmann, *Coming of God*, p. 159.

39 Moltmann, *Coming of God*, pp. 148, 154.

40 Bauckham is critical of Moltmann's claim that his position is one-sided, since not all in the early church held millenarian views without being triumphalist ('Millennium', p. 130).

41 Stanley J. Grenz, *The Millennial Maze: Sorting out Evangelical Options* (Downers Grove: InterVarsity Press, 1992), pp. 184ff.

42 Bauckham, 'Millennium', p. 133.

43 Bauckham, 'Millennium', p. 132.

44 Bauckham, 'Millennium', p. 137.

45 Bauckham, 'Millennium', p. 138.

46 Moltmann, *Coming of God*, pp. 201–202. Emphasis added.

47 Tim Chester, *Mission and the Coming of God* (Milton Keynes: Paternoster, 2006), p. 60.

48 Brandon Lee Morgan, 'Eschatology for the Oppressed: Millenarianism and Liberation in the Eschatology of Jürgen Moltmann', *Perspectives in Religious Studies* 39.4 (2012), p. 385.

49 See Gregory K. Beale, *The Book of Revelation*, New International Greek Testament Commentary (Grand Rapids: Eerdmans, 1999).

50 Bauckham, 'Millennium', p. 146.

51 See Walter J. Hollenweger, *Pentecostalism* (Peabody, Mass.: Hendrickson, 1997), p. 1.

52 Kärkkäninen, *Pneumatology* (Grand Rapids: Baker, 2002), p. 14.

53 Jürgen Moltmann, *The Spirit of Life* (London: SCM, 1992), p. 17.

54 David A. Höhne, 'The Spirit's Perfecting Work on Emotions', in *True Feelings* (Nottingham: Apollos, 2012), p. 132.

55 Michael Welker, *God the Spirit* (Minneapolis: Fortress, 1994), p. 1.

56 Tim Blanning, *The Romantic Revolution* (New York: Modern Library, 2012), p. 5.

57 Calvin, *Institutes* I.13.18.

58 Walter Bauer, William F. Arndt, Wilbur Gingrich and Frederick W. Danker, *A Greek–English Lexicon of the New Testament* (Chicago: University of Chicago Press, 1979), p. 866.

59 Calvin, 'Romans', p. 224, Calvin uses the term 'the Spirit of regeneration'.

60 Calvin, *Institutes* III.1.1.

61 See above ch. 1 and Matt. 26:39; Mark 14:36; Luke 22:42.

62 Calvin, 'Romans', p. 240.

63 Colin Gunton, '"Until He Comes": Towards an Eschatology of Church Membership', *International Journal of Systematic Theology* 3.2 (2001), p. 192.

64 See Robert B. Pippin, 'On "Becoming Who One Is" (and Failing)', in Nikolas Kompridis (ed.), *Philosophical Romanticism* (London: Routledge, 2006), pp. 91–118.

65 Miroslav Volf, 'Soft Difference: Theological Reflections on the Relation Between Church and Culture in 1 Peter', *Ex auditu* 10 (1994), p. 19.

66 John Wesley, *A Plain Account of Christian Perfection* (London: Epworth, 1960), p. 29.

67 Wesley, *Perfection*, p. 28.

68 Wesley, *Perfection*, p. 52.

69 Wesley, *Perfection*, p. 52.

70 Calvin, 'Romans', p. 225. Emphasis added.

71 Moltmann, *Coming of God*, p. 194.

72 Gunton, 'Church Membership', p. 188.

73 Colin E. Gunton, 'Election and Ecclesiology in the Post-Constantinian Church', in *Reformed Theology* (Grand Rapids: Eerdmans, 2003), p. 149. Emphasis added.

74 Gunton, 'Church Membership', p. 197.

For further reading

Gregory K. Beale, *The Temple and the Church's Mission*, New Studies in Biblical Theology, vol. 17 (Leicester: Apollos; Downers Grove: InterVarsity Press, 2004)

——, *Revelation: A Shorter Commentary* (Grand Rapids: Eerdmans, 2015)

Gerald Bray, *Yours Is the Kingdom: A Systematic Theology of the Lord's Prayer* (Nottingham: Inter-Varsity Press, 2007)

Raymond E. Brown, 'The *Pater Noster* as an Eschatalogical Prayer', in *New Testament Essays* (London: Geoffrey Chapman, 1965), pp. 217–253

William J. Dumbrell, *The Search for Order: Biblical Eschatology in Focus* (Grand Rapids: Baker, 1994)

——, *The End of the Beginning: Revelation 21–22 and the Old Testament* (Eugene, Ore.: Wipf & Stock, 2001)

Stanley J. Grenz, *The Millennial Maze: Sorting out Evangelical Options* (Downers Grove: InterVarsity Press, 1992)

Colin E. Gunton, '"Until He Comes:" Towards an Eschatology of Church Membership', *International Journal of Systematic Theology* 3.2 (2001), pp. 187–200

——, 'Election and Ecclesiology in the Post-Constantinian Church', in *Reformed Theology* (Grand Rapids: Eerdmans, 2003), pp. 97–110

George E. Ladd, *The Presence of the Future* (Grand Rapids: Eerdmans, 1974)

Christopher W. Morgan and Robert A. Peterson (eds.), *Heaven* (Wheaton: Crossway, 2014)

Stephen Motyer, *Come, Lord Jesus! A Biblical Theology of the Second Coming of Christ* (London: Apollos, 2016)

Karl Rahner, 'The Hermeneutics of Eschatological Assertion', in *Theological Investigations*, vol. 23 (London: Darton, Longman & Todd, 1961–92), pp. 326–346

Kim Riddlebarger, 'Eschatology', in *Reformation Theology: A Systematic Summary* (Wheaton: Crossway, 2017), pp. 721–755

Cornelis P. Venema, *The Promise of the Future* (Edinburgh: Banner of Truth, 2000)

Paul Williamson, *Death and the Afterlife*, New Studies in Biblical Theology, vol. 44 (London: Apollos; Downers Grove: InterVarsity Press, 2017)

Index of Scripture references

307

310

Index of names

315

Index of subjects

317

Jesus Christ: **ascriptions and roles:**
Bread of Life, 183, 186; 'God
with us', 9–11; high priest, 28,
133, 210–213, 217–218; judge,
175–179, 210, 221; king, 109–113;
kinsman redeemer, 107–109, 153,
172, 210, 250, 262–263; Lamb,
90, 171, 178; Passover, 121;
prophet, 216; Son of God, 40, 60,
85–86, 110–113, 132–133, 152,
203, 214–215, 218, 263; Son of
Man, 46, 90, 170–172, 214–216,
225; Word (Logos) 74–75, 142;
person, life and work: ascension
and exaltation 124, 132, 213–216;
baptism, 109, 129, 141, 152;
cleansing of the temple, 118–119;
heavenly session, 28, 178, 192,
208, 212, 217; miracles, 113–114,
126, 169; passion and death,
25–29, 50–51, 52, 83–84, 85,
121–122, 171, 212–213; prayers,
24–29; prophetic ministry,
169–170; temptation, 25, 83,
110–113, 152; triumphal entry,
118; **in Scripture and theology:**
apocalyptic, 38; creation and
redemption, 21, 22, 46, 51–54;
election, 141–142; God's will, 33,
140, 168–171; messianic
narrative, 107–125; resurrection
of the dead, 204–208; sonship,
39–40; time and eternity, 6,
44–48; *see also* Christology;
incarnation, the; Messiah, the;
resurrection, of Christ; second
coming; Trinity
Jews and Gentiles, 174
Judas, 117, 239
judges (Old Testament), 99–100, 176
judgment, 24–25, 84, 172, 175–179,
209, 221; *see also* day of
judgment
justification by faith, 14–15

kingdom of God, 95–136; and the
church, 131–134, 175, 181;
discernment of, 96–97; on earth,
53–54, 125–134; and the Holy
Spirit, 129–131; in Jesus'
preaching, 169–170; and
judgment, 176; and the Messiah,
99–125, 127–129, 168; in
millennialist thought, 246–247;
modern/liberal interpretations,
4–5; and the new creation,
134–136; in Old Testament
narrative, 98–107; and
resurrection, 151, 178, 201–202;
and the Trinity, 32, 98–99, 230
kingship, 101–107, 108, 153–155,
176–177, 201–202
kinsman redeemer, 100–101, 103;
Jesus as, 107–109, 153, 172, 210,
250, 262–263

Lazarus, 188
liberal Protestantism, 4, 5, 47, 51,
239
limited atonement, 212
Logos (Word), the, 74–75, 142
Lord's Prayer, xv–xvi, xvii, 31–34
Lord's Supper, 133, 183–184, 219,
224, 238
love: in the Christian life, 195, 255,
257; and covenant, 156, 158; of
God for creation, 226–230, 241,
264; of self, 256; in the Trinity,
41, 50–51, 236

martyrs, 242, 247, 250
mediation: through Abraham, 159;
and forgiveness, 219, 222,
223–224; Holy Spirit's agency in,
20, 41, 83, 88, 133, 136, 173, 240,
253, 254; through humanity, 164;
through Israel, 157; in judgment,
179, 225, 230, 231, 234; in the
messianic narrative, 45, 67, 69,

Printed and bound by CPI Group (UK) Ltd, Croydon, CR0 4YY

25/03/2025

14647345-0004